THE OECD JOBS STRATEGY

D0674718

WITHDRAWN

TECHNOLOGY, PRODUCTIVITY AND JOB CREATION

BEST POLICY PRACTICES

ORGANISATION FOR ECONOMIC CO-OPERATION AND DEVELOPMENT

ORGANISATION FOR ECONOMIC CO-OPERATION AND DEVELOPMENT

Pursuant to Article 1 of the Convention signed in Paris on 14th December 1960, and which came into force on 30th September 1961, the Organisation for Economic Co-operation and Development (OECD) shall promote policies designed:

- to achieve the highest sustainable economic growth and employment and a rising standard of living in Member countries, while maintaining financial stability, and thus to contribute to the development of the world economy;
- to contribute to sound economic expansion in Member as well as non-member countries in the process of economic development; and
- to contribute to the expansion of world trade on a multilateral, non-discriminatory basis in accordance with international obligations.

The original Member countries of the OECD are Austria, Belgium, Canada, Denmark, France, Germany, Greece, Iceland, Ireland, Italy, Luxembourg, the Netherlands, Norway, Portugal, Spain, Sweden, Switzerland, Turkey, the United Kingdom and the United States. The following countries became Members subsequently through accession at the dates indicated hereafter: Japan (28th April 1964), Finland (28th January 1969), Australia (7th June 1971), New Zealand (29th May 1973), Mexico (18th May 1994), the Czech Republic (21st December 1995), Hungary (7th May 1996), Poland (22nd November 1996) and Korea (12th December 1996). The Commission of the European Communities takes part in the work of the OECD (Article 13 of the OECD Convention).

Publié en français sous le titre :

STRATÉGIE DE L'OCDE POUR L'EMPLOI
TECHNOLOGIE, PRODUCTIVITÉ ET CRÉATION D'EMPLOIS
Politiques exemplaires

HC
79
T4T44
1998

© OECD 1998

Permission to reproduce a portion of this work for non-commercial purposes or classroom use should be obtained through the Centre français d'exploitation du droit de copie (CFC), 20, rue des Grands-Augustins, 75006 Paris, France, Tel. (33-1) 44 07 47 70, Fax (33-1) 46 34 67 19, for every country except the United States. In the United States permission should be obtained through the Copyright Clearance Center, Customer Service, (508)750-8400, 222 Rosewood Drive, Danvers, MA 01923 USA, or CCC Online: http://www.copyright.com/. All other applications for permission to reproduce or translate all or part of this book should be made to OECD Publications, 2, rue André-Pascal, 75775 Paris Cedex 16, France.

FOREWORD

With the rise of the knowledge-based economy, entailing globalisation and an enormous expansion in new information and economic opportunities but also a worrisome tendency for polarisation between technology winners and losers, the OECD Member countries are seeking new and more appropriate policy responses to the societal challenges surrounding innovation and diffusion of technology. While there are great similarities in the fundamental challenges confronting governments, country-specific conditions, including differences across countries in the policy-making process itself, make it difficult to conclude on general recommendations for policy in this evolving area. There is thus tremendous scope for mutual learning among countries, from the experience of success as well as failure.

This study examines this new policy environment and draws conclusions regarding what works and does not work in government efforts in regard to technological change. Forming part of the OECD Jobs Study, it concludes a two–year programme launched at the May 1996 Council meeting at Ministerial level and identifies "best practices" in innovation and technology diffusion policies. Related issues, raised at the 1996 *G7 Jobs Conference* in Lille, are also addressed – in particular: *(i)* the creation of high-performance workplaces, *(ii)* investment in intangible assets, and *(iii)* consistency in structural and macroeconomic policies.

The report has been prepared under the aegis of the Joint Expert Group which is comprised of the three main committees of the Directorate for Science, Technology and Industry. Substantive inputs were also directly provided by the Committee for Scientific and Technological Policy and the Industry Committee. The Information, Computer and Communications Policy Committee contributed to Chapter 10 on demand in new growth areas. The work on intangible assets reported in Chapter 11 was undertaken in co-operation with the Directorate for Education, Labour and Social Affairs. Co-operation with the Economics Department contributed to the analysis of linkages between macroeconomic policy and structural reform, addressed in Chapter 4

This report is published on the responsibility of the Secretary-General of the OECD.

TABLE OF CONTENTS

Part II – Best Policy Practices

List of Tables

List of Figures

List of Boxes

INTRODUCTION AND MAIN CONCLUSIONS

Introduction

Technological change drives long-term economic growth and improved standards of living. It is however a process of "creative destruction". New technologies destroy jobs in some industries, especially among the low-skilled, while creating jobs which are often in different industries and require different skills. Historically, this process has led to net job creation, as new industries replace old ones and the skills of workers adapt to changing and expanding demand. Today's rapid technological change coupled with the restructuring underway in OECD economies leads some to associate technology with unemployment and social distress. However, technology *per se* is not the culprit. Its economy-wide employment impact is likely to be positive provided that the mechanisms for translating technology into jobs are not impaired by deficiencies in training and innovation systems and rigidities in product, labour and financial markets.

OECD countries increasingly seek wide-ranging and coherent policy reforms to enhance the contribution of technology to growth, productivity and jobs. As of today, this potential contribution remains largely untapped, with policies not yet fully adapted to the characteristics and problems of knowledge-based economies. While weaknesses remain in the framework conditions for technological change, innovation and technology diffusion policies themselves continue to be too piecemeal, with insufficient consideration of the linkages within national innovation systems and to the broader structural reform agenda. There is too much focus on measures assisting the development of new technologies in the small high-tech segment of the economy and too little on fostering economy-wide innovation and technology diffusion. There is also scope for improving policy effectiveness, notably through more use of market-based instruments and hard evaluation of the impact of policy initiatives.

This report assesses the policy reform efforts of OECD countries, identifies "best policy practices" in different technology policy areas and presents recommendations. It is part of the follow-up process to the 1994 *Jobs Study*, which included a number of wide-ranging policy recommendations aimed at reducing unemployment and raising living standards, and formed the basis for in-depth examinations of individual countries. The 1997 report, *Implementing the OECD Jobs Strategy*, examined progress made, and provided suggestions on how to make different policies mutually strengthening and reform more politically feasible, *e.g.* through co-ordination of different policies. In the area of innovation and technology diffusion policies, which formed part of the original OECD Jobs Study recommendations, the 1996 *Technology, Productivity and Job Creation* report provided new evidence on the role of technology in economic performance, and recommended further policy action (summarised in Box 1). Building on those findings, this report contributes to the ongoing reform process in OECD countries in two ways:

- by identifying the appropriate roles of government in regard to the linkages between technology, productivity and job creation in a policy environment characterised by increased globalisation, the move to the knowledge-based economy, the systemic nature of technical advance, and changing patterns of government funding and firms' innovative strategies;

- by assessing innovation and technology diffusion policies in OECD countries and providing country-specific recommendations as to how technology policies should be improved, as well as how they could be better implemented and integrated with other reforms.

Box 1. **Innovation and technology diffusion policies – the 1994 and 1996 recommendations**

Among the recommendations of the 1994 *Jobs Study*, notably on macroeconomic policy, labour-market flexibility, entrepreneurship, reform of employment security provisions and unemployment benefit systems, active labour-market policies and skill formation, was the following:

– *enhance the creation and diffusion of technological know-how by improving frameworks for its development.*

On the basis of the analytical work in the 1996 *Technology, Productivity and Job Creation* report, this recommendation was further developed into proposals for:

– *enhancing productivity through improved knowledge creation, access and distribution;*
– *promoting organisational change to achieve more effective knowledge management;*
– *co-ordinating technological and human capital development;*
– *stimulating new demand;*
– *realising the innovative and job-creating potential of SMEs.*

The report is structured in two parts. Part I provides the background for the policy assessment. The empirical evidence on the role of technology in the knowledge-based economy is initially reviewed (Chapter 1). The mechanisms of innovation and diffusion in the national innovation systems of OECD countries are then explored (Chapter 2). This is followed by an analysis of the changing patterns of public and private research and development (R&D) efforts and their implications (Chapter 3). The first part concludes with the rationale for and tasks of innovation and technology diffusion policy, structural and macroeconomic framework conditions in OECD countries and the feasibility of reform (Chapter 4). On this basis, Part II assesses country efforts and draws lessons for countries in a number of areas. These concern: the evaluation of innovation and technology policies (Chapter 5); management of the science base (Chapter 6); financial support to industrial R&D efforts (Chapter 7); technology diffusion policies and initiatives (Chapter 8); policies for new technology-based firms Chapter 9); and policies for facilitating growth in new demand (Chapter 10). The report is completed by a discussion of policies for high-performance workplaces and intangible investment (Chapter 11).

The remaining parts of the Introduction sum up the findings. The main recommendations are presented in Box 2, while Table 1 at the end of the Introduction indicates where country-specific best practices and policy recommendations can be found in Part II.

Box 2. Summary of main policy recommendations

1. Innovation and technology diffusion policies need to become an integral part of the broader policy agenda through:

- *better co-ordination with structural reform in product, labour and financial markets and in education and training systems as well as with macroeconomic policy (Chapter 4);*
- *openness to international flows of goods, people and ideas coupled with policies increasing the absorptive capacity of domestic economies (Chapters 4, 7 and 8).*

2. Policy should help realise the productivity benefits of technical change by:

- *improving the management of the science base via increased flexibility in research structures, and strengthening university-industry collaboration (Chapter 6);*
- *ensuring that long-term technological opportunities are safeguarded through adequate financing of public research and incentives for inter-firm collaboration in pre-competitive research (Chapters 6 and 7);*
- *raising the efficiency of financial support for industrial R&D while removing the impediments to the development of market mechanisms for financing innovation, e.g. private venture capital, as an alternative to traditional R&D support (Chapter 7);*
- *strengthening technology diffusion mechanisms by encouraging more competition in product markets and through better design and delivery of programmes (Chapter 8);*
- *strengthening incentives for comparable measurement and reporting by firms of intangible investment to improve the management and composition of investment (Chapter 11);*

3. Policy should ensure favourable conditions in which technical progress can contribute to job creation by:

- *helping to reduce mismatches between demand and supply for skills and improving the framework for firms to adopt new organisational practices (Chapter 11);*
- *facilitating the creation and growth of new technology-based firms by fostering greater managerial and innovation capabilities, reducing regulatory, information and financing barriers and promoting technological entrepreneurship (Chapter 9);*
- *promoting new growth areas such as Internet-based services and environmental goods and services through regulatory reform which encourages flexible technological responses and entry (Chapter 10).*

4. The efficiency and leverage effects of innovation and technology diffusion policy initiatives need to be strengthened via:

- *improving techniques and institutional mechanisms for evaluation (Chapter 5);*
- *adopting new mechanisms for supporting innovation and technology diffusion through greater use of public/private partnerships (Chapters 7 and 8);*
- *removing obstacles to international technology co-operation by improving transparency in foreign access to national programmes and securing a reliable framework for intellectual property rights (Chapter 7).*

5. Reforms need to be made politically feasible through:

- *improved inter-ministerial co-ordination, involving major stakeholders and monitoring of implementation, which can ensure consistency and credibility in policy formulation (Chapters 4, 5 and 11).*

The policy environment

Despite modest gross domestic product (GDP) growth over the past four years, unemployment in many parts of the OECD area remains unacceptably high, and wage and income disparities have widened in most countries, posing risks to social cohesion. At the same time, OECD economies are experiencing a wave of technological change, as indicated by the swift pace of scientific discovery, high patenting activity by the private sector, the rapid diffusion of new technologies, such as information and communication technologies, and a growing share of knowledge-based industries. The policy challenge facing OECD governments with respect to technological change needs to be viewed within the context of the emerging knowledge-based economy. Key aspects of this transformation are:

- *Many OECD countries continue to have high structural unemployment, weak employment growth, and increasing wage dispersion.* Low or declining unemployment has tended to be associated with rising employment rates in the business sector (Figure 1). Compared to the

1980s, the 1990s saw significant wage moderation, an increase in wage rate dispersion (notably in New Zealand, the United Kingdom and the United States), and a considerable proportion of individuals remaining trapped in low-paid jobs in many countries. Wage differences among sectors within countries have widened in general, often reflecting technology-based wage premia. In services, the highest relative wages are in finance, insurance and business services, and in transport and communications services – two segments that use information and communication technologies extensively. Wages in high-technology manufacturing (computers, electronics, aerospace, pharmaceuticals) are 20-25 per cent above the manufacturing average (except in Japan), and the gap has tended to widen.

Figure 1. **Structural unemployment and business sector employment rates**

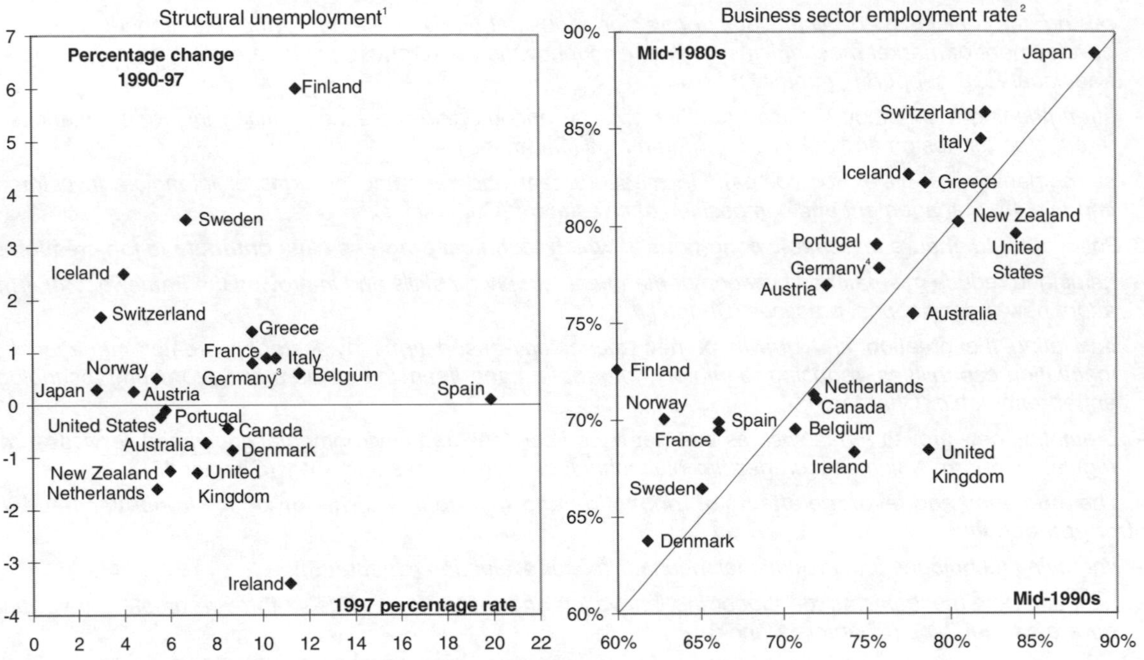

1. Structural unemployment data are based on Secretariat estimates of the non-accelerating wage rate of unemployment (NAWRU) made for the *OECD Economic Outlook* 60, 1996.
2. Numbers engaged in the business sector as a percentage of the labour force.
3. Percentage change between 1991 and 1997; data cover unified Germany in 1995.
4. Data prior to 1991 cover western Germany only.

Source: OECD, *Economic Outlook* 62, December 1997.

- *Jobs are shifting from low-skilled to high-skilled workers.* Employment growth in the last decade has been mainly fuelled by growth in white-collar, high-skill jobs (*e.g.* professionals). Despite this general trend, low-skill employment also increased in some countries, while in others employment in some high-skilled occupations has declined. More generally, the content of skills in both high- and low-skilled occupations is changing rapidly. In many countries (Finland, France, Germany, Italy, the United Kingdom), white-collar high-skill jobs are the only ones that showed an increase, while improved job opportunities for low-skilled white-collar workers (*e.g.* administrative, sales and service workers) were evident in Canada, the United Kingdom and the United States. In manufacturing, in all countries where employment declined overall, white-collar high-skill jobs actually increased. In services, both high- and low-skill white-collar employment increased, but growth was primarily driven by white-collar high-skilled jobs (Australia, Canada, Finland, France, Germany, New Zealand

and the United Kingdom; the contribution of high- and low-skilled employment to service employment growth was equal in Italy, Japan and the United States).

- *Aggregate productivity growth remains modest, but many firms see strong productivity growth and job gains through the combination of technological change, organisational change and upskilling.* Evidence from firm-level studies in a number of countries suggests that R&D-performing and/or technology-using firms have higher than average productivity and employment growth, but that other factors, such as worker training, organisational structures and managerial ability, are critical. There is a tendency for a smaller average size of firm, and small and medium-sized enterprises (SMEs) are of increasing importance for net job creation although their average productivity remains lower than that of larger firms. At the sectoral level, productivity growth in high- and medium-high-tech manufacturing is significantly higher than elsewhere in the economy. The manufacturing sector in most countries is characterised by fast productivity growth and a drop in employment, while services have experienced weaker productivity growth and robust employment growth. Productivity growth in the business sector as a whole has typically grown by between 1 and 2.5 per cent per annum since 1980, with the relationship to employment growth varying significantly across OECD countries. Many of the European countries have had satisfactory productivity performance but poor employment growth (Finland and Poland being the outliers), while countries such as Australia, Canada, Mexico, New Zealand and the United States combined better long-term employment performance with lower productivity growth overall (Figure 2).

- *There is a shift to services, and to high-tech and innovative activities.* Two-thirds of OECD business activity and 70 per cent of jobs are in the services (highest in Australia and the United States, lowest in Finland and Norway). While 40-60 per cent of all business R&D is performed in high-tech manufacturing, an increasing share of R&D is performed in the services, notably in Australia and the United States (30-40 per cent), but also in the United Kingdom. While manufacturing has declined in importance, its high-tech segment has been very dynamic in terms of sales and productivity (especially in Japan, the United Kingdom and the United States), although less so in terms of jobs. More broadly, technology-based industries in both manufacturing and services accounted directly for between one-quarter and one-third of total growth in business output between 1980 and 1995. Among G7 countries, their contribution was largest in Japan, followed by Canada, Germany, the United Kingdom and the United States; it was lowest in Italy.

- *Increasing diffusion of new products and processes generates substantial productivity and employment gains throughout the economy.* Service industries as diverse as social and personal services, transport and storage, real estate and business services, or wholesale and retail trade, are the main buyers of technologically sophisticated machinery and equipment. Among the G7 countries, the importance of service firms in this type of indirect investment in intangibles has become particularly high in the United Kingdom and the United States. Technology diffusion had a particularly significant impact on service productivity in a number of countries. Large investments in information and communication technologies in the service sectors of Canada, Japan, the United Kingdom and the United States are linked to fast-rising employment.

Figure 2. **Employment and labour productivity growth in different parts of the economy**

Average annual growth rate, 1980-95

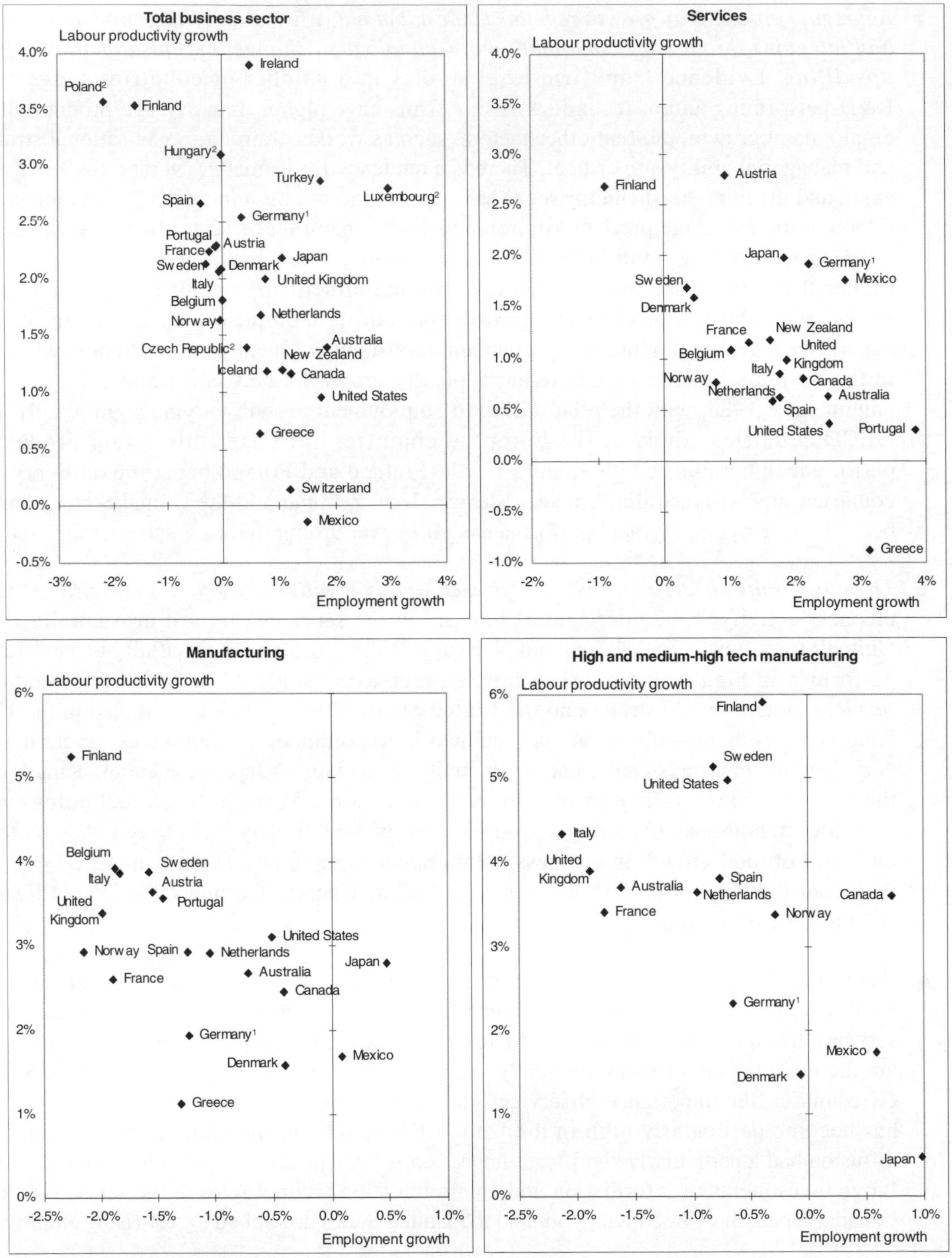

1. Data cover western Germany only.
2. Data cover the 1985-95 period.

Source: OECD, STAN database and *Economic Outlook* 62, December 1997.

- *Differences in the specialisation of innovation systems in OECD countries continue to shape policy challenges and priorities.* OECD countries have distinct sets of strengths and weaknesses, especially in terms of their ability to respond to change and to exploit the potential of new technologies. For some (the United Kingdom and the United States), a major task is to ensure the rapid take-up of scientific discoveries in "science-based industries". For others, issues of specific importance include: strengthening basic research capabilities (*e.g.* Japan); increasing the knowledge content of "resource-based" clusters of industries (Australia, Canada, Denmark, Finland, Norway); redefining the traditional missions of innovation and technology policy away from defence (*e.g.* France, the United States); managing the transition from imitation to innovation (*e.g.* Korea); or coping with the consequences of the internationalisation of R&D strategies of large firms (Germany, the Netherlands, Sweden, Switzerland).

- *Globalisation is knitting dense and diversified linkages among national innovation systems.* The technology content of international trade is rapidly increasing, with the share of high-tech products (computers, semiconductors, pharmaceuticals, telecommunications, aerospace and scientific instruments) growing faster than any other commodities. Technology embodied in imported capital and intermediary goods has contributed significantly to productivity growth, especially in Canada, Denmark and the Netherlands. International technological alliances and purchases of foreign patents and licences have grown. In catch-up economies (Ireland, Korea, Mexico), absorption of international technology, both high- and low-tech, has been fundamental to productivity and economic growth. Corporate innovation activity is still predominantly located close to firms' headquarters, especially in Japan but also in France, Germany, Italy and the United States. Nevertheless, there is a marked tendency towards internationalisation of R&D, which is most pronounced for firms based in smaller home countries (Belgium, Finland, the Netherlands, Sweden, Switzerland).

- *Government financing for R&D has declined in many countries.* The share of R&D efforts financed by governments has stagnated since the early 1980s (Figure 3). In the budget-conscious 1990s, the level of government-financed R&D has declined (at fixed prices) in many OECD countries (including all G7 countries except Japan). This has affected support for technology more than for science as funding for defence and economic objectives (energy, agriculture, etc.) generally fell whereas that for health, the environment and the advancement of knowledge rose. In consequence, government-financed R&D in industry fell, particularly in countries where defence R&D contracts are important (France, the United Kingdom and the United States), although there has sometimes been an offsetting increase in space R&D contracts. Lower public funding of R&D for economic objectives resulted in some cases from privatisation of energy and telecom operators and laboratories (France, Norway). Despite the relative decline in R&D, the scientific community continues to exhibit high productivity, while engaging in closer links with the business sector and with scientists across the world. Simultaneously, scientific research has become the leading source of innovations in fields such as biotechnology, blurring the distinction between science and technology.

- *Private-sector R&D has generally levelled off, and there are signs of an orientation away from basic exploratory research towards more market-driven and short-term innovative efforts.* A prolonged stagnation of private R&D expenditures started in the mid-1980s/early 1990s (especially in Germany, the United Kingdom and the United States), due to slower economic growth, declining government support for industrial R&D and high real interest rates. The recent recovery (notably in the United States) has not led back to previous R&D

intensities. There are also indications of an orientation away from basic exploratory research towards more market-driven, short-term efforts, due in part to firms' difficulties in securing economic returns and research funding. Market pressure, on the other hand, has raised efficiency in R&D, especially in the United States. While to date productivity and growth have not suffered serious adverse consequences from the changing patterns of business R&D (since it is mainly long-term research which has suffered), effects may show up in the future.

Figure 3. **The evolution of public and private R&D efforts between the mid-1980s and the mid-1990s**

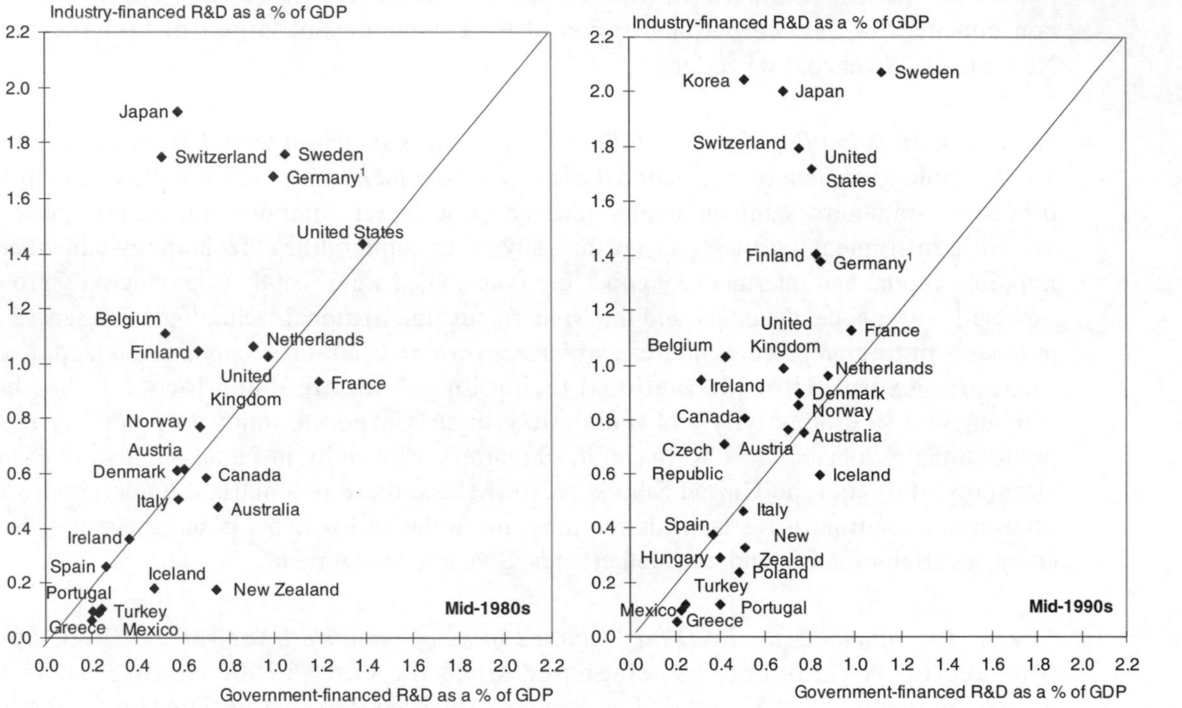

1. Data prior to 1991 cover western Germany only.

Source: OECD, MSTI database, 1997.

Best policy practice and main recommendations

Against the background of a changing environment and clearly spelled out rationale for policy (Box 3), this report assesses best policy practices (Box 4) and draws lessons. However, measuring and comparing outcomes of innovation and technology diffusion policy across countries is often difficult, especially at the macro level, due to the long time lags between policy implementation and results, and because so many interacting conditions have a bearing on the latter. This study develops principles for successful policy, while the methodology for assessment varies between areas, ranging from econometric analysis (*e.g.* tax incentives for R&D) to more qualitative evaluations (*e.g.* technology diffusion programmes). Throughout, there is an attempt to make use of and systematise the lessons learned from previous assessments, taking into account specific national conditions. The main findings are presented below under five sub-headings, covering the breadth of the innovation and technology diffusion policy area: the interplay with broader framework conditions and structural reforms; policies for realising the productivity benefits of technical change; policies enabling technical progress to contribute to job creation; reforms for improving the efficiency and leverage effects of initiatives; and measures for making reforms politically feasible

Box 3. The rationale for and limits of government action: market, government and systemic failure

The traditional rationale for technology policy has been that of market failure. Governments intervene to provide for public goods, as well as to mitigate externalities, inefficient market structures and barriers to entry, imperfect markets for information, etc. The need to temper intervention because of the limited effectiveness of government action has long been recognised. However, the nature of the factors shaping technical progress increasingly calls for measures to address "systemic failure", the lack of coherence among institutions and incentives. This occurs when there are mismatches between the different components of innovation systems (such as conflicting incentives of markets and non-market institutions).

This suggests a task for government that goes well beyond technology policy defined in a narrow sense, *i.e.* encompassing only government actions and regulations managed by ministries and public agencies having technological development as their main mission. The present report extends the boundaries of technology policy to include all measures and programmes targeting innovation and technology diffusion, irrespective of institutional arrangements and division of labour within government. This places technology policy in a horizontal – and somewhat uncomfortable – position, challenging the ability of governments to co-ordinate policies dealing with science, industry, finance, education, etc.

Box 4. Best-practice policy as a learning tool

The search for best practice is based on the identification of policies that "work" in a specific country, and on an understanding of the general principles that can be derived from the observed experience. The next step is to examine how best practice can be transferred to other national contexts. In the area of innovation and technology diffusion, it is difficult to provide "off-the-shelf" policy prescriptions. Because factors specific to countries and points in time impinge on what can be achieved or should be attempted by policy makers, few policies represent best practice in an absolute sense. Therefore, the search for best practice evolves by necessity towards the prescription of "context-related" good practices. The notion of best practice must be understood as a learning tool, rather than a normative concept. The search for best practice must be directed to areas where countries pursue objectives in regard to a common rationale and be guided by a common set of assessment criteria regarding policy efficiency, although it cannot be dependent on their full applicability.

Technology policies need to become an integral part of the broader policy agenda

While there is a clearly defined but institutionally diffuse role for innovation and technology diffusion policy, measures in this area need to complement broader structural reforms in order to translate technological developments into growth, productivity and jobs. The impact of technology policies, narrowly defined, will be modest unless they are consistent with, or complemented by, broader reforms. Policy makers should formulate technology policy in such a way that it is:

- *Complementary to reforms in product, financial and labour markets and reforms in education and training*. In an increasingly integrated world economy, product market reforms enable more rapid diffusion of technology and information, and strengthen incentives for firms to innovate and adapt goods and services to changing consumer needs. Financial market reforms facilitate new technology-based entrepreneurial initiatives. Labour market reforms contribute to innovation, facilitate the use of new technologies, and allow technical change to translate into more jobs. Such reforms need to be complemented with wide-ranging changes in education and training systems to improve labour-force skills and competences. While most OECD countries have liberalised financial markets, countries that have also reformed product and labour markets, such as Ireland, the Netherlands, New Zealand and the United Kingdom, have experienced considerable improvements in economic performance. Further progress in structural reform, such as more flexible product and labour markets in many European countries; greater attention to broad-based upskilling in countries with widening income distributions, such as the United Kingdom and the United States; regulatory reform of product and financial markets in Japan and Korea as well as in Europe; and a further strengthening of framework conditions in transition economies, can help improve performance and reduce barriers to innovation and technological change.

- *Co-ordinated with macroeconomic policy.* A stable macroeconomic framework is a precondition for innovative activity. In the past, fiscal imbalances and uncertainty about inflation led to high real interest rates. This, combined with the general climate of uncertainty created by unsustainable policies, increased the cost of capital and reduced incentives for innovative activity. Technological progress, on the other hand, affects macroeconomic performance and policy in a number of ways, including via its impacts on growth, prices, measurement of output and inflation, and the stability of tax bases. Mutually strengthening developments in the two areas may set the stage for either vicious or virtuous circles. Breaking out of vicious circles may require more or less comprehensive policy action. In Western Europe, macroeconomic uncertainty and high real interest rates have in the past combined with slow restructuring and weak innovative effort. International technology co-operation can spur direct investment, technology diffusion, industrial restructuring and strengthen prospects for long-term economic performance, thereby helping to make structural reform and European integration more feasible. Countries which have suffered severe economic shocks, such as Finland and Japan, have formulated policy packages, with science and technology policy as a key ingredient, designed to break out of vicious circles.

- *Consistent with the globalisation process, through openness to international flows of goods, people and ideas and policies increasing the absorptive capacity of domestic economies.* The globalisation of markets for goods and services and of production networks is closely related to the internationalisation of technology and knowledge. Insofar as there are identifiable losers from globalisation, tensions arise. Technology policies must allow domestic firms, especially SMEs, to improve their absorptive and innovative capacity to benefit from the globalisation process. In small, open economies where advances in technology have centred on the performance of a limited number of increasingly globalised firms (*e.g.* Finland and Sweden), efforts have been made in recent years to improve the science-industry interplay. Still, enduring weaknesses in reward structures and taxation impede the attraction and upgrading of skilled individuals, thereby limiting the ability of the domestic economy to take full advantage of the internationalisation of knowledge. The virtuous circle of technological advance, growth and job creation set off in Ireland has strongly benefited from that country's success in attracting foreign direct investment. Japan and Korea have benefited from technology imports and their mastering of incremental innovations, but need now to upgrade their domestic innovative capacity. In Germany, public investment in the R&D infrastructure aims at raising inward flows of R&D and foreign know-how. For technology policy to achieve results, however, it must be complemented by broader structural reforms.

Realising the productivity benefits of technical change

Technological progress directly increases the productivity of innovating firms, and indirectly increases economy-wide productivity through its diffusion and adoption. As information and communication technologies become pervasive, the potential for productivity gains shifts from high-tech manufacturing to the overall economy, and notably to the expanding service sector. The realisation of these potential productivity gains can be helped by regulatory reform in product and factor markets, policies that allow domestic firms to take advantage of international sources of technology, and also policy initiatives providing services to firms aimed at increasing their capacity to absorb new technologies, as well as to engage in collaborative research with other firms.

Policies have a role to play also in encouraging innovation and growth in the knowledge base of an economy. This involves initiatives aimed at improving the management of the science base, as well as reforming support schemes of industrial R&D so as to increase their leverage effect on firms' R&D efforts. However, such policies may be ineffective in the absence of measures which help firms improve their performance in terms of non-technological aspects of innovation, *e.g.* adoption of new organisational structures and upgrading of workforce skills. Policy makers need to:

- *Improve the management of the science base via increased flexibility in research structures and strengthen incentives for university-industry collaboration.* Government support to the science base has been relatively protected at a time of budget stringency. An important current issue is the appropriate balance between core and contract-based resources in financing research institutions. While in some countries there is a risk that the share of contract-based resources is becoming excessive, in many others (notably in Continental Europe) increasing that share will stimulate the flexibility of research structures and their responsiveness to economic and social needs. There are benefits to be gained from greater involvement by industry and other stakeholders in setting research priorities (including cross-disciplinary research). The experience of a number of countries (Australia, Canada, Sweden, the United Kingdom and the United States) which have created centres of excellence, co-operative R&D centres, etc., is instructive in this respect. The research Framework Programmes of the European Union have for the last 15 years focused on supporting co-operation between universities, research centres and firms as well as increasing the international mobility of scientists. The organisation of academic research should both stimulate scientific excellence and facilitate mobility of ideas and people. A number of countries need to take measures concerning the status of university researchers, employment conditions, and other factors influencing mobility, including possibilities for creating their own firms.

- *Ensure that long-term technological opportunities are safeguarded through adequate financing of public research and incentives for inter-firm collaboration in pre-competitive research.* Increasing market pressure has led many firms to improve the efficiency of their research activities in terms of economic outcomes. However, it has also reduced the funding of basic, exploratory research, whose outcomes are uncertain or difficult to appropriate. In addition to the appropriate funding of public research within increasingly tight government budgets, it is important that policy induces such research by firms, or at least does not deter them from undertaking it. Many public programmes (the Advanced Technology Programme in the United States, the research Framework Programmes and Eureka in Europe) aim at encouraging co-operation between firms, and sometimes universities, on such "generic technologies". The regulation of concentration (mergers and acquisitions) and R&D co-operation increasingly takes this aspect into account. Antitrust policies in Europe, Japan and the United States have adapted to such concerns since the early 1980s. Still, governments generally need to improve the balance between allowing co-operation upstream, where it helps to keep research costs down and allows partners to benefit from each other's competencies, and enforcing competition downstream, when it comes to production and marketing, where it allows consumers to benefit from lower prices.

- *Raise the efficiency of financial support for industrial R&D while better weighing its merits relative to other instruments for financing innovation.* R&D investments are an important factor behind productivity gains at the firm level. While there is a sound economic rationale for some public support to industrial R&D, in the form of either tax incentives or targeted R&D subsidies, in most countries there is room for improving such schemes. R&D tax incentives (used by about half of OECD countries) can be effective in increasing private R&D expenditure but their cost effectiveness depends on other features of the tax system and on their detailed design. Efficiency gains could be obtained by reducing their generosity in some countries (Canada, Spain), or by fine-tuning their inducement mechanism (Australia, France, Japan). Beyond their great variety in terms of size, objectives and design features, measures to support pre-competitive R&D through targeted grants often share a common weakness, defective articulation between mechanisms for selection (of projects and recipients) and funding, the latter remaining relatively crude in contrast with the increasing sophistication of market financing tools (*e.g.* venture capital). Many programmes to promote near-market R&D and innovation on a project basis have had mixed results; this explains recent efforts to streamline or reform them (as in Austria). As removing the impediments to the development of market mechanisms for innovation financing becomes increasingly attractive, countries should assess the appropriateness of the current scope and design of their financial support for industrial R&D.

- *Strengthen technology diffusion mechanisms by fostering competition in product markets and through better design and delivery of programmes.* Innovations are translated into aggregate productivity and employment growth through the process of technology diffusion. This process can be strengthened through open trade, competition and regulatory reform. Better designed and integrated public initiatives can help this process by increasing the ability of firms to access and exploit technologies. Enhancing competition and liberalisation of infrastructure and services has a strong potential for spurring innovation and diffusion in growing sectors such as telecommunications as well as in mature sectors, particularly in Austria, France, Germany and Spain. Australia, Finland, the Netherlands and the United Kingdom have consolidated the institutional framework for diffusion policies so as to reduce overlap, while in France there exists a potential for overlap between national and regional initiatives. Denmark, the Netherlands and Spain have taken measures to improve the functioning of technology transfer centres. Technology extension services and information provision have been made more effective through greater industry participation and cost-sharing in Canada, Germany, Switzerland and the United States, although in Germany many technical centres remain heavily dependent on public support. Australia, Canada and the United States have integrated diffusion issues more explicitly in technology development projects; similar action is warranted in Korea, Mexico and Spain. Schemes to promote greater technology uptake have been made more effective in Austria, Norway, the Netherlands and the United Kingdom through evaluation and a better targeting of firms.

- *Strengthen incentives for comparable measurement and reporting by firms of intangible investment to improve the management and composition of investment.* While investment in intangible assets underpins productivity growth, there may be a tendency for firms to underinvest because of the lack of visibility of such assets in reporting practices. Strengthened incentives for their disclosure can improve resource allocation through better internal management and improved external capital market assessment. There are scattered examples of good practice at the firm level, for example in Swedish firms, and experimentation in US firms. However, there are also disincentives to reporting, such as not wanting to reveal strategic information, concerns about taxation treatment and about becoming locked into static reporting practices. Denmark is pioneering initiatives to encourage firms to disclose more systematic comparable information, based on current best practice. Similar initiatives in other countries will be important for further progress, and to enable a better understanding of the benefits of improved reporting, as well as a more favourable balance between its costs and benefits. However, in the absence of government initiatives, it is unlikely that individual efforts by firms will lead to internationally comparable reporting practices.

Ensure the conditions for technical progress to contribute to job creation

Technology policy has both direct and indirect impacts on job creation, including the number and types of jobs created. Favourable impacts cannot be taken for granted, as is suggested by a sometimes negative relationship prevailing between productivity growth and employment performance over extended periods of time. Although technology policies must not seek to protect jobs at the expense of productivity and competitiveness, a number of OECD countries are in need of policy adjustment in order to strengthen job outcomes. Reducing the potential mismatch between the skills in supply and those in demand, while ensuring complementarity between technology and human capital policies is one area for reform. Regulatory reform initiatives that generate increased flexibility and adaptability in labour markets and provide incentives for investment in human capital are critical in this respect, as are technology policies that encourage training and changes in organisational structures in smaller firms that fall largely outside the scope of traditional public training schemes.

Technology policy can further help to improve the conditions for the creation and growth of new technology-based firms (NTBFs). More broadly, it can help create an environment conducive to the articulation of demand and jobs, including in new growth sectors such as Internet-based services or environmental goods and services. NTBFs contribute directly to job creation. Even more importantly, they create and diffuse new goods and services and thereby help instil a culture of innovation, encourage investments in skills and improve economy-wide dynamic allocative efficiency. Higher incomes from technology-induced productivity growth not only increase demand for technology-intensive goods and services but also in low technology areas, thus stimulating employment. Policy measures in this respect are multiple, ranging from encouraging risky innovative activity (*e.g.* the establishment of venture capital funds, tax credits, tax treatment of capital gains) in close co-ordination with structural reform in financial markets, to targeted diffusion programmes and appropriate regulatory conditions that allow growth in new markets such as electronic commerce or environmental services. Policy should:

- *Help overcome mismatches between demand and supply for skills and improve the framework for adoption of new organisational practices.* The productivity and job gains associated with new technologies are best realised when firms make complementary investments in organisational change and upskilling. Canada, New Zealand, the United Kingdom and the United States have improved previously uneven performance in this respect; nevertheless, to varying extents they still need to expand and improve vocational and technical education and training. Nordic countries (Denmark, Finland, Iceland, Norway and Sweden) and many continental European countries as well as Japan have traditionally done well in these respects but a number of them must combine greater firm-level flexibility. Expanding or improving the content of vocational and technical education is an issue for Austria, Belgium, Germany, Iceland, the Netherlands, Norway and Switzerland. Improving links with business an important issue for Finland and France, while Austria, Germany, Japan and the Netherlands should facilitate mobility between vocational/technical and academic studies. Expansion and improvement of vocational education is of prime importance for the group of "catch-up" countries, including Italy, Greece, Portugal and Spain. Nordic and continental European countries and Japan have a strong infrastructure and traditions supporting diffusion of information on new work organisation and work practices, but this institutional infrastructure needs to become more demand-driven as well as more closely co-ordinated with education and training programmes. More generally, the incentives for firms to offer training and for individuals to upgrade their skills need reviewing and strengthening in most OECD countries.

- *Facilitate the creation and growth of new technology-based firms by fostering greater managerial and innovation capabilities, reducing regulatory, information and financing barriers and promoting technological entrepreneurship.* Dynamic NTBFs tend to display above-average employment growth, while contributing indirectly to growth and jobs through higher productivity, lower prices and greater product variety. The difference between the United States and other countries in the dynamism of NTBFs is neither the rate of start-ups nor the rate of survival of new firms (with a few exceptions such as Japan and Sweden). It is the share of start-ups that take place in technologically progressive activities and the proportion of these firms that enjoy fast growth. Policies aimed at encouraging entrepreneurship in general, and risky innovative activity in particular, are important, especially in countries such as Japan where rates of business start-up are very low. Governments must also address the specific factors which restrain the number of valuable entrepreneurial technology-based projects, raise obstacles to their transformation into business start-ups, and weaken subsequent market selection processes to the detriment of firms with growth potential. Increasingly this must include measures which spur greater management and innovation capabilities within firms, raising their potential for growth and investment in technology and skills. Regulatory barriers to entry should be reduced, and private venture capital industry promoted (including specialised financial market segments and "business angel" networks). This may be achieved through tax incentives for investors (as in France and the United Kingdom); programmes to leverage private investment (*e.g.* in Australia, Germany and the Netherlands); or relaxing investment rules for pension funds, banks and insurance companies (*e.g.* in Australia, Finland and Italy). Direct financial support should be concentrated on early stages of innovative ventures (seed capital, pre-investment appraisal). Disincentives to "technological entrepreneurship" (regulations discouraging spin-offs from large firms and universities) and obstacles to risk-taking (*e.g.* bankruptcy law which excessively penalises failure, lack of stock options which improve the risk/reward ratio for highly-qualified staff) should be removed or modified.

- *Promote new growth areas such as Internet-based services and environmental goods and services through regulatory reform which encourages flexible technological responses and new entry.* The emergence of new industries to replace declining ones is important for growth and job creation. In new areas such as network-based services and environmental goods and services, government measures have helped foster market-driven innovation, technology diffusion and economic expansion. Policies to facilitate growth need to integrate and co-ordinate different policy targets (encouraging positive social impacts of Internet-based services, the goals of environmental and technology policy), combine consistent regulation and economic incentives covering supply- and demand-side market behaviour of individuals and firms, and avoid locking-in to particular technologies. Jobs in network-based services have been created in access providers and new media due to infrastructure liberalisation, technological innovation and flexible service conditions. Best practices are found in Canada, Finland, the United Kingdom, the United States and the European Commission. High- and low-skill jobs are being created to supply environmental goods and in new services such as eco-auditing; the distribution of jobs is shaped by combining flexible application of regulations with economic incentives encouraging innovation. Best-practice policies are found in Canada, Germany, Japan, the Netherlands, New Zealand, Nordic countries and the United States.

Improve the efficiency and leverage effects of innovation and technology policy initiatives

There is a need for improvement in the efficiency and leverage effects of innovation and technology diffusion policies via:

- *Improved techniques and institutional mechanisms for evaluation.* The increasing emphasis on evaluation partly reflects tight government budgets, but is also emblematic of a trend towards more accountability, transparency and the desire to minimise distortions from government policies while maximising their leverage effect. Only a few countries (Australia, Canada, the United Kingdom and the United States) systematically evaluate the whole range of technology programmes based on socio-economic criteria and with resource allocation and priority-setting as goals. While evaluation in these countries is mature and institutionalised, further efforts are needed to allow better comparison of the relative efficiency and effectiveness of different policy tools. In Europe, the European Commission has helped to put evaluation on the policy agenda in certain countries by developing methodologies and supporting networks of evaluators. It has also recently introduced a rationalised evaluation scheme covering monitoring and five-year assessment of the EU research programme and Framework Programme. Among European countries, Denmark, Finland, France, Germany, the Netherlands, Norway, Sweden and Switzerland have well-developed evaluation practices, but tend to use evaluation mainly for improving programme management. Their approach provides part of the information necessary for managing the systemic nature of modern innovation systems, but fails to provide a sufficient basis for allocating public funds between competing uses. The approach taken to evaluation in New Zealand is similar, while in Japan a number of recent initiatives apply a more rigorous methodology to evaluating socio-economic impacts of programmes. In Greece, Ireland, Italy, Portugal and Spain, as well as in the Czech Republic, Hungary, Mexico, Poland and Turkey, evaluation remains ad hoc, and there is a need to institutionalise the process by developing the methodological tools and mechanisms that will help embed evaluations in policy making.

- *Adoption of new mechanisms for supporting innovation and technology diffusion through greater use of public/private partnerships.* Public/private partnerships seem particularly well suited for correcting market failures in certain areas (*e.g.* development of generic industrial technologies) while minimising some systemic failures, by fostering co-operation between different actors (examples of such programmes exist in Australia, Austria, Japan, the United States and the European Commission). In comparison with traditional R&D subsidies, they entail a more competitive selection of participants, an increased influence from the private sector on project selection and management, as well as greater leverage of public funding on private resources. Public/private partnership schemes have the potential to enhance synergies between market-driven R&D and R&D responding to governments' needs in accomplishing their direct missions (*e.g.* defence, public health, environment), provided that they can be designed so as to minimise the potential risks of capture by private sector participants, as well as dead-weight losses. Realising this potential is of particular importance for countries with a large public research sector (*e.g.* France, the United States). It involves different types of adjustment to policy practices, for example: the need to improve synergies between mission-oriented national programmes and diffusion-oriented regional initiatives (*e.g.* in Austria, Germany and the Netherlands), or to make the technology diffusion infrastructure more flexible in supporting diffusion, adoption and innovation in a broad range of firms and activities (*e.g.* in Nordic countries).

- *Removal of obstacles to international technology co-operation by improving transparency in foreign access to national programmes and securing a reliable framework for intellectual property rights.* International discrepancies in the access of foreign firms to government-funded research programmes have been reduced, especially following positive initiatives in Japan. Rules (*e.g.* reciprocity requirements or conditions regarding exploitation of research results) and practice now differ as much from programme to programme as from country to country. They should be made more transparent, particularly in the United States where each of the many agencies involved in technology policy applies its own eligibility criteria. There is scope for improving other aspects of the regulatory framework for transborder co-operation among private enterprises [*e.g.* in the area of intellectual property rights (IPRs)]. Despite progress in harmonization under the aegis of the World Intellectual Property Organization (WIPO) and the World Trade Organization (WTO) [Agreement on Trade-related Aspects of Intellectual Property Rights (TRIPS Agreement)], the lack of predictability in IPRs and standards, enforcement and litigation still hampers firms' global operations, particularly in new technology fields.

Making reforms politically feasible

Adoption of best policy practices hinges on the political ability to implement them. Achieving this requires overcoming institutional inertia as well as addressing social cohesion problems arising from transition costs and redistribution of incomes and jobs, primarily away from workers who are low-skilled or whose skills are becoming obsolete. A fundamental question is whether the signals sent by policy to individuals and firms are consistent and credible.

Key factors for success in this respect are the extent to which co-ordination can be achieved between ministries and relevant stakeholders can participate in the formulation of policy. Denmark, the Netherlands, Finland, the United Kingdom and the United States have all made significant improvements in this area. New forms of interaction with the private sector, *e.g.* in the form of P/PPs, which have helped dynamise research systems and better link them to economic and societal goals, have been developed in Germany, the Netherlands and the United States, as well as within the framework of the new Innovation Action Plan of the European Union.

Appropriate incentive systems are needed to engineer policy co-ordination. Financial pressures can be used creatively to spur change in governance, and to adopt assessment mechanisms designed to induce innovative behaviour. Checks must be put in place against government failure, such as institutions furthering their own special interests, and adopting a partial rather than an economy-wide perspective. The benefits of awareness and transparency may be magnified by "audits" and international benchmarking of how policy organisation and formulation relate to economic behaviour and performance, inducing a critical process of self-examination in governments.

Technology policies need to be part of a broader package developed in consultation with the social partners to ease transition problems. One strategy is to begin with those measures which appear to be the most feasible, universally supported and whose effects are likely to be the most evident. Once these measures have been in existence for some time and their effects have been evaluated, necessary corrections can be implemented and more difficult decisions can be pushed through. Science and technology policies in Finland, Iceland, Japan and the Netherlands have been able to evolve along these lines. Even when "big bang" policies have been introduced, technology policy has generally evolved gradually over a period of decades (*e.g.* New Zealand). On the other hand, the ability to advance may hinge on the political will to push through difficult decisions, handle the associated transition costs and demonstrate positive outcomes. In some countries, a crisis situation has helped muster support for reform (*e.g.* Finland, Japan). It is important that policy makers exploit such opportunities as they arise, thereby preventing conditions from deteriorating to a degree which makes it extremely difficult to repair the damage.

Measures that promote broad-based upskilling and lifelong learning can help to raise the mobility and employability of workers and mitigate the costs of job displacement. Social security programmes and transfers protecting social cohesion will continue to play an important role in preserving a social fabric conducive to trust; itself a major building block for risk-taking, innovation and creativity in a broader sense. At the same time, it is crucial that policies be designed in such a way that they do not undermine incentives for work, upskilling, organisational change or restructuring. OECD countries face a major challenge in putting into place, and successfully communicating to the general public, a comprehensive policy framework which allows for a mutual strengthening of social cohesion, on the one hand, and technological progress and change on the other.

Finally, policy makers should pursue international policy co-ordination, which may help achieve consistency in national reforms. It can help underpin domestic policy efforts, for instance in the area of diffusion and the science-industry interface, and to secure broader public acceptance. Again, improved understanding of the contribution that technology can make to better standards of living will be crucial for the feasibility of such co-operation. OECD governments further need to ensure that mobilisation of efforts takes place at the regional and local levels, *e.g.* through the design of administrative and fiscal frameworks. Along with the goal of transparency of policies and resulting impacts, governments should design incentives which spur competition among local authorities in initiatives for change rather than in mere attraction of financial support.

Overview of the main country-specific findings

Table 1 presents an overview of the main country-specific findings of the report. It shows national strengths and weaknesses and serves as a guide to the best practices and policy recommendations in the report. In summarising the evaluation of national challenges and policies in different innovation and technology diffusion policy areas, it distinguishes between five situations: *(i)* case of best policy practice; *(ii)* partial best-practice policy, with minor policy recommendation; *(iii)* minor policy recommendation; *(iv)* partial best-practice policy, with remaining major weakness; *(v)* major weakness.

This report defines best policy practice as a learning tool rather than a normative concept; the table should not be interpreted as a ranking of countries. Neither should it be used to prioritise policy reforms within individual countries since it is not based on a series of country reviews and does not cover all areas of innovation and technology diffusion policy. Identified best practices are examples of successful national responses to generic problems that comprise elements (*e.g.* the general approach or a specific instrument) which could be emulated with appropriate adaptation in other countries. The report provides numerous examples of such best practices, although there are fewer in some areas than in others.

Areas where best practices are few and far between are precisely those where a systemic policy approach is inherent to success, namely: the institutional settings for policy formulation, implementation and evaluation, as well as the promotion of NTBFs and new demand. In other areas, such as technology diffusion or the management of the science base, where examples of best practices abound, they do not translate everywhere into satisfactory performance because their impact depends in part on conditions created by other policies. For example, efforts to make the science base contribute more to economic growth must be echoed by an increasing uptake of scientific inputs by the business sector – especially by NTBFs and in new growth areas. Industrial renewal brought about by firm creation and expansion of new markets will in turn enhance the effects of schemes for promoting technology diffusion.

For each country, the table indicates where policy adjustment and learning from best practices of other countries is required. Broadly speaking, three groups of countries can be distinguished. Some countries (*e.g.* Australia, Canada, Finland, the United Kingdom and the United States) exhibit few pronounced weaknesses and generally require only incremental improvements. However, except in the case of Finland, vocational and technical education and training constitute the weak point of the innovation systems of these countries and threaten long-term performance, requiring further expansion and improvement or reductions in drop-out rates. In Finland, as in Sweden, an important challenge is to make the infrastructure for diffusion better serve interactions between small and large firms. In Canada, financial support to industrial R&D should be rationalised. There is also room for improvement in overall co-ordination of innovation and technology diffusion policies in most of these countries, including the United States.

By contrast, a number of OECD countries face a comprehensive agenda of far-reaching policy reforms. They include all new Member countries (the Czech Republic, Hungary, Korea, Mexico, Poland), where the institutional set-up for innovation and technology diffusion policies is still incomplete; European countries with less policy experience in this area (Greece, Ireland, Portugal, Spain, Turkey); but also more advanced countries such as Austria and Italy which face lasting problems of policy co-ordination that weaken efficiency in every technology policy area. The remaining Member countries, including Japan and all other European OECD countries, fall somewhere in the middle and show more contrasted profiles of strengths and weaknesses. The weaknesses, *e.g.* in France, Germany and Sweden, partly reflect rigidities in the public research sector and related difficulties in adjusting financing and regulatory policies to the requirements of the emerging entrepreneurial model of knowledge generation and use.

Table 1. **Overview of best policy practice and policy recommendations in individual areas of innovation and technology diffusion policy**[1]

	Chapter 4[2]	Chapter 5	Chapter 6	Chapter 7	Chapter 8	Chapter 9	Chapter 10		Chapter 11
	Institutional framework for policy formulation and implementation	Evaluation	Managing the science base	Financial incentives to industrial R&D efforts	Technology diffusion policies and initiatives	Promoting new technology-based firms	Facilitating growth in new demand: Internet-based	Environment	High-performance workplaces and intangible assets
Australia	●/□	●	●/□	●	●/□	□	●/□	□	○
Austria	○	○	□	□	●/□	○	□	□	□
Belgium	○	□	□	○		○	□	○	□
Canada	●/□	●	●/□	●/○	●/□	●/□	●	●	●/○
Czech Republic		○	○		○	○		○	
Denmark	□	□	●	□	●/□	□	□	□	●
Finland	●	□	●	●/□	□	●	●	●	●/□
France	□	□	○	●/○	●/□	●/○	□	□	□
Germany	□	□	□	□	●/□	●/□	□	□	●/○
Greece	○	○	○		●/○	○	○	○	○
Hungary		○	○		○	○		○	
Iceland			●				□	□	□
Ireland	□	○	●	□	□	□	○	○	●/□
Italy	○	○	○	○		□	○	○	○
Japan	○	□	●/○	○	●/□	○	●/□	●	●/○
Korea	□	○	○	□	●/○	○	□	○	□
Luxembourg							□	□	
Mexico	○	○	○	●/○	○	○	□	○	○
Netherlands	●/□	□	●	□	●/□	□	●	●	●
New Zealand		□	□				●/□	●/□	□
Norway	□	□	□	□	●	□	□	●	●
Poland	○	○	○	○	□	○	□	□	○
Portugal	○	○	□				○	○	○
Spain	○	○	●/○	○	●/○	○	○	○	○
Sweden	□	□	●/□	□	□	○	●/□	●	□
Switzerland	□	□	□	●/□	●/○	○	□	□	□
Turkey	○	○	○	□	□		○	○	○
United Kingdom	□	●	●/□	●/□	●	□	●	□	●/○
United States	○	●/□	●/□	●/□	●/□	●	●	●/○	●/○
EC	●/○	●/□		●/□	●/○	□	●	●	●

Key: ● represents case of best policy practice; □ represents minor policy recommendation; ○ represents major weakness calling for policy adjustment.

1. The table should be interpreted with caution and should not be read as a ranking of countries. Five situations are distinguished: *i)* case of best policy practice; *ii)* partial best-practice policy, with minor policy recommendation; *iii)* minor policy recommendation; *iv)* partial best practice policy, with remaining major weakness; *v)* major weakness. A blank means that available information was insufficient to draw conclusions.
2. This column is also based on judgement derived from other chapters.

Source: OECD Secretariat.

Part I

Policy Framework

CHAPTER 1. TECHNOLOGY, GROWTH AND EMPLOYMENT IN THE KNOWLEDGE-BASED ECONOMY[1]

1.1. Context and background: the macroeconomic performance of OECD economies

1. Technological change has a dual role in the debate on unemployment and job creation: that of the villain, and that of the knight in shining armour. New technologies are widely blamed for job loss among the low-skilled, while at the same time being held up as providing the solution to unemployment through the creation of new high-skill jobs paying good wages in emerging sectors. While this dual role may be exaggerated, technology both creates and destroys jobs. More fundamentally, it transforms the structures of economies, and their ability to grow and create wealth and jobs.

2. This chapter explores the relationships between technology, growth and employment. It examines how technology is transforming OECD economies from industrial to knowledge-based – directly based on the production, distribution and use of knowledge and information – becoming in the process more than ever the engine of economic growth. It then reviews evidence from firm-level, sectoral and aggregate data on the relationship between technology and productivity, before discussing the impact of technology on employment, skills and wages. These relationships need to be viewed in the context of the macroeconomic performance of OECD economies in the 1990s, and, in particular, growth and labour market developments (reviewed in detail in OECD, 1997*a*), namely:

- Weaker economic growth than in the 1970s and 1980s; higher unemployment rates (the 8 per cent rate for the whole OECD area is double the level of 20 years ago), and significant variation by country and region; a large share of long-term unemployed (particularly in Europe, with the exception of the Nordic countries[2] and Austria); higher youth unemployment rates; large regional unemployment differences (Belgium, Italy, Spain).

- Lower employment growth than in the 1970s and 1980s, with the United States creating twice as many jobs as Japan and four times as many as the European Union during the last cycle for each percentage point of growth; with business employment growth associated with decreases in structural unemployment in many countries (Ireland, the Netherlands, New Zealand); with weak or declining employment growth associated with increases in structural unemployment

1. The analytical work underpinning this chapter has benefited from financial support from the European Commission (DG XII) in the framework of the preparation of the *Second European Indicators Report on S&T Indicators*, 1997.
2. Throughout this publication, the term *Nordic countries* refers to the following: Denmark, Finland, Iceland, Norway and Sweden.

(Finland, Germany, Iceland, Norway, Portugal, Sweden, among others); and with government employment the main source of job opportunities in countries with high unemployment rates.

- Higher unemployment rates among the less educated and less skilled; a change in the employment mix, with a shift away from low-skilled jobs and towards high-skilled ones; but also some increase in job losses among skilled white-collar workers (especially in industries such as finance, insurance and business services), and increased job opportunities for low-skilled white-collar workers (though not at the same rate as high-skilled ones) in countries experiencing an economic upturn (Canada, the United Kingdom, the United States).

- A high degree of job turnover in most OECD countries, with many jobs created and destroyed each year; different employment adjustment mechanisms (with European workers less likely to become unemployed but, once unemployed, competing less successfully for relatively few vacancies; a higher risk of becoming unemployed in the United States, but generally short-lived unemployment spells); and an increasing sense of job insecurity.

- An increase in temporary job arrangements in some high unemployment European countries (France, Italy, Spain), partly compensating for declines in permanent employment, as well as in some countries with strong employment gains (Ireland, the Netherlands); an increase in part-time employment in almost all countries (but which remains a fairly small fraction of total employment, except in the Netherlands).

- A slower rate of increase in real compensation per employee in most countries compared to the 1980s; significant wage moderation as shown by wage shares in business gross domestic product (GDP), with real wages failing to increase in line with labour productivity (particularly in Europe); an increase in wage rate dispersion in the 1980s and early 1990s in the United Kingdom and the United States and to a lesser extent New Zealand, and a more compressed wage group in Germany and Norway (in Canada, France and Japan the tendency towards a wider wage distribution in the 1980s faded in the 1990s); a significant increase in the proportion of individuals trapped in low-paid jobs in many countries.

1.2. Technology, structural change and growth: the move to knowledge-based economies

3. Through its effects on production methods, consumption patterns, and the structure of economies, the spread of information and communication technologies (ICTs) is playing a key role in the transformation of OECD economies from industrial to knowledge-based. Economies have always relied on knowledge to develop new products and improve productivity; what distinguishes the current period is the speed with which knowledge is accumulated and associated economic activities developed. Countries differ with respect to where they are in this process of structural transformation, due to their starting points, varying technological and industrial specialisations, and different institutions and attitudes to change.

The changing composition of production and employment

4. This structural transformation has a number of dimensions. The first is the shift of economic activities between sectors in the economy and the associated reallocation of jobs. As OECD economies become richer, an increasing proportion of consumption and production activities take place in the service sector. Technological change is both directly and indirectly responsible for much of this shift. It facilitates the development of new services based on the use of information technologies (ITs) and, most importantly, it contributes to generating economy-wide productivity gains which are translated into higher incomes and hence more differentiated and service-oriented consumption patterns.

5. The shift to services is statistically well-documented. Approximately two-thirds of all business activity in the OECD area is conducted in the service sector, which accounts for about 70 per cent of all jobs. These shares have increased over time in all countries. Important structural differences remain, however, with the service share in business-sector value added highest in Australia and the United States, and lowest in Finland and Norway. This shift is even more pronounced in employment terms; reflecting its lower productivity, the share of services in total business employment is typically higher than in value added (Figure 1.1, top panel). At the same time, there is evidence (which cannot be easily captured in standard statistics) that the dividing line between industry and services is moving; many business service activities traditionally undertaken by integrated manufacturing firms have been spun off and are now undertaken by firms located in the service sector.

6. Compositional shifts are also occurring within manufacturing, as OECD economies move to higher quality and more differentiated activities. While manufacturing is declining in terms of both value added and employment, its high-technology segment (*i.e.* computers, electronics, aerospace and pharmaceuticals) has expanded in most countries (Figure 1.1, middle and bottom panels). This is especially the case for value added: high-tech production is high and rising in Japan, the United Kingdom and the United States. It is less so for jobs: reflecting the rapid productivity growth in this sector, the share of high-tech jobs in manufacturing has increased substantially only in France, Japan and the United Kingdom (and also in Finland, but the share remains very low); in the Netherlands and the United States it continues to be high, despite a relative decline since 1980 (such a decline can be partly traced to outsourcing of activities by firms in the high-tech manufacturing sector to the service sector).

Box 1.1. **Some definitions: from high-tech to knowledge-based industries**

The importance of technology-based activities in the economy has traditionally been approximated by the share of *high-technology manufacturing industries* (aerospace, computers, electronics, pharmaceuticals). This measure is becoming increasingly inadequate as it focuses only on the producers of technology and ignores its use. For example, firms in many manufacturing industries outside the high-tech segment (*e.g.* in plastics, cars, textiles or chemicals) are increasingly adopting technology-intensive production techniques. While their products are not high-tech in the traditional sense of the word, technology is fundamental to their production.

More importantly, given its size in the economy, the service sector is becoming an important user and even developer of new technologies (OECD, 1996*a*). Information and communications technologies are pervasive in most services, especially in communications, and in finance, insurance and business services. For this reason, this chapter adopts a broader measure of the *technology-based* or *knowledge-based* share in the economy. In addition to high-tech manufacturing, the category includes two other sectors: communication services; and the finance and insurance services sector. This definition of "knowledge-based" industries focuses on their "technology content", *i.e.* the extent to which they develop or use intensively new technologies. Hence, while education and even health are clearly "knowledge-based", they are not included.

7. More broadly, the direct contribution of technology- or knowledge-based industries to growth is explored in Figure 1.2 (see Box 1.1). The figure (top panel) shows the contribution of different sectors to business-sector value-added growth between 1980 and 1994 in the G7 countries. Knowledge-based industries typically accounted for about a quarter of total growth in output. Their contribution was largest in Japan, followed by Canada, Germany, the United Kingdom and the United States; it was lowest in Italy. In most countries, the contribution of high-tech manufacturing was the weakest of the three sectors (except in Japan and the United Kingdom), with service production providing the bulk of growth.

Figure 1.1. **Structural shifts in value added and employment**

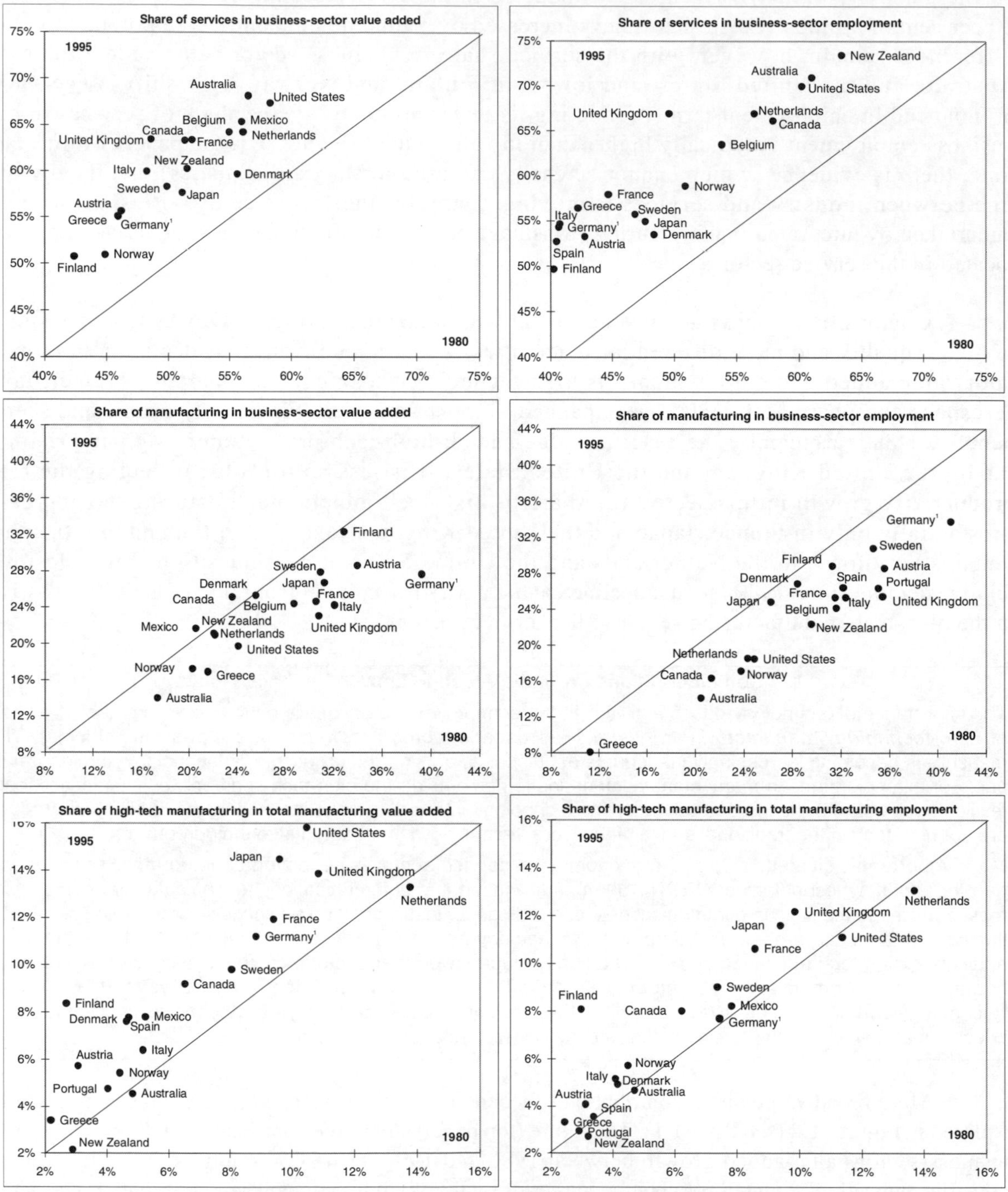

1. Data cover western Germany only.

Source: OECD, STAN and ISDB databases, 1997.

Figure 1.2. **The direct contribution of knowledge-based industries,[1] 1980-95**

Contributions to average annual growth rate of business sector value added, employment and labour productivity[2]

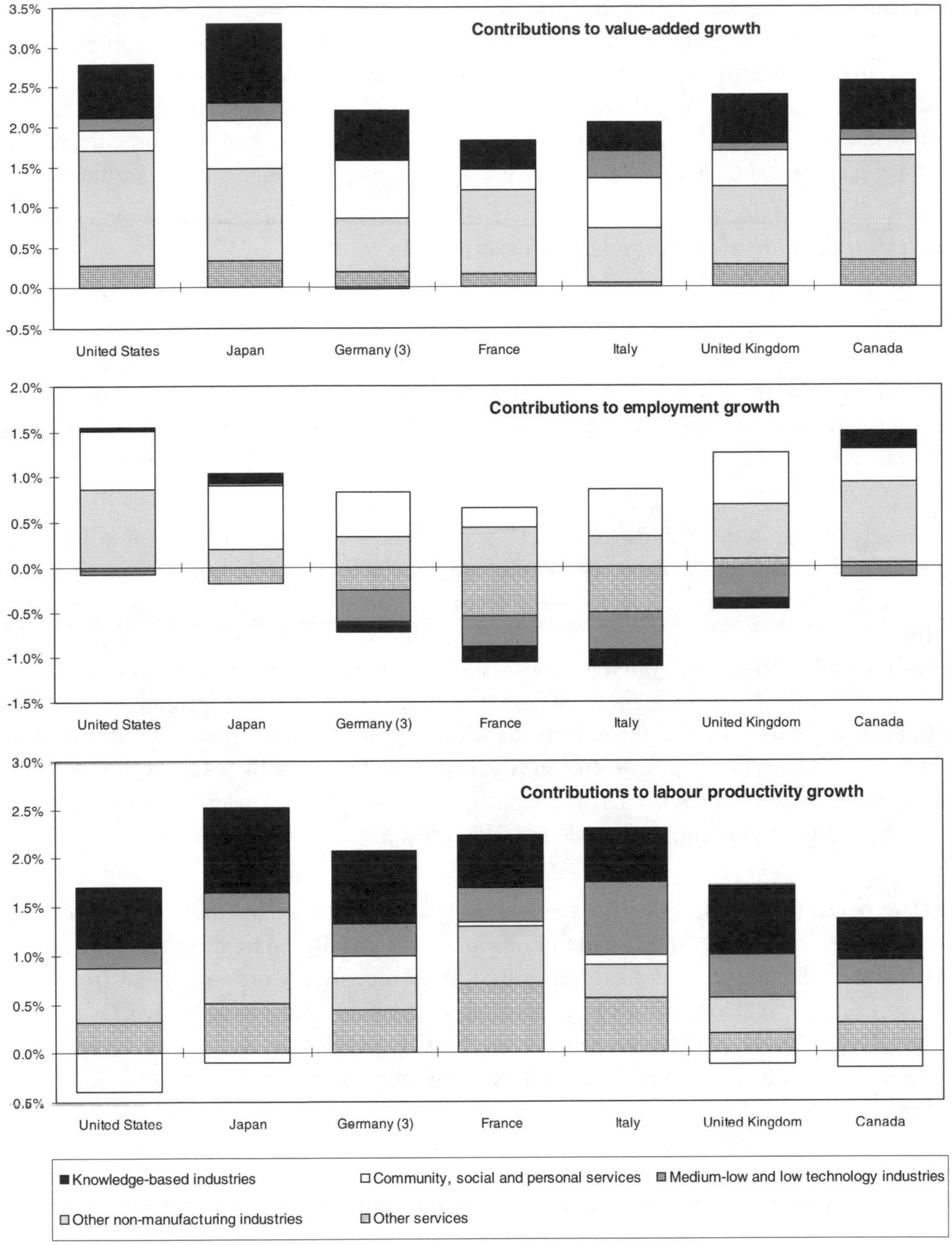

1. The knowledge-based industries group includes high- and medium-high-technology manufacturing, communication services, finance and insurance.
2. Contributions of sectors are calculated by the growth rates weighted by average shares in business sector GDP and employment.
3. Data cover western Germany only.

Source: OECD, STAN and ISDB databases, 1997.

8. While useful as an approximation of the direct contribution of technology-based production, such estimates give an incomplete picture of the importance of technology. Technology contributes to growth through many channels: directly through the production of technology-intensive goods and services; and more importantly, indirectly through its impact on prices, productivity, wages and incomes. As goods and services embodying new technology are widely adopted, production and consumption patterns change. Inventions such as the semiconductor, the computer, and applications such as the Internet, as well as advanced materials, the jet engine and new drugs, have all changed the way goods are produced and distributed, and altered demand patterns for business services, leisure, travel, health and education.

Changing investment patterns: intangibles, ICTs and skills

9. In addition to changes in the sectoral composition of production (which represents the output side), another important dimension of the structural transformation of OECD economies is the changing pattern of investment (the input side). This involves a tilt towards intangible investments *e.g.* in research and development (R&D), other forms of innovation-related assets, hardware and software, ICTs and in the upgrading of skills.

10. The level and growth of business R&D expenditures are the most often used indicator of innovative capacity. In practice, the capacity to innovate depends on a multitude of factors, ranging from the efforts made by firms themselves through investments, to the skill level of the workforce, or the "learning" ability of firms and the general environment within which they operate (Chapter 2). For small firms, some of these non-R&D innovative investments may be more important than R&D expenditures proper, suggesting that R&D alone is not a sufficient indicator of innovative behaviour. However, R&D remains critical as it plays a dual role: both in the development of new products and more efficient production processes, and in helping firms to identify, follow and potentially take advantage of knowledge initially developed elsewhere – it enhances their learning or "absorptive" capacity. This suggests that firms need a research capability to assimilate knowledge developed elsewhere.

11. R&D expenditures undertaken in the business sector dipped in the early 1990s in a large number of countries, reflecting in part the economic cycle and in part defence restructuring (see Chapter 3 for further discussion), but have recovered more recently. More important from the point of view of the structural transformation of economies is the fact that business R&D is increasingly undertaken in different parts of the economy. While most expenditures are still concentrated in a few high-technology manufacturing industries, such as computers, semiconductors and aerospace (which account for between 40 and 60 per cent of the business R&D effort), services account for an increasing share. This trend is particularly apparent in Australia and the United States, where 30-40 per cent of R&D is performed by the non-manufacturing sector – mainly by service firms (Figure 1.3), and is also the case in the United Kingdom. It is less evident in other European countries and Japan, partly because these countries have not yet extended their R&D surveys to provide better coverage of service firms.

12. The increasing share of services in total business R&D can be traced to different factors. First, a certain amount of research has traditionally been performed in the services (commercial R&D firms, design and engineering firms, etc.), and the generally increased weight of such activities in the economy has thus raised their share of R&D. Second, research is being carried out in completely new areas, such as product development where IT, entertainment and information exchange converge (multimedia, CD-ROM publications, etc.). Third, some activities formerly carried out by manufacturing are now assured by service "spin-off" firms. Software firms, which are now considered to be a part of the service sector, are one example.

Figure 1.3. **R&D in the manufacturing and non-manufacturing sectors, 1980-95**

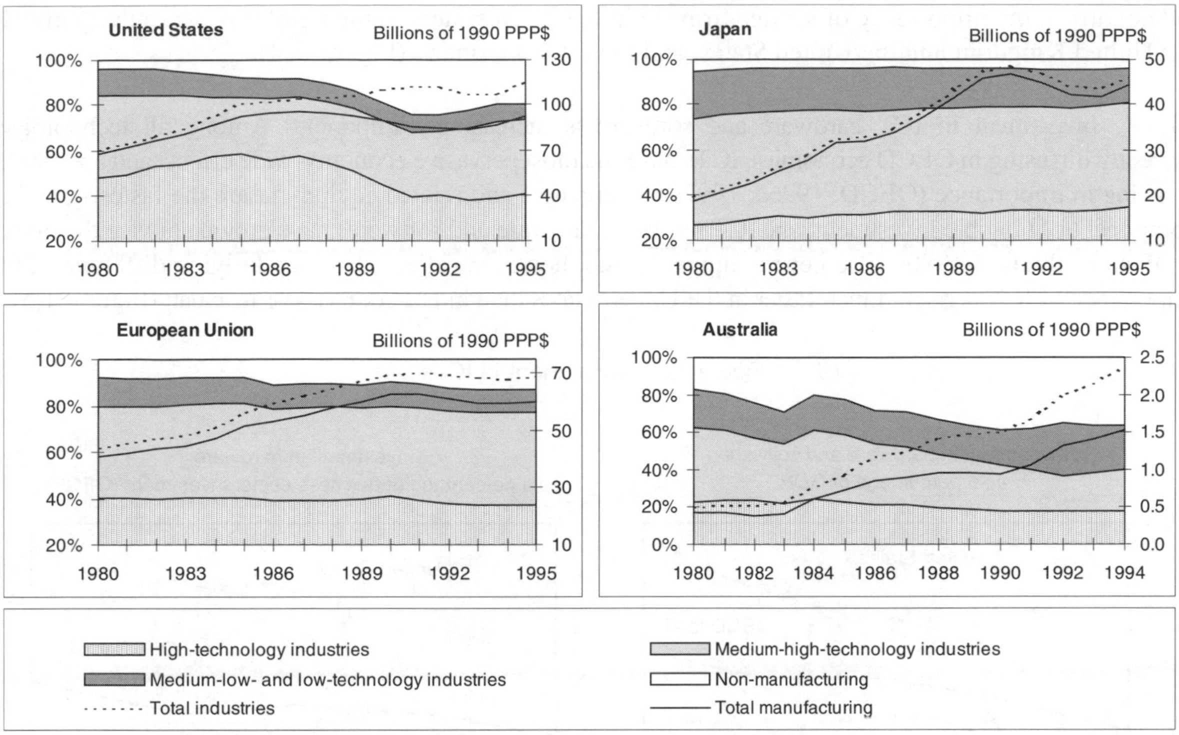

Source: OECD, ANBERD database, December 1997.

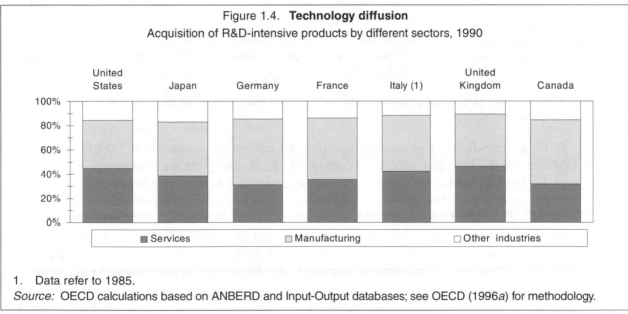

Figure 1.4. **Technology diffusion**

Acquisition of R&D-intensive products by different sectors, 1990

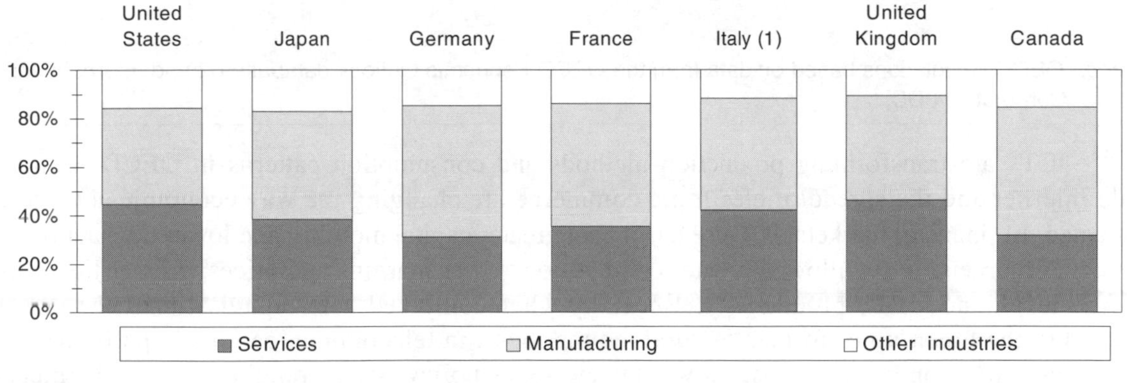

1. Data refer to 1985.

Source: OECD calculations based on ANBERD and Input-Output databases; see OECD (1996*a*) for methodology.

13. In addition to directly investing in intangible assets such as R&D, service firms invest indirectly through the purchase of R&D-intensive investment goods. In most countries, despite its growing role in developing new technologies through R&D expenditures and other innovation-related efforts, the service sector is principally a user of technology. Service industries as diverse as social and personal services (an industry category covering, among other things, equipment purchases by the

health industry), transport and storage, real estate and business services, or wholesale and retail trade, are the main buyers of technologically sophisticated machinery and equipment. Among the G7 countries, the importance of service firms in indirect investment in intangibles is particularly high in the United Kingdom and the United States, and lowest in Germany (Figure 1.4).

14. Investment in ICT hardware and software is increasingly important. Among all technologies currently diffusing in OECD economies, ICTs have the most pervasive economy-wide effects and are rapidly growing in importance (OECD, 1996*a*; 1997*b*). Computers and related equipment are the fastest-growing component of tangible investment, and ICT markets (hardware and software) have grown at twice the rate of GDP since the mid-1980s. The general upward trend, however, reflects large underlying differences; the importance of ICT is rising much faster in the United States than in EU countries or in Japan (Figure 1.5).

Figure 1.5. **Investment in ICTs**

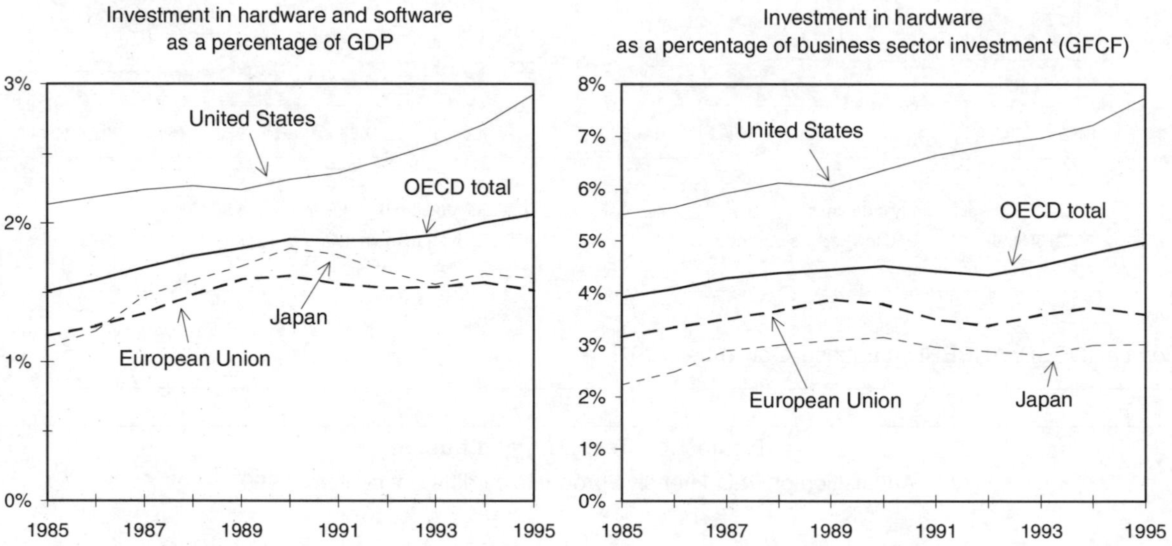

Source: OECD calculations based on data from the OECD Economic Outlook database 62 and International Data Corporation (IDC).

15. ICTs are transforming production methods and consumption patterns in OECD economies, while Internet and the spread of electronic commerce are changing the way economic activities are conducted. In financial markets, ICT use has meant greater capital mobility and lower transaction costs. In product markets, it has allowed greater competition, lower margins and prices, greater flexibility at the firm level, and higher productivity, especially when combined with organisational change. ICTs have led to the break-up of former "natural monopolies", in telecommunications in particular. Their widespread diffusion has also raised a whole new set of policy issues, ranging from their impact on macroeconomic policy to concerns about the adequacy of existing regulatory frameworks.

16. Intangible investments also include training expenditures and skill formation. Despite the lack of adequate internationally comparable statistics in this area, the available evidence points to increasing investment in training by firms and governments (Chapter 11). Levels of education have risen steadily, increasing the supply of highly skilled manpower. At the same time, demand for highly skilled workers has risen steadily, while that for the unskilled has declined significantly. As revealed by occupational data, these trends are reflected in the changing distribution of skills in total employment. Over the last 10-15 years, there

has been a significant increase in the share of white-collar high-skilled occupations in total employment, which now accounts for between a quarter and a third of all jobs in most large OECD countries (Figure 1.6).

Figure 1.6. **Trends in the distribution of skills in total employment**

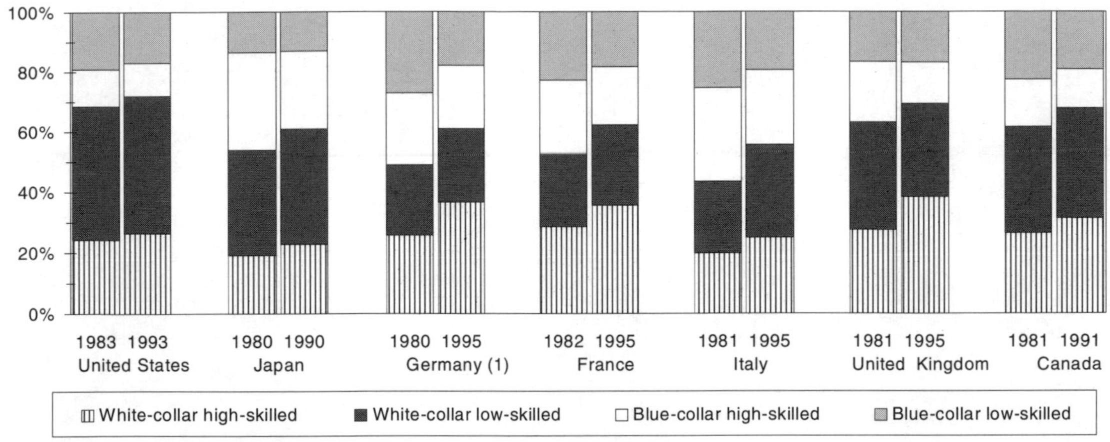

1. Data cover western Germany in 1980 and unified Germany in 1995.
Source: OECD and Eurostat data.

Globalisation and technology: the driving forces of transformation

17. A third dimension of the structural transformation of OECD economies from industrial to knowledge-based concerns the role of globalisation and its interaction with technological change. A well-documented deepening of the economic interdependency between firms and countries is taking place, through increased trade, foreign direct investments, international sourcing of production inputs and inter-firm alliances, including the internationalisation of R&D activities. This process has been made possible to a large extent by the falling cost of telecommunications and the increased availability of ICTs. It has also been spurred by deregulation of financial and product markets, a process that owes part of its impetus to technical change. In turn, increased international competition acts as an incentive for firms to create new products or more efficient production processes; and the expansion of international trade and production provides firms with more resources to finance innovative efforts, especially in countries with small domestic markets.

18. The direct role of technology in this process is reflected in the changing patterns of international trade. An increasing share of trade is in similar but differentiated products (intra-industry trade), and involves a growing share of high-tech products. Exports from high-technology industries have risen faster than average, now accounting for about 17 per cent of OECD manufacturing exports. Between 1980 and 1994, the share of high-tech products such as computers, semiconductors, pharmaceuticals, telecom products, aerospace and scientific instruments has grown faster than that of any other type of commodity (Figure 1.7). These figures, however, highlight only the most visible aspect of the relationship between technology and globalisation. Technological change combines with increased economic interdependency to intensify and alter the nature of global competition across a widening spectrum of industries. In industries characterised as low- or medium-tech, technology and associated organisational change increasingly provide an edge in productivity and enable product differentiation, crucially shaping competitiveness and value added. At the same time, globalisation adds to pressures for adjustment and restructuring, which can particularly hurt unskilled workers as well as firms in industries vulnerable to foreign competition.

Figure 1.7. **Dynamism of high-technology exports**

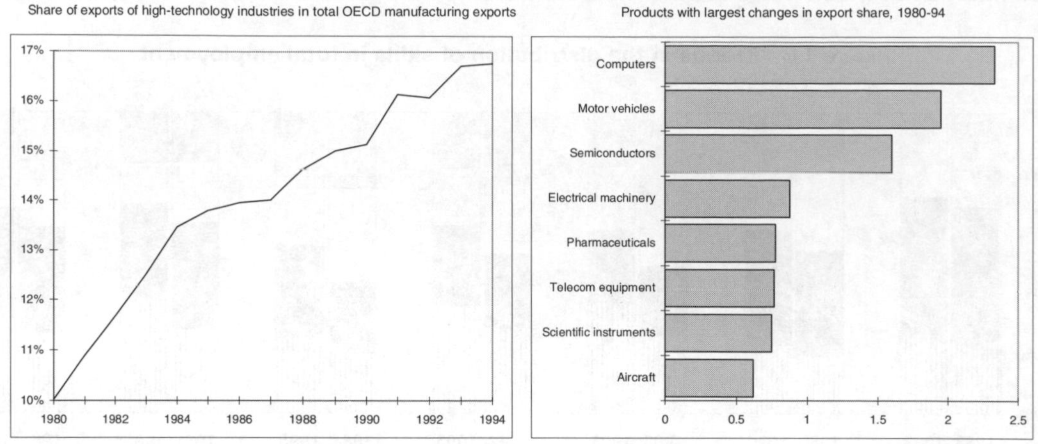

Source: OECD, STAN database, December 1997.

1.3. Technology and productivity: microeconomic evidence and macroeconomic puzzles

19. Productivity gains drive economic growth, so that understanding the role of technology in the growth process requires examining how it affects productivity at the micro and at the aggregate level. Empirically, the technology-productivity link is most clearly seen at the firm level, especially when other complementary investments, such as organisational change and changes in production methods and training, are taken into account. It is still visible at the sectoral level, although weaker, given the variety of firm characteristics and behaviour. At the level of total manufacturing or of the business sector as a whole, it is difficult to empirically establish a clear link between an indicator of technology effort such as R&D and productivity growth.

20. The difficulty in establishing this relationship empirically can be traced to a number of factors. One is that both innovative effort and productivity tend to be mismeasured, a problem which may have become more severe with the growing share of services in economic activity (see Box 1.2 on the "Solow paradox"). Another is the lag between the time when innovative efforts take place and when they translate into productivity gains. A third is the difficulty in disentangling the impact of technology from that of other factors affecting productivity, such as infrastructure, the accumulation of physical and human capital, economies of scale, market structure, demographic change, international trade or the degree of competition. But, most importantly, it is because economy-wide productivity gains from new technologies are mainly generated during the process of diffusion of new products and processes throughout the economy.

21. The impact of technology on productivity is crucially conditioned by the policy environment and the framework conditions within which firms operate. Excessive regulations or distortionary taxes which inhibit risk-taking and the creation of new technology-based firms (NTBFs) will reduce productivity growth associated with the development of new products and processes. Rigidities in labour markets can retard the adoption of changes in production necessary to realise the potential of new technologies. In product markets, monopoly structures in industries developing new technologies allow them to appropriate benefits of innovation but limit productivity gains in user industries. Similarly, excessive regulation in services blunts incentives to modernise through the adoption of new technologies.

Box 1.2. **The productivity paradox: towards a solution?**

Since the first oil shock and until recently, OECD countries have simultaneously experienced a slowdown of productivity growth and exceptionally rapid technical advance, giving rise to what has been labelled the "Solow paradox".

Part of the paradox can be traced to measurement issues. Both technical change and productivity are mismeasured. R&D statistics capture only part of the innovative effort and do not provide information on the results of that effort. In terms of productivity, there are serious problems with the measurement of output, especially in the services. New technology is increasingly adopted in service sub-sectors where mismeasurement is notorious (*e.g.* the health industry and financial institutions and insurance). To the extent that the weight of services in GDP has steadily increased over time, overall mismeasurement has probably increased. Another source of mismeasurement concerns qualitative changes brought about by innovations. Conventional price indices fail to fully capture changes in quality and thus understate the growth rate for output and productivity in innovative industries such as computers.

Other explanations focus on adaptation lags associated with learning and on the changing nature of technical advance. Using new technologies efficiently requires time, effort and major investments in training and organisational change. Mastering a radically new technology is a long process, as the example of the dynamo at the end of the 19th century shows (David, 1991). It took time before complementary technologies, such as the electrical engine, were efficient enough to realise electricity's productivity potential. At the same time, there is some evidence that innovative effort may be increasingly devoted to product differentiation, increased quality, rapid introduction of innovations, or just-in-time delivery. Such activities, although they have high private rates of return, generate fewer externalities (spillovers). As other firms derive less benefit from them, the overall productivity of research tends to fall.

These explanations contribute to a better understanding of the productivity paradox, without completely resolving it. Nevertheless, the inclusion of more sophisticated measures of technology goes some way towards providing a better explanation of productivity growth. An example is the strong link established between measures of embodied technology diffusion and productivity in the ICT segment of the service sector; another is the mounting firm-level evidence on the positive effects of technology and productivity.

From firm-level to sectoral and aggregate productivity

22. The growing body of empirical evidence on the determinants of productivity at the firm level suggests that aggregate productivity patterns may give a misleading picture. There is a large variation of behaviour and characteristics among firms within industries, including with respect to development and use of technology. Many firms in low-tech industries make substantial innovation-related efforts. The recent availability of establishment- or firm-level data in a number of OECD countries has allowed technology-productivity relationships to be explored at the micro level (OECD, 1996*b*). Such firm-level research illustrates that developing or adopting new technology spurs higher productivity, but that a number of other factors, such as worker training, organisational structures and managerial ability, are also critical (see Chapter 11 for further discussion on these issues). Recent OECD work based on firm-level data for France, Japan and the United States has shown that R&D-performing firms tend to have higher labour productivity levels and growth rates than non-R&D firms, although this is more the case in France and the United States than in Japan (Figure 1.8). Studies for the United States (Conference Board, 1997) and Canada (Baldwin *et al.*, 1995) have found that technology users are more productive than non-technology users. Results from other countries reach similar conclusions.

Figure 1.8. **Technology and productivity at the firm level in France, Japan and the United States**
Labour productivity levels expressed relative to non-R&D firms in initial period (=1)

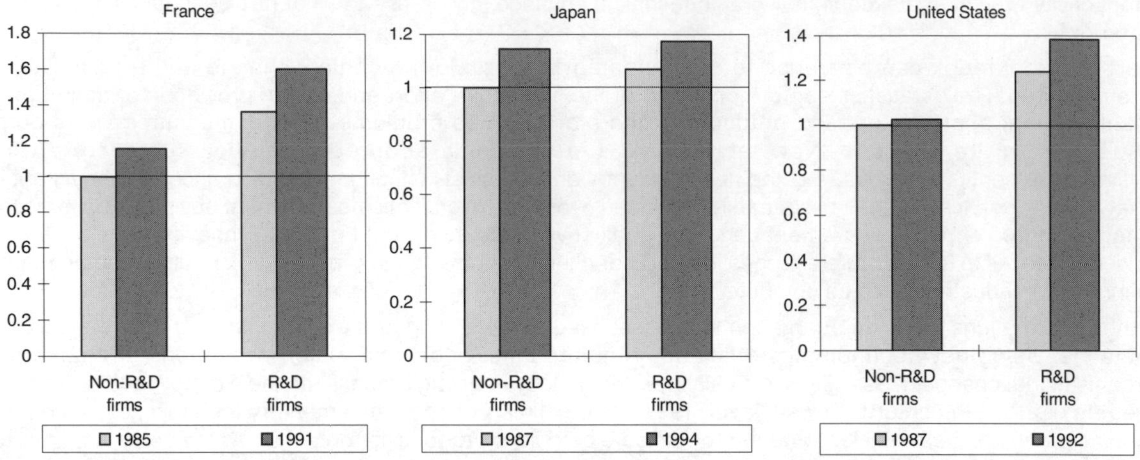

Source: OECD Secretariat.

Figure 1.9. **Labour productivity growth in different parts of the economy**
Average annual growth rates,[1] 1980-95

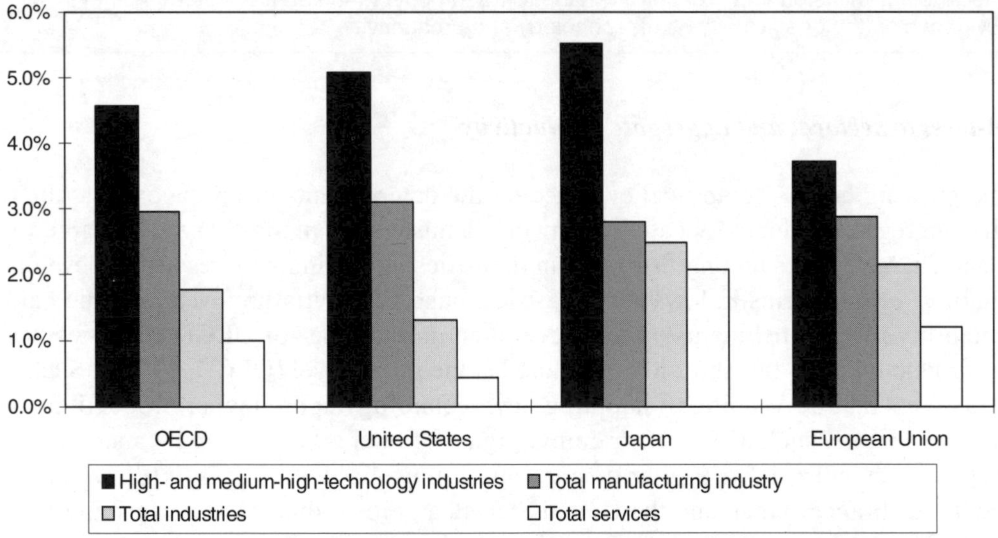

1. OECD total and EU data are estimates. Calculations for total services cover the 1985-94 period only.
Source: OECD estimates based on ANA, STAN, ADB, ISDB databases and Labour Force Statistics database, 1997.

23. Aggregate productivity trends reflect the structure of economies as well as productivity in different segments. Partly as a result of innovative effort, productivity tends to be higher in manufacturing than in the services. Productivity growth in service-oriented economies such as the United States is lower than that in economies with a bigger manufacturing sector (such as Germany or Japan). The impact of technology is particularly visible in the productivity performance of the high- and medium-high-tech segments of manufacturing, which has been much faster than in manufacturing as a whole (Figure 1.9). Moreover, while productivity increases in high- and medium-high-technology industries have been mainly driven by output increases, productivity growth in medium-low- and low-technology manufacturing can be mainly traced to labour shedding.

Technology diffusion: the key to economy-wide productivity gains

24. Understanding the relationship between technology and productivity requires moving beyond an exclusive focus on R&D efforts in the high-tech segment of manufacturing. Given the small size of this segment, even strong productivity gains linked to intensive innovative efforts will not necessarily translate into strong aggregate productivity growth. For example, even within manufacturing, the high-tech sector accounts for only 30 per cent of total manufacturing labour productivity growth in Japan, 25 per cent in the United States, and 20 per cent in Germany and the United Kingdom (Figure 1.10). For the business sector as a whole, productivity gains in the high- and medium-high-tech manufacturing industries combined account for between 15 and 35 per cent of total business-sector productivity growth (highest in the case of the United States, lowest in France, Germany and Italy). Productivity growth in knowledge-based industries (*i.e.* high- and medium-high-tech manufacturing, communication services, finance and insurance) accounts for almost half of total business-sector productivity growth in the United States, over one-third in Canada, Japan and the United Kingdom, 30 per cent in Germany, and a quarter in France and Italy (Figure 1.2 above).

25. Beyond such decomposition exercises, the more general issue is that, despite the importance of investment in R&D for productivity growth, it is less the invention of new products and processes and their initial commercial exploitation that generate major economic benefits than their diffusion and use. Innovating firms do not fully appropriate the productivity benefits of successful innovations. Rather, these become embodied in goods and ultimately contribute to higher productivity for the economy as a whole. This suggests that potential barriers to efficient technology diffusion can act as a brake on economy-wide productivity gains.

Figure 1.10. **Contributions to manufacturing labour productivity growth**
Contributions of different industries to average annual growth rate,[1] 1980-95

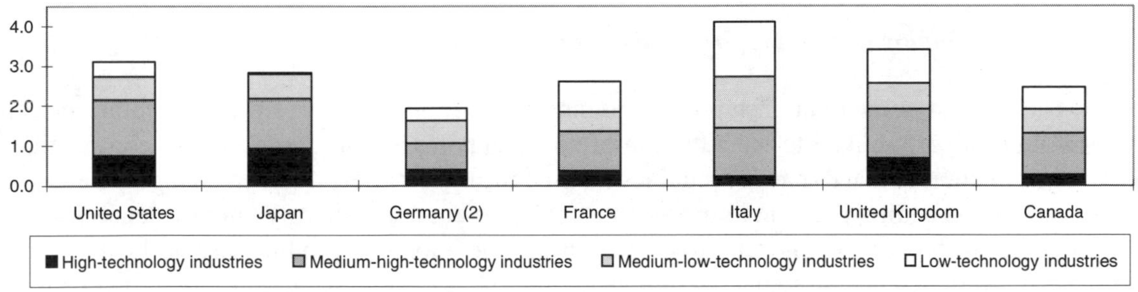

1. Contributions of sectors are calculated by the growth rates weighted by average shares in business sector GDP and employment.
2. Data cover western Germany only.

Source: OECD, STAN database, 1997.

26. For many industries (especially outside manufacturing), buying and assimilating technologically sophisticated machinery and equipment, often ICTs, is the main way of acquiring technology. Together with training, such capital-embodied technology raises the technological level of an industry's capital stock, and improves productivity. The importance of such embodied technology for total factor productivity (TFP) was explored in a recent OECD study (OECD, 1996*b*). A formal breakdown of economy-wide TFP growth in the 1970s and 1980s based on estimates of the impact of R&D and of technology diffusion showed that for the ten OECD countries covered by the analysis: *(i)* technology diffusion has contributed substantially to TFP growth, often accounting for more than half of productivity growth in a given period; *(ii)* its contribution typically exceeds that of direct R&D efforts; and *(iii)* technology diffusion had a much greater impact on TFP growth in the 1980s than in the 1970s.

27. The impact of technology diffusion is felt most strongly in the services, which are increasingly active as developers and users of new technologies, and in particular in the ICT segment of services. In addition, productivity growth is strongly dependent on international technology diffusion. As technology diffusion among OECD countries has increased, foreign R&D has had a major impact on domestic productivity. Cross-border trade in technology and the dynamic role played by multinational enterprises and research-intensive industries bring benefits whose distribution differs across firms, industries and countries. While for large countries such as France, Germany, Japan and the United States, domestic technology diffusion continues to be more important for TFP growth than technology imports, for countries such as Canada, Denmark and the Netherlands, the reverse is true. But in all countries, the role of imported technology was more important in the 1980s than in the 1970s, a result consistent with the increased importance of technology-intensive goods in exports.

1.4. The impact on employment, skills and wages: potential gains and current problems

28. The impact of technology on employment, wages and the structure of skills in individual firms and industries or in the economy as a whole is the result of complex interactions, which have been reviewed in detail in a number of recent OECD studies (OECD, 1994; 1996*b*; 1997*c*). While historically technical change has gone in hand with growth in employment and wages and with stable unemployment, many OECD countries are experiencing high unemployment levels and sluggish job growth in a period of rapid technical advance. This raises questions about the adequacy of existing mechanisms for translating new products and higher productivity growth into more and better jobs. The key to the technology-employment relationship, and by implication the role for policy, is hence twofold: first, understanding how innovation affects the behaviour of firms, and ensuring that the right environment is present for firms to benefit from developing or introducing new products and processes and hence create jobs; and second, understanding the mechanisms of the transition from the firm level to the sectoral and economy-wide picture and removing existing barriers in this respect.

Technology and employment at the firm and aggregate level

29. The interest in the relationship between innovation and jobs at the firm level comes both from concerns about layoffs linked to the adoption of new technologies and more intense competition and from the important role that dynamic technology-based firms are believed to play in modern economies. In effect, the job shedding inherent to modern technologies contrasts sharply with evidence from many studies that innovators as a whole tend to create jobs, as the improved productivity or the new products developed through new technologies are translated into increased demand and jobs. The phenomenal success of a number of such firms, especially in the United States, has driven home the realisation that economies benefit greatly from an environment where such entrepreneurial initiatives can flourish.

30. Much recent research has used firm-level data to investigate the relationship between technology and employment in a number of OECD countries. These studies broadly find a positive relationship between innovation and employment at the firm level. They show that R&D performing firms tend to experience positive growth in employment, often superior to that experienced by non-R&D performing firms. In addition, they suggest that NTBFs tend to achieve faster rates of growth and employment than other start-ups. This evidence of a positive relationship suggests that some firms cope better than others with new technologies. These differences are explored in more detail in Chapter 9.

31. Such studies offer valuable insights and convincing evidence that the introduction of new technologies can lead to job gains at the level of the firm; they nevertheless fail to appreciate the full contribution of small technology-based dynamic firms to overall welfare, including employment growth. For instance, the impact of technologically advanced firms goes well beyond the jobs they generate

directly in the process of producing goods and services. The impact of technology on employment at the industry level depends on the nature of the jobs created, the extent to which they substitute for other jobs, and also on the effect on rival firms in a given industry as well as in other industries or countries.

32. In turn, sectoral impacts say little about aggregate employment or unemployment. Technology is accompanied by physical or intangible investments, which generate demand and employment in supplier industries and in capital goods. In addition, whether they decrease prices or create new products, innovations result in higher wages and profits, thus increasing real incomes, demand for goods as well as for services and, consequently, creating jobs. The fact that these compensating effects have not worked in many countries suggests problems that policy needs to address. Finally, when workers are displaced by labour-saving technology, this is likely to put downward pressure on wages and partly offset labour substitution. The net outcome on employment depends on the nature of technological advance, the degree of substitution between inputs, the degree of labour market flexibility and mechanisms for upgrading labour skills, and the role of institutions. The impact on unemployment also needs to consider the effect on the supply and demand of different kinds of labour. A host of new technologies, from time-saving devices to new drugs, have changed labour participation rates and more generally transformed the nature of work. The failure of equilibrating mechanisms to work adequately can be traced to skill mismatches, labour-market rigidities and to problems in the institutional and regulatory structure of economies.

33. The interaction between technology and jobs at the sectoral and aggregate level is closely related to the structural transformation that the OECD economies are undergoing and which was examined earlier. The shift to services and to high-technology activities within manufacturing is apparent in the employment trends of different sectors. For the OECD area as a whole, service employment is rising rapidly, and particularly in two very different segments: community, social and personal services; and finance, insurance, and business services. High-technology manufacturing jobs have increased slightly since 1980, but show a very cyclical pattern (*i.e.* rising fast throughout the 1980s and declining faster than other manufacturing jobs between 1990 and 1994) (Figure 1.11).

Figure 1.11. **Employment trends by industry, total OECD**

1980=100

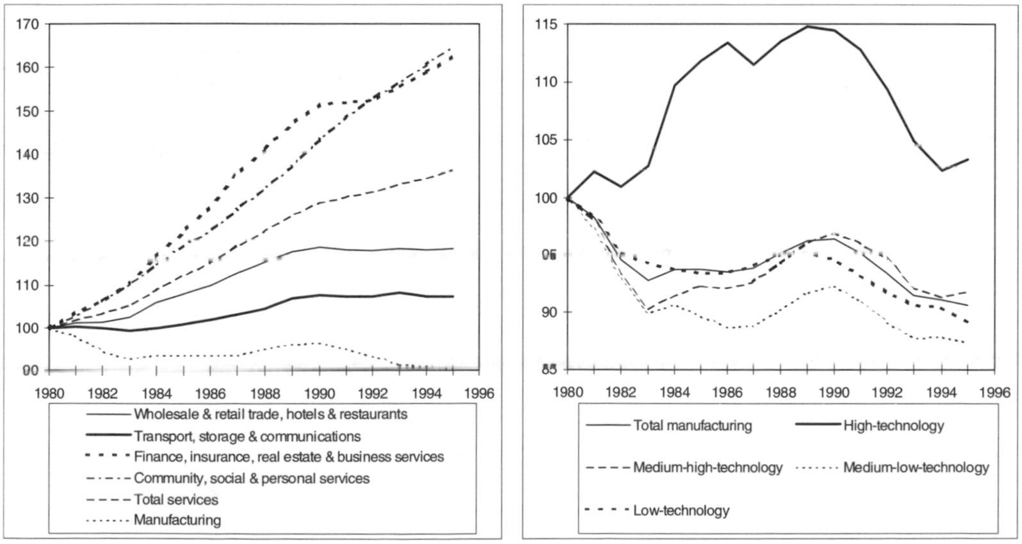

Source: OECD, STAN, ISDB databases and Labour Force Statistics database, 1997.

34. The slight pick-up of high-tech manufacturing jobs since 1994 should not disguise the fact that they remain a very small part of the total and cannot be expected to contribute in any significant way to overall employment growth. Such jobs have had a negative impact on the change in total business-sector employment between 1980 and 1995 in most G7 countries, with a very slight positive contribution only in Canada and Japan. As Figure 1.2 (middle panel) above shows, by far the largest contributions to overall employment growth came from jobs in community, social and personal services (Germany, Italy, Japan, the United States), finance, insurance and business services (France, the United Kingdom), and wholesale and retail trade (Canada). More generally, an assessment of the overall impact of technology on jobs should not concentrate on the high-tech sector but should look more widely at how innovations and their application change employment opportunities and requirements throughout the economy.

35. The lack of dynamism of manufacturing jobs is also apparent when examining the relationship between productivity and employment growth. The manufacturing sector – and especially its high-tech segment – is characterised by strong productivity gains, in large part due to its innovative efforts. Yet these gains are not translated into employment growth. Figure 1.12 shows that while manufacturing productivity increased in practically all countries during the 1980s and early 1990s, manufacturing employment declined in most in the 1980s and in all between 1990 and 1995. Furthermore, the lack of a positive relationship between productivity gains and job gains suggests that while the technology-based productivity improvements may occur overwhelmingly in manufacturing, the technology-related job gains are in the services. This partly reflects the "contracting out" of activities previously conducted within manufacturing firms, and partly the process of technology diffusion discussed above.

36. In services, technology directly affects the quantity and quality of jobs via the introduction of new processes and the creation of new products (*e.g.* automated teller machines, computers used in financial services, scanners in supermarket checkouts). More important, however, is the indirect impact through the additional demand for services arising from higher incomes. As incomes increase, demand for services increases more than proportionately. To the extent that technology raises productivity, it is the main force behind medium-term increases in wages and incomes.

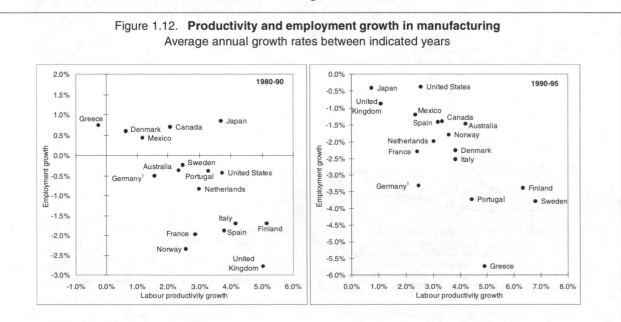

Figure 1.12. **Productivity and employment growth in manufacturing**

Average annual growth rates between indicated years

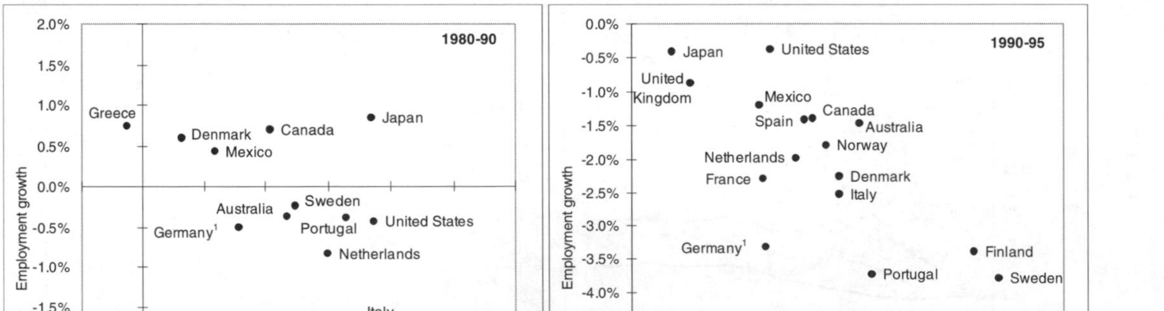

1. Data cover western Germany only.

Source: OECD, STAN database, 1997.

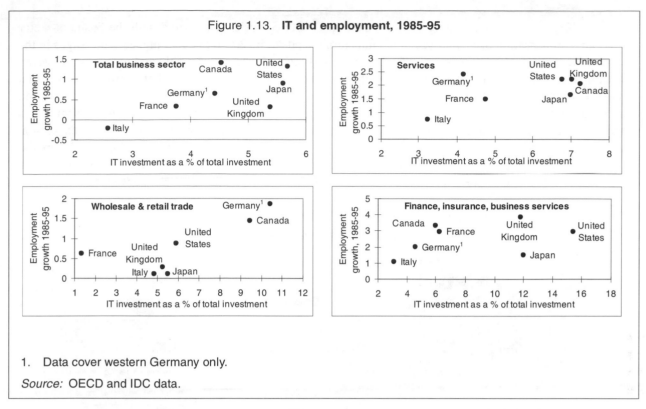

Figure 1.13. **IT and employment, 1985-95**

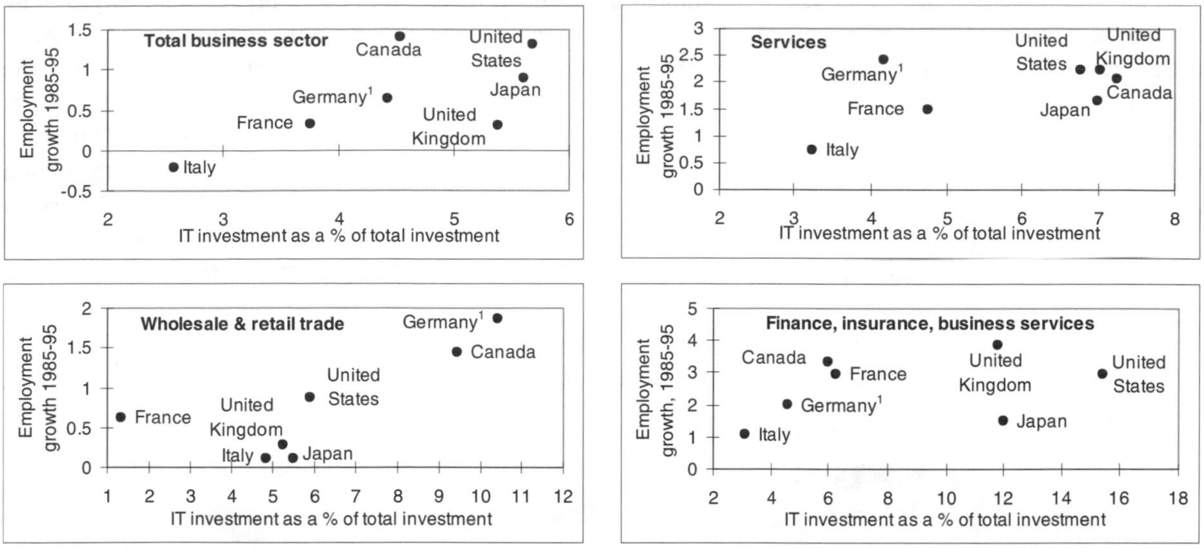

1. Data cover western Germany only.

Source: OECD and IDC data.

37. While the overall impact is difficult to establish empirically, the evidence available from countries with an increasing share of employment in services suggests that even though the diffusion of technology in the services will increase productivity and provoke the same kind of restructuring that has occurred or is occurring in the manufacturing sector, new demand and new job creation will more than replace the activities and jobs lost. By plotting employment growth against the intensity of IT (defined as the share of IT investment in total investment), Figure 1.13 provides some evidence to this effect. It suggests that employment gains in the 1980s were larger in countries that invested more in the application of new technologies (Canada, the United Kingdom, the United States). This is true economy-wide, but also for the service sector as a whole, as well as for segments as different as wholesale and retail trade, and finance, insurance and business services, where labour-saving technologies have been broadly introduced. These employment gains underscore the importance of an appropriate regulatory environment and flexible product and labour markets, which help translate investments in new technologies into new services, higher demand and more jobs.

The impact on wages and skills

38. Another dimension of labour market developments important for understanding the technology-employment relationship concerns quality of employment in terms of wages and skills. Technology both destroys and creates jobs, but beyond net employment gains or losses, it is increasingly apparent that workers with different skill levels are affected differently. While technical change renders the skills of some highly trained employees obsolete, it tends to be mainly associated with the decline in wages or employment opportunities of unskilled workers, as well as favouring wage premiums or better job prospects among skilled or "knowledge" workers. This raises important policy issues ranging from the training or other active labour market policies needed to upgrade the skills of those who benefit least from the introduction of new technologies in the workplace to the investment policies needed to help human capital develop and realise its potential.

39. Wages differ significantly across sectors in OECD countries. Compared with the business-sector average, compensation per employee in manufacturing tends to be 20-30 per cent higher, with wages in the service sector as a whole typically just below average (Figure 1.14). Substantial variations exist, however, within both services and manufacturing. Within services, relative wages are higher in two segments that make extensive use of ICTs: finance, insurance, real estate and business services, and transport and communications services. Within manufacturing, compensation per employee in the high-tech segment is typically 20-25 per cent above average, and the gap has tended to widen over time. Japan is an exception, with the highest relative wages in the medium-high-tech segment of manufacturing. This trend seems to corroborate evidence from firm-level studies (reviewed in OECD, 1996*a*), which suggests that there is a technology-related wage premium (due to higher productivity, rent sharing or efficiency wages).

Figure 1.14. **Relative wages in different parts of the economy**[1,2]

Relative compensation per employee in nominal terms

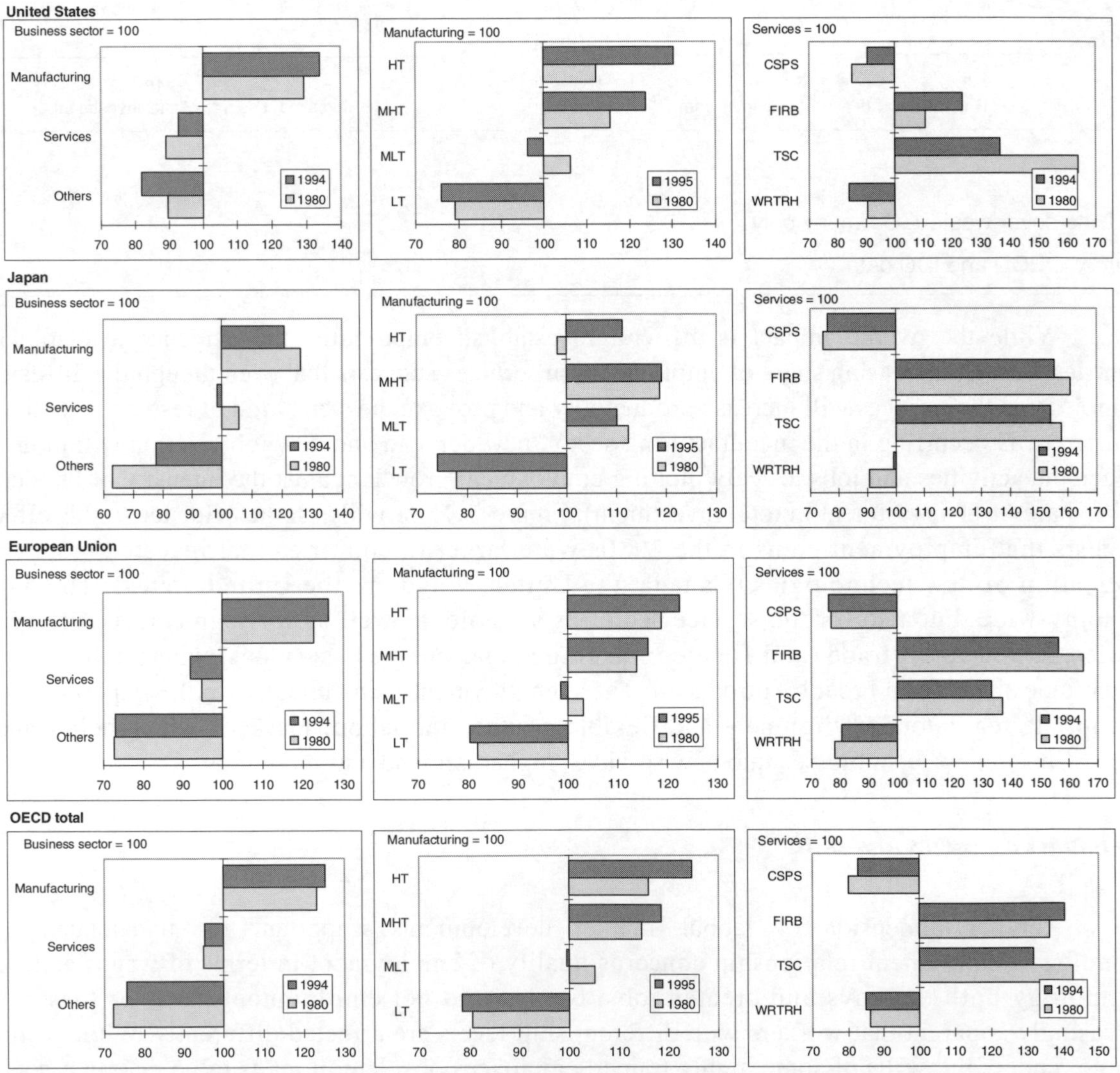

1. HT = High technology; MHT = Medium-high technology; MLT = Medium-low technology; LT = Low technology; CSPS = Community, social and personal services; FIRB = Finance, insurance, real estate and business services; TSC = Transport, storage and communications; WRTRH = Wholesale and retail trade, hotels and restaurants.
2. The data do not adjust for variations in hours worked in different parts of the economy.

Source: OECD, STAN database, December 1997.

40. In terms of skills, the data clearly show that employment growth has been mainly fuelled by the growth in white-collar high-skill jobs. In many EU countries, these are the only jobs that showed an increase. Figure 1.15 shows the contributions of jobs with different occupational characteristics to employment growth in the economy as a whole, as well as in manufacturing and services. Of the countries shown, growth in occupational categories other than white-collar high-skill accounted for more than half of total employment growth only in Ireland and the United States. This increased importance of white-collar high-skilled jobs is not simply a structural effect due to the increase in the significance of service activities (which employ overwhelmingly white-collar workers). As Figure 1.16 shows, an "upskilling" process is taking place in both manufacturing and services.

Figure 1.15. **Upskilling in total employment growth**
Contributions to average annual growth between indicated years

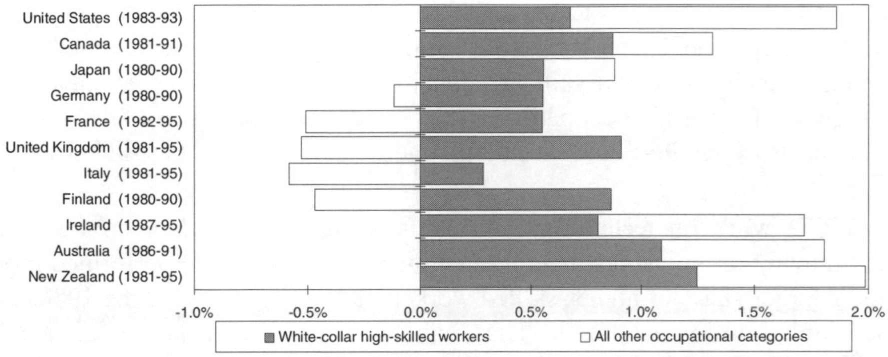

Source: OECD Secretariat estimations from national data, International Labour Office, Eurostat, 1997.

Figure 1.16. **Upskilling in manufacturing and service employment growth**
Contributions to average annual growth between indicated years

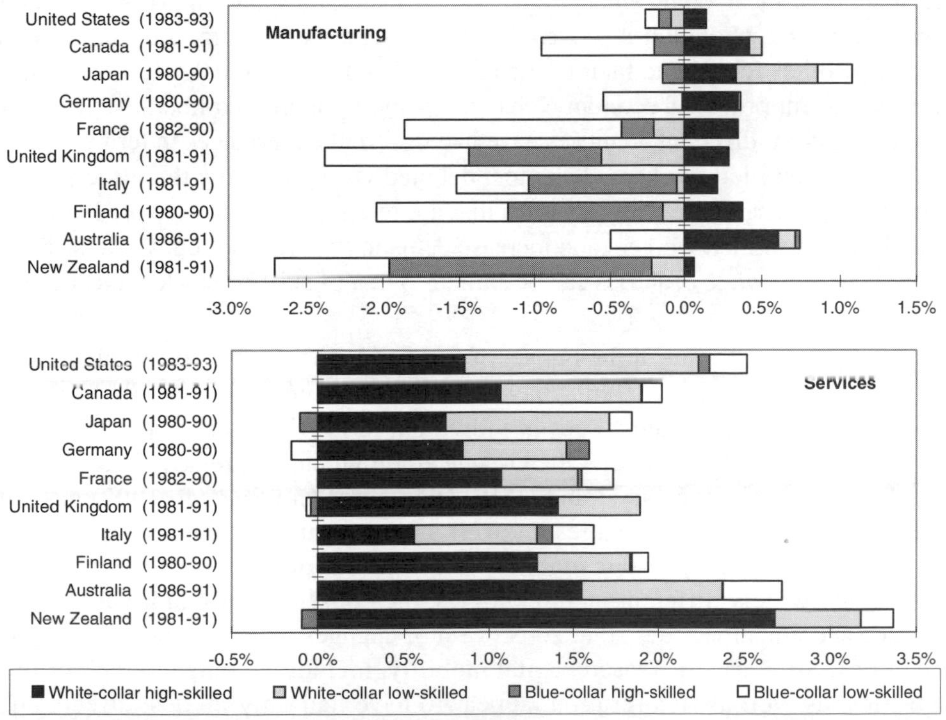

Source: OECD calculations based on national data, 1997.

41. In manufacturing, the decline in employment is associated in many countries with a decline in blue-collar low-skilled jobs (Australia, Canada, France, Germany, the United States), but also in blue-collar high-skill ones (Finland, Italy, New Zealand). In all countries where manufacturing employment declined overall, white-collar high-skill manufacturing jobs actually increased. In the services, employment growth entailed increases in both high-skill and low-skill white-collar jobs, but in most countries in Figure 1.16 growth was primarily driven by white-collar high-skilled jobs (Australia, Canada, Finland, France, Germany, New Zealand and the United Kingdom). Only in Italy, Japan and the United States is the contribution of white-collar low-skilled employment higher than that of white-collar high-skilled jobs.

42. In general, the generation and diffusion of new technologies, shifts in the composition of final demand, and shifts in labour supply all underlie changes in the skill composition of employment and in the importance of different occupational categories to job growth. Even though it is hard to identify the impact of each, it is generally agreed that when new technologies are introduced into production processes, the demand for low-skilled workers drops and that for high-skilled workers rises. At the same time, and in addition to this upskilling, technology can also have a "deskilling" effect. As new technologies perform a greater variety of tasks, the skills required for certain occupations may be reduced. There is, in fact, evidence that IT is reducing the requirements of middle-management jobs, traditionally thought of as skilled.

43. Recent OECD work on technology and skills using industry data on R&D and workers' qualifications has shown that industries that invested more in research and performed more innovative activity employed a larger share of higher-skilled workers at the beginning of the 1980s and continued to upgrade human capital during the decade. Thus, increased upskilling is not merely a consequence of some labour-biased technological shock. Sectoral human capital formation and innovative effort can be read as a mutually reinforcing and cumulative process which can have a lasting effect on industrial performance (OECD, 1996*a*). The employment effects of technological advance, and technology policy for that matter, are strongly influenced by this interplay.

44. While there is a clear complementarity between technology and skills at the microeconomic level, for the economy as a whole it has proven difficult to separate the effects of technological change from a wide array of other forces and factors such as trade and institutional effects. During the 1980s, many countries underwent profound economic change, including increased liberalisation of product and labour markets. In addition, different countries have had different experiences in terms of changes in the supply of skilled and unskilled workers. The most debated issue concerns the effects of trade and of globalisation more generally. Trade with countries that are relatively rich in unskilled labour can reduce domestic demand for low-skilled workers and increase demand for high-skilled workers. Thus, the effect of trade with low-skill, low-wage countries can be similar to that of skill-biased technical change.

45. Studies addressing the issue of the impact of trade and globalisation on employment and wages in OECD countries (OECD, 1994; 1996*b*) have broadly concluded that, while trade can have an important impact on employment and wages in individual industries that are particularly exposed to foreign competition, the overall impact on OECD-wide employment and relative wages is low. A recent paper from the International Monetary Fund (IMF) (Slaughter and Swagel, 1997) has surveyed the literature on the impact of trade on wages, as well as on the impact of capital mobility through international sourcing of goods, labour mobility and international technology flows. The survey concludes that despite widely different methodologies, the consensus of empirical research suggests that increased trade accounts for about 10 to 20 per cent of changes in wages and income distribution in advanced economies. Similarly, increased capital mobility, including "outsourcing" of production to low-wage countries, as well as immigration, appear to have had only modest effects on the labour markets of advanced countries.

46. The studies reviewed in the IMF survey do not dispute that further globalisation can increase the sensitivity of wages and employment to external shocks and thereby contribute to greater job insecurity. The vast majority conclude, however, that the most important influence on labour markets in the 1980s and 1990s has been a technology-driven shift in labour demand away from less skilled workers and towards more skilled workers, resulting in increased wage inequality or increased unemployment among the low-skilled. In practice, however, it remains difficult to separate empirically the impact of technology from that of globalisation and other factors. Technical change and globalisation are mutually reinforcing processes.

1.5. Concluding remarks

47. In this chapter it has been argued that the role of technology needs to be seen in the context of an ongoing transformation of OECD economies from industrial to knowledge-based economies where the creation and distribution of knowledge and technology underpins the process of growth. This transformation has a number of dimensions. It involves sectoral shifts, with a move to service activities whose nature is being radically changed by technology, and an increased importance of high-tech activities within manufacturing. It also involves more intangible investment in R&D and in upgrading skills, as well as specific investment in ICTs. Finally, it involves more international interdependence, through technology-intensive trade, foreign investment, and international sourcing and collaboration between firms.

48. In this new environment, understanding how technology affects productivity and employment means moving beyond the traditional focus on R&D-intensive manufacturing activities. Innovations increasingly occur throughout the economy, not least in the service sector. More importantly, it is the economy-wide diffusion and use of technology that generates aggregate productivity gains. These gains are realised when firms undertake organisational change to accompany process and product innovations and when the regulatory environment and framework conditions are conducive to innovative activity.

49. The impact on jobs is the result of the interplay of innovation with product and labour market conditions and with the regulatory environment. While R&D-intensive innovative firms have a better-than-average jobs record, the bulk of the impact of technology on employment and wages is indirect, and occurs in sectors other than those in which the new technology was originally developed. As new technologies increase productivity growth, and as consumption patterns become more diversified and shift towards services, the employment losses associated with technology tend to be concentrated among the less skilled and in manufacturing, while the new jobs tend to require higher skills and typically be found in the services. For the overall impact to be positive, the conditions need to be in place for more efficient processes to translate into lower prices and higher incomes, and new products into new demand.

CHAPTER 2. THE MECHANISMS OF INNOVATION AND TECHNOLOGY DIFFUSION

2.1. Introduction

50. Determining how governments could better harness technical change to the benefit of economic growth, job creation and social progress requires an understanding of the processes through which technology is generated, diffused and applied. Innovation allies curiosity-driven research with problem-solving and profit-driven applied R&D, thus creating and matching new technological and market opportunities. Not only does it produce technical change, it also shapes the socio-economic impacts of change. While public attitudes and expectations towards technological innovation are evolving in line with social concerns (unemployment, environmental problems, ageing populations, etc.), innovation modes themselves are undergoing profound changes. These changes – which have major consequences for the strategic orientation and instruments of government policy – are summarised in the first section of this chapter.

51. Policy responses may differ significantly among countries, reflecting their industrial and technological specialisation, their institutional setting and varying perceptions of what policy can and should do. The second part of this chapter introduces the concept of the "national innovation system" which can serve as an instrument to understand these country specificities, and why they translate into different policy priorities, strategies and instrument choices.

Innovation as a creative, interactive and integrated process

52. The process of innovation and technology diffusion is undergoing substantial change. The main driving forces are increasing market pressures (stemming from globalisation, deregulation, changing patterns of demand and new societal needs), as well as scientific and technological developments (*e.g.* increasing multidisciplinarity in the production of new knowledge, diminishing cost of information access and processing).

53. In this new mode, the production of goods and services is becoming more and more knowledge-intensive – more science-intensive via the better use of existing stocks of scientific knowledge, more technology-intensive via diffusion of capital and intermediary goods, as well as more intensive with regards to the skills required to manage the increased complexity and uncertainty of knowledge. Technology diffusion now involves much more than the mere purchase of advanced equipment. Indeed, genuine innovative efforts such as organisational and managerial change are often required to fully exploit the potential of new technologies. This is most visible in the implementation of ICTs.

54. The types of knowledge used in the process of innovation are diverse, comprising the results of basic and/or applied research, but spanning beyond R&D to cover also the production and engineering

knowledge derived from hands-on experience with production processes. Further, innovation builds on codified knowledge (in the form of publications, patents, blue-prints, etc.) from an increasing range of disciplines and technological areas as well as on different forms of tacit knowledge (*i.e.* embedded in the "know-how" and dexterity of individuals, in organisational routines and the like). Increasingly, R&D acquired in the process of diffusion via the purchase of intermediary products and capital goods complements direct R&D carried out in firms. However, technical knowledge becomes economically useful only when its production and use is merged with managerial and organisational knowledge (in firms, laboratories, universities, etc.). It yields economic benefits and justifies private investment in its assimilation and production only when it can be embodied in traded goods and services.

55. The fact that innovation does not always involve huge R&D expenditures does not mean that science is becoming less important to technological development. On the contrary, the scientific content of innovation seems to be increasing and the scientific roots of innovation are diversifying and changing in relative importance. Several studies (*e.g.* Reger and Schmoch, 1996; Narin *et al.*, 1998) point to the growing importance of science-based industries, on the one hand, and to a growing take up of scientific research in a broad range of industries, on the other hand. This reflects movements on the scientific front, demand-side effects (*e.g.* ageing, environmental concerns) and technology fusion (*e.g.* bio-informatics after mechatronics). Therefore, the ability to use the results of scientific research in innovation remains of critical importance.

The firm as the nodal point of innovation

56. Firms are the main carriers of technological innovation. Their capacity to innovate is partly determined by their own capabilities, partly by their capacity to adopt and apply knowledge produced elsewhere. Increasing complexity, costs and risks in innovation enhance the value of networking and collaboration to reduce moral hazard and transaction costs, spurring a multitude of partnerships between firms with complementary assets. These take the form of acquisitions and alliances as well as traditional market-mediated relations (*e.g.* purchase of equipment, licensing of technology). Firms also exchange information and engage in mutual learning in their roles as customers, suppliers and subcontractors.

Internal innovation competence

57. To reinforce their innovation competence, many firms are investing heavily in new ICTs, as well as increasingly in "intangibles" (*e.g.* skills and qualifications, purchase of technologies and know-how, and organisational restructuring to realise the potential of ICTs) (Chapter 1 and Chapter 11). Given this diversity of inputs, a too-narrow focus on R&D would overlook the importance of other types of innovative efforts such as design or market analysis and would also overlook the important variations in the R&D content of innovation and innovative performance of sectors (Table 2.1). Firms and industries with low R&D intensities may be highly innovative. Similarly, the reduction of business R&D observed in the 1990s (Chapter 3) need not necessarily indicate a general reduction in innovative efforts, although it does signal significant changes in their composition and orientation. At the same time, there is increasing evidence of suboptimal innovation capabilities in a majority of firms – especially small and medium-sized enterprises (SMEs). This is due in part to market and systemic failures which translate into lack of competencies to manage innovation and organisational change (Chapter 4).

Table 2.1. **Breakdown of innovation expenditures**
Percentage share

	R&D	Patents and licences	Product design	Market analysis	External spending
Australia	35.1	4.1	. .	7.6	. .
Belgium	44.7	1.5	11.3	6.6	21.2
Denmark	40.1	5.3	15.8	8.2	9.0
Germany	27.1	3.4	27.8	6.1	29.2
Greece	50.6	6.4	. .	13.2	11.7
Ireland	22.2	4.3	22.0	38.5	20.4
Italy[1]	35.8	1.2	7.4	1.6	47.2
Luxembourg	29.3	8.9	8.4	4.3	26.4
Netherlands	45.6	6.1	7.6	19.8	20.2
Norway	32.8	4.2	14.2	5.5	17.6
Portugal	22.9	4.1	24.5	5.4	16.8
Spain	36.4	8.0	. .	8.8	6.3
United Kingdom	32.6	2.7	28.4	8.9	15.9
Average	33.5	4.6	24.0	6.6	22.4

1. Adjusted according to ISTAT (*Istituto Nazionale di Statistica*). Data do not total 100 per cent as "other expenditures" are not included in the table.

Source: Bosworth *et al.* (1996); Community Innovation Survey (CIS) Data; ISTAT, 1995; Australian Bureau of Statistics (ABS), 1994.

External linkages of firms – networks and clusters

58. As regards external links, the number of actors involved in the process of innovation is increasing (*e.g.* enterprises – large and small, universities, public and co-operative research labs, hospitals). There is also a widening variety of types of interactions (user-producer interactions, outsourcing and contracting of R&D, formation of R&D alliances and research joint ventures to pool resources, formal and informal links with the scientific community, etc.) (Figure 2.1). Firms are more likely to innovate successfully if they are able to rapidly access and implement acquired knowledge. This accounts for a positive relationship between internal innovation capabilities and the use firms can make of external linkages. Firms with higher internal innovative efforts have a greater capability to co-operate with other actors and adopt knowledge produced outside the firm (Colombo and Garrone, 1994).

59. Networking has become an effective innovation technique in its own right. Indeed, some authors (*e.g.* Wolfe, 1997) argue that networking must now be considered on an equal footing with hierarchy and the market as co-ordination mechanisms. Empirical studies have confirmed that collaborating firms are more innovative than non-collaborating ones (Smith *et al.*, 1996). Even non-collaborating firms do not work in isolation, but are involved in a number of interactions (*e.g.* they purchase embedded technologies, consultancy and intellectual property and scan for ideas from a variety of sources).

Figure 2.1. **Types of networks**

Type of network (Survey of 8 European countries[1])	% share
Weak or no network linkages	12.9
Equipment supplier (ES) dominated networks 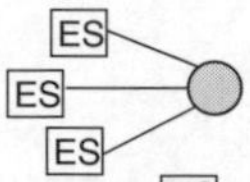	14.4
Marketing-oriented networks: users (US) and competitors (CO) 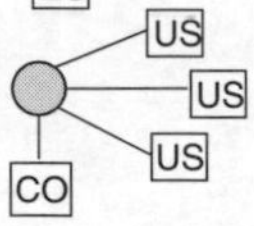	16.0
Marketing-oriented networks: equipment & component (CM) suppliers and users 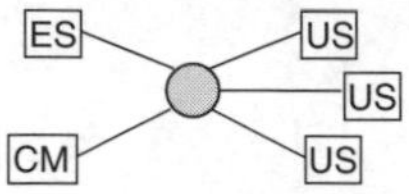	15.8
Marketing-oriented networks: equipment & component suppliers, users and competitors 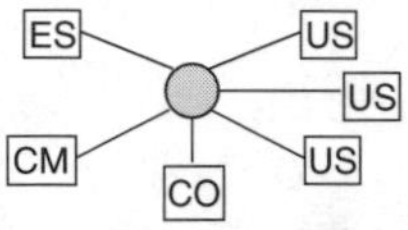	21.9
Complete innovation networks, including government laboratory and university (GU) 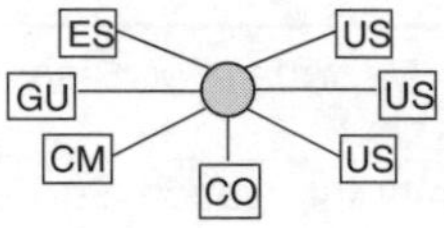	19.1

1. Belgium, Denmark, France, Germany, Ireland, Italy, the Netherlands, Norway.

Source: DeBresson *et al.* (1997).

60. A related type of interaction concerns industrial clusters[3] involving dense and long-lasting links. Typically clustering will be organised around a common market with a few central actors providing unique sources of knowledge-based competitive advantages. It comprises not only close interactions between firms, but also between firms and specialised supporting institutions and infrastructure (business associations, co-operative research institutes, specialised education institutions, etc.). Clusters can involve seemingly casual relationships that would not be characterised as collaboration, but are nonetheless repetitive and stable. They have the effect of internalising some spillovers that would otherwise be dissipated outside the firm, which thus benefits from the knowledge infrastructure reinforced by community linkages. Clusters often have a specific geographic base and may constitute "regional innovation systems" – examples range from Silicon Valley to Italy's textile districts.

The broader context – the national innovation system

61. Interactions between the actors involved in the innovation process take various forms (Figure 2.2). They include the traditional market-mediated innovation chain where firms innovate singly and trade technology through licences, embodied R&D in outputs, etc., but also comprise a wider range of interactions. Firms enter into inter-firm co-operation entailing trust and informal flows of knowledge going beyond formal agreements. Extended networks and clusters of industries commonly involve many players, including institutions which are not primarily market-driven

3. For an overview of recent studies, see the contributions to the OECD Workshop on Cluster Analysis and Cluster-based Policies (Amsterdam, October 1997) at <http://www.oecd.org/dsti/sti/s_t/inte/nis/membersonly/indclus.htm>.

(*e.g.* business associations, political entities, scientific institutes). Each of these interactions form "innovation systems" of their own, with distinct properties.

Figure 2.2. **Interactions in innovation systems**

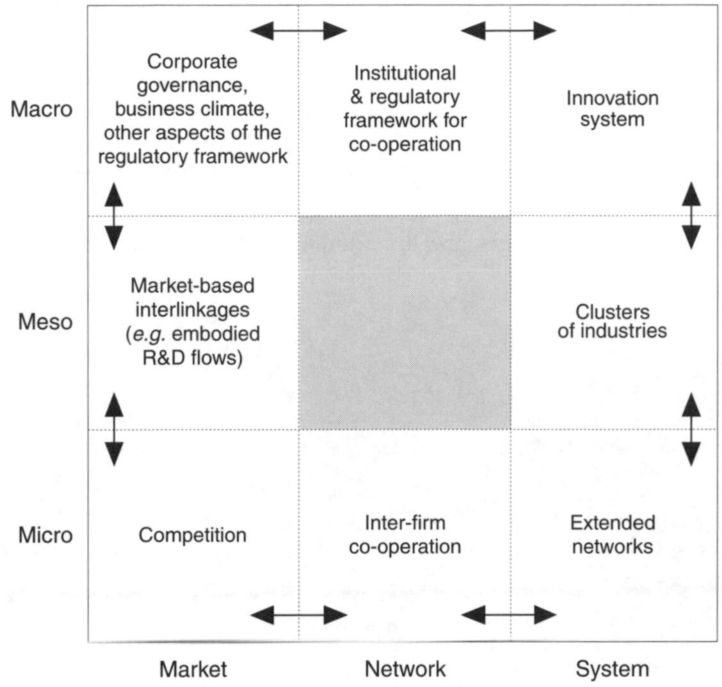

Source: OECD Secretariat.

62. Those market and non-market institutions within a country which influence the direction and the speed of innovation and technology diffusion can be said to constitute a "national innovation system" (NIS) (Box 2.1). Such systems are characterised by distinctive attributes (specific patterns of scientific, technological and industrial specialisation, specific organisation of institutions and policy priorities) and different structures of interactions (*e.g.* between the enterprise sector and the science system; collaboration between firms). The main actors in a NIS are firms, public and private research organisations, and government and other public institutions. These actors are influenced by a variety of factors: the financial system and corporate governance, legal and regulatory frameworks, the level of education and skills, the degree of personnel mobility, labour relations, prevailing management practices, etc. (Figure 2.3). The interplay between the innovative activities of firms and these institutions strongly shapes national technological capabilities and influences the direction and speed of technological change. If market and non-market institutions do not interact well, technological change will be slowed and/or its contribution to economic growth and welfare reduced.

Box 2.1. **The concept of a national innovation system**

National innovation systems are defined as the "... set of distinct institutions which jointly and individually contribute to the development and diffusion of new technologies and which provide the framework within which governments form and implement policies to influence the innovation process. As such it is a system of interconnected institutions to create, store and transfer the knowledge, skills and artefacts which define new technologies." (Metcalfe, 1995).

From this perspective, the innovative performance of an economy depends not only on how the individual institutions (*e.g.* firms, research institutes, universities) perform in isolation, but on "how they interact with each other as elements of a collective system of knowledge creation and use, and on their interplay with social institutions (such as values, norms, legal frameworks and so on)." (Smith, 1996).

63. Innovation systems also exist at levels other than the national one, as for example world-wide, regional or local networks of firms and clusters of industries. These systems may or may not be confined within the borders of a nation, but national characteristics and frameworks always play a role in shaping them. This also holds true with regard to the internationalisation of innovative activities which to a large extent reflects foreign investors' perceptions of the relative strengths of national innovation systems (*e.g.* the existence of scientific centres of excellence or the supply of skilled scientists, engineers and competitive suppliers). Thus, the concept of a NIS provides a tool for analysing country specificities in the process of innovation as well as a guide for policy formulation. It highlights interactions and interfaces between various actors and the working of the system as a whole rather than the performance of its individual components.

Figure 2.3. **Actors and linkages in the innovation system**

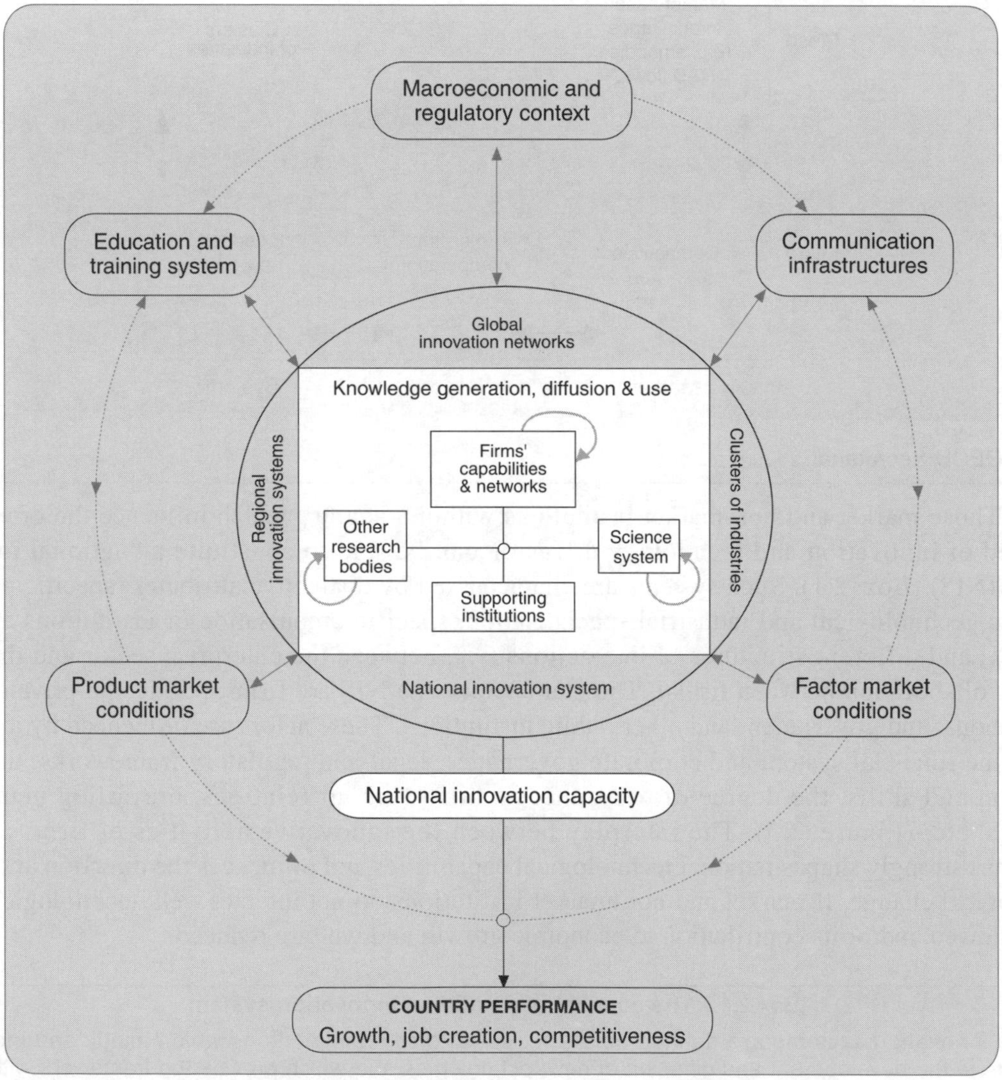

Source: OECD Secretariat.

2.2. Country specificities in the patterns of innovation

64. The characteristics of innovation processes described above are of a general nature. However, how these trends translate into concrete innovative activities will differ across countries depending on their industrial specialisation, specific institutional settings, policy priorities, etc. (Patel and Pavitt, 1994). Historical experience shows that such differences tend to remain even when countries face the same technological and economic developments (Vertova, 1997). Their persistence can be explained by the interplay of endogenous, self-reinforcing processes of investment in fixed capital, R&D and education, building on and extending advantages in the mastering of specific technologies, economies of scale, resource endowments, and a variety of institutional factors which vary across countries. Countries thus have a strong tendency to develop along certain "technological trajectories", shaped by past and present patterns of knowledge accumulation and use.

65. In this process, countries have developed distinct national innovation systems, with unique characteristics that have to be taken into account when deriving recommendations for national technology and innovation policies [see OECD (1997*d*) for an overview of these differences]. A brief description of the relative roles of the business sector, the government, and the higher education sector in terms of their R&D spending (HERD), as well as an overview of the main linkages within national innovation systems are given below as an illustration of the problems faced by technology policy in different countries. For instance, national innovation systems differ with regard to their size and level of development, structure (*i.e.* weight and range of functions performed by the actors), scientific and technological specialisation patterns, and the density and quality of the linkages among actors.

Size and structure

66. Large and highly developed countries offer markets with advanced customers and opportunities to reap economies of scale while maintaining diversity in R&D activities. To reap these benefits, innovators in smaller high-income countries generally have to internationalise more rapidly and concentrate on a narrower range of fields (*e.g.* the development of mobile communications in Finland and Sweden). They will profit most from free flows of technology across borders and thus should keep their innovation systems open and create adoption capabilities to capture the benefits of inflows of technology. Their innovation systems will be strongly shaped by the clusters in which they exhibit relative strengths, and the development of institutions will be centred around these clusters. For example, a significant part of the advanced innovation systems of small high-income countries is structured around resource-based and related industries (*e.g.* Norwegian fishery and oil sectors, Finland's forestry cluster, Danish dairy products). A common feature is that the development of resource-based clusters has been promoted by government though substantial public R&D efforts and the creation of specific institutions to support value-adding innovation. Smaller countries face proportionally higher costs in maintaining institutions (*e.g.* in education and science) that cover a broader range of subjects than can be taken up by their industries. On the other hand, technological change in ICTs combined with liberalisation and globalisation reduces the scale advantages of large countries.

67. The level of R&D activity as well as its evolution differs considerably among countries (Figure 2.4), reflecting not only industrial structures but also development strategies. Some countries are trying to forge ahead (Finland), others are catching-up from initial low levels and are still somewhat behind (Greece, Mexico, Portugal, Turkey), while yet others are approaching the OECD average (Australia, Iceland, Ireland). Some countries with high levels of R&D efforts in the past are either stabilising or slightly reducing their efforts (France, Germany, Japan, the Netherlands, the United Kingdom, the United States). Others are showing signs of stagnation (Austria, Belgium, Canada,

Norway, New Zealand) or are at risk of falling behind (Italy, Spain). Countries are clearly facing different tasks for technology and innovation policy, ranging from promoting a more R&D-intensive development trajectory ("from imitation to innovation"), through keeping abreast of developments at the "technology frontier", to ensuring higher social returns from already high levels of investment in R&D.

Figure 2.4. **Level and growth of gross expenditure on R&D (GERD)**[1]

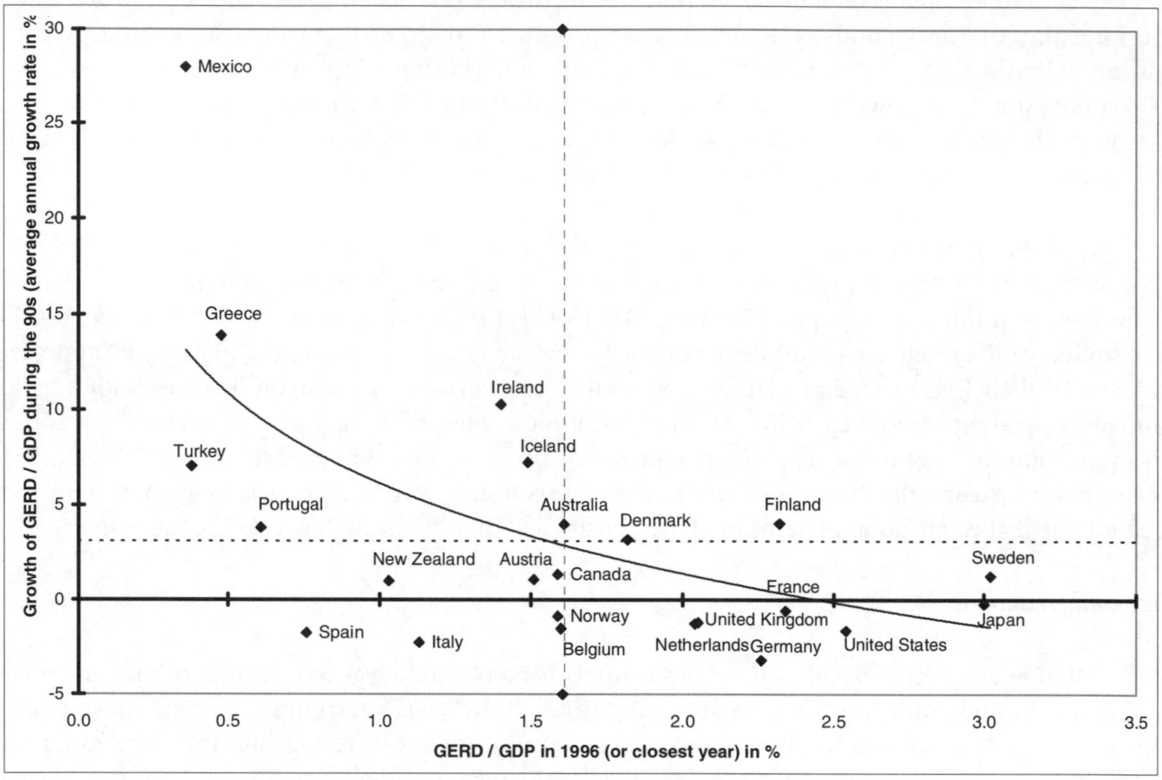

1. Dotted lines indicate the unweighted OECD average.
Source: OECD, MSTI database, November 1997.

68. The role of government is another distinguishing feature of national innovation systems, reflected in the levels and structures of public R&D financing (see also Chapter 3). In "catch-up" countries (Greece, Hungary, Mexico, Poland, Portugal, Turkey), government R&D expenditure accounts for a relatively higher share of total R&D than in more advanced economies, pointing to the need to build up a scientific and technological infrastructure in these countries and the relative technological weakness of the business sector. At the other end of the spectrum are countries in which the business sector provides the lion's share of R&D funding (Belgium, Ireland, Japan, Sweden, the United States). The orientation of publicly funded R&D in a given country depends on the overall objectives of government policies and the specific role of science and technology (S&T), all of which have an important historical component in terms of national preoccupations and institutions. Over the long term there has been a trend away from the "traditional" missions of the post-war period (defence, energy) towards other R&D objectives reflecting changing societal demands, such as the emerging problems of ageing populations, environmental issues and concerns about competitiveness. Despite this common trend, striking differences persist. Notwithstanding recent restructuring and downsizing, the defence cluster still plays an important role in France, Sweden, the United Kingdom and the United States. For the majority of countries the most important civil objectives are "advancement of research" and "promotion of industry (or agriculture)" (Canada, Greece, Iceland, Ireland, New Zealand, Norway and Portugal).

69. The role of the higher education sector can serve as an indication of the relationship between the science system and the rest of the innovation system. One indicator is the share of HERD financed by government (see Chapter 3 and Chapter 6 for an extensive treatment of this issue). This share is declining in the majority of OECD countries, but remains very high in some (*e.g.* Austria). In others, the enterprise sector represents a significant financial contributor for universities. In those countries with a strong orientation of public funding towards the higher education sector in the form of "general university funds" (GUF) (again, Austria), issues arise as to how to balance this with the growing tendency of research to become more directly oriented towards technological innovation and of development to become more short-term.

Patterns of scientific and technological specialisation

70. The science bases of the respective NIS are quite different, even when their specialisation is measured by looking only at those fields which are likely to have the greatest impact on technological development (*e.g.* biology, engineering sciences, chemistry; OECD, 1997*d*). Specialisation patterns were stable in the period from 1981 to 1993; recent developments have made them look more dissimilar in the 1990s than in the 1980s. Dissimilarities can be partly explained by country size (*e.g.* the broader science base of the United States), standard of living (*e.g.* the high shares of clinical medicine and biomedical research in the richer countries that spend more on their health systems) and industrial specialisation (*e.g.* engineering sciences in Germany and Japan).

71. On the other hand, certain countries display considerable similarities. This applies to Germany and Japan due to their common specialisation in engineering, technology, chemistry and physics. France, Germany and Italy (as well as the eastern European countries), similarly resemble each other in their specialisation in chemistry, physics and mathematics. The United States is a case apart insofar as its scientific efforts are more evenly spread – hence the pronounced difference with most other countries. The United Kingdom and the Nordic countries are relatively specialised in clinical medicine. In the United Kingdom, this focus was further accentuated in the 1990s. Despite this pronounced specialisation, the science base of the United Kingdom – like that of the United States – appears to be fairly strong over a broader range of fields, as indicated by citation shares.

72. National innovation systems also differ in their patterns of technological specialisation. An examination of long-term historical developments (Vertova, 1997) as well as of more recent trends (Pavitt and Patel, 1996), points to the following features:

- A limited number of countries show strong similarities in technological specialisation; there are no overall signs of convergence (Figure 2.5).

- For the majority of countries, there is a significant positive correlation between past and present patterns, an indication that technological capabilities accumulate over time and that development is strongly path-dependent (Table 2.2). This does not exclude rapid structural change in some countries, but even for these countries the coefficient of correlation with previous periods is positive.

73. "Clustering" of countries with similar technological specialisation (Figure 2.5) shows strong similarities between smaller, mainly resource-based economies (although to a lesser degree in the 1990s than in the 1980s) as well as some similarities between the larger European countries. It also reveals the unique specialisation patterns of Japan and the United States. At the same time structural change is reflected in the changing composition of country "clusters" over time. Important structural changes can be observed for Denmark and Spain, as well as for Finland and Ireland.

Figure 2.5. **Technological (dis)similarities across groups of countries**[1]

Based on patenting

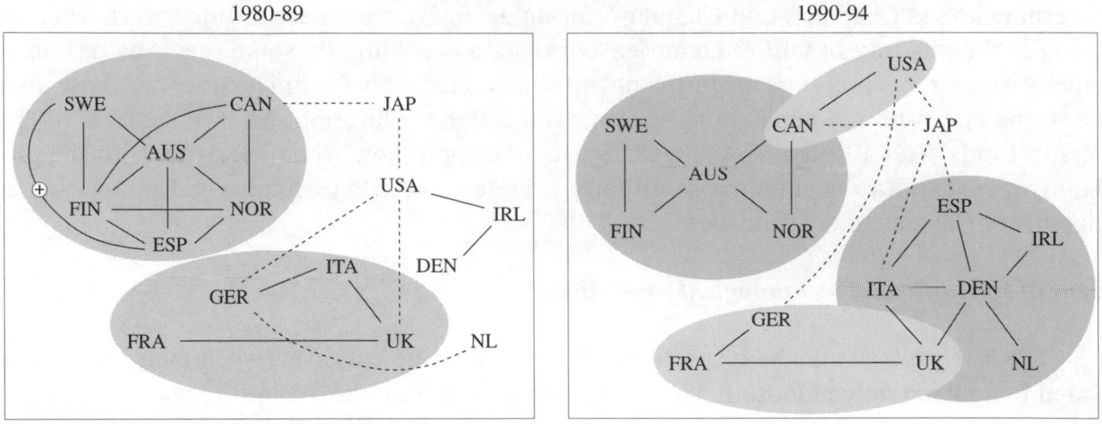

1. Dotted lines indicate a significant correlation (dissimilarity) between the patterns of Revealed Technological Advantage (RTA) of countries; straight lines indicate significant correlation (strong similarity) (at a 5 per cent significance level).

Source: OECD Secretariat.

Table 2.2. **Comparison of technological specialisation**[1] **between periods**

Pearson correlation coefficient

	1980-89/1990-94	1963-68/1985-90
Australia	0.914*	0.28
Canada	0.912*	0.67*
Denmark	0.849*	0.47*
Finland	0.540*	0.59*
France	0.685*	0.82*
Germany	0.960*	0.35*
Ireland	0.643*	0.05
Italy	0.834*	0.32
Japan	0.956*	0.45*
Netherlands	0.647*	0.66*
Norway	0.965*	0.35*
Spain	0.581*	0.53*
Sweden	0.789*	0.73*
United Kingdom	0.831*	0.23
United States	0.949*	0.55*

* Denotes statistical significance at the 5 per cent level.

1. Technological specialisation is measured by the RTA which indicates relative shares of patenting in one country compared to the OECD total.

Source: OECD Secretariat calculations from ANPAT database; Pavitt and Patel (1996).

74. Technology and innovation policy has to reflect these specialisation patterns by *(i)* fostering complementarity between scientific and technological specialisation patterns; *(ii)* taking them into account when designing selective policies (*e.g.* oriented toward specific clusters); *(iii)* acknowledging that specialisation patterns do not – and cannot – change rapidly.

Linkages within national innovation systems

75. As outlined above, innovation performance depends crucially on interactions among the main actors (firms, research institutions, government, etc.) that make up an innovation system, which in turn depend on the incentives or barriers confronting the various individuals, companies and institutions. Such interactions take a number of forms: co-publishing in scientific and technological research; citation of publications and purchase of patents and licences; acquisition of technologies embodied in capital goods and personnel; use of informal networks of researchers; innovation impulses from user-producer interactions, etc. As a general trend, most forms of interactions and knowledge flows have intensified, contributing to an overall increase in the knowledge-intensity of economic activities. But the importance and the quality of the various linkages differ from country to country, depending on the structure and specialisation pattern of the respective NIS.

Links within the science system

76. The production of scientific knowledge is undergoing a major transformation (Gibbons *et al.*, 1994). In the so-called "new mode of production of knowledge", the production of scientific knowledge cuts across disciplines, institutions and, increasingly, countries (Chapter 6). Advancement of science is no longer the sole realm of universities and specialised research bodies, but involves a widening range of other institutions (corporate R&D labs, hospitals, etc.) – both nationally and internationally. Further, scientific knowledge is increasingly produced with an eye to its application.

77. At the beginning of the 1990s, co-authored articles amounted to more than 50 per cent of all scientific articles, with internationally co-authored articles accounting for more than 20 per cent (Table 2.3). The share of co-authored articles involving at least one researcher based in another country has increased, but in most countries by less than national (or intra-regional) collaboration. Also, the accelerated development of the "scientific home base" in some countries has led to a decline in the "degree of internationalisation" (*e.g.* China, the East Asian and Pacific countries, South and Central America).

78. The United States is still the linchpin of international scientific collaboration. A little less than one-quarter of all internationally co-authored articles involve US researchers – far more than any other country. Nevertheless, as the overall share of scientific publishing in the United States is even greater (one-third of the total), its degree of internationalisation is lower than that of most other countries. Countries differ with regard to the openness of their science systems. Some (*e.g.* India, Japan and the former USSR) show a low degree of internationalisation that cannot be explained by the size of their scientific home base, but reflects less open science systems. Other countries with a comparable number of publications show a much higher propensity to collaborate internationally (*e.g.* Australia, Germany, the United Kingdom). Some new poles of collaboration are emerging, as exemplified by increased collaboration among European countries, and between East Asian countries and China. On the other hand, linkages among eastern European countries have eroded considerably as a result of the collapse of the old scientific systems.

Table 2.3. **Patterns of international collaboration in science and research**
Number of scientific articles, 1988-93

	Total	*Of which:* co-authored (per cent of total)	*Of which:* internationally co-authored (per cent of total)	Country's share of total (per cent)	Country's share of internationally co-authored (per cent)	Degree of internation-alisation[1]
United States	908 125	53	14	33.1	22.6	0.69
United Kingdom	210 685	47	22	7.7	8.3	1.08
Germany	192 629	46	26	7.0	8.9	1.27
France	142 805	58	28	5.2	7.1	1.37
Italy	79 833	67	29	2.9	4.1	1.42
Southern Europe, other	66 741	52	29	2.4	3.4	1.42
Nordic countries	105 636	62	31	3.8	5.8	1.52
Western Europe, other	146 424	57	34	5.3	8.9	1.66
Japan	219 280	46	11	8.0	4.3	0.54
Canada	120 454	53	25	4.4	5.4	1.22
Former USSR	172 854	21	8	6.3	2.5	0.39
Eastern Europe, other	66 296	50	33	2.4	3.9	1.61
Israel	28 957	64	33	1.1	1.7	1.61
Mideast, other	10 528	46	28	0.4	0.5	1.37
Africa	36 851	56	34	1.3	2.2	1.66
Australia / New Zealand	69 393	47	22	2.5	2.7	1.08
India	52 336	29	11	1.9	1.0	0.54
South / Central America	42 967	58	36	1.6	2.8	1.76
China	30 437	49	27	1.1	1.5	1.32
East Asian NIEs[2]	29 846	50	23	1.1	1.2	1.13
Asian / Pacific, other	14 499	61	44	0.5	1.1	2.15
Total	2 747 576	51	26	100.0	100.0	1.00

1. Share of international co-authored articles divided by the country's share of all articles.
2. Newly Industrialised Economies.

Source: National Science Foundation (1996); OECD Secretariat calculations.

79. All in all, scientific collaboration is increasing, although to a greater extent at the national/regional level than internationally. The "home base" and the "neighbourhood" continue to matter in the "global research village", but openness to cross-disciplinary and cross-country scientific co-operation is increasing in importance.

Links between science and technology

80. An important interface in a NIS is that between the science system and the enterprise sector (addressed in detail in Chapter 6). Especially in countries with a large share of science-based industries and/or a large higher education sector, building bridges from university research to technological innovation is an important task for policy. However, industries and hence countries with different

industrial specialisation patterns differ greatly in their reliance on the science base and few have strong direct links with basic research (*e.g.* pharmaceuticals, organic and food chemistry, biotechnology and semiconductors) (Figure 2.6). This widens the scope for polices aimed at managing the science base beyond the support of university-industry co-operations. Scientific knowledge stemming from basic research (the production of which is the main activity of universities) is rarely a direct input into technological innovation except for the above-mentioned science-based industries. However, in many industries it is an essential indirect input in the process of technological innovation (Martin and Salter, 1996; Chapter 6). It can be accessed and used by innovating firms in various ways and forms (published information, embedded in new instruments and methodologies, via personal contacts and participation in scientific networks, embodied in the skills and abilities of graduates, spin-off firms, joint R&D ventures and projects, etc.). For most of these interactions, significant localisation effects can be observed – especially for those that involve informal contacts on a regular basis. Therefore, spillovers are concentrated in some clusters of industries, facilitated by geographic proximity and the existence of a "technological infrastructure" comprising related business services, the existence of other innovative firms, etc.

Figure 2.6. **Structure of knowledge spillovers and dependence of technology on science**[1]
Clustering on the basis of European patent data, 1989-92

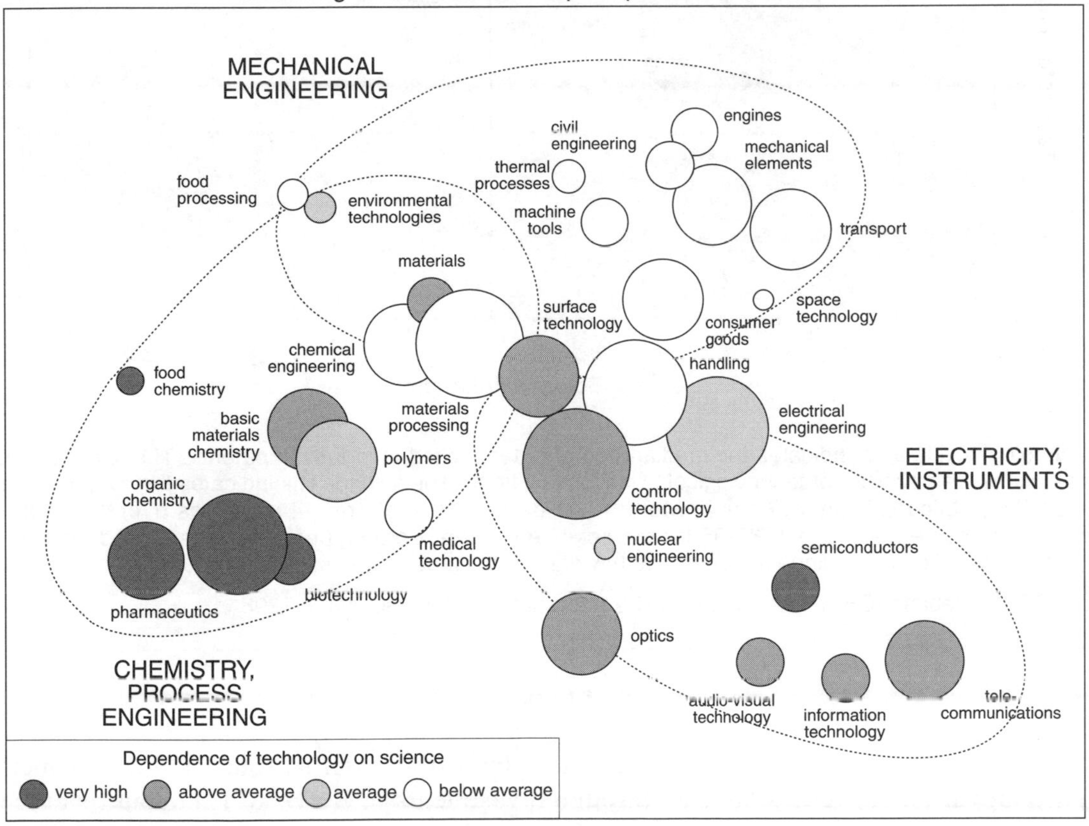

1. Circles are proportional to the number of world-wide patents.
Source: Swiss NIS report (adapted from Schmoch *et al.*, 1996).

81. The importance of the "science link" differs from one country to another according both to industrial specialisation and to the organisation of the interactions (especially incentives for researchers and enterprises) between the science system and the enterprise sector. Some innovation systems show a

stronger link (Canada, Denmark, Ireland, the United Kingdom and the United States).[4] In other countries, like Germany, Japan and Korea, but also to a lesser extent in Austria and Italy, innovation has been geared more towards engineering excellence and the rapid adoption and adaptation of technological innovation (as reflected in rapid "technological cycle times", Figure 2.7). Although there will continue to be room for competitive advantages not based on tight linkages between scientific knowledge and technological innovation, the interplay between industry and the science base is of increasing importance for technical progress and economic performance and is thus an important target for technology and innovation policy.

Figure 2.7. **Science and technology linkages and innovation**[1]
All patents

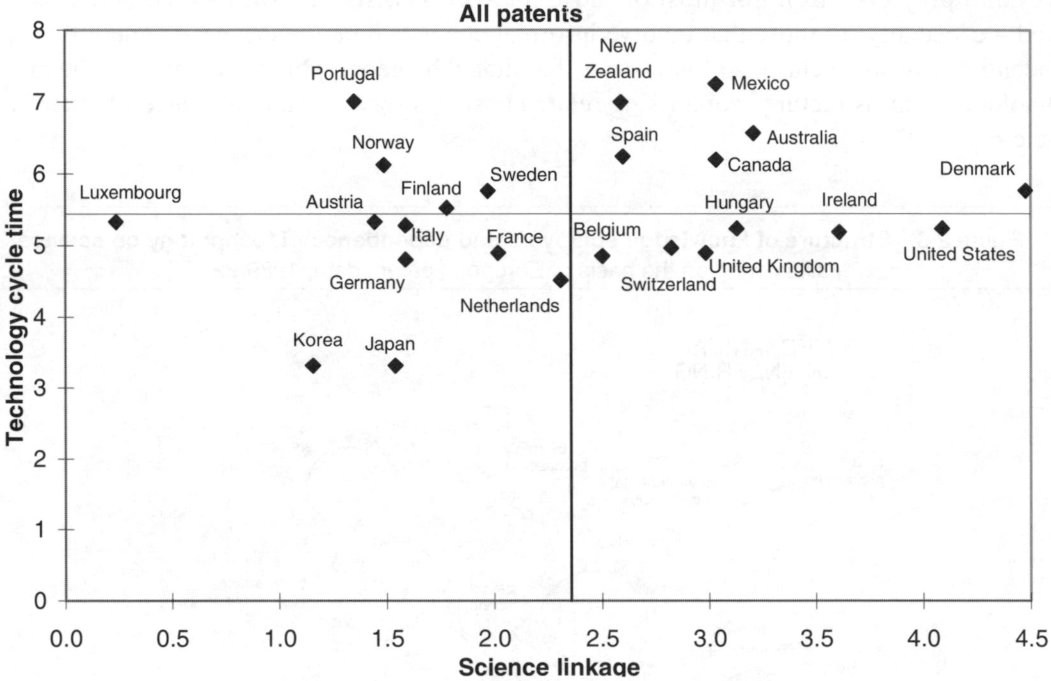

1. Technology cycle time indicates the median age of patents cited in industrial patents. The lower the median, the quicker the "take-up" of technological inventions by firms. The science link indicates the average number of scientific publications in industrial patents. The data used are straight averages over 1980-95 for the technology cycle time, and 1985-95 for the science linkage. Both values were normalised by the sample standard deviations. The lines represent the unweighted average for the sample of countries.

Source: TP-2 database (CHI Research), OECD Secretariat calculations, March 1998.

Inter-firm linkages

82. As described above, firms increasingly use flows from external sources to complement their internal innovation capacities built up through investments in R&D, ICT, human resources and organisational re-engineering. "Networks of innovation" have become the rule rather than the exception, and most innovative activity involves interaction of multiple actors. The configuration of these interactions shows some common country characteristics and differences. Some of the main channels of technology transfers and sources of information for innovation are depicted below.

4. Measured here as the intensity of citation of scientific publications in industrial patents.

83. Innovation surveys found that, as regards channels of technology transfer, the purchase of equipment, customer-supplier relations and the hiring of skilled personnel are by far the most important in many countries (Table 2.4). Customer-supplier interactions are shaped not only by market relations, but also by institutional factors, trust, the existence of business and technological fora, etc. (Lundvall, 1992). The importance of other sources of technology transfer, such as consultancy, differs, perhaps reflecting both the quantity and quality of existing services and government initiatives (*e.g.* in Denmark and Norway; see also Chapter 8 on diffusion-oriented programmes).

Table 2.4. **Relative importance[1] of technology transfer channels**

	Australia	Belgium	Denmark	France	Germany	Ireland	Italy[2]	Luxembourg	Norway	United Kingdom
Use of others' inventions	4	4	3	2	5	2	5	4	2	2
Contracting out of R&D	8	5	6	5	6	3	6	5	5	6
Use of consultancy services	5	3	4	4	3	5	3	5	3	4
Purchase of other enterprises	7	7	7	7	7	6	8	8	6	7
Purchase of equipment	1	6	2	3	4	4	1	3	8	5
Communication services from other enterprises	2	2	1	1	1	1	2	1	1	1
Hiring of skilled personnel	3	1	5	6	2	7	4	2	4	3
Other	6	8	8	..	8	8	7	7	7	8

1. Importance was ranked from 1 (highest) to 8 (lowest).
2. Adjusted according to ISTAT. "Other" includes "purchase of projects". The table does not allow for direct comparison, as the response rates differ considerably across countries.

Source: Bosworth *et al.* (1996); CIS data; ABS, 1994.

84. Again, technology diffusion via embodied R&D in capital goods and intermediaries has increased in importance *vis-à-vis* direct R&D. When technology flows are analysed by broadly defined "technology clusters" (*e.g.* IT, material technology, fabrication technology, transportation and consumer good technologies), ITs account for a rapidly increasing share of acquired technologies, with a large proportion also accruing to material technologies (OECD, 1996*a*). These technology clusters are "generic" and provide inputs to a wide range of other industries, while other clusters such as transport technologies and consumer good technologies are of importance to a limited number of sectors. Although the technology content of trade flows has generally increased, a few sectors have become the main "gateways" for technology flows, for example chemicals in Denmark and the Netherlands, aerospace in the United Kingdom, motor vehicles in Germany. This reflects the differentiated patterns of technological specialisation and capabilities of the respective national innovation systems, and can provide guidance for setting technology and innovation policy priorities.

85. The sources of information used by innovating firms are also quite diversified (Table 2.5). Suppliers (of equipment and components) and customers are by far the most important external sources, while universities, government labs and technical institutes rank comparatively low on average. But this average hides the fact that in many advanced countries, networks spanning beyond

customer-supplier relations have evolved and a substantial number of firms participate in "complete networks" including suppliers, competitors, users, public research institutes and universities (see again Figure 2.4). Some innovation systems seem to be very conducive to co-operation among all actors of NIS, as demonstrated by the high share of complete network activities illustrated in Figure 2.1 (*e.g.* Denmark, Germany and the Netherlands).

86. Analysis of the innovation strategies of Europe's largest industrial firms (Arundel *et al.*, 1995) provides additional information on international differences with regard to the importance of the geographic location of sources of technological knowledge. In general, sources located in the home country are most important, although the difference with flows from other countries is not always very significant. Public sector research scores highest, pointing to the importance of a well-developed national research infrastructure for these large firms (Figure 2.8). Innovation systems able to provide such an infrastructure not only raise the technological competitiveness of home firms, but are also more likely to attract technology-oriented foreign direct investment (FDI).

Links between national innovation systems

87. The increasing openness of national innovation systems to external knowledge flows is reflected in the share of technology acquired from abroad embodied in capital and intermediary goods; purchases of foreign patents and licences; technological alliances between firms of different countries; and, in science, the number of internationally co-authored publications. It also shows in the innovation activities of multinational firms, as indicated by their patenting patterns and the location of their R&D facilities.

88. Corporate innovation activity as measured by patents is still predominantly located close to the firm's headquarters (Table 2.6), especially for large countries like France, Germany, Italy, Japan and the United States, although there is a tendency towards internationalisation, applying especially to firms from smaller countries (Belgium, the Netherlands, Switzerland) or in the United Kingdom, which hosts a number of companies with globally dispersed activities. In terms of R&D expenditure, the R&D carried out in foreign subsidiaries as of 1994 corresponded to only 11 per cent of the total R&D of 12 major OECD countries.

89. Nevertheless, there is a tendency for R&D activities to be spread. Foreign R&D is mainly established through the acquisition of existing firms and research facilities, but there is also a tendency for firms with strong own-technology to rely on greenfield operations (Andersson and Svensson, 1994). In some cases R&D is shifting away from addressing local market needs to establishing competence centres carrying out R&D for the whole corporation. While, in general, the R&D intensity of domestic firms is higher than that of foreign subsidiaries (Figure 2.9), the relationship between a company and its foreign subsidiaries is influenced by the relative technological position of the country of origin and the host country, as well as by industry- and firm-specific factors (Table 2.7).

Table 2.5. **Sources of information for innovation**[1]

	Australia	Belgium	Denmark	France	Germany	Greece	Ireland	Italy[2]	Luxembourg	Netherlands	Norway	Portugal	Spain	United Kingdom	All countries
Within the enterprise	3[3]	1	2	1	7	1	2	1	2	2	2	1	5	1	1
Within the group of enterprises		6	8	7	11	. .	8	9		8	9	10	. .	8	13
Suppliers of material and components	4	4	3	5	4	7	5	5	3	3	4	. .	9	3	5
Suppliers of equipment	5	3	4	4	6	. .	6	3	1	4	3	4	3	5	3
Clients or customers	1	2	1	3	1	2	1	2	4	1	1	5	1	2	2
Competitors	2	7	5	8	4	3	3	6	8	6	7	7	2	4	6
Consultancy firms	8	13	13	13	10	. .	11	7	9	11	12	6	7	12	8
University/higher education	9	10	11	12	8	6	10	11	11	10	11	8	11	9	10
Government laboratories	11	12	10	11	11	. .	13	13	13	9	10	9	12	13	12
Technical institutes	11	11	9	10	13	. .	9	12	12	13	8	11	8	11	11
Patent disclosures	9	9	12	9	9	. .	12	10	10	12	13	12	10	10	9
Conferences, journals	7	7	7	6	3	4	7	8	6	7	6	2	6	7	7
Fairs, exhibitions	6	5	6	2	2	5	3	4	5	5	5	3	4	6	4

1. Sources were ranked by importance from 1 (highest) to 13 (lowest).
2. Adjusted according to ISTAT.
3. For Australia, the first two categories are combined. The table does not allow for direct comparison, as the response rates differ considerably across countries.

Source: Bosworth *et al.* (1996); CIS Data and ABS, 1994.

Figure 2.8. **Importance of sources of technological knowledge by region**[1]

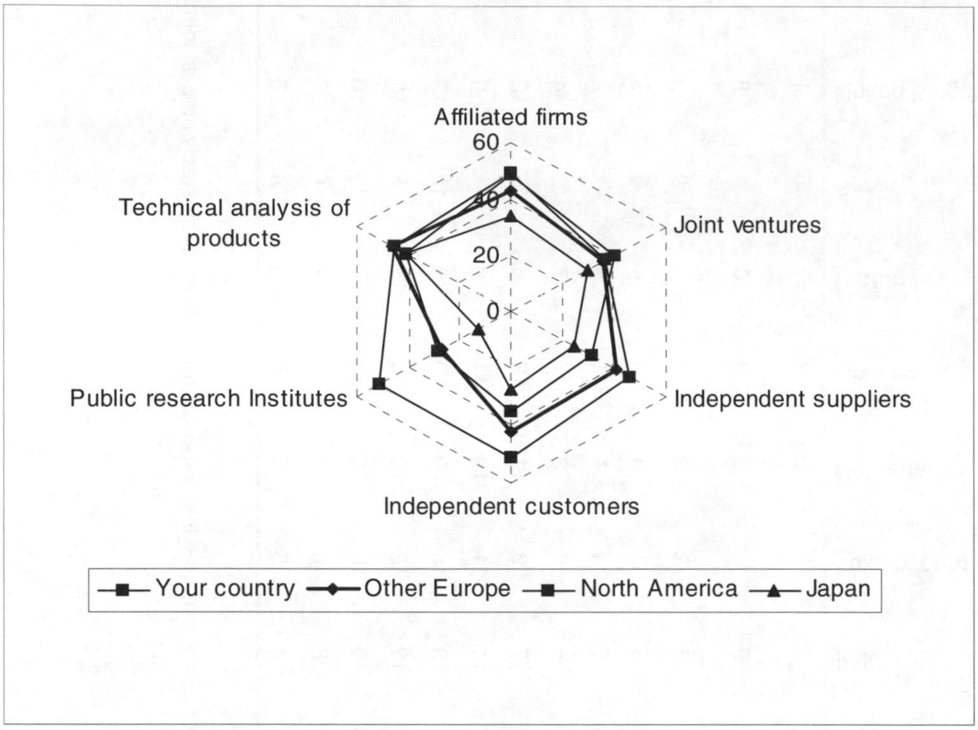

1. The further away from the centre, the more important the source.

Source: Arundel *et al.* (1995).

Figure 2.9. **Share of foreign affiliates' R&D and turnover (or production) in total manufacturing R&D and turnover, 1994 (or nearest year)**

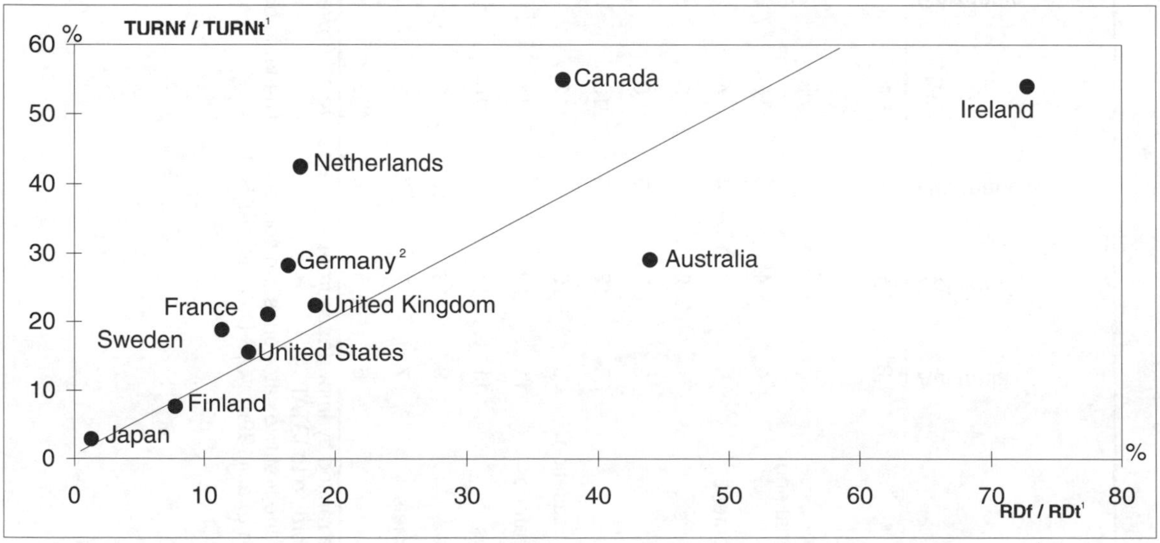

1. TURNf / TURNt: foreign affiliates' turnover / total firms' turnover;
   RDf / RDt: foreign affiliates' R&D / total firms' R&D.
2. Sample of the 500 most R&D-intensive firms.

Source: OECD, AFA, STAN and ANBERD databases, November 1997.

Table 2.6. **Geographic location of large firms' patenting activities in the United States**
1985-90, percentage

	No. of firms	Home	Abroad	Of which: United States	Europe	Japan	Other
Japan	139	99.0	1.0	0.8	0.2	. .	0.0
United States	243	92.2	7.8	. .	6.0	0.5	1.3
Italy	7	88.2	11.8	5.3	6.2	0.0	0.3
France	25	85.7	14.3	4.8	8.7	0.3	0.6
Germany	42	85.1	14.9	10.4	3.9	0.2	0.4
Finland	7	82.0	18.0	1.6	11.5	0.0	4.9
Norway	3	67.9	32.1	12.7	19.4	0.0	0.0
Canada	16	67.0	33.0	24.9	7.3	0.3	0.5
Sweden	13	60.8	39.2	12.6	25.6	0.2	0.8
United Kingdom	54	57.9	42.1	31.9	7.1	0.2	3.0
Switzerland	8	53.3	46.7	19.6	26.0	0.6	0.5
Netherlands	8	42.2	57.8	26.1	30.6	0.5	0.6
Belgium	4	37.2	62.8	22.2	39.9	0.0	0.6
All firms	569	89.1	10.9	4.1	5.6	0.3	0.8

Source: Patel (1997).

Table 2.7. **Nature of R&D activities of foreign affiliates in countries of destination**

Parent company's technological position	Affiliate's technological position[1] in destination country: High	Medium	Low
High	• Development of new technology • In close link with universities and other local laboratories	• Laboratory of production support • Specialised laboratory • Technology transfers from the parent company	• Laboratory of production support • Technology transfers from the parent company
Medium	• Technology watch • R&D effort more important than the parent company's	• Specialised laboratory	• Laboratory support • Technology transfers from the parent company
Low	• Technology watch	• Technology watch	

1. The technological position reflects various quantitative and qualitative measures: the R&D effort, patents, scientific publications, high-technology exports, links between universities and industries, structure and quality of scientific and technological personnel.
Source: OECD Secretariat.

90. Thus, in most OECD countries, domestic firms are more R&D intensive than foreign affiliates (*e.g.* Canada, France, Germany, the Netherlands, Sweden and the United Kingdom), in a few R&D intensity is roughly balanced (Finland, Japan, the United States), while it is higher in foreign affiliates in Australia and Ireland. Again, this reflects the varying features of the respective national innovation systems. Foreign R&D in the United States is attracted by the quality of research institutions, while locating R&D in Ireland is motivated more by the need to upgrade and adapt products and processes. From the perspective of the United States, foreign R&D expands already intensive knowledge interactions, but is also a source of knowledge outflows. In Ireland, foreign R&D is a major driving force in the technological catching-up process. From the perspective of a home country, the internationalisation of R&D reduces the concentration of R&D by domestic firms at home, and risks dismantling some of the home country's innovative capacity. Such risks may loom particularly large for small countries whose R&D base is strongly dominated by a small number of large multinational firms (Krugman, 1991). On the other hand, foreign R&D strengthens the ability of firms to increase their sales abroad, expand their overall resources and investment and absorb foreign technology more effectively.

2.3. Conclusion

91. A number of trends in the characteristics of technological innovation and in innovation systems have important policy implications:

- Innovation has become a complex activity, involving many different types of knowledge and actors. Smooth interplay between these actors is essential for successful innovation. Inter-firm collaboration, networking and the formation of clusters of industries are examples of such interactions.

- Countries provide the environment for innovative activities through their institutions, infrastructures and policies which influence the direction and the speed of innovation and technology diffusion.

- Because of their unique history, countries' production and innovation systems have different specialisation patterns, capital stock and institutions. This gives them a distinct set of strengths, but also limits their ability to manage certain kinds of change.

- Countries can be viewed as "national innovation systems", with distinctive attributes (specific pattern of scientific, technological and industrial specialisation, specific policy priorities) and specific structures of interactions (*e.g.* between the enterprise sector and the science system, collaboration between firms).

- The increasing segmentation of economic activity, as firms focus on core strengths and learn to combine and contract for complementary inputs, creates more horizontal links within and between countries. Thus, innovation systems are increasingly interlinked across national borders. Nevertheless, national characteristics and the strengths and weaknesses of the respective systems remain decisive for performance.

- Lastly, while there is a tendency for national innovation systems to adjust so that economic performances converge, they do so in distinctive ways that preserve some of their specific features.

CHAPTER 3. CHANGING PATTERNS OF PUBLIC SUPPORT AND PRIVATE R&D EFFORTS

3.1. Context and background

92. The role of innovation activities, and hence of R&D, in creating growth and jobs in the knowledge-based economy is broadly recognised, as has been shown in the preceding chapters. Despite this general awareness, resources devoted to R&D declined during the 1990s in many OECD Member countries, both in absolute terms and compared with total national product. This decrease stems first from a reduction in government funding of R&D, although business also weakened its commitment to R&D compared with production levels.

93. At the same time there is evidence of a reorientation of business R&D expenditures towards more applied projects with a foreseeable and quick payoff, responding clearly to market demand, and a fear that the decline in government funding may have a negative effect on the level of basic or long-term research. There is a danger that shrinking technological opportunities due to lower reserves of basic knowledge may result in less innovation in the future. On the other hand, increasing market pressure and associated firm responses seem to be having a positive effect on the efficiency of R&D. In this context, the question arises as to whether, and how, changing trends and patterns in R&D will affect productivity and economic growth.

94. Various aspects of the relative, and sometimes absolute, decline in government-financed R&D are reviewed in the following section. Possible causes are examined in terms of changes in the objectives of government R&D budgets and/or in government's use of different financial instruments and of the growing internationalisation of R&D funding. The impact of the decline is followed through to see which sectors of performance, and which activities, are affected. An examination is then undertaken of total R&D funding, that of the science system and, finally, an effort is made to measure total government support for industrial technology, including some non-R&D programmes. The nature, causes and consequences of changing patterns in business R&D are addressed in the final section.

3.2. Government funding of science and technology

95. In 1975, half the R&D in the OECD area was financed by governments. By 1995, the share was down to about one-third. This decline in the contribution of governments to national R&D efforts (gross domestic expenditures on R&D-GERD) has taken place in the majority of Member countries with only minor reversals, for example the burst in government financing in the United States in the early 1980s. By 1997 the projected federal share of US R&D – 31 per cent – was "the lowest ever reported since surveys began" (National Science Foundation, 1997*a*).

96. During the 1980s, governments generally increased their funding of R&D and their share of GERD declined only as a result of the greater dynamism of R&D financed by industry. In the 1990s, government-financed R&D grew less rapidly than GDP in the majority of Member countries and actually fell at fixed prices in about half, including France, Germassny,[5] Italy, the United Kingdom and the United States, and, in some years, Canada. In those countries where government-financed R&D grew, the rate was generally about 4 per cent per annum, rising to 6 per cent in Denmark and Japan, and 11 per cent in Ireland.

97. Support for S&T, like all other policy areas, has come under pressure due to budgetary stringency. Indeed, it seems that R&D has not maintained its share of total government discretionary expenditure during the 1990s in any of the G7 countries with the exception of Japan (Figure 3.1).

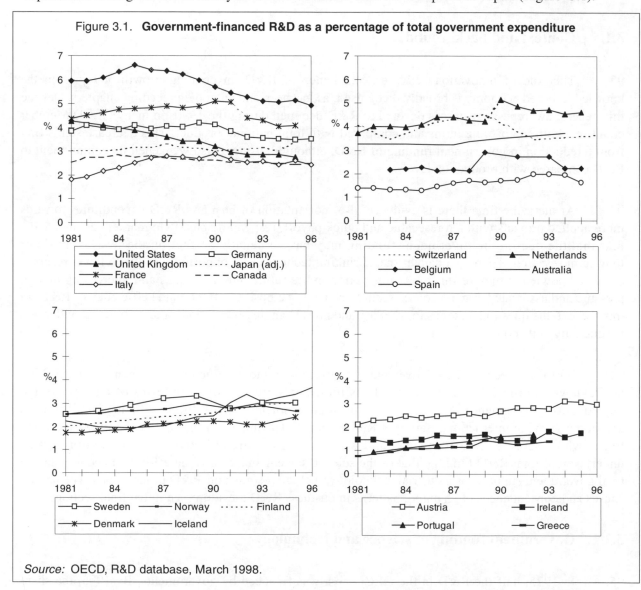

Figure 3.1. **Government-financed R&D as a percentage of total government expenditure**

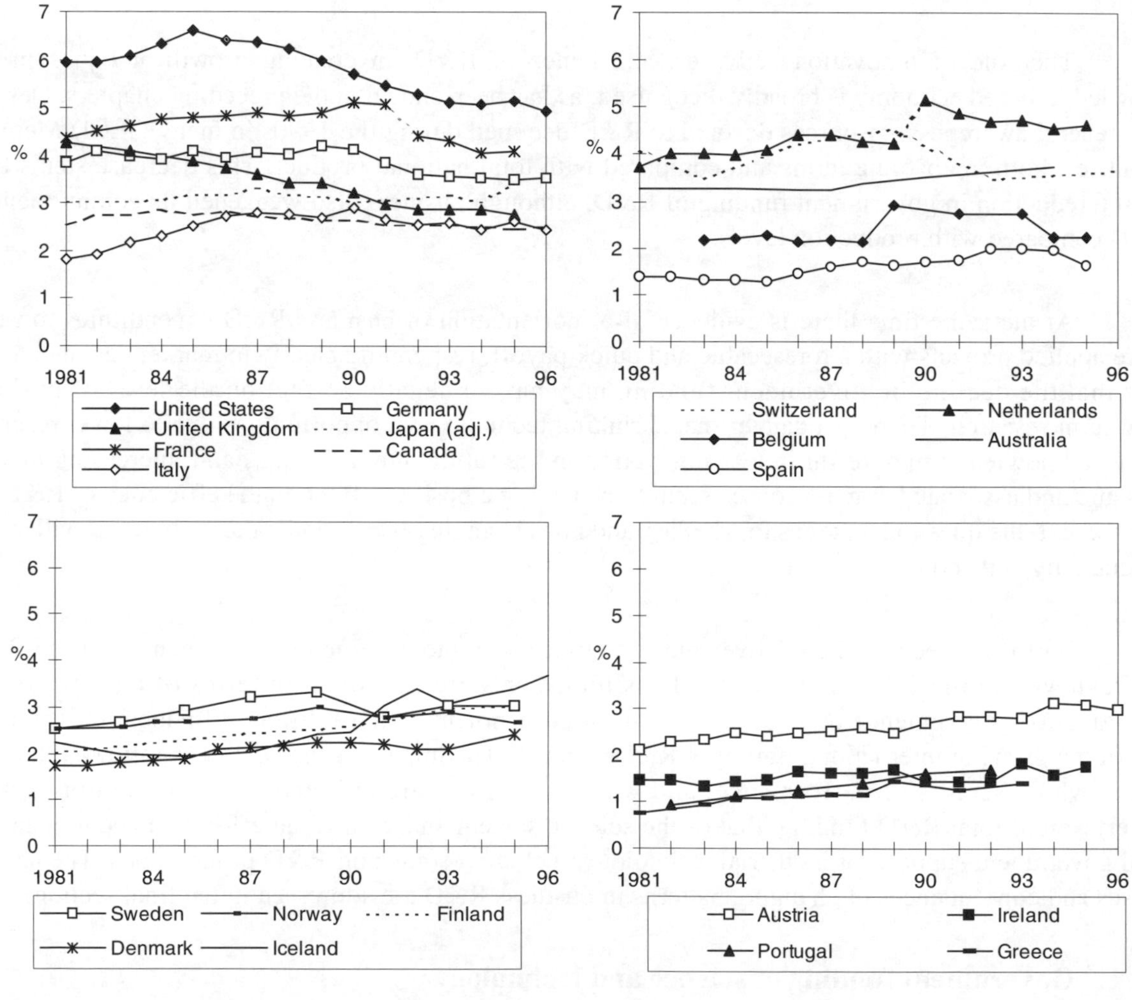

Source: OECD, R&D database, March 1998.

5. Allowing for the break in series caused by re-unification.

Trends in the structure of total government R&D funding

Ministerial responsibilities

98. The change in the level of total government R&D funding is the result of decisions about the priority of different government aims and objectives and the importance of R&D for these aims. In some countries such as France, Germany or the Netherlands, these choices are made mainly in one large ministry, responsible for more than half of the government funds committed to R&D. The more usual pattern is typified by Australia, Denmark and Japan where two-thirds or more of funds are spent by the Ministry of Education (which is responsible for funding the universities) and a S&T ministry or agency. Canada is representative of countries where decisions on R&D funding are spread over a large number of ministries and agencies, with the National Research Council, the largest spender, responsible for only 14 per cent of the total (Statistics Canada, 1997*a*).[6] In the United States about 90 per cent of federally funded R&D comes from four mission-oriented departments or agencies [Department of Defense (DOD), Department of Health (DOH), National Aeronautics and Space Administration (NASA), Department of Energy (DOE)] which not only finance R&D for their own missions, but also support R&D programmes which in other countries come under the responsibility of S&T ministries. The official science agency, the National Science Foundation (NSF), supplies less than 5 per cent of the funds (National Science Foundation, 1997*b*).

Changing objectives of government R&D

99. Because of these differences in institutional practices and because ministerial responsibilities can change quite drastically over time, international comparisons are usually based on a functional breakdown of funding (see for example the review of national specificities in Chapter 2).

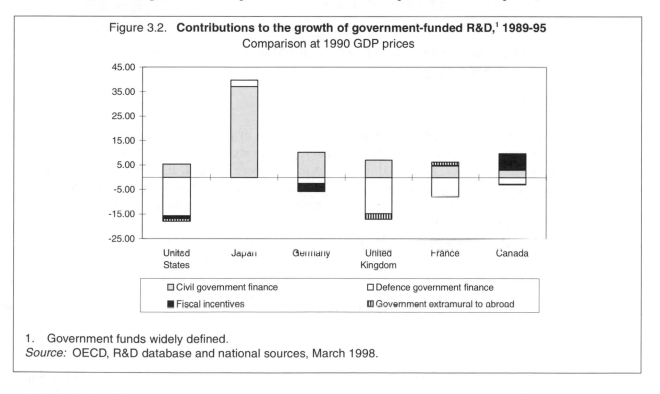

Figure 3.2. **Contributions to the growth of government-funded R&D,[1] 1989-95**
Comparison at 1990 GDP prices

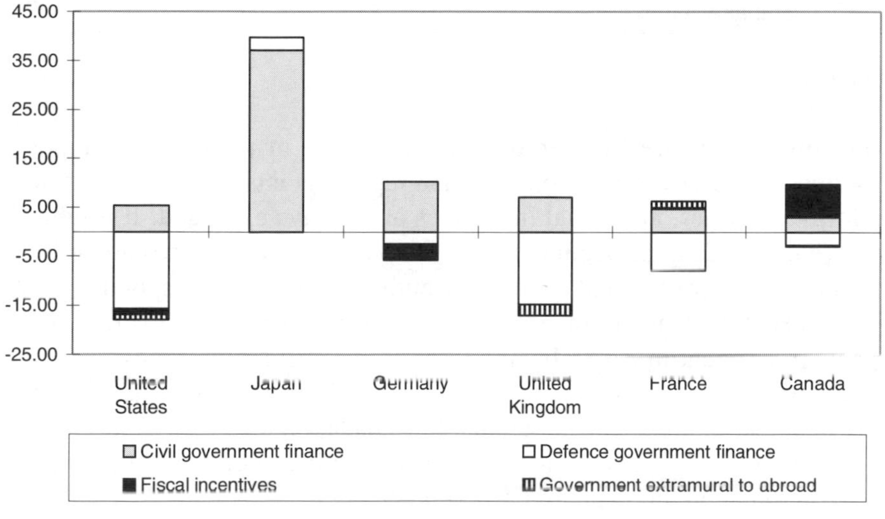

1. Government funds widely defined.
Source: OECD, R&D database and national sources, March 1998.

6. However, the portfolio of departments and agencies reporting to the Industry Minister has a high percentage of the total.

100. The drop in defence R&D largely explains the decline in government-financed R&D in France, the United Kingdom and the United States in 1989-95 (Figure 3.2). However, according to R&D budgets, funding for energy actually declined in more countries than did funding for defence, followed by exploration and exploitation of the Earth and atmosphere, and promotion of agriculture, forestry and fisheries (Figure 3.3). Budget R&D funds generally increased for advancement of knowledge and for "welfare" objectives such as environmental protection, social services and health.

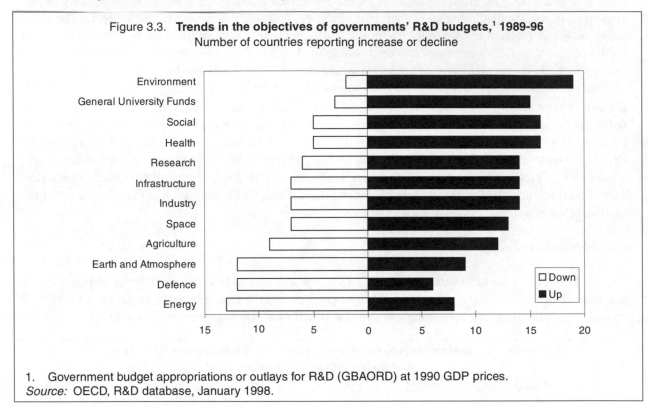

Figure 3.3. **Trends in the objectives of governments' R&D budgets,[1] 1989-96**
Number of countries reporting increase or decline

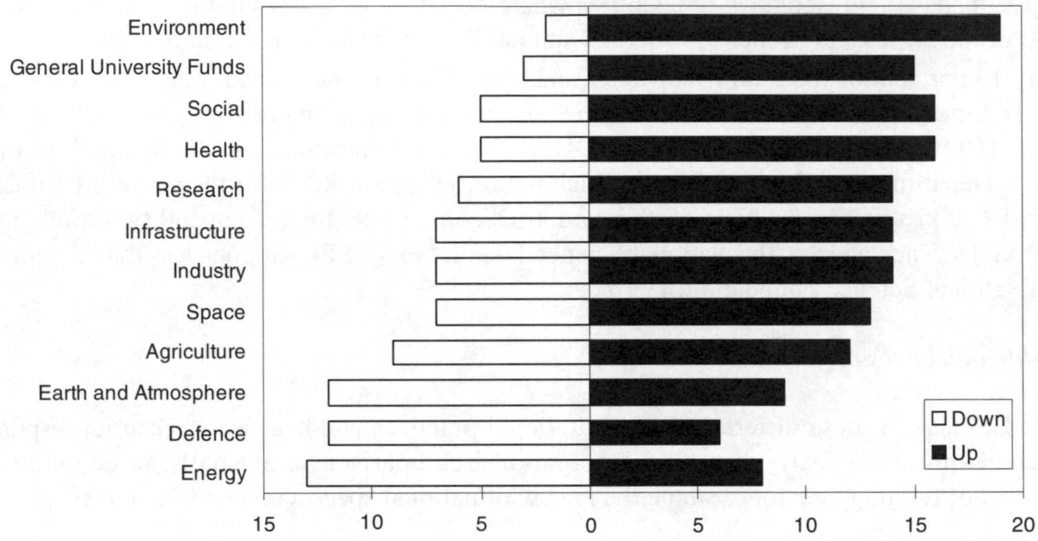

1. Government budget appropriations or outlays for R&D (GBAORD) at 1990 GDP prices.
Source: OECD, R&D database, January 1998.

Role of fiscal incentives

101. Governments can finance R&D through a wide range of financial instruments. The standard R&D series described so far cover only contracts and regular grants. The treatment of loans and grants which may be forgiven varies, and fiscal incentives are always excluded. It might be argued that if fiscal incentives were included, the decline in government R&D funding would be less marked. At the end of the 1980s the cost to government of fiscal incentives for R&D corresponded to only 1 per cent of government-financed R&D in Japan, rising to about 3 per cent in France, Germany and the United States, and 10 per cent in Australia and Canada. The effect on trends was, thus, negligible in Japan and was actually negative in Germany and the United States in that the cost of fiscal incentives fell more rapidly than that of contracts and grants. In Canada, on the other hand, government financing would have grown in 1989-95 if fiscal incentives had been included, and in Australia growth would have been even higher than on the standard basis (Figure 3.2).

Sector of performance of government-financed R&D

102. Governments spend their resources in different sectors of the economy depending on the type of programme and the institutional arrangements in the country. In most, the higher education sector is the major recipient of funds, followed by the government sector itself, with the business enterprise sector somewhat less important, and a very small share of funds going to the private non-profit (PNP)

sector. The concentration in the higher education sector is particularly marked in small, highly R&D-intensive countries such as Austria, the Netherlands, Switzerland and Sweden. In the United States the business enterprise sector is the largest single recipient of funds, followed by higher education and only then by government. In Japan, in Korea, in the central and east European Member countries, in France, and in a number of countries with low R&D spending, governments spend more in their own institutes than in the higher education sector. In Japan and Portugal, PNP institutes receive more government R&D funding than industry and the share of government-financed R&D performed in this sector is also above average in the United States (Figure 3.4).

Figure 3.4. **Government-financed R&D by national sector of performance, 1995**

As a percentage of GDP

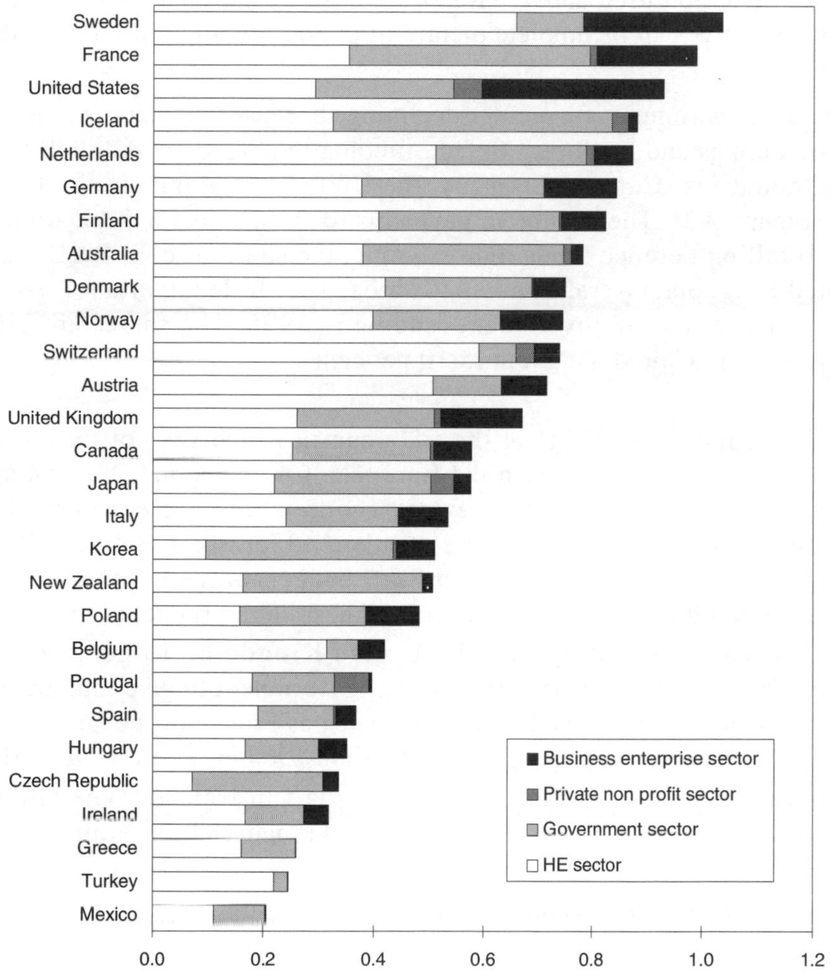

Source: OECD, R&D database, March 1998.

103. During the period under review (1989 to 1996), Germany and the central and east European Member countries restructured their national innovation systems. Less drastic changes affected the level and structure of government R&D funding in other Member countries. In many, governments were devolving S&T responsibilities and agencies from the public to the private sector. For example,

since the end of the 1980s, France Télécom and Giat industries were privatised in France and a number of units were transferred to the business sector in the United Kingdom.

104. Between 1989 and 1995 the share of government-financed R&D carried out in the business enterprise sector fell almost without exception and funding was down at fixed prices in all the G7 countries. Finance for R&D performed by government also fell, both as a share of the total and at fixed prices with some exceptions, notably Japan. Finance of HERD continued to grow.

International flows of government funds

105. The increasing internationalisation of R&D activities means that the traditional measure of the government contribution used above – R&D financed by national government and carried out on national territory – gives an incomplete picture of public funding (OECD, 1998*a*).

106. Is national government financing declining because greater use is being made of international programmes and facilities? In fact, funding to abroad actually fell between 1989 and 1995 in four G7 countries (Canada, Germany, the United Kingdom and the United States), but grew in France (Figure 3.2). The decline in payments to abroad, as for R&D on national territory, was partly due to falling defence funds. For example, the share of civil R&D carried out abroad grew in the United Kingdom. Overall funding to abroad is of little importance in the United States, where it was only 1 per cent of government funding in 1995. The shares are higher in Canada, France, Germany and the United Kingdom (5-10 per cent).

107. Total public support for R&D in the EU countries involves not only R&D financed by national government but also funds from the European Commission. The Commission finances R&D through two mechanisms: *(i)* framework funds which are earmarked for R&D; and *(ii)* structural funds, a share of which are subsequently used for R&D. Between 1985 and 1995, the share of the former in the combined civil direct R&D budgets of the European countries rose from 3 to 7.5 per cent, making the Commission the fifth highest public funder after France and Germany (about 25 per cent each) and Italy and the United Kingdom (10 per cent each).[7] Adding Commission framework funds to those from national government to give total public R&D finance has little effect in countries with large R&D efforts such as France or the United Kingdom, a little more in small R&D-intensive countries such as Belgium, Denmark or the Netherlands, but would double spending in Greece and would increase it by half in Ireland.[8] The latter countries also benefit from structural funds which are already included in national government finance.

Government-financed R&D in the science system

108. Although S&T systems are and should be closely integrated in the context of "national innovation systems", it is worthwhile distinguishing between government's traditional role in funding "scientific research" (Figure 3.5) and the more complex one of financing "technology" and, more particularly, "industrial technology".

7. For details of Commission programmes and other public sector co-operation in Europe, see Chapters 9 and 10 of European Commission (1997*a*).
8. Data are derived from national surveys and not from European Commission sources.

Figure 3.5. **Structure of government financing of the science system**

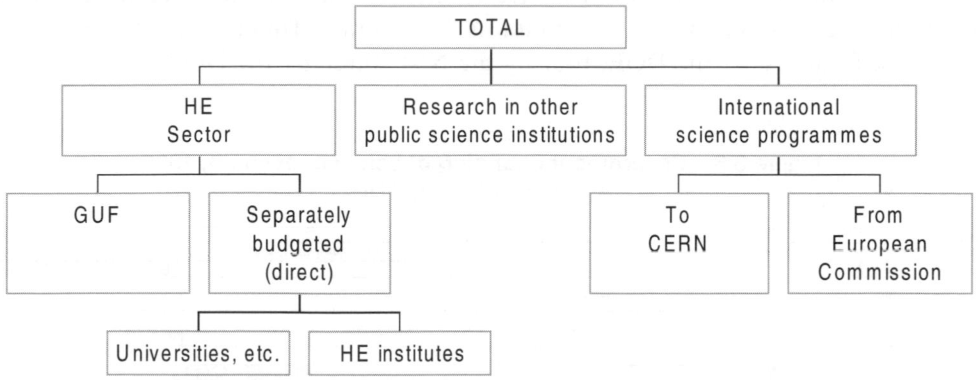

Source: OECD Secretariat.

The higher education sector

109. For most countries, the universities are the largest single component of the national science system. Over the period 1989-95, the share of HERD financed by government fell in virtually all Member countries. The actual sums involved increased over the period (at 1990 GDP prices) in all except Canada and Sweden, although growth was minimal in Belgium, Finland, Germany and Spain. Government funding grew at over 10 per cent per annum in Iceland and Ireland.

110. Governments fund university R&D activities in a number of ways. Traditionally they provided general support via block grants from the Ministry of Education, part of which was used by university staff to carry out R&D. Such funding (GUF), which is difficult to measure,[9] is still very important in small, highly R&D-intensive countries such as the Netherlands, Sweden and Switzerland (Figure 3.6). Governments may also provide grants to encourage research "for the advancement of knowledge" or grants (or contracts) to obtain the knowledge needed for government missions such as defence or health care. In terms of shares of the two components, that of GUF has declined in the majority of countries and that of direct support has grown. The actual amounts of direct funding increased at 1990 prices in all countries except Sweden, Switzerland and possibly Greece (Figure 3.7), with growth particularly marked in Australia, Austria, Iceland, Ireland and Turkey. It is more difficult to examine trends in GUF as a number of countries revised their R&D estimates during the period. Funding was actually lower in 1995 than in 1989 in Belgium, Canada, Finland, the Netherlands, New Zealand, Sweden and Turkey. Only in Ireland did GUF grow at over 10 per cent annually over the period 1989-95.

111. In some countries the science system also includes research institutes which carry out the same type of R&D activities as universities. They may be linked to the latter and included in the higher education sector. The largest single case in the OECD area is the *Centre National de la Recherche Scientifique* (CNRS) in France which receives the lion's share of direct funding of

9. GUF is usually estimated by applying standard R&D content percentages to readily available sets of data on the block grant. The method assumes that university teaching staff spend the same proportion of their time on R&D in the 1990s as they did in the 1980s, whereas anecdotal evidence suggests that the weight of teaching and administration is increasing at the expense of R&D.

HERD. Similar bodies such as the *Consiglio Nazionale delle Ricerche* (CNR) in Italy and the Research Councils in the United Kingdom are treated as part of the government sector. In the United States the higher education sector contains 17 federally financed R&D centres (FFRDCs), of which nine are financed by the DOE, four by the NSF, three by the DOD and one by NASA.

Figure 3.6. **Government financing of science research, 1995**
As a percentage of GDP

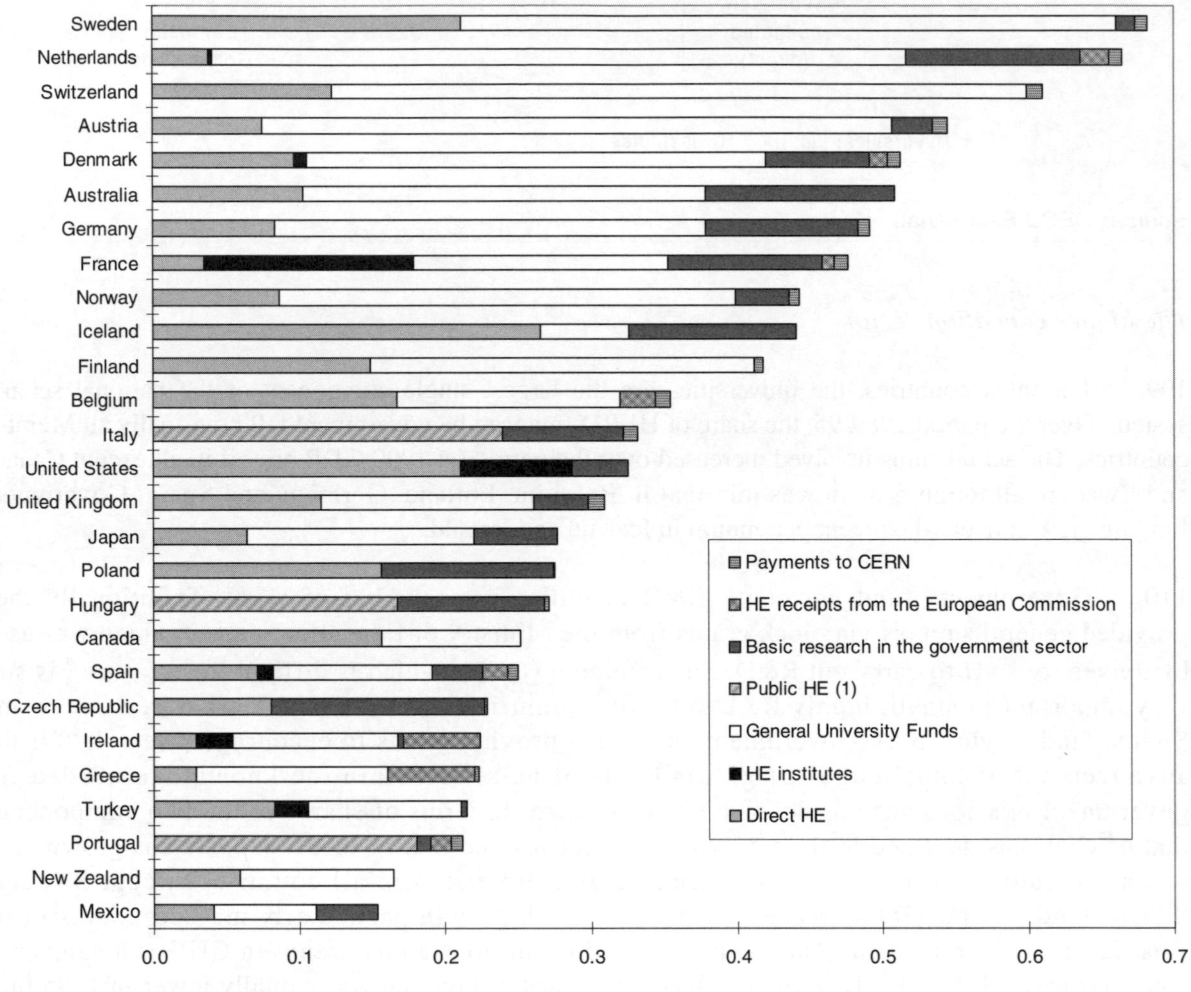

1. Sum of direct HE and GUF not separately available.
Source: OECD, R&D database, national publications and data supplied by CERN, March 1998.

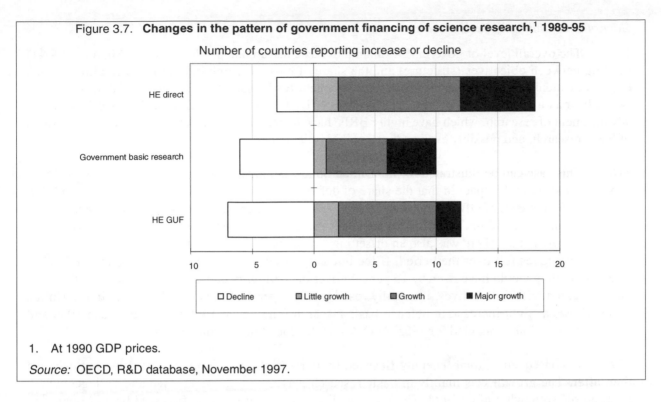

Figure 3.7. **Changes in the pattern of government financing of science research,[1] 1989-95**

Number of countries reporting increase or decline

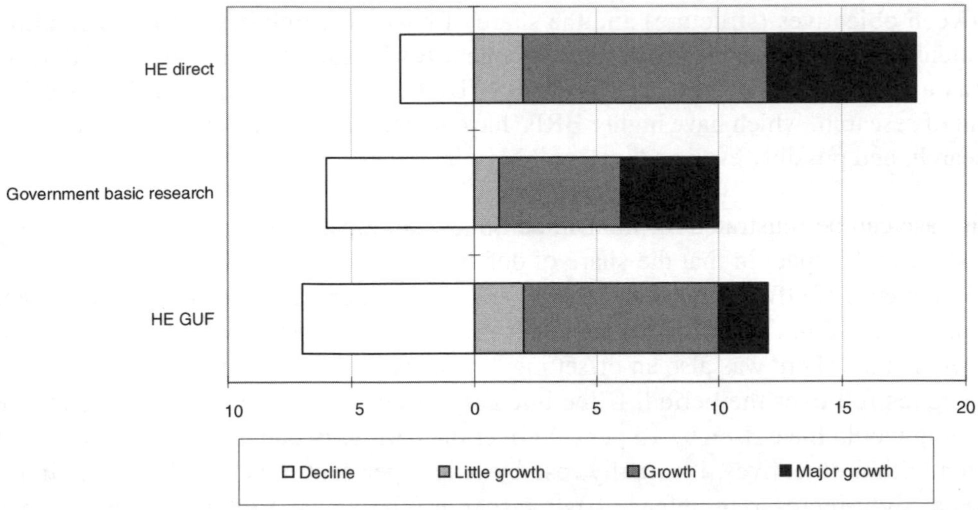

1. At 1990 GDP prices.

Source: OECD, R&D database, November 1997.

Science in the government sector

112. Since it is not possible to separate expenditure on "scientific" research in the government sector from standard R&D data, spending on "basic research" has been used as a proxy.[10] This type of funding is particularly important in the central and eastern European Member countries and is also significant in Australia, France, Germany and the Netherlands (Figure 3.6). The share of government support for the national science system going to basic research in government establishments fell in some two-thirds of countries and rose in one-third (Figure 3.7). Spending actually fell at fixed prices in six countries (Germany, Ireland, Sweden, Turkey, the United Kingdom and the United States), while growth was significant in Austria, Denmark, Iceland and Japan.

International funds for science

113. The measure of government support for science would be incomplete if the major international facilities are excluded. CERN (*Conseil Européen pour la Recherche Nucléaire*), the largest of these, represents only a small share of funding in most countries (Figure 3.6). CERN expenditure is scheduled to decline in 1997 at current prices.

114. The inclusion of funds from the European Commission would significantly increase direct public support to HERD in Greece and Ireland, and also in the Netherlands where, however, direct funding is still very low. The effect is modest in Belgium, Denmark and Spain, and insignificant in France, the only G7 European country for which data are available.

10. Data are not available for Belgium, Canada, Finland, Greece and New Zealand.

Government funding of basic research

115. The overall level of government funding of basic research depends on the distribution of R&D funding between objectives (structure) and the share of basic research in total R&D funding of each objective (intensity). Insofar as the share in government R&D budgets (GBAORD) of defence, which typically has a very low basic research intensity (BRI), has decreased and those of health and advancement of research, which have higher BRIs, have increased, one can expect that the overall share of basic research, and possibly even its level, will have increased.

116. This case can be illustrated for the United States (National Science Foundation, 1997*c*). There was a clear structural impact in that the share of defence R&D, with a BRI of under 0.5 per cent, fell from 66 to 54 per cent of GBAORD between 1989 and 1995, whereas health, with a BRI of about 5 per cent, rose from 13 to 17 per cent. The share of "advancement of research" with the highest BRI (10 per cent) remained stable. There was also an offsetting "intensity" effect in that the share of basic research of most objectives fell over the period. If the intensity in 1995 had been the same as in 1989, basic research funding would have risen by 15 per cent over the period. Because of the decreased priority for basic research within objectives, it actually rose by only 8 per cent. Overall GBAORD in the United States shows a slight increase in defence basic research funding (at 1990 prices) between 1989 and 1995, with a decline scheduled for 1995-97 (National Science Foundation, 1997*b*).

117. In consequence, total federally financed basic research grew from 1990 to 1994 but declined thereafter. The growth was mainly in basic research performed in universities and colleges which levelled off somewhat after 1994. The main decline was in government-financed basic research in industrial firms. In 1992 about 20 per cent of their basic research was directly government-financed, rising to over 25 per cent for the whole business enterprise sector (including FFRDCs). By 1997 these shares were down to 3 and 10 per cent respectively (National Science Foundation, 1997*d*) (Figure 3.8).

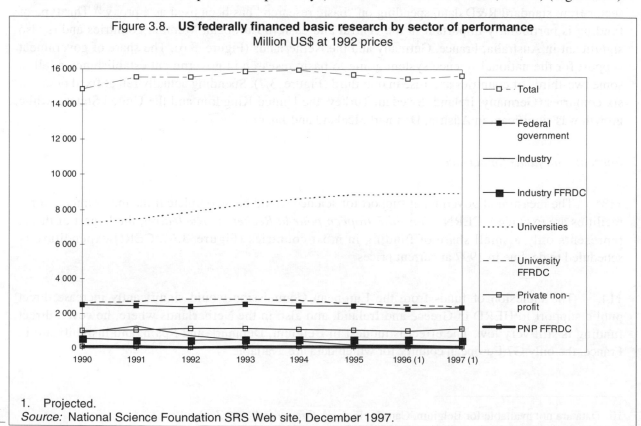

Figure 3.8. **US federally financed basic research by sector of performance**

Million US$ at 1992 prices

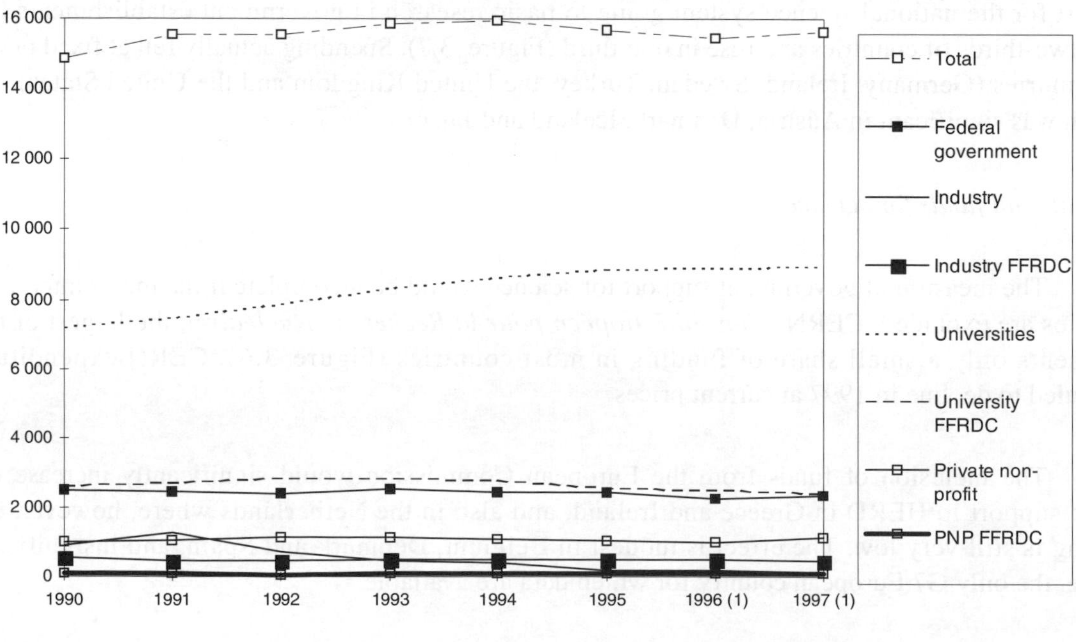

1. Projected.

Source: National Science Foundation SRS Web site, December 1997.

118. Data on government financing of basic research are not widely available outside the United States. R&D budgets show that basic research funding continued to grow at fixed prices in the United Kingdom (Office of Technology Assessment, 1995) and Germany (to 1992 only, Bundesministerium für Bildung, Forschung und Technologie, Wissenschaft, 1996).

Trends in government support for technology

Declining support for non-industrial technology

119. The main aim here is to examine the level and structure of government-funded industrial technology. However, as noted above, certain "technological" objectives such as energy and agriculture have contributed to the overall decline in government support for R&D in many Member countries. In about half the countries funding also declined for "infrastructure" (comprising transport and telecommunications as well as urban development). Agricultural S&T was an established cluster in its own right in many national innovation systems in which government funds were significant. The decline in government finance may affect the universities but is also bringing about rationalisation of the non-market institutes concerned and, in some countries, the gradual privatisation of both agricultural R&D and agricultural extension programmes. Energy, transport and telecommunication agencies are also undergoing privatisation in Member countries, and one must assume that the R&D concerned is being picked up by the resulting private enterprises.[11]

Types of government support for industrial technology

120. Classic R&D data show that the percentage of GBAORD going to "industrial development" as a socio-economic objective is generally declining, as is the share of R&D in the business enterprise sector which is financed by government. However, both of these indicators give an incomplete picture of the range of ways in which governments can support industrial technology.

121. These can be divided into three broad groups (Figure 3.9): financial incentives; mission-oriented contracts, procurement and grants; S&T infrastructure and diffusion. The first category includes all programmes designed to encourage industrial firms to carry out R&D (or other innovation activities) by reducing the cost through grants, loans, fiscal incentives, etc. The second covers government payments to industrial firms to carry out R&D to meet government needs, notably for defence or space objectives. The third covers ways in which governments can assist firms without giving them money: *(i)* by financing R&D activities aimed at industrial development in institutes and universities; *(ii)* by supporting technological research in academic and similar units; and *(iii)* by funding non-R&D programmes either supporting post-R&D stages of the innovation process or diffusion and extension programmes.

11. For example the public enterprise Norwegian Telecom became the private company Telenor AS. Where these firms still receive funds from government once in the business sector, the amounts will be treated in the next section on industrial technology.

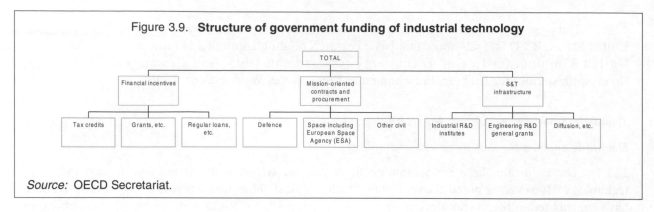

Figure 3.9. **Structure of government funding of industrial technology**

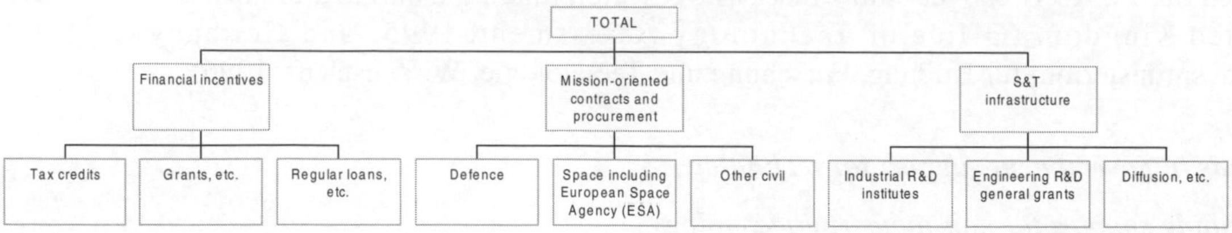

Source: OECD Secretariat.

122. The balance between these three broad areas, and between the types of funding within each area, can be seen as reflecting each country's "strategy" for funding industrial technology. Comparing the sums involved with industrial GDP allows them to be viewed in a national context [without making precise comparisons which are not justified by the quality of the data (Young, forthcoming)] (Figure 3.10). The pattern varies considerably across countries. In the United States, federal support for industrial technology is almost all paid to firms, with the largest share in the form of contracts and procurement. The pattern is similar in France and the United Kingdom, although these countries make more use, respectively, of financial incentives (France) and funding via the infrastructure (United Kingdom). In Australia and Canada, financial incentives are the largest category, followed by contracts and procurement. Funding in the Netherlands is distributed fairly evenly across categories. In Finland, Japan and Mexico over half the funds are for support via the S&T infrastructure.

123. Total funding of industrial technology grew steadily in Japan in the first half of the 1990s and also increased significantly, after some variations, in Australia and Finland. It fell in France, Germany, the United Kingdom and the United States. There was some growth over the period in Canada, Mexico and the Netherlands.

Figure 3.10. **Government funds for industrial technology**

As a percentage of industrial GDP

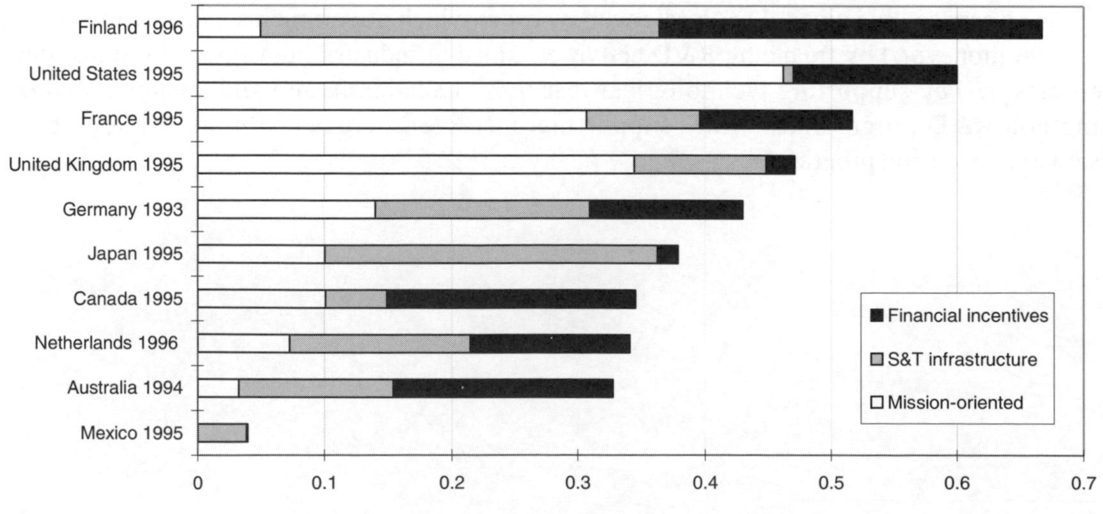

Source: OECD, Secretariat calculations based on R&D database, PSI database and information supplied by Member countries, March 1998.

Funding of manufacturing technology via financial incentives[12]

Level and structure of funding

124. In the OECD area as a whole, funding of research development and innovation (RDI) in manufacturing industry via financial incentives grew by over 10 per cent between 1989 and 1992, and fluctuated thereafter. The share of RDI funds in total public support to manufacturing industry rose slightly from 17 per cent in 1989 to almost 19 per cent in 1993. Funding was lower in 1995 than in 1989 (at 1990 GDP prices) in all the G7 countries except the United States, but grew in the European Commission and in many smaller Member countries.

Types of programmes

125. Over the period 1989 to 1995 OECD Member governments financed some 280 manufacturing support programmes whose primary policy objective was R&D and technological innovation. More than half provided general incentives for R&D activities, while about one-third promoted selected technologies, notably IT and energy saving. The remaining programmes focused on research co-operation between firms and research institutes, including support for hiring R&D personnel or for temporary employment of R&D personnel from research institutes, international R&D co-operation and the funding of technology parks or R&D venture capital.

126. Governments generally adapted financial flows in existing programmes to meet the changing policy focus, rather than introducing new programmes or phasing out old ones. Thus over half the programmes were in use throughout the period and only about one-quarter were introduced in 1990 or later. At the overall OECD level, there do not appear to be any significant qualitative differences between recent R&D support measures and those introduced in the late 1980s.

127. This picture changes slightly when other R&D-related programmes are included: *(i)* programmes with R&D as their secondary policy objective – for example, an SME programme that provides R&D venture capital; and *(ii)* programmes with R&D as the economic activity supported – for example, a sectoral programme for selected industries that provides financial assistance to R&D activities. The inclusion of these programmes adds about 120 programmes and about 18 per cent to the total net cost of financial incentives for manufacturing RDI.

128. An examination of these other programmes reveals several new insights. First, about one-third concern SMEs. Second, their inclusion raises the weight of IT and energy saving in financial incentives for selected technologies. Moreover, 20 per cent of these programmes promote RDI in environmental technologies. Third, it is interesting to note that almost half the secondary policy objective programmes and programmes supporting R&D activities were implemented in 1990 or later. This means that recent shifts in the policy focus of public support to industrial R&D are better reflected in this category of programmes than in programmes which have R&D as their primary policy objective.

Use of different financial instruments

129. Approximately half the OECD Member countries support manufacturing RDI through classic financial instruments such as grants and conditional loans, with little or no use of other schemes. This

12. This section on financial incentives is based on national reports to the OECD database on public support to manufacturing industry (PSI).

group includes the European Commission, Germany, the United Kingdom (at the end of the period), plus Finland, Iceland, Ireland, New Zealand, Portugal and Switzerland. Such programmes also predominate in Belgium and Sweden (Figure 3.11).

130. In Canada, Denmark, Japan and the Netherlands, governments made use of a broader variety of financing instruments. In Australia, Canada and the Netherlands, R&D tax concession programmes channelled the lion's share of total financial incentives for R&D in the manufacturing sector. This category is also important in France, Japan, the United States and, in the earlier years of the period, Germany. These programmes are examined at greater length in Chapter 7.

131. Relatively few countries make major use of the other types of financial instrument (regular loans, guarantees and equity holdings), although they are the main forms of support in Austria and Hungary and are also applied in Italy, Japan, Norway and Turkey. Funding for such schemes appears to fluctuate from year to year. The limited use of loans, guarantees and equity capital compared to other financial instruments is surprising, as their fund raising capacity and potentially lower budgetary impact should make them more attractive to governments than the more widely used grants and tax concessions where there is no difference between the net and gross cost to government.

Figure 3.11. **Funding of financial incentives for RDI in manufacturing industry by financial instrument**

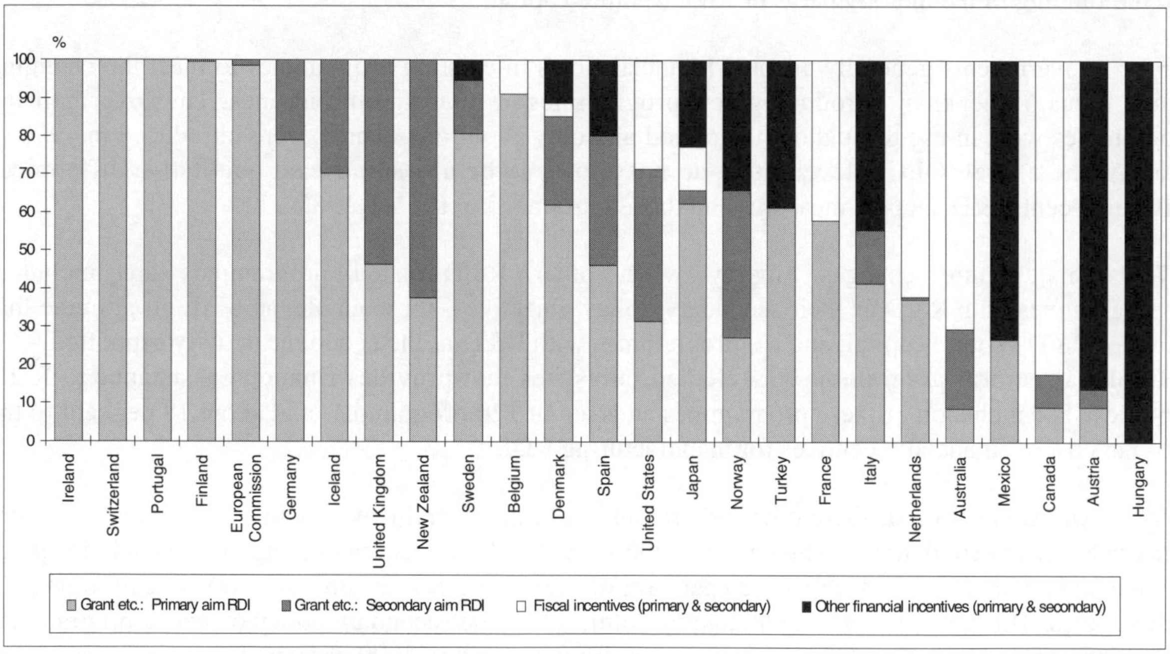

Source: OECD, PSI database, December 1997.

Mission-oriented contracts and procurement

132. As might be expected, the reason for the major difference in the level of mission-oriented R&D in France, the United Kingdom and the United States, on the one hand, and the other countries, on the other, is the amount of defence R&D (Figure 3.12). In France, Germany and the United States there was a 20 per cent decline in payments to the business enterprise sector for defence R&D between 1989 and 1995 (at 1990 GDP prices). This decline continues through to 1997 and probably 1998 in the United States. In Canada much of the decline in funding via financial incentives (other than fiscal ones) is explained by the ending of a programme aiding the defence industries.

Figure 3.12. **Government funding of industrial technology via mission-oriented contracts and procurement**
As a percentage of industrial GDP

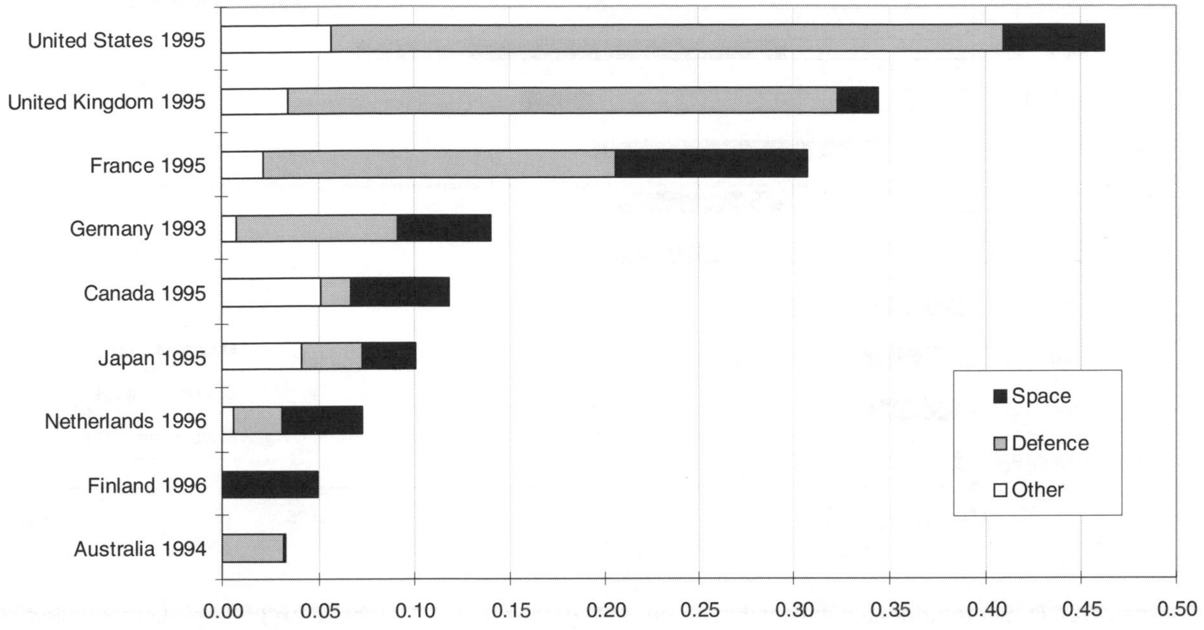

Source: OECD, Secretariat calculations based on R&D database, PSI database and information supplied by Member countries, March 1998.

133. Space R&D contracts to industry are most important in France. Some countries include some space programmes in financial incentives. Funding of industrial R&D via space programmes grew in all the countries in depicted in Figure 3.12, with the exception of the United Kingdom.

Funding of industrial technology via the S&T infrastructure

134. S&T infrastructure covers government funding of R&D and related activities which are intended to support industrial technology but are not carried out by industrial firms. The first component is R&D for industrial development carried out in R&D institutes, government departments or universities. These activities may be part of the business enterprise sector or in the government or private non-profit sectors. Such R&D activities are particularly important in Australia and Finland and are significant in Japan, the Netherlands and the United Kingdom (Figure 3.13).[13] In general, government funding of institutes such as the Commonwealth Scientific Industrial Research Organisation (CSIRO) in Australia or of the Netherlands Organisation for Applied Scientific Research (TNO) is declining.

13. In France, they are represented here only by co-operative research institutes in the business enterprise sector.

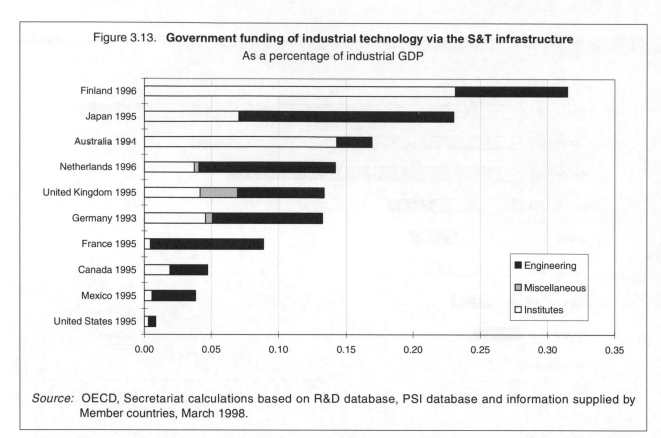

Figure 3.13. **Government funding of industrial technology via the S&T infrastructure**
As a percentage of industrial GDP

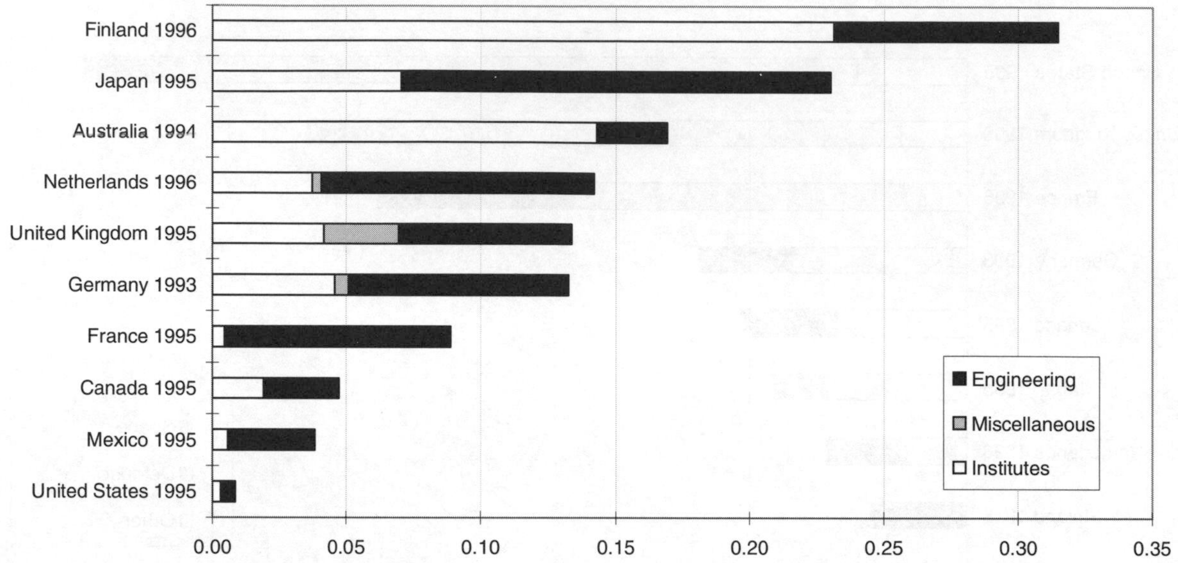

Source: OECD, Secretariat calculations based on R&D database, PSI database and information supplied by Member countries, March 1998.

135. The second component is funding of engineering research via the objective "advancement of knowledge", which includes non-oriented R&D in general and GUF. This is strictly speaking part of the science system, but it may also serve as a proxy for the general support for academic technological R&D.

Role of provincial government in funding industrial technology

136. Although provincial and local governments are taking an increasing interest in encouraging industrial technology in their regions as a means of attracting or generating jobs, their financial contributions are not yet very important in the majority of Member countries. For example, in Canada provincial governments spent about C$ 250 million on industrial technology (about 10-15 per cent of the total) (Statistics Canada, 1997*a*; 1997*b*). Such schemes more often involve co-operation between the different levels of government, as in the United States where the states provide about 10-15 per cent of co-operative technology support (Berglund and Coburn, 1995).

Closing remarks on government S&T funding

137. Government support for R&D has levelled off in a number of OECD countries in the 1990s, including all the G7 except Japan. The decline in defence R&D has contributed in the G7 countries and there has been a general downturn in support for R&D for energy. Internationalisation does not seem to have had a major effect on the level and structure of funding except in small countries whose R&D is heavily funded by the European Commission. Changes in the structure of government funding away from defence and economic objectives towards health and advancement of knowledge have increased the share of basic research in total public R&D funding. Governments fund industrial technology in a wide variety of ways and no common trends seem to emerge from the funding series. This section has reviewed such funding from the government point of view. The following one relates the sums involved to R&D in the business enterprise sector.

3.3. Causes and consequences of changing innovative efforts

138. Over the last decades there has been a considerable variation in business expenditures on research and development (BERD) among the OECD countries. On average, they grew by over 3 per cent in the 1970s and by about 5 per cent in the 1980s. Beginning in the mid-1980s, a prolonged levelling off began in a first group of countries (Canada, the Netherlands and the United States), and in the early 1990s in a second group (France, Germany, Italy, Japan and the United Kingdom). The patterns are similar in terms of R&D intensity (the ratio of BERD to business sector GDP) (Figure 3.14). The slowdown occurred in almost all OECD countries, with the exception of Australia, Iceland and Ireland. In some countries, notably Germany, Italy, Japan and the United Kingdom, BERD has even decreased in real terms in the 1990s. On average, growth in BERD amounted to about 1 per cent a year between 1990 and 1995 (Table 3.1).

Figure 3.14. **Trends in R&D intensities in the business sector**[1]

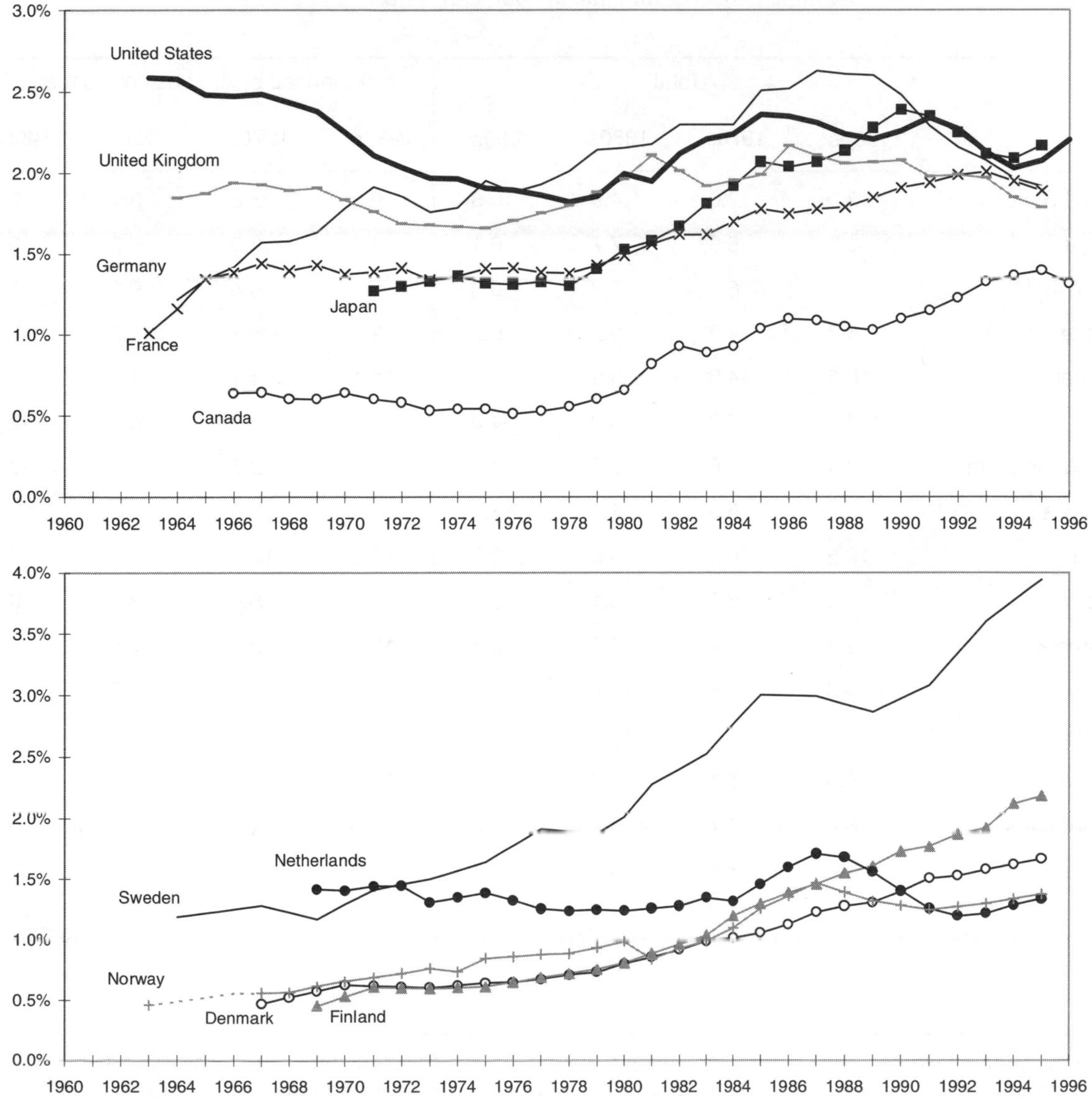

1. BERD divided by GDP of the business sector.
Source: OECD, Economic Outlook 60 and R&D database, February 1998.

139. Beginning in 1995 there were signs of a revival in business R&D, notably in the United States. Since the deep trough of 1992-94, there has been a slight increase in R&D spending in most European countries, although most growth rates remain low. The upsurge has been stronger in Nordic countries.

140. There are concerns among governments that the observed levelling off signals a more permanent change, and could indicate a lasting decline in productivity growth with even wider economic consequences. Moreover, there are indications of a tilt in innovative efforts away from basic long-term research towards more short-term efforts, and from applied research towards development, also with possible negative long-term effects. To gauge the scope and impacts of these developments and the possible implications for policy, it is important to know what factors are driving this change. In this section, the focus is on explaining the evolution of business R&D and the possible consequences of changes in innovative efforts for technological and economic performance and their policy implications.

Table 3.1. **Growth of R&D in the business sector**
Average annual growth rate at 1990 GDP prices, percentage

	Total				Financed by the business sector			
	1960s[1]	1970s	1980s	1990s[2]	1960s[1]	1970s	1980s	1990s[2]
United States	2.0	2.0	4.9	0.8	6.2	3.8	5.7	2.6
Canada	3.9	5.0	7.7	6.1	4.9	5.6	6.2	6.0
Japan	..	6.4	9.2	-0.6	..	6.4	9.2	-0.7
France	5.7	4.3	5.2	0.7	9.9	5.2	5.2	2.5
Germany	10.5	4.5	3.9	-1.5	11.1	4.1	4.7	-1.0
Italy	10.4	3.3	8.2	-4.0	9.6	2.6	6.5	-2.6
United Kingdom	2.4	2.6	3.3	-1.2	2.2	2.5	4.2	-0.8
Australia	..	6.9	11.0	13.1	..	2.9	12.8	12.5
Austria	16.5	10.2	4.5	2.5	17.6	10.0	4.6	..
Belgium	..	6.3	3.1	0.9	..	6.4	3.2	0.7
Denmark	13.1	4.1	7.6	5.6	12.7	3.1	7.5	4.2
Finland	19.3	6.6	10.4	3.9	..	6.5	10.5	4.1
Iceland	..	..	15.2	17.6	..	..	20.4	17.3
Ireland	14.5	5.1	10.0	20.5	14.3	3.7	10.7	20.6
Netherlands	0.0	1.7	3.7	1.2	0.0	1.1	3.8	0.0
Norway	9.2	8.1	5.7	3.5	10.3	6.4	7.0	5.0
Spain	22.7	11.9	11.8	-1.7	21.7	11.9	9.7	-0.7
Sweden	4.9	5.6	5.8	7.3	8.1	6.2	6.0	7.3
Switzerland	2.4	1.2	3.7	-4.8	3.1	1.4	3.5	..

1. First year available: 1963 – France, Ireland, Italy, Norway, Switzerland, United States; 1964 – Austria, Germany, Spain, Sweden, United Kingdom; 1966 – Canada; 1967 – Denmark.
2. Last year available: 1996 – Canada, France, Germany, Iceland, Italy, Spain, United States; 1995 – Belgium, Denmark, Finland, Ireland, Norway, Sweden, United Kingdom; 1993 – Austria, Switzerland.

Source: OECD (1997*e*); R&D database, January 1998.

3.4. Driving forces behind changing R&D

141. Examinations of 18 OECD Member countries between 1965 and 1996 (Guellec and Ioannidis, forthcoming), show that the rate of economic growth is the single most important factor explaining variations in business sector R&D. The level of spending has been strongly pro-cyclical: BERD accelerates when GDP accelerates and slows down, or decreases, during economic downturns. This is related to the importance of liquidity constraints and the availability of cash for R&D, and most likely to a pro-cyclical element in firm expectations.[14] The prolonged recession of the early 1990s was a major factor behind the levelling off in R&D. In Germany and Japan, which were hit by exceptional macroeconomic shocks in the early 1990s, the business cycle exerted a particularly strong impact on R&D as well as on physical investment.

142. Real interest rates have been at historically high levels in most OECD countries since the early 1980s. As will be further discussed in Chapter 4, interest rates influence the costs of undertaking R&D, as well as other investments. For firms with a high degree of indebtedness, which was common throughout the OECD in the second half of the 1980s, debt repayment reduces available cash flow. Interest rates seem to have exerted a certain downward effect on R&D expenditures from the mid-1980s onward, although the effect is of limited magnitude and has diminished further in the 1990s – in line with the lower indebtedness of firms in recent years.

143. Government funding of industrial R&D plays a prominent role in the determination of business funding of R&D. According to Guellec and Ioannidis' estimates, a 1 per cent increase in government funding of business-performed R&D has no significant immediate effect on business funding (slight substitutability in the year it is received, exactly balanced out in the next year), but it generates a 0.2 to 0.3 per cent increase in business funding in the long term.[15] It appears that the leverage effect is a long-range one, suggesting that government funds are allocated mainly to long-term projects – consistent with their goal. The share of industrial R&D financed by government has declined steadily over the past three decades, especially in countries where it used to be the highest (*i.e.* France, the United Kingdom, the United States). Lately, it has dropped even more sharply (see the previous section). The change in government funding played a strong role for R&D especially in France, the United Kingdom and the United States, where it spurred an increase in R&D in the early 1980s, and subsequently contributed to the decline from the mid- or late 1980s.

144. There are other possible explanations of a more structural nature for the changes in R&D. These emanate from industrial restructuring, the globalisation of R&D, the intensification and changing patterns of competition and the advancement of information and communication technology:

- Total R&D expenditure can be expected to depend on industrial structure, notably the share of services and high-tech manufacturing. Although they represent some two-thirds to three-quarters of GDP in OECD countries, services account for at most one-fifth of total BERD. An increasing share of services in the economy directly reduces the aggregate R&D intensity. However, there has been a trend towards intensification of R&D in services, and the sources and processes of technical change in services (especially those that are unrelated to R&D) are poorly

14. On average, one percentage point of GDP growth leads to slightly less than 1 percentage point of R&D growth in the next year and 1.7 percentage points in the longer run.
15. In monetary terms, this means that, in an "average" OECD country, US$1 dollar of government subsidy generates US$1.2 of business-funded R&D in the long run (in addition to government funding).

captured in the statistics. Therefore, it is not clear to what extent the growing share of services may be associated with a slowdown in innovation efforts. At the same time, within manufacturing, the share of R&D-intensive sectors increased sharply in the early 1980s and decreased as abruptly thereafter. The aerospace industry and the computer and electronic industries accounted for most of this shift as both industries rely heavily on defence funding, which followed a similar pattern. Overall, the stagnation in R&D cannot be attributed to sectoral shifts, as reflected in the reductions that occurred within virtually all industries.

- On balance, the expansion by firms of R&D abroad does not occur at the expense of R&D and innovative capacity in the country of origin, although there are individual cases of substitutability (OECD, 1997*f*). To the extent that so-called "hollowing out" of research does occur, it affects individual countries but not the OECD as a whole since R&D activities are not transferred on any substantial scale to non-OECD countries.

- Deregulation (*e.g.* telecoms, power industry), along with globalisation and the advancement of ICT, may reduce the return to innovators. Assisted by patents, intellectual property rights (IPR) or simply impediments to codification and diffusion of information, innovators are able to advance along their learning curves and increase market shares while their competitors are delayed in imitation. By reducing the scope for such gains, sharpened competition may lead to less R&D. On the other hand, there is no universal linkage between competition and R&D or innovation in a broader sense.[16] Industries which have been deregulated do not, in fact, demonstrate any particularly large decline in R&D. Although there are cases in which former monopolies have reduced their expenditures, the reductions tend to be offset by spending by new competitors; witness the surge of innovation in the telecom industry in the last 15 years.

145. At the same time, the progress and diffusion of ICT has lowered the cost of circulation of information, making scientific and technological information more broadly accessible and information about suppliers and changing customer needs less costly. By substantially raising the return to absorption of already existing technology, the information society may favour imitation at the expense of innovation. On the other hand, ICT companies are among the greatest spenders on R&D and those experiencing the most rapid rate of increase. Furthermore, better access to information reduces the cost of innovation and enhances the productivity of research. Speedier imitation by competitors also provides innovators with incentives to intensify their innovative activities in search of new applications. Innovation and a stream of new products become an even more necessary condition for firms to maintain market shares and profit margins.

146. However, the improved circulation of knowledge, along with sharper competition, appears to have consequences for the orientation of research. The degree to which the returns from R&D can be appropriated is changing – creating particular problems for basic research which leaves more scope and time for competitors to imitate or build upon results. This puts greater pressure on firms to concentrate on innovative efforts whose results can be effectively appropriated. In addition, more competitive markets for finance and corporate ownership lead to more tightly controlled R&D budgets, as investors press for immediate returns. It is true that special financial devices such as venture capital, and

16. The issue of whether innovation is spurred by competition or market concentration is an old one, first raised by Joseph Schumpeter early in the 20th century. Much theoretical as well as empirical literature on the subject has not delivered a clear answer (Symeonidis, 1996). The linkages between market structure and innovation vary widely across industry and over time. Technological and institutional features specific to each industry and period determine variegated equilibrium relationships between innovation and market structure.

specialised markets such as NASDAQ (National Association of Securities Dealers Automated Quotation) have developed more effective risk financing for long-term, risky projects than have the traditional intermediaries in many banking systems. However, given the lack of adequate measurement of intangible assets, there are disincentives for investment in such assets within firms as well as *vis-à-vis* external resource contributors (Chapter 9), favouring applied or targeted research at the expense of more exploratory research. Even venture capital is increasingly allocated to relatively low-risk projects: the share of seed and start-ups in venture capital in the United States has dropped from 22.9 per cent in 1980 to 12.0 per cent in 1996 (Venture Economics Investor Services, 1997). With firms under increasing pressure to present credible prospects for visible gains, more information is required to persuade resource contributors that they are not investing in "dream projects".

147. Various firm-level observations underscore the significance of these changes (Office of Technology Assessment, 1995). There has been a flow of reporting by R&D managers to newspapers about the increased focusing of their company's research on applied matters, which provide "value for money", and the expanding search for valuation methods of R&D projects.[17] Overall, increased competition in product and capital markets appears to have only marginally affected the level of R&D, but rather to have impacted on its pattern, shifting research towards more applied and visible activities at the expense of "blue sky", exploratory research. Not all basic research has been downgraded, since in many and increasingly important fields basic research feeds directly into industrial applications (*e.g.* biotechnology, computer science), providing measurable returns. It is rather the "exploratory" type of basic research – the purpose and contribution of which is to increase the pool of knowledge required for applied follow-up in the longer run – which may have been hurt. According to a survey of American companies (*R&D Magazine*, 1997), the average length of research projects has been reduced from 21.6 months in 1991 to 16.7 months in 1996, which is consistent with a more applied focus (although it may also signal greater efficiency). Government funding was highlighted above as favouring long-term research in business; its reduction has reinforced market pressures on applied R&D. This is further underpinned by the reported perception of firms that the exploratory component of their research activity should be funded by government because of a too-low private rate of return (*R&D Magazine*, 1997).

148. The size and reorientation of R&D may also have been affected by a growing importance of other innovative efforts not captured by R&D statistics. For instance, except for Germany and Japan, there has been a decline in the average size of manufacturing firms in OECD countries since the 1970s, with the share of SMEs increasing markedly, particularly in employment but also in overall production, trade, etc. Compared to large firms, SMEs have less ability to cover fixed costs, and to separate R&D from their other expenditures and thus report it for inclusion in official statistics. The increased networking among firms, and between firms and public institutions as described in Chapter 2, further indicates that industry is developing other ways to draw upon basic research.

149. Overall, together with reductions in government funding and structural change, macroeconomic factors such as economic growth and, to a lesser extent, the level of real interest rates, have played an important role in explaining past variations in R&D efforts. Along with improved macroeconomic conditions and a recovery in economic growth, R&D expenditures have picked up

17. For instance, *The Economist* (1997), commenting on the Glaxo-Wellcome merger in pharmaceuticals: "After grumbles from (mainly Wellcome) scientists who disliked the new firm's insistence that all research needed clear commercial applications, a lot of dreamier types were persuaded to quit". *Financial Times* (1996*a*), Vanessa Houlder, reporting on a conference on R&D evaluation: "Once, R&D managers could take pride in the overall size of their research budget; now they are coming under pressure to assess the business value of individual projects."

since 1994 or 1995 in Japan, the United States and several other countries. Between 1995 to 1997 (predicted), business-funded R&D in the United States has surged by more than 15 per cent in real terms. In European countries growth rates of R&D, although still low, appear to be recovering. At least a partial reversal of the levelling-off is probable. However, a continued pressure on government funding and sharper competition, along with the increased codification and diffusion of technology, may continue to affect R&D. Not only may R&D be prevented from returning to its previous trend, but there may be a shift away from investment in long-term, exploratory research.

3.5. Economic consequences of changing R&D efforts

150. Innovative efforts, and R&D in particular, are undoubtedly the major factor behind technical change and long-term economic performance. This being said, the extent to which reduced R&D expenditure hurts technical change and economic growth is far from clear, especially in the short term. For instance, increased efficiency in R&D, or a greater applied focus, may well outweigh the short-term effects of reduced (basic) R&D. However, such an offsetting effect is less likely in the long term.

151. An examination of productivity growth across countries in recent years displays no effect of the levelling off. For various reasons detailed in Chapter 1, it is difficult to measure productivity growth and assess the possible effects of the R&D levelling off on productivity. Still, there is conclusive evidence at the firm level that R&D-performing firms experience both higher productivity levels and higher productivity growth than other firms (Crépon and Mairesse, 1994; OECD, 1997*g*). In addition, the entrance by new, often innovative firms and the termination of more weakly performing ones (partly driven by technical change), favours higher productivity growth (OECD, 1997*h*). On the other hand, empirical studies show that average productivity rises during economic downturns, as less productive firms go out of business and less productive labour is shed. The economic downturn in many OECD countries, and the subsequent rise in average productivity, may thus have masked possible negative effects of the levelling off in R&D in the first half of the 1990s.

152. The impacts of diminished technology breakthroughs would generally not be expected to show up immediately, whether in the form of lower productivity or other, related effects. There are lags between R&D and commercially relevant innovation, between innovation in the laboratory and production, and between production and broad commercial diffusion which can trigger higher aggregate productivity growth. The magnitude of these various lags varies greatly across industries, but is commonly estimated at between two and ten years (US Bureau of Labor Statistics, 1987). Since the levelling off started in the mid-1980s in the United States, possible effects on productivity could have manifested themselves as of the mid-1990s. Lack of evidence of an impact at this stage does not mean that there has been no impact at all. As has been argued above, it is long-term oriented research which has been reduced, not applied research which determines productivity in the short and medium run. A shift in R&D expenditures towards short-term, high-payoff projects may even have the effect of spurring higher productivity growth. However, any expansion thus triggered should be of a transitory nature. The question is to what extent it may have occurred at the expense of long-term growth potential.

Box 3.1. Estimating the effects of R&D on patents

The number of patents granted by the US Patent and Trademark Office (labelled LGR) is regressed on business-performed R&D expenditures, funded by business (LRP) and funded by government (LRG). Regressions are in logarithm, using the Seemingly Unrelated Regression (SURE) method for controlling for shocks affecting different countries simultaneously. Country and year dummies control for country- and time-specific effects. According to the US Patent and Trademark Office, the average length of time between application and grant of a patent was around 19 months in the 1990s, less than in previous decades. Two years have been assumed as the minimum lag between R&D and patents in the regression. The estimates are performed over the 1975-95 period for 18 OECD Member countries.

Results of the estimation are as follows:

	LGR(-1)	LGR(-2)	LGR(-3)	LRP(-2)	LRP(-3)	LRG(-2)	LRG(-3)
Coefficient	.495	.325	-.073	.260	-.171	.031	.043
Student	10.4	6.3	-1.7	7.8	-5.1	3.0	3.9

Log likelihood: 689.63; R-squared (adjusted): 0.9977; Durbin-Watson: 1.97.

Short-term coefficients are those referring to LRP(-2) and LRG(-2) respectively. For business-funded research the long-term coefficient is equal to: (.260-.171)/(1-.495-.325+.073) = .352; for government-funded research, it is: .292.

The "rate of return" of R&D in terms of patents granted is calculated by multiplying the above elasticities by the share of each source of funds in total BERD.

$$dGR/dRP = \varepsilon(RP) \cdot GR/RP$$

where $\varepsilon(RP)$ is the elasticity for business-funded research.

Then the rate of return of government funding relative to business funding is:

$$(dGR/dRG)/(dGR/dRP) = \varepsilon(RG)/\varepsilon(RP) \cdot (RP/RG)$$

From the above table, we have $\varepsilon(RG)/\varepsilon(RP)$ = 0.12 for the short run and 0.83 for the long run. If we take the last year in the regression (1993 for R&D variables), the "average" OECD government contributed to 18 per cent and business to 82 per cent, which gives $RP/RG = 4.5$. Using instead the average value for 1975-93 $RP/RG = 2$. Multiplying these two ratios by $\varepsilon(RG)/\varepsilon(RP)$ gives the range of relative returns: 0.2 to 0.5 for the short run and 1.5 to 3.5 for the long run.

153. One beneficial effect is that tighter monitoring of research activities by company managers, with more careful selection of projects and strengthened cost control, has led to increased efficiency in applied research. This view is supported by the increase in the share of US companies (presumably those most subject to strengthened market pressure) in patents granted in the 1990s as compared with other countries, whereas their share in R&D was decreasing.[18] Another possible factor of improvement in the efficiency of research is the growing number of R&D co-operation agreements between firms (Vonortas, 1997), which enhance the sharing of competences while avoiding duplication of projects.

18. The share of US firms in patents granted by the US Patent and Trademark Office (USPTO) rose from 53.3 per cent in 1988 to 57.4 per cent in 1995, as their share in business-performed R&D decreased from 50.7 per cent in 1986 to 46.7 per cent in 1993 (the average delay between research and patenting is assessed to be around two years). The share of US in European Patent Office granted patents was 22.4 per cent in 1988, 23.3 per cent in 1990, 25.3 per cent in 1996. It must be noted that the share of US companies in patent applications decreased, which tends to show that the improved share in grants is due not to an increase in the propensity to patent, but really to higher quality inventions.

Finally, research itself is affected by technical change, which increases productivity. Laboratories are major users of computers, which have, for instance, allowed a wide use of simulation techniques instead of the full-scale, and costly, experiments or prototypes necessary in the past (*e.g.* in the chemicals and aerospace industries). Overall, there is presumption of improved efficiency of research, but it does not offset, in terms of output, the reduction in resources devoted to this activity.

154. Compared to the short-term impact, there are greater risks of adverse implications for long-term growth, which is influenced primarily by science and basic research, and how the output is exploited in the economy. Translating basic science into visible economic gains takes time: 30 years is the length of time usually recognised by studies of basic science (Adams, 1991; Cockburn and Henderson, 1996). While it is difficult to assess the possible effects of current changes in basic research on economic performance, there are indications of risks in the medium to long term. On average, one dollar of government funding in OECD countries is associated with a short-term return, in terms of the number of patents granted, of about one-half of the return to private money, but the figure is between 1.5 and 3.5 for the long run (Box 3.1). In other words, reduced government funding poses more serious questions for technical progress in the long compared to the short term.

155. In summary, no alarming immediate consequences can be observed from the levelling off of R&D which took place in the late 1980s and early 1990s. Because the reduction appears to have been associated with a shift towards short-term, applied R&D and a push towards more stringent administration, there may have been offsetting positive impacts on productivity in the short and medium term. The risk of negative impacts is greater in the long term, especially if the expansion of the fundamental knowledge base continues to be checked. This could result in a gradual weakening of potential technological opportunities, eroding the basis for innovation as well as the potential gains from technology diffusion – and eventually hampering long-term economic growth and job creation.

CHAPTER 4. THE POLICY CHALLENGE

4.1. Introduction

156. The broader context for individual policy areas and issues are presented in this chapter. The rationale for policy intervention, and some of the pitfalls, are first examined under three headings: market failure, government failure and systemic failure. The task of technology policy and the approach to best policy practice adopted in this study are introduced in the next section. Consideration is then given to the broader set of structural and macroeconomic framework conditions within which firms operate and technology policy is set. The issue of feasibility in reform is addressed in the final section.

4.2. Policy rationale

157. The basic economic justification for S&T policies in the post-war period (in addition to the fulfilment of government and public needs such as defence, health, environment) has been the "market failure" argument. Markets may fail to operate efficiently for a variety of reasons, including asymmetric information, economies of scale, indivisibilities and external effects. Research is primarily affected by two types of market failures: imperfect appropriation of returns and uncertainty.

158. First, as the social rate of return from research is commonly higher than the private rate of return, the innovator is able to capture only part of the gains, with the rest accruing to consumers and/or competitors [see surveys of the literature by Nadiri (1993) and Mohnen (1996)]. Moreover, many innovations contribute to further innovations without the original innovator receiving any reward. While such "spillovers" increase the benefits from R&D, the downside is that less resources are devoted to innovation than would be socially desirable, especially in areas where appropriability is difficult (*e.g.* basic research). In surveys firms rank fear of imitation by competitors high among the factors hampering innovation (Licht *et al.*, 1997).

159. Second, uncertainty is inherent to innovation. It is generally difficult to predict the cost and duration of a project and the commercial success of its outcome. With failures common, either at the development stage (*e.g.* the technical avenue happened to be a dead end) or at the commercial stage (*e.g.* no demand, price too high), projects are funded only when the expected return is higher than that on alternative, less risky, uses of resources. While this reflects the priorities of risk-adverse investors with respect to individual projects, the interests of society as a whole tend to be different since there are gains to be made from pooling risk. Moreover, problems arise due to asymmetric information and imperfect contracts (*e.g.* moral hazard, adverse selection), especially since firms, in order to keep their edge, may be reluctant to provide outsiders with all the information necessary to assess the project. Large firms may have an advantage over small and new firms for two reasons. First, large firms have a relatively greater capacity to fund research out of retained earnings. Second, large established firms are likely to have built up a reputation among financiers.

160. The strength of the market failure argument lies in its clarity. It suggests a simple criterion for judging when government intervention is appropriate and ensures that the creativity of private initiative in finding market solutions is not underestimated. However, although its scope has been widened by theoretical and methodological advances (*e.g.* in contract and game theory), it still has limitations in capturing key elements of technical progress. This includes diffusion of technology, which, if insufficient, may hamper innovation in the first place and which is strongly influenced by actors not driven predominantly by market incentives (*e.g.* universities, mission-oriented public research organisations). The market-failure argument thus has its limits as a guide for policy making.[19]

161. Other concerns arise regarding government intervention. For instance, a patent system, if too strong (*i.e.* one which over-protects patentees) can reduce both the development of further incremental innovations and the rate of diffusion. Conversely, if too weak, it may damage the preconditions for innovation. Public programmes encouraging R&D co-operation between firms can lead to collusion in product markets. Government failure typically occurs if governments intervene where markets would have worked if left alone. Even where market failures exist, government intervention is not necessarily justified, because markets may still perform better on their own. Lags in information and delays in implementation limit the scope for successful government involvement in rapidly evolving fields. Administrative costs and "pork barrelling" may also outweigh the benefits of public intervention.

162. Furthermore, some observable market imperfections reflect constraints imposed by government on the development and operation of market mechanisms, rather than their inherent failure. It is generally better to eliminate such imperfections by easing the constraints (*e.g.* through deregulation or competition policy) rather than invoking government support policies. On the other hand, certain functions by definition belong to the public sphere because they cannot be reproduced by markets. Government failure also occurs when a government does not intervene, or does so insufficiently, in situations where intervention would have been necessary to realise social gains. This may apply to genuine public goods such as basic education or innovation-inducing regulatory frameworks (OECD, 1997*i*).

163. It should be stressed that governments face less clear-cut incentives for change than the private sector. Government departments do not compete on the market; dynamic and entrepreneurial public servants cannot launch new departments; and inferior service does not necessarily eliminate laggards. The experimentation, without much social cost, inherent in new firm creation, is not natural to public services. Moreover, government behaviour is systematically influenced by vested interests; increased discretion for policy makers may raise the return to exertion of political pressure, diverting resources to lobbying.

164. Theories that emphasize the "systemic" nature of technological change add another dimension to the rationale for technology and innovation policy. They seek to capture that overall technology performance depends not only on how specific actors (firms, research institutes, universities, etc.) perform, but on how they interact with each other as elements of an "innovation system". As shown in Chapter 2, interactions within as well as between OECD countries are becoming increasingly important for technological performance. If market and non-market institutions interact poorly, the potential for technological change may be slowed and/or its contribution to economic growth and welfare reduced. Mismatches between components of an innovation system are referred to as "systemic failure". Recent

19. See the proceedings of the Conference on "New Rationale and Approaches in Technology and Innovation Policy", forthcoming in August 1998 as a special edition of the *STI Review*. The conference, which took place in Vienna on 30-31 May 1997, was jointly organised by the Austrian Ministries for Science and Transport and for Economic Affairs and the OECD.

research on national innovation systems (OECD, 1997*j*), has pointed to the presence of such mismatches (*e.g.* in the interface between publicly funded research and the enterprise sector).

165. The inherent uncertainty of knowledge generation underlines the importance of the systemic perspective. A greater number of innovations will be associated with a greater number of failures. The more strongly the provision of financing is conditioned on the factors associated with success, the lower the anticipated failure rate. At the same time, while some success factors can be predicted, others cannot. The ability to make qualified distinctions in this respect is associated with venture capitalists. Policies will be effective in spawning the creation and growth of innovative firms only to the extent that there are entrepreneurs who are willing to take on risk, and financiers who are both willing to fund it and knowledgeable about those factors associated with success which are predictable. Hence, systems that discourage experimentation and do not allow failure limit the willingness of individuals to engage in innovative activity.

166. The specification of policy rationale needs to include aspects such as timing and duration of a measure. In fact, government interference is often costly simply because initially productive measures perpetuate their own existence. In the case of systemic failure, determining adequate policy timing takes on additional dimensions. Systemic failure commonly motivates a series of actions which may be of a more or less punctual nature (*e.g.* consolidating connected responsibilities scattered among ministries, undertaking regulatory reform or putting in place sound principles for mandatory evaluation), and where the exact sequencing makes a difference. In this context it should also be considered how technology interrelates with policy. For instance, regulatory reform may be essential for the scope and orientation of innovation while innovation can help to spur political support for adjusting or eliminating costly regulations (OECD, 1997*i*). In the health-care industry, due to the way in which private and public insurance systems have been organised (Weisbrod, 1991), innovation has induced the development of technologies which are cost inefficient.[20] Conversely, the recent emergence of new contractual forms [*e.g.* Health Maintenance Organizations (HMOs) in the United States] has put downward pressure on these costs. In electricity and communication services, the development of alternative technologies for transmitting voice and data communications has led to the entry of new firms in an industry dominated by public monopolies. By weakening the case for a "natural monopoly", innovation has in effect forced deregulation, enabling enhanced innovation and lower prices for consumers, and generating demand for new products and services.

167. Another important aspect is that policy rationale must guide government action in countries which are at different levels of technological and economic development, including catch-up economies. The market failure rationale points to the fact that at any stage of economic development there are invariant common core principles to which governments in market economies should adhere. The systemic failure rationale provides complementary guidance to address the implications of the evolutionary nature of technology and innovation policy, as some countries need not only to adapt to global conditions but also to progressively build the complete set of institutions characterising efficient national innovation systems. The risk of government failure is all the more important to consider in that context since, at some stages of development, the government has an active role to play in strengthening market mechanisms, making their weaknesses transitory and shaping supporting institutions, while at other stages it has not.

---

20. Customers and direct providers (*i.e.* physicians) lack incentives to keep costs down. Under these conditions, innovation has thus contributed, along with increased demand, to the sharp rise in health-care costs over the last decades.

may amplify or mitigate the negative impacts of market failures on innovation performance. For example, in Japan the relative weakness of university research combined with the high concentration of business research in a few scale-intensive manufacturing sectors and the underdevelopment of venture capital explain the present emphasis on actions to widen the technological base of long-term growth and competitiveness. In contrast, in the United States, a priority task for technology policy is to leverage the huge mission-oriented public R&D and to promote R&D co-operation among firms within the prevailing business culture and corporate governance system. In deciding on priority actions to correct for market failures, governments have also to take into account the impact on national capabilities to achieve broader social and political goals (*e.g.* national security). For example, minimising dependency on imported energy is a greater concern in some countries (*e.g.* France, Japan) than in others.

175. Governments address current challenges with administrative structures and policy instruments which have largely been shaped by responses to past problems. This "path-dependency" of technology policy increases the risk of government failure. National technology-policy institutions have developed comparative advantages and corresponding administrative culture, techno-structures and specialised tool kits which may be a disadvantage in accomplishing evolving priority tasks in a changing environment. With regard to the capacities and traditions of S&T policy institutions, important international differences are reflected in:

- the division of responsibilities between central and sub-central levels of government;
- the "institutional matrix" (prerogatives of ministries and missions of other public or semi-public bodies) through which solutions are applied to problems, which involves a more or less complex set of organisations and leaves, in the short term, only limited room for discretionary changes in policy;
- government/industry relationships, including permeability to lobbying by interest groups, and the scope for public/private partnerships in designing and implementing policies;
- government-vested interest in given "development trajectories", as reflected in particular in the stock of public "scientific and technological" investment (*e.g.* mission-oriented programmes and research organisations).

176. These structural features serve as both constraints on policy choices in the short term and possible targets for policy reform in the longer term. They define national "contexts" which must be taken into account in comparative policy analysis.

Best practice as a learning tool

177. In the area of innovation and technology diffusion, it is difficult to provide "off-the-shelf" policy prescriptions. Because factors specific to countries and points in time impinge on what can be achieved or should be attempted by policy makers, few policies represent best practice in an absolute sense (except in very broad terms or at the very detailed level of designing specific policy instruments). Furthermore, observation of varying performance levels and practices across countries, in combination with ongoing socio-economic changes, indicates that evaluation and adaptation of best practices is an evolutionary phenomenon.

178. At the same time, the diversity of conditions and experiences at the country level, together with the difficulties involved in providing "standard" solutions, provides a forum for assessing and

comparing relationships between practice and performance. There is a vast accumulated stock of observations, as well as ongoing experimentation, to draw on. Assessing why some countries are more successful than others in achieving a given goal can enable countries to learn from each others' experience, from similarities as well as differences, and apply the resulting insights to improving their policy responses to key challenges.

179. This learning process must, however, be fuelled by organised information collection and evaluation of actual outcomes of policies against objectives that are more or less common to Member countries. Hence, through a process of identifying best-practice policies in another country, extracting those components which are most relevant to its own situation and desired goals, and adopting the appropriate policies, a country can move from a position of lower efficiency to one of higher efficiency (Path 1 in Figure 4.1). Even once it has reached this new position, there is still potential for further improvement, as each country renews its search for best-practice examples in other countries. To the extent that exchange of experience also can help countries co-ordinate policy adjustments to generate greater mutual benefits, additional gains arise.

Figure 4.1. **The learning wheel**

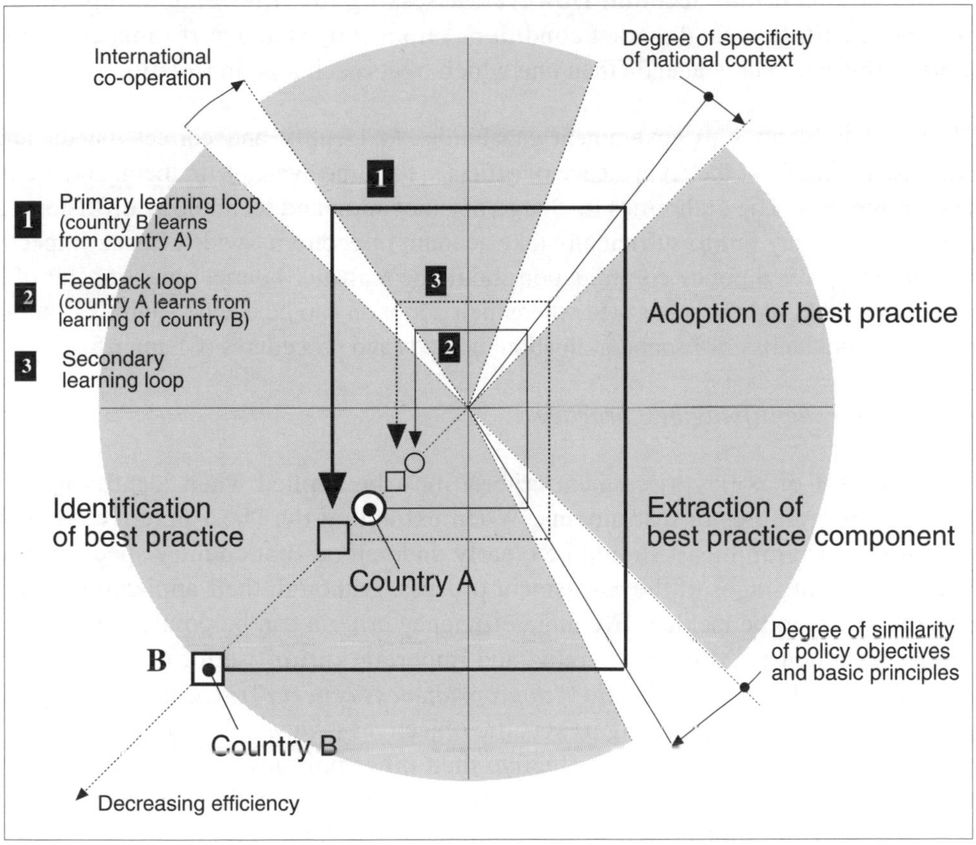

Source: OECD Secretariat.

180. The notion of best practice must be understood from this perspective, *i.e.* as a learning device rather than a normative concept, recognising that:

- There is not necessarily a unique best practice for a given policy objective. There may be several routes to success, each of which is specific to a type of NIS at a given point in time.

Hence, the distance from the epicentre in Figure 4.1 should only be interpreted as measuring "efficiency" in a strict sense, not the scope for harmonization of policy.

- Given differences in political feasibility and incentive structures for actors within national innovation systems, countries will not always be in a position to draw the same lessons from recognised best policy practice.

- It is crucial to distinguish between major and minor policy objectives, and thus major and minor lessons from shared experience. Government action should thus be limited to the most important and urgent issues, as well as those most likely to be better addressed by policy than by markets. Governments cannot and should not be expected to implement every policy that has proven useful elsewhere.

- There is a risk of "not seeing the forest for the trees" and attributing success to programmes, whereas an international comparison would have shown that performance is primarily explained by other factors. In accordance with the systemic failure argument, the indirect effect of framework conditions and the interaction between different policy measures must always be taken into account. However, assessing the interrelated impacts of different policies, institutions and market conditions on incentives and performance represents a far more ambitious policy agenda than one which treats each area in isolation.

- There are limitations to government capabilities to identify and correct market and systemic failures, arising from the competence of officials, the time available to them, and the influence of vested interests. The authorities in charge of innovation and technology diffusion policies in a narrow sense may fail to sufficiently take account of economy-wide effects. Expectations with regard to improved policy co-ordination should be realistic. International transfer of best policy practices should only be advocated where their adoption can be decided and their implementation monitored on the basis of sound evaluation methods and procedures (Chapter 5).

Efficiency criteria for identifying best practices

181. A common set of policy assessment criteria must be applied when identifying best-practice policy strategies, programmes or instruments. When extracting the "best-practice component" of a national measure or programme, it should be clearly understood that country specificity will play a different role at different stages of the assessment process. Although their applicability clearly varies depending on the issues to be tackled, five main efficiency criteria can be pointed out: *(i)* Is the policy (programme or instrument) addressing a sound and important (prioritisation) objective which can be related to a clearly identified market failure (*"appropriateness criteria"*)? *(ii)* Is the policy (programme or instrument) cost-effective in achieving its specific objectives (*"own efficiency criteria"*)? *(iii)* Is the policy (programme or instrument) more effective than other policies (programmes or instruments) which would achieve the same goals (*"superiority criteria"*)? *(iv)* How does the policy (programme or instrument) interact with other policies (programmes or instruments) and to what extent does its efficiency depend on conditions created by other government actions (*"systemic efficiency criteria"*)? *(v)* To what extent, and how, have results from evaluation fed back into policy design and implementation, and how does policy design ensure a degree of flexibility in responding to unpredictable changes (*"adaptive efficiency criteria"*)?

182. In practice, governments rarely apply all of these efficiency criteria. They represent an ideal of what governments should be aiming for in evaluation rather than a reflection of current practices. The search for best practice should always be inspired by them, but cannot be dependent on their full

applicability. Informed judgement as to "what works" and "what does not work" at the overall policy level and at the level of specific policy measures will have to fill the gap. On this basis, the next part of this report goes on to assess technology policies in individual areas. Before that, however, the ensuing sections provide the broader framework for technology policy, including political feasibility.

4.4. Structural and macroeconomic framework conditions for technology policy

183. Beyond the interplay between different parts of what may be labelled "technology policy", broader framework conditions determine the general climate in which technical progress is taking place. So-called structural conditions continue to vary markedly across countries despite substantial reforms in OECD countries in recent decades (see Box 4.1 for a review). In the following, some of the most important framework conditions from the viewpoint of technology are considered.

184. *Product market* competition influences the preconditions for technical progress in several ways. The traditional view that market concentration is associated with innovative activity is supported less and less by the evidence. First, competition creates incentives for firms to innovate. In rapidly evolving industries, non-innovators – technology laggards – face the threat of losing market shares and having to reduce prices. In fact, empirical evidence as well as theoretical findings suggest that firms which trace technological leaders innovate more (Lerner, 1997). In the absence of impeding regulation, the speed of innovation often turns initially monopolistic market structures into contestable ones. Second, competitive markets will underpin the most efficient selection of technologies and innovations. Third, by reducing prices, competition makes it less expensive to acquire technology embedded in intermediate products, in turn reducing the scope for market dominance. On the whole, there is a rather complementary relationship between competition and technological advance. At the same time, there are cases where the characteristics of innovation (network externalities, economies of scope in production and R&D) lead to monopolistic positions which have to be checked by appropriate competition policy.

185. The availability of funding for risky investment is crucial for innovation as well as for entrepreneurial activity in a broader sense. *Financial markets* are characterised by various inefficiencies and barriers to exchange among OECD countries, including in the area of corporate governance. This applies to: *(i)* the degree of competition in financial intermediation, which influences how savings are allocated; *(ii)* the exposure of business corporations to the open scrutiny of capital markets, which allows competing and alternative assessments of the risks and prospects of business corporations and thereby increases the quality of resource allocation, differs partly as a consequence of variations in the ownership and capital structures of corporations; *(iii)* conditions for the emergence of active investors, who play a leading role in the monitoring and funding of business corporations – as epitomised by venture capital operations. Meanwhile, there are numerous policy measures reducing risk to individual investors or improving the risk-reward ratio (*e.g.* venture capital funds, tax credits, tax treatment of capital gains).

186. *Labour market* conditions play an important role for technical advance itself as well as for its impacts on productivity and, in particular, employment. Not only do mobility and flexibility represent a prerequisite for industrial restructuring, but high costs of reducing the workforce in the case of failure make it more risky to invest in the first place. At the same time, the availability of skilled labour, and the incentives for upskilling, are key to the effective use of new technologies. A highly educated population will use, demand and more easily accept new technologies and products. Because investment in human capital tends to be associated with externalities and individuals face problems in borrowing against future income, governments assume responsibility for a well-functioning educational system. However, the skill requirements brought about by technological change go beyond the educational system, requiring a workforce able to continuously learn and adapt.

Box 4.1. **Review of structural reforms affecting the framework conditions for technology**

Product markets used to be highly regulated. Extensive regulatory reforms have been undertaken in the United Kingdom, the United States, and, more recently, in Australia and New Zealand. The last decade has also seen extensive regional reform, especially in the European Union, where many markets previously reserved for national monopolies are now opening up. Nevertheless, product markets often remain highly regulated at the national level, especially in services, thus restricting competition and the availability of information on products, suppliers and customers.

Financial markets have been partly liberalised through domestic deregulation as well as the elimination of restrictions to international capital movements. All countries have moved towards more competition in financial intermediation, and the role of institutional investors in venture capital has grown tremendously since the 1980s. Important country differences remain, however, *e.g.* in corporate governance and exit mechanisms for investors. The first wave of so-called second-tier markets in Europe and Japan performed poorly, notably compared to NASDAQ in the United States. A number of new approaches were attempted in the 1990s, including EASDAQ (European Association of Securities Dealers Automated Quotation), AIM (Alternative Investment Market) in the United Kingdom, METIM (*Mercato Telematico per le Medie Imprese*) in Italy, *Nouveau Marché* in France, *Neue Markt* in Germany, and JASDAQ (Japanese Association of Securities Dealers Automated Quotation), etc. The ownership and capital structures of corporations are governed primarily by domestic regulations and thus differ considerably across countries.

In ***labour markets***, the United States has long displayed greater scope for flexibility and market forces than many continental European countries, where labour markets have tended to be more highly regulated in terms of working times, hiring and dismissal obligations and high levels of non-wage labour costs. In the 1980s, the United Kingdom pushed through extensive deregulation, with Australia and New Zealand following more recently. The Netherlands has introduced measures to increase mobility and flexibility in the context of a consensual tripartite system setting wage and working conditions. Most European countries have been examining ways of liberalising their working time arrangements (*e.g.* annualised working time, different work-time arrangements), and allowing greater flexibility in non-standard working (part-time, short-term, etc.).

Against the background of increasing income disparities, or the development of long-term unemployment particularly for low-skilled workers, some countries have counteracted a deterioration in ***social cohesion*** through comprehensive sets of actions, including labour market reforms and training programmes. A number of countries are seeking to fend off widening income differences with minimum wages, social security programmes, etc.

In relation to ***government charges***, a long period of rising taxes on households/individuals and companies has in the last decade given way to a more mixed picture. Along with globalisation, taxes and charges have generally been reduced on mobile production factors, while overall government expenditures have stabilised or even declined. Countries stand out in different respects, with the Nordic countries, along with a few continental European countries such as France, displaying the highest tax pressures overall, while Germany and Japan have the highest corporate tax rates. Throughout, there have been general efforts towards less-distortive interventions, a streamlining of government bureaucracies and a reduction of transaction costs in general.

Business networks have developed on the initiative of firms which have felt a need for improved co-operation, for instance, in order to cope with high fixed costs in a climate of intensified competition. Governments have also fostered the building of such networks in a number of areas, including exchange of information on markets, prospective partnerships and exports, R&D, etc. Such efforts have been particularly noticeable in countries such as the United States, where the business climate favours individual effort.

In ***S&T structures***, there has been relatively little change due to the presence of strong institutional rigidities. An important exception has been New Zealand, which has pursued radical reforms involving "privatisation" of a large part of government research and generalising the principles of contracting out government support. Nevertheless, the process of allocating resources on a contractual basis has in most countries introduced an element of increased flexibility.

187. Capturing the gains of innovation requires organisational skills and investment in intangible assets, including upskilling of the labour force. Well-functioning educational systems, incentives for upskilling and opportunities for organisational adjustment facilitate increased productivity and job creation. The policy response to the premium attached to knowledge and human capital, and to the reduced employment opportunities for less-skilled workers, has fundamentally two dimensions. It needs to combine attempts to reduce skills mismatch through training and investment in human capital with regulatory reform in product and labour markets to ensure that the wealth created through new products and processes can be translated into higher demand for services that are intensive in low-skilled employment.

188. Furthermore, technical advance typically benefits indirectly from social cohesion. By spurring favourable conditions for trust, social cohesion can ease technical change by reducing the perceived costs associated with the risk of failure, fostering knowledge circulation and generation within as well as between firms. On the other hand, social cohesion is often defended in ways which stifle flexibility and weaken incentives for upskilling, organisational change and entrepreneurial activity. Since exploiting the gains of technology involves the displacement of jobs and changing patterns in demand for skills, shifting the relative positions of various categories of workers – to the advantage of some and at the expense of others, technical change requires a combination of conditions which allow for long-term investment and a preparedness for change.

189. *Government charges*, taxes and related compliance costs matter for all firms, but may particularly impede firm start-up and the growth of small firms based on innovation. Some of these costs limit innovative activity directly, by protecting existing technologies at the expense of new and potentially superior ones. Others stifle innovative activity indirectly. Registration costs, rules dampening the mobility of individuals between public research facilities and industry, and competition laws can prevent the partnering of firms and the start-up of NTBFs. The fundamental preconditions for *business networks* are notably shaped by a culture of co-operation, the venues for partnering between firms and the availability of information on prospective partners. Inter-country differences in these respects influence the ability of firms to share the costs of innovation as well as the channels for diffusion of technology. *S&T structures* form important framework conditions in regard to basic research, technical and industrial research and the science-industry interface. Conditions in this respect are determined notably by the balance between university, government and industry in the performance of the R&D effort and by the flexibility of related research structures.

190. Innovation and technology diffusion interact with broader framework conditions in ways which vary across OECD countries. Table 4.1 outlines some key, stylised features of these framework conditions, broadly characterised as strengths (bold), weaknesses (normal text) or neutral areas (italics) as of the 1990s for the United States, Continental Europe, East Asia and the transition economies in eastern Europe, respectively. In broad terms, the main patterns can be described as follows.

191. In the United States, well-functioning product and factor markets, as well as attitudes and demand in regard to new products, form largely favourable framework conditions for innovation and technology diffusion (notwithstanding problems with broad-based upskilling and widening income differences). A strong science base, coupled with the size of its economy, enables the United States to benefit from an intense clustering and attraction of knowledge-intensive activities. Australia, New Zealand and the United Kingdom have undertaken reforms to make their framework conditions (in particular product and labour markets) more similar to those of the United States, although their S&T systems are of course very different.

in Canada and the United States, both countries with mature expansions, and similar tendencies in a number of other economies, have given rise to concerns about possible deflation.

Effects of technological change on macroeconomic variables

197. Technical progress has a potential to reduce upward pressures on prices. Reasons include:

- Improved and smoother adaptation of supply to changes in demand through ICT, reducing the size of inventories and making low levels of inventory less inflationary.
- Increased competition from globalisation and increased market access, partly induced by technology. For example, in electricity and communication services, technological advances have lowered barriers to entry and spurred deregulation by weakening the case for a natural monopoly. The development of alternative technologies for transmitting voice and data communications has also led to the entry of new firms in an industry dominated by public monopolies. Globalised production and supply have softened national capacity constraints and enhanced productivity improvements by domestic producers.
- Organisational change and the adoption of incentive structures – often made possible by ICT – that tighten the link between productivity and wages and diminish the scope for inflation caused by wage rises that are not matched by productivity increases (for a further discussion of organisational change, see Chapter 11). Technology can thus make low levels of unemployment less conducive to inflationary pressure, lowering the level of structural unemployment at which inflation emerges (NAIRU).

198. An important distinction is whether or not these technological developments have led to a rise in the level of capacity or to a rise in its rate of growth. If technological change is a continuing force, it has the potential to change the assessment of the possibilities for growth in a significant way. If there has only been a one-off rise in the level of potential output or if the current situation is linked to temporary factors, no fundamental change in potential growth patterns will ensue. The distinction is hard to make at this point and both interpretations are consistent with recent developments in the United States, where a prolonged boom with high capacity utilisation and falling unemployment has not yet, as of early 1998, produced much sign of increased inflationary pressure.

199. The size and stability of tax bases are also influenced by technology. The advancement of ICT, and the globalisation of goods and factor markets make resources more internationally mobile and tax bases more volatile. The plausible consequence is a shift, at least in part, of the tax burden away from relatively mobile activities to those which are less mobile, including housing, labour and consumption. A related point is that increased mobility of capital through electronic networks may increase tax avoidance and evasion. In the absence of downward adjustment in public expenditures or international co-ordination in tax policy, this would result in a weakening of public finances, with possible repercussions on innovative behaviour and economic performance in general. On the other hand, ICTs provide openings for savings in government expenditures, for instance because their use can lead to efficiency improvements in the administration and delivery of public services. As well, indirect savings can result from reduction in fraud.

200. Irrespective of its actual impact on prices, technical progress is currently complicating the measurement of prices due to the pace at which new products and product qualities evolve. Increased choice and improved product quality are often incompletely captured in official price statistics and resulting measures can overstate price changes and understate real industry output or the purchasing

power of consumers. Mismeasurement has also come into focus because inflation rates are low and even small measurement errors may be important.

201. In principle, monetary policies that use inflation targets could be misled by an upward bias in inflation. Overestimation of inflation, if not taken into account, could lead to disinflation objectives that are unnecessarily low. However, not all countries apply inflation targets and some of those that do take account of a potential bias in their policy formulation. Yet, if biases vary over time, as well as across countries, this might complicate the formulation of inflation targets, with adverse consequences for the conduct of monetary policies.

202. Government expenditures may be affected by an upward bias in inflation when beneficiaries are over-compensated due to indexation of transfer payments. Obviously, such effects vary directly with the degree of indexation across OECD countries. On the revenue side, if tax brackets are adjusted to reflect inflation, an upward bias in the price index would lead to lower tax revenues than an unbiased inflation measure. OECD Secretariat estimates show that among OECD countries the effects on government budget balances of an overestimation of the consumer price index would be largest in Italy and the United States.

203. In addition to formal indexing of government expenditure, private contracts can be indexed (such as housing rents or insurance contracts), implying allocative inefficiencies if inflation measures are biased. Informal indexing also takes place, for example, in wage negotiations where reported price measures enter as one of the yardsticks. In particular, statutory or implicit indexation has played an important role in wage formation in France, Greece, Italy, Spain and Switzerland.[21] If the true rate of inflation is lower than the measured one (and this is not discounted by economic agents), relative wage adjustments may not take place to the full extent needed, with potential implications for real activity. Even if a bias was recognised by economic agents, full wage adjustments may not take place in a situation of low levels of inflation combined with nominal wage floors.[22]

204. Biased signals for technology policies can also emerge if measured rates of productivity growth remain low despite sizeable investment in ICTs (the "Productivity Paradox", Chapter 1) and R&D efforts. A case in point are service industries – many of which have invested heavily in ICT without a discernible pick-up in productivity growth rates. A significant upward bias in national accounts deflators, if increasing over time, could shed light on the productivity paradox and partly explain the productivity slowdown reported for many OECD countries since the early 1970s.

Vicious and virtuous circles

205. Due to the interdependence of macroeconomic conditions and policies, on the one hand, and technical change, on the other, mutually strengthening developments in the two areas may set the stage for vicious or virtuous circles. Breaking out of vicious circles may require more or less comprehensive policy measures. For instance, low growth and decreased tax revenues put pressure on government budgets. Recurring fiscal deficits place upward pressure on interest rates, increasing the cost of capital

---

21. If wage indexation were to affect real wages, however, there could be effects on negotiated wages, which could limit the impact of this bias.
22. The assessment is further complicated by the fact that another determinant of nominal wage growth, the growth rate of productivity, will be understated if inflation is overstated. Net effects on nominal wage growth would then depend on the respective size of the bias in inflation and productivity growth (the two need not be equal at the sectoral level) and the elasticities with which they bear on wages.

to firms and reducing innovative efforts, while mitigated technical change hampers long-term productivity and output growth.[23] In Western Europe over the last decade, macroeconomic uncertainty and high real interest rates have combined with slow restructuring and a weak innovative effort.

206. The transition economies have been able to implement important systemic reforms, renew with sustained growth and secure greater macroeconomic stability but their science and skill base has been eroding as a result of budget constraints and emigration. Inflows of FDI have had limited impacts in the face of slow progress in changing the management structures of newly privatised firms, as in the Czech Republic and Hungary, hindering technology diffusion among domestic firms. Furthermore, against a background of instability, structural reforms and technology policies have had unintended effects, as in Poland where high interest rates meant that efforts to promote access by SMEs to capital via government funds undercut the activities of newly privatised banks.

207. Conversely, opportunities exist for virtuous circles. For instance, price stability facilitates innovative activity, while innovation reduces inflationary pressure and, coupled with organisational change, may favour a stronger connection between productivity and wages, further reducing inflationary pressures from low levels of unemployment. The United States may have entered a virtuous circle of this sort in the 1990s. Furthermore, the process of European integration coupled with structural reforms may help to strengthen long-term economic performance by increasing mobility and inward FDI, and improving international technology co-operation. A few countries which were particularly hard-hit by harsh changes in economic conditions and performance, notably Finland and Japan, have within a short period bolstered their S&T policy as part of a broader package aiming to restore long-term growth. Ireland provides an example of a country which has been able to boost economic growth and jobs through a combination of macroeconomic stability, labour market and regulatory reforms, exploitation of support from the European Commission and investment incentives spurring inward FDI and technology. This has fostered the development of endogenous innovation capacities.

208. Summing up, the contribution of technology to the economy is strongly influenced by a range of conditions which stretch beyond technology policy. To be effective, technology policy needs to work in tandem with broader framework conditions, including macroeconomic and structural policies. There is a need for better policy co-ordination across the board. Strengthening the integration of policy efforts can help to create positive synergies between reforms in different areas. This may enhance the contribution of technology policy to economic growth and, conversely, enhance the scope for manoeuvre in macroeconomic policy.

4.5. Making reform politically feasible

209. Policy makers not only need to recognise what comprises "best policy practices", they must also be able to implement them. Problems of political feasibility arise for two basic reasons:

- The first is institutional inertia. It is a well-known fact that societies and institutions defending existing territories in a context of shrinking resources, tend to vigorously resist change. Institutional inertia is inherent to all economies and societies, although it can take different forms. In the United States, for instance, the laissez-faire ideology combined with corporatist

23. A possible counterfactor, observed in Chapter 3, is that R&D may become more applied and produce relatively more short-term gains. There is still a risk of a weakened long-term record, with both R&D and economic growth stuck along an inferior growth trajectory.

attitudes can prevent reform, *e.g.* in health and education, which would be conducive to more widely spread innovation. The Nordic countries and Germany find it difficult to envisage reforms that would put excessive, even transitory, strain on a consensus-based approach to policy formulation and implementation. Japan is characterised by both a tendency to avoid issues which escape a consensual policy agenda and strong rivalry between ministries in interpreting and implementing this agenda. France has a powerful centralist administration characterised by highly rigid structures combined with a high social legitimacy, reflecting features of the French education system.

- A second obstacle relates to the distribution of the gains from policy reform, and whether a sufficient number of stakeholders can expect to benefit. The winners and losers from technical change are not the same. The losers are typically low-skill workers facing shrinking job opportunities, and non-innovating firms unable to keep up with global competition, although the quest for change in skills and restructuring of work organisation increasingly applies to workers and managers in a wide variety of industries, occupations and positions. Moreover, losses are likely to be felt more quickly than gains.

210. A key question is whether the signals sent by policy to individuals and firms are consistent. One aspect of this is whether policy can be expected to be durable. Policy does not have to be continuous or irreversible, but it is crucial that expectations about how it will change over time make economic sense, thus facilitating planning and investment decisions.

211. For policy to be consistent and credible, broad support within government for long-term objectives is required as well as mechanisms to underpin long-term commitment to these objectives. In many cases this will require co-ordination of decision making across different policy areas and traditional delineations of administrative competences. Synchronised policy packages may be necessary to ensure a sufficient number of winners within a socially acceptable time frame. For instance, to be both socially acceptable and politically feasible, increased labour market mobility and incentives for upskilling may need to be coupled with improved training for low-skilled workers. Policies enhancing the diffusion of technical and organisational change, especially among SMEs, can strengthen incentives for investment in employee skills and foster job creation. Several responses to these issues, which can be highlighted as best practice in coping with institutional rigidities, are described below, and avenues for possible improvements pointed out.

212. In a number of countries (*e.g.* Finland, the Netherlands, Norway), the setting of a "common goal" among ministries for developing the information society demonstrates the potential for progress once the challenges have been clearly identified. To be efficient, however, co-ordination schemes may require rationalisation of responsibilities and liabilities within governments. This is difficult without sanctioning at the highest level of authority. Such leadership may take different forms, including the establishment of a Science and Technology Policy Council at the prime minister level, with wide responsibility including in budget matters (such as in Finland or Japan), ad hoc initiatives co-ordinating macroeconomic and microeconomic policies for the purpose of fostering innovation launched by the prime minister (as in Australia's "investing for growth" initiative) and active leadership at the presidential level (as in the United States with the strong involvement of the vice presidency in technology policy). Mechanisms of this kind make it possible not only to establish solid, coherent and credible technology policies, but can also help to break down the walls compartmentalising government administrations.

213. The *Green Paper on Innovation* published by the European Commission in 1995, and the subsequent Innovation Action Plan, represent a systematic attempt to co-ordinate various fields of policy, in this case in the EU as a whole, towards the common goal of strengthening the overall

innovation capacity of firms and public institutions (Caracostas, 1998). However, implementing the good policy principles underlying the Innovation Action Plan and the Fifth Framework Programme for Research and Technological Development (RTD) clearly represents a long-lasting effort. In particular, it will be necessary to overcome the difficulties involved in co-ordinating actions pursued both at national level and jointly by the 15 Member States, *i.e.* resulting from the heterogeneity of national innovation systems in Europe and of the corresponding policy institutions.

214. Awareness and transparency are key factors in policy co-ordination. Ministries in different areas have to become conscious of the potential of technology, and the stifling effect of rules and regulations which cause technological lock-in. It is also important that the policy-making process include checks against government failure to provide some guard against the inherent risk of authorities or institutions furthering their own interests and activities by, for instance, going beyond sound rationale for policy, neglecting the administrative and bureaucratic costs of policy interference and adopting a partial rather than an economy-wide perspective. A set of evaluation mechanisms should be in place to continuously monitor policy relevance and efficiency and encourage "policy learning". Various evaluation tools are available, but they should be used to maintain pressure on institutions over the long term rather than on a one-off basis. In addition to evaluation exercises concerned with either the optimisation of resource allocations or with institutional examinations – the topic of Chapter 5, "audits" can help to identify administrative obstacles to change and innovation. So far, audits have been used in conjunction with regulatory reform, but have not been perceived or managed as durable processes. "Continuous audits" can be implemented systematically, particularly in the areas of procurement policies, tax structures, university regulations, trade and transport, etc. To complement such initiatives, overall policy reviews, such as those carried out by the OECD, have proved useful in stimulating policy debates at the national level, although they do require appropriate follow-up. As stressed at the OECD Industry Ministerial of February 1998, international benchmarking of how policy organisation and formulation relate to economic behaviour and performance can throw light on major discrepancies and induce a process of self-examination in governments.

215. Technology policy benefits not only from inter-ministerial co-ordination within central governments; the involvement of other key stakeholders may be pivotal. Input from the private sector can increase the likelihood that policies are tuned to the functioning of markets, and may be crucial for long-term credibility. Similarly, the support of the social partners, such as unions, may be necessary, for instance, to restrain wage inflation, increase business investment in training, reduce friction costs in organisational change and increase the potential for job creation.

216. The introduction of market-oriented instruments and economic accountability – where possible – is one of the most efficient ways to stimulate change in attitudes and behaviour. A significant part of university and public laboratory financing should come from contractual and precarious resources in order for research to remain attentive to "market needs" (Chapter 6). This principle, which has become common wisdom in countries adhering strongly to market principles, may also inspire a number of other countries which can benefit from (re)dynamising their research systems (including Germany and the Netherlands). The use of matching funds is another successful practice that has been generalised in OECD countries, giving rise to various forms of "public/private partnerships" linking industry, university and government (Chapter 7).

217. Support for technology policy can be bolstered by subjecting its targets to public debate involving the various stakeholders. This is most obviously valuable in the case of "government missions", which are currently undergoing significant changes in some countries (Chapter 3) – *e.g.* a re-orientation of public R&D away from defence and nuclear energy towards health, the environment

and industrial competitiveness. This discussion process can be implemented in several ways. A number of countries have recently engaged in extensive "technology foresight" exercises (*e.g.* Australia, Austria, France, Germany, Japan, the Netherlands, the United Kingdom, the United States). While the first generation of these exercises mainly comprised studies "for" and "by" technology experts, more recent approaches (the Austrian and Dutch exercises) have emphasized the involvement of a greater number of actors and aimed to establish societal consensus for technology policy.

218. Governments further have a responsibility to ensure that decompartmentalisation and mobilisation of energies take place regionally and locally – the basic level at which innovative initiatives flourish – *e.g.* through the design of administrative and fiscal frameworks. Along with the goal of transparency of policies and resulting impacts, it is important that governments design incentives which spur competition among local authorities in initiatives for change rather than in mere attraction of financial support. In this way, local authorities as well as other constituencies can better sense what it takes to attract mobile businesses and resources as well as create conditions in which new enterprises and jobs can develop. Although progress has been made in OECD countries, further effort is warranted to ensure appropriate co-ordination among various government actors in providing adequate autonomy and incentives for change among local authorities.

219. Policy co-ordination is desirable also at the international level in order to harness the benefits from globalisation of trade, investment and technology. Again, this can be exemplified by the process of European integration, including monetary union, which has a potential for reducing uncertainty for trans-European trade, increasing competition and reducing costs, and improving conditions for inward FDI – a major channel for diffusion of technology. However, additional structural reforms necessary for industrial restructuring, are hampered by insider-outsider problems as well as concerns over social cohesion. Measures relating to technology have an important role in enabling workers (especially low-skilled workers) to adjust, and firms (especially non-innovative SMEs) to absorb and exploit technology in order to raise productivity and compete in larger markets. Whereas there is relatively high mobility among researchers, both geographic and sectoral, in the United States, national and cultural barriers in Europe (the Nordic area represents a partial exception) continue to hamper mobility and, hence, flows of technology and know-how. Harmonization of policies in areas such as diplomas and IPRs, joint initiatives in regard to science-industry interplay across European borders, co-operation in science policy with third countries, etc., would improve mobility. Thus, the inclusion of technology policy, and realisation of its benefits, in comprehensive policy packages can help to pave the way for reforms in other areas which would otherwise not be politically feasible. Failure to realise the potential positive impacts of technology weakens public support for necessary structural reform as well as for monetary union and economic integration in a broader sense.

220. Finally, timing matters for political feasibility. Policies may need to be packaged so as to ease transition problems, and developed in consultation with major stakeholders. One strategy is to begin with those measures which appear to be the most universally supported and whose effects are likely to be the most evident, through a process of consultation involving the key social partners. Once such measures have been in existence for some time and their effects have been carefully evaluated, necessary corrections can be implemented. Moreover, if the first set of reforms is successful, the ground is better prepared for a further, more deep-seated series of actions. S&T policies implemented in some of the Nordic countries (Finland, Iceland), as well as Japan and the Netherlands, were inspired by these principles and have resulted in a number of in-depth re-orientations. Experience shows that significant changes to systems occur gradually over a period of one or two decades even when "big bang" policies are introduced (*e.g.* New Zealand). At the same time, the ability to make progress in reform also hinges on the political initiative and stamina to push through difficult decisions and the ability to handle the

associated transition costs and demonstrate convincing outcomes. In some countries, a crisis situation has been an important factor in mustering support for reform (*e.g.* Finland, Japan). Public awareness of the need for change has increased and the dire prospects for broad groups of society in the absence of reform have fuelled public acceptance. Especially for countries faced with the risk of severely damaging their knowledge base in the process of institutional upheaval, it is important that policy makers exploit opportunities for reform. The transition economies in eastern Europe face urgent problems in this respect (Chapter 6).

Part II

Best Policy Practices

CHAPTER 5. POLICY EVALUATION[24]

5.1. Introduction

221. Evaluation is central to formulating policy best practice. Governments need to know whether their support of innovation and technology is using the right policy tools, is well administered, is achieving the desired results, and at what cost. Evaluation is carried out to ensure that the underlying rationale for policy is valid, to avoid incoherence and contradictions, to ensure transparency and "value-for-money", to improve and refine existing policies and eliminate non-performing ones, with the aim of arriving at best practice in policy design. Political issues usually loom large, often providing the impetus behind evaluation but also sometimes constraining the implementation of results.

222. OECD countries demonstrate a growing interest in the evaluation of government programmes and policies, partly because of budget stringency and the need to better allocate increasingly scarce public resources. More fundamentally, however, the focus on evaluation is emblematic of a broader reassessment of the role of government and of market mechanisms across a number of policy areas. Accountability, transparency and the desire to minimise distortions arising from government policies while maximising their leverage are driving the trend towards evaluation. At the same time, new developments in technology policy with an increased emphasis on diffusion and adoption, organisational change and innovative behaviour have raised new methodological challenges for evaluation.

223. Against this background of a higher profile for evaluation and changes in its implementation, policy makers have to grapple with a number of questions. What methods and criteria should be used in evaluation? What are the best institutional mechanisms? Should evaluation focus on individual policies, or address strategic issues and look at systemic links in the innovation system? How should evaluation feed back into policy design? In an attempt to address some of these questions, evaluation practices in place in OECD countries are compared and reviewed in this chapter. The aim is to gather information on the methods, procedures and institutional settings most likely to yield acceptable evaluations of past or existing policies and to guide future policy making.

224. The chapter is structured as follows. Following this introduction, the next section discusses the scope, coverage and evolution of evaluation in innovation and technology. Without attempting a full-scale review, the third section examines the characteristics of evaluation practices in OECD

---

24. The preparation of this chapter has benefited greatly from the information on evaluation practices received from Member countries, followed a request by the Secretariat. Substantial input was also provided by the numerous papers and discussions in the Conference on Policy Evaluation in Innovation and Technology that took place at the OECD Headquarters on 26-27 June 1997. The proceedings of that conference have been published as OECD (1997), *Policy Evaluation in Innovation and Technology: Towards Best Practices*.

characteristics taken or not into account, etc.). Another is the attitude towards the appropriate role of the state in the economy (whether evaluation is seen as a tool to improve and refine government interventions or to constrain government action).

231. The methodologies used in evaluations diffuse easily among countries and professional communities. Practices, however, are institution-, country- and area-specific – some researchers even refer to "national systems of evaluation". Some countries have only recently begun to develop an "evaluation culture", others have a long-standing tradition of both project and programme evaluations (for a description of different evaluation practices in a number of OECD countries, see European Commission, 1994). While each country's evaluation practices are distinctive, there are enough similarities across countries to enable them to be classified into three groups. These groups are fairly homogeneous in terms of the role that evaluation plays in the policy-making process, the criteria used and methodologies employed. Nevertheless, the similarities should not be overplayed; significant institutional differences exist within each group as well as some differing evaluation practices. These are highlighted in Table 5.1, in which some best practices and weaknesses in evaluation are summarised.

The first group: an emphasis on resource allocation issues

232. Australia, Canada, the United Kingdom and the United States share many evaluation practices. Their focus on evaluation can be traced to tight government budgets, but more importantly to explicit attempts to rationalise government action. The desire to evaluate and apply performance indicators is symptomatic of the move towards "new public management" with an emphasis upon accountability. This is evident in the United States where the Government Performance and Results Act (passed by Congress in 1993), requires all agencies to set quantitative performance targets and report on progress. It is also clearly articulated in the United Kingdom through the use of the ROAME-F (Rationale, Objectives, Appraisal, Monitoring, Evaluation, Feedback) statement developed by the Department of Trade and Industry which gives guidelines for evaluation and is used throughout government (Bradbury and Davies, 1998). In Australia and Canada, this trend can be seen in a number of recent broad reviews of government initiatives, as in the R&D Report (Industry Commission, 1995) and the "Mortimer Report" (Review of Business Programs, 1997) in Australia, or in "framework documents" such as Industry Canada (1995).

233. In the above countries, evaluation is very much a part of the policy landscape, with a comprehensive range of activities within government departments and agencies. Formal requirements for regular evaluation of programmes typically exist. Evaluations are commissioned and conducted either through independent public organisations (*e.g.* the General Accounting Office and the Office of Management and Budget in the United States, the Industry Commission in Australia), or directly from ministries (*e.g.* the Department of Trade and Industry in the United Kingdom, Industry Canada in Canada), or both. In addition to research evaluation in institutes and universities, there are regular evaluations of programmes providing financial support for R&D, technology extension services, public/private partnerships, etc.

Table 5.1. **Best practices and weaknesses in evaluation**

	Economic rationale and objectives, additionality	Evaluation of actors and institutions	Evaluation of innovation and technology programmes	Use of quantitative methods in evaluation	Use of qualitative methods	Institutionalised rules and procedures for evaluation	Regularity of evaluations	"Systemic" approach to evaluation	Policy feedback and learning
Australia	●	●	●	●		●	●	●	○
Austria	○	○	●	○	●	○	○	○	○
Belgium	○			○	●		○	○	
Canada	●	●	●	●	●	●	●	●	
Czech Republic	○	●	○			○	○	○	○
Denmark		●	●			●	●		○
Finland	○	●	●	○	●		●	●	●
France	○	●	○		●	●	○	○	○
Germany		●	●	○	●		●	○	
Greece	○		○	○	●	○		○	○
Hungary	○	●	○			○	○	○	○
Ireland			●	○				○	
Italy	○				●	○	○	○	○
Japan	○		○			○	○	○	○
Netherlands	●	●	●	●				○	●
New Zealand	●		○	●			○	●	○
Norway	●			●					○
Portugal	○			○	●	○	○	○	○
Spain	○		○		●			○	○
Sweden	○	●	●	○	●		●		
Switzerland	●				●	●			●
United Kingdom	●		●	●	●	●	●	○	●
United States	●	●	●	●	●	●	●	○	○
European Union		●	●	●	●	●	●		●

Key: ● represents strengths (best practices); ○ represents weaknesses; no symbol signifies insufficient information or absence of major strength/weakness.

Source: OECD Secretariat.

234. Evaluation tools cover the full spectrum from quantitative to qualitative and vary from peer reviews to sophisticated econometric techniques. The United States has pioneered the use of micro-level data sets for evaluating the impact of manufacturing extension programmes on the performance of client firms, while in Australia rigorous and sophisticated cost-benefit techniques have been used to evaluate fiscal incentives for R&D. In general, there is a strong emphasis on evaluation as a guide for resource allocation, with socio-economic objectives and criteria very much in evidence in the evaluation process. There is a clear move away from an exclusive preoccupation with administrative issues in spending government funds towards attempts to measure the economic impacts of programmes in a broader sense.

235. Together with the development of more formal quantitative techniques, evaluation in these countries is concerned with improving the operational aspect of programmes, often at a sub-central level of government. A number of case studies provide valuable information for the improvement of ongoing or future policy initiatives (in the case of Canada, see McDonald and Teather, 1997). However, less effort has been devoted to assessing the relative efficiency and effectiveness of different policy tools in achieving a given policy objective. There are also few cross-portfolio evaluations (*i.e.* evaluation of the impact of a number of policy initiatives taken together), which take into account how different programmes can interact and reinforce (or inhibit) each other in sophisticated and mature national innovation systems. Stated differently, in many instances evaluations have focused almost exclusively on measuring the economic returns of particular government initiatives without exploring the broader and more difficult issues of the ways in which these initiatives can promote learning and affect the behaviour of firms and institutions.

The second group: a focus on institutions and structures

236. A second group of OECD countries have equally developed evaluation practices, but a distinctively different overall approach to evaluation. Denmark, Finland, France, Germany, the Netherlands, Norway, Sweden and Switzerland all have either legal frameworks that require research evaluation and the evaluation of technology programmes or a receptive policy attitude towards evaluation. Strictly economic objectives and criteria in evaluation are, however, less explicit. There is more concern with formative-type evaluations, and less with evaluation as a means to improve the allocation of public funds among competing uses. Accordingly, there is greater emphasis on methodologies that stress the qualitative aspects of programmes and focus less on providing quantitative estimates of rates of return of specific government initiatives or on the economic impacts of particular measures on firm performance.

237. In France, the scope of the institutional structure and evolution of the evaluation system has gradually widened from an initial focus on scientific institutions to include programmes and institutions of technology and innovation policy.[26] However, the long evaluation cycles of the institutions responsible for evaluations have limited the possibilities for periodical re-evaluation of all institutions and programmes; concerns have also been raised as to the influence of evaluations on policy making or the rearrangement of the institutional framework (Larédo, 1997). More recently attempts have been

26. Note submitted to the OECD Secretariat, March 1997: *Ministère de l'économie et des finances, "L'évaluation des politiques et programmes portant sur l'innovation et la technologie en France"*. This shift was marked by the establishment of the *Comité national d'évaluation de la recherche* (CNER) in 1990 supplementing the *Comité national d'évaluation* (CNE) dating from 1984, in the evaluation of research institutions, national programmes and universities in addition to policy instruments such as the research tax credit.

made to evaluate the impact of support for technology diffusion policies and initiatives aimed at innovating SMEs.

238. In Germany, evaluation practice is well developed and covers a host of decentralised institutions, as well as S&T programmes. The Ministry of Education, Science, Research and Technology (*Bundesministerium für Bildung, Wissenschaft, Forschung und Technologie* – BMBF) includes an internal evaluation group, and there are attempts to combine strategically oriented evaluations for project funding with those of institutional funding of S&T organisations. An important development has been a recent review of evaluation practices ("meta-evaluation") commissioned by the BMBF. This review identified a number of weaknesses in the current evaluation system: insufficient attention to underlying assumptions of economic and technological problems; often unsuitable standardised procedures; and few horizontal evaluation studies of related policy initiatives (Kuhlmann, 1995; 1997).

239. In Finland, evaluations have been carried out frequently from the beginning of the 1980s onward (Luukkonen, 1997). The coverage spans from institutions carrying out or financing basic research (*e.g.* university institutes, Academy of Finland) to research centres doing applied research (Technical Research Centre of Finland – VTT) and the various national technology programmes financed by the Technology Development Centre (TEKES). As in other countries, evaluations initially focused on the scientific quality of research organisations, research institutes and research funding agencies, based on peer review methods. Professional evaluators are increasingly carrying out evaluations on a more elaborate methodological basis. Nevertheless, the focus is on the conduct of the programme and the achievement of technological or scientific goals rather than on the economic impact.

240. In the Netherlands, a strong "evaluation culture" has evolved, but without having led to institutionalised procedures (Rip and van der Meulen, 1995). Evaluation efforts are fairly frequent, but "patchy"; systematic evaluations have been established only for strategic innovation-oriented programmes and for university research. Evaluation is seen as the responsibility of intermediary institutions and is both commissioned and implemented by them. It is considered as one aspect of ongoing quality assurance, rather than an attempt to improve resource allocation or assess the strategic goal achievement of the various instruments of technology policy. Recent evaluation initiatives include that of the R&D allowance scheme, which provides for a reduction in the employers' wage tax and social insurance contributions (Dorsman, 1997).

241. Similar practices exist in other countries in this group. In Sweden, universities and R&D funding agencies conduct *ex ante* and *ex post* evaluations which feed into a government bill on publicly financed R&D.[27] The Swedish National Board for Industrial and Technical Development (NUTEK) evaluates R&D programmes in mid-term via peer reviews, looking at relevance and efficiency issues. NUTEK itself has recently been evaluated. The recent adoption of "management by objectives" as the guiding principle in the public sector has made monitoring and evaluation the main instruments for funding decisions in government. In Denmark, the evaluation practices of the Agency for Development of Trade and Industry involve monitoring of technological service institutes (*Godkendte Teknologiske Serviceinstitutter* – GTS), administration of programmes aimed at the promotion of innovation, and co-administration of R&D programmes with other ministries.[28] The evaluations of the GTS institutes

27. Note submitted to the OECD Secretariat, January 1997: NUTEK, "Information on Policy Evaluation Practices in Innovation and Technology in Sweden".

28. Note submitted to the OECD Secretariat, January 1997: "Evaluation Practices of the Danish Agency for Development of Trade and Industry".

are based on peer reviews; the evaluation reports are not made public (Birch, 1997). Innovation support programmes are evaluated on a regular basis, taking account of some impacts on trade and industry.

242. In Norway, evaluations have focused on individual projects and programmes. The S&T institutions and R&D policy have not been subject to comprehensive evaluations. The realisation that this approach is not suitable for more demanding policy assessments with a broader scope lies behind the recent launching of a "Forum for evaluation of industrial development strategies and instruments".[29] The idea is to move away from previous practice based on peer reviews within a closed group of "evaluation experts" towards creating more openness and competition and a real "evaluation market". This involves focusing on impact assessment at the expense of "process evaluation", as well as developing databases with capabilities for studies based on micro data, and *ex post* cost-benefit-oriented evaluation studies.

243. In Switzerland, although the legal framework is still lacking to a large extent, an "evaluation culture" is evolving and evaluation is more frequently used as a planning and management instrument in research policy. Evaluations of the strategic research programmes ("Swiss Priority Programmes") and of several research centres have been carried out. The Swiss National Science Foundation has run a National Research Programme (*Nationale Forschungprogramm* – NFP) on the "efficiency of government measures", which both evaluates specific policies and undertakes methodological research ("meta-evaluations"). Some interesting methodological work using micro-level data for the evaluation of diffusion-related programmes is also under way (Arvanitis and Hollenstein, 1997).

244. The role of the European Commission deserves particular mention. By virtue of the large number of its RTD programmes, and its structural interventions more generally, the Commission has played an important role in advancing the state of the art of evaluation practice in Europe.[30] During the 1980s, its impact on the evaluation practices of individual countries has been through organising evaluations, developing methodologies and supporting networks of evaluators. Recently, a rationalised evaluation scheme comprising continuous monitoring and five-year assessments of the European RTD programmes has been introduced. The scheme employs independent expert panels and covers mid-term appraisal, *ex post* evaluation and recommendations for future activities. It is to be used as a tool for programme management and to provide timely and independent feedback to policy formulation. In addition to the work of the Evaluation Unit of DG XII dealing specifically with technology policy, more general methodological guidelines for the conduct of evaluations have been issued (European Commission, 1997*b*), while evaluation efforts are also undertaken in the context of the structural funds to less-developed regions.

The third group: ad hoc evaluation efforts

245. In the remaining OECD countries, evaluation is a more recent, ad hoc phenomenon. While the legal framework for evaluation often exists, evaluations have not yet become a regular fixture of policy making. The methodologies used tend to be qualitative, relying on expert advice, with few attempts to quantify the impacts of interventions. Evaluations tend to be formative rather than summative, limiting

29. Note submitted to the OECD Secretariat, January 1997: Royal Ministry of Trade and Industry, "Assessment in Innovation and Technology Policy – Current Practices in Norway".

30. In Europe the diffusion of evaluation practices has been driven by EU programme evaluations and the building of a common set of tools and a pool of professionals in the MONITOR/SPEAR programme (for example, as developed in European Commission, 1992).

their use as a guide for allocating resources. However, a wide variety of practices can be seen among this group. A number of countries (Austria, Belgium, Italy, Japan, New Zealand) have in place at least part of an "evaluation system"; some evaluations of both institutions and programmes are undertaken, and there are at least some examples of attempts to apply more rigorous methodological approaches to evaluate the socio-economic impacts of programmes. Others (the Czech Republic, Hungary, Korea, Mexico, Poland, Turkey) have yet to build up a full institutional framework for evaluation. Finally, in a number of European countries (Greece, Ireland, Portugal), existing evaluation efforts are closely linked to the support programmes of the European Union.

246. In Japan, most evaluations are carried out in-house by government agencies, with a focus on projects rather than programmes and policy options, and with technological rather than economic objectives predominating. The recent establishment of an evaluation division within the Ministry of International Trade and Industry (MITI) may signal a change towards greater institutionalisation and professionalisation of the evaluation process. In Italy, there is little evaluation of programmes, which are mostly carried out by scientific decision makers rather than independent evaluators. From a methodological point of view, the recent use of the Community Innovation Survey for policy evaluation (Pianta and Sirilli, 1997) is worthy of note.

247. In New Zealand, the major evaluations have focused on the performance of publicly funded scientific research, rather than on innovation and technology programmes as such.[31] While few evaluations of innovation policies have been completed, there is ongoing discussion on methodological issues related to evaluations (Piric and Reeve, 1997), as well as a recent pilot study analysing the benefits and outcomes arising from meat research, with a methodology combining cost-benefit analysis and case-study research.

248. Among the European countries in this group, evaluation activities in Belgium are carried out at the regional as well as at the federal level, although evaluations are not required by law or other formal requirement. While evaluations of scientific institutions have taken place, evaluation of programmes and policies is not frequent (one recent example is the evaluation of the multimedia programme). Institutions for carrying out evaluations have only recently been set up at the regional and federal levels. Feedback into technology and innovation policy has been limited due to the infrequency and low visibility of evaluations.[32]

249. In Austria, evaluations of technology programmes and policies began in the early 1990s and were mainly centred around either targeted technology programmes or participation in international programmes (Fritz *et al.*, 1997; Stampfer, 1997). The principal funding institutions for R&D and main public performers of basic and applied R&D have yet to be evaluated. Methodologies have tended to focus on programme conduct and direct effects on programme clientele. Although some studies take account of economic effects, there is in general no analysis of broader socio-economic impacts. Commissioning institutions are predominantly the responsible ministries, but no system exists to verify that the results of evaluations are taken up. EU membership could have a significant impact on the development of an "evaluation culture". To comply with European standards, a wave of *ex ante* project and programme evaluations have been undertaken, mainly in the context of the structural funds.

31. Note submitted to the OECD Secretariat, January 1997: Foundation for Research, Science and Technology, "Information on Policy Evaluation Practices in Innovation and Technology".

32. Note submitted to the OECD Secretariat, January 1997: *Direction Générale de la Recherche/Région Wallonne de Belgique, "Les pratiques d'évaluation des politiques dans le domaine de l'innovation et de la technologie"*.

250. In Greece, Ireland and Portugal, the diffusion of evaluation practice can be traced directly to the growing importance of European Commission-funded technology programmes and structural interventions whose implementation requires the existence of an evaluation process. In these countries, despite the setting-up of "evaluation units" in the relevant ministries and the existence of a number of methodologically robust evaluation efforts, a genuine "evaluation culture" has yet to emerge. In Spain, where European Commission structural funds have played a lesser role, research evaluation has developed over the last few years, mostly addressing technical issues; R&D policy and programme evaluation is less institutionalised (Sanz-Menéndez, 1995).

251. In all the new OECD Member countries (the Czech Republic, Hungary, Korea, Mexico, Poland), evaluation efforts are very much in their early phase of development. There are numerous evaluation initiatives but no formal co-ordination or institutional structure for evaluation. The central European "transition" countries in particular have a strong tradition of scientific research and have consequently built up "peer-review" mechanisms for the assessment of research quality and the allocation of funds. Economic evaluations have been built up only since 1990, following the restructuring of the whole institutional set-up. In the Czech Republic, economic evaluations by the Enterprise Development Agency are increasingly used in the context of support for applied R&D.[33] In Hungary, a system of project and programme evaluation for basic research has long been in existence. Following a pilot evaluation project on applied R&D carried out with the methodological assistance from Sweden's NUTEK, a long-term evaluation strategy for all Hungarian applied R&D programmes using performance indicators has been defined. The evaluation of institutes is also being developed.[34]

5.4. Best-practice principles for policy evaluation

252. Drawing on the accumulated experience with innovation and technology policy evaluation in OECD countries, in this section we attempt to draw out what can be said to constitute best practices with respect to three different dimensions of evaluation: *(i)* the basic rationale, objectives and criteria; *(ii)* the coverage of innovation and technology policy evaluation efforts and the tools and methodologies used; and *(iii)* the conduct of evaluations and the institutional set-up within which they take place. In each of these areas, "best practices" are defined as approaches, rules and procedures that are desirable from a conceptual and theoretical point of view, that seem to have worked in practice and that have some measure of generality (*i.e.* are not completely country-specific). These best-practice evaluation principles are those that if widely applied would be most likely to maximise the leverage effect of government interventions while minimising potential distortions. They are summarised in Box 5.2.

---

33. Note submitted to the OECD Secretariat, January 1997: "Information on Policy Evaluation Practice in Innovation and Technology Programmes in Purview of the Ministry of Industry and Trade, Czech Republic".

34. "Policy Evaluation Practices in Innovation and Technology in Hungary", report to the Joint Expert Group on Technology and Job Creation, January 1997.

Box 5.2. **Best-practice evaluation principles: a summary**

Rationale, objectives and criteria for evaluation:

- establish a realistic hierarchy of objectives, so as to allow quantitative *ex post* assessment of their attainment wherever possible;
- clearly establish the economic rationale for the policy intervention and use it in the evaluation; carefully balance market and systemic failures against potential government failure;
- identify and attempt to measure the additionality implied by the policy intervention.

Coverage of evaluations and use of different tools and methods:

- evaluate as broadly as possible all existing innovation and technology policies;
- attempt "portfolio" evaluations;
- develop the use of quantitative techniques (*e.g.* cost-benefit analysis, econometrics based on the use of micro-level data) where appropriate;
- combine results of quantitative and qualitative techniques when interpreting evaluation results.

Conduct of evaluations and institutional setting:

- design the evaluation together with the programme to be evaluated;
- ensure that evaluations are user-driven;
- formulate guidelines and a "code of conduct" for evaluations, ensuring their independence, funding and regularity;
- ensure feedback and learning by, *inter alia*, establishing a requirement for responding to evaluations and a presumption in favour of publication of evaluation results.

Rationale, objectives and criteria for evaluation

253. Identifying the rationale, the objectives and the criteria to be used for assessing the success or failure of different government initiatives is the starting point of any evaluation effort. Yet, often, insufficient attention is paid to this stage of the evaluation. Objectives are vague and inappropriate, making any attempt to verify whether they have been met either trivial or close to impossible. The rationale behind the policy intervention is often misunderstood; even clearly stated objectives do not justify policy intervention. In innovation and technology policy, evaluation is complicated by the fact that the objectives against which results are judged are often multiple and complex, mirroring the complex relationship between technical progress and its socio-economic impacts. Objectives can be direct (*e.g.* inciting additional R&D expenditures, increased mobility of personnel, greater university-industry collaboration, increased access to new technologies by SMEs, etc.) or indirect (*e.g.* increasing the knowledge base of the economy, boosting productivity or the acquisition of skills, creating jobs). Furthermore, links between particular policies and direct objectives are often hard to establish. The more indirect the objective, the more difficult it is to establish cause and effect.

254. This complexity implies that policy makers need to establish a hierarchy of objectives when designing and evaluating programmes. Stating objectives in very general terms, such as increasing welfare or improving competitiveness, while useful in situating the initiative in its political context, is useless in the operational sense of examining whether or not the policy has attained its objectives. For this, intermediate or lower-level objectives need to be clearly spelt out. In the case of innovation policy, for example, it is clear that "additional R&D", "greater use of advanced technologies" or "more university-industry links" are not ends in themselves, but rather the means to realise the socio-economic benefits of research. While it is difficult to argue how a particular policy contributes to raising the knowledge base or the productivity potential of an economy, it is easier to argue in logical steps: to show empirically that it has boosted R&D and that R&D translates into productivity gains.

255. It is also important to distinguish between strictly economic and more general socio-economic objectives. Technology policy is increasingly concerned with complex socio-economic impacts (such as health, environment or working conditions). From society's point of view, even "non-economic" aspects have an economic interpretation (*e.g.* expenditures on pollution control must balance the marginal social benefit of pollution abatement to its marginal social cost). Such calculations are not always feasible in the context of innovation policies with broader direct or indirect socio-economic impacts. Singling out the first-order direct economic effects is nevertheless useful, since it helps in judging whether the rationale for the intervention is valid and allows a more accurate examination of whether the objectives have been achieved.

256. Another issue concerns identifying objectives that are appropriate given the nature of the policy intervention. There is a tendency in many countries to motivate specific initiatives by relating them to general economic objectives that are currently high on the political agenda. Employment is a case in point (Box 5.3). While technology policy has an important impact on job creation through a host of channels, it would not be reasonable to set employment objectives in, say, a programme of financial support for industrial R&D. Although more and better jobs is an ultimate objective of such a policy (via the higher productivity and incomes, and the creation of new products that the policy will generate), to specify an explicit employment objective could be counter-productive, often leading to attempts to justify the policy by pointing to the jobs directly created, with the implication that the policy has failed when such jobs do not materialise. The resulting calculations are dubious, and can lead to misguided initiatives.

257. In addition to unclear objectives, the rationale for a particular government initiative is often not spelt out or is misunderstood. The rationale for policy to stimulate technological development is the recognition that there is a difference between the expected private rate of return and the social rate of return, with the private rate being too low to induce firms to engage in innovative activities that would be beneficial from a societal standpoint. The specific sources of market or systemic failure that create this wedge between private and social returns and that justify government involvement have to be explained. Specifying these is not a gratuitous exercise; too often, the policy initiative is not the most appropriate to counteract the specific failure. If, for example, the problem lies in inefficient financial markets that prevent the financing of NTBFs, it may be preferable that policy direct address those specific inefficiencies rather than helping firms through grants or soft loans. The process of identifying the specific source of market failure provides valuable lessons for the design of the policy initiative.

258. Furthermore, in setting out a rationale, the case should be made that government actions can improve on imperfect market outcomes. The accumulated experience of three decades of technology policies, together with recent advances in innovation theory, have shown the limits of a simple "market failure" rationale to policy. "Government failure" is preponderant, making it all the more important to account for costs of programmes as well as for benefits, including those costs associated with the distortions to economic incentives that policy initiatives can bring about.

Box 5.3. Employment impacts in the evaluation of technology policies

Concerns about unemployment in many countries have led to attempts to measure employment impacts when evaluating technology programmes. Unfortunately, the political imperative of pointing to the job gains associated with a particular technology policy initiative has often come at the expense of analytical rigor in measuring employment impacts. While there are clear links between technical change and employment creation, the links are seldom direct and are not easily measurable. Hence, a requirement that an innovation policy initiative lead directly to more jobs, while in principle a desirable aim, can in practice produce perverse results. The difficulties in accounting for job gains associated with technology support were examined in a recent European Commission "handbook" aimed at measuring the employment effects of structural interventions (European Commission, 1996*a*). That report notes that the reliability of estimation of employment effects diminishes substantially when moving from direct job creation programmes through subsidies to indirect job creation through productivity growth, additional demand or new firm creation.

There are at least three pitfalls to be avoided in calculating employment effects. The first is a failure to distinguish between gross and net jobs. Net effects are gross effects (new jobs observed or forecast), minus dead-weight (the jobs that would have been created anyway in the absence of the programme), substitution (jobs that went to people other than those that would have been employed in the absence of the programme), and displacement or crowding-out (when the policy initiative reduces activity and jobs elsewhere in the economy). The second pitfall is the transition from direct to global job impacts. In technology policies, job creation is rarely as significant in the targeted firm as it is in other parts of the economy. Indirect job impacts occur through supplier effects (inter-industry sourcing of inputs), and through income multiplier effects (through the higher incomes brought about by productivity-enhancing policies). Long-term supplier effects that occur when policy improves the knowledge base of the economy and its underlying growth rate, are also very important. A final hurdle relates to the translation from job creation to unemployment reduction. Ultimately, policy makers care about unemployment rates, and unemployment is determined by the interaction of the demand and the supply of labour. Even policies whose net job impact is positive need to take into account their effect on the supply for labour, through their impact on activity rates.

Some recent Member country experiences point to the difficulties involved in calculating net job impacts when evaluating innovation and technology policy initiatives. In France, the evaluation of the *Grands Projets Innovants*, a programme of support to industrial innovation, included an assessment of jobs created per million francs of subsidies. Similarly, in the context of the evaluation of EUREKA projects, project managers are asked about the number of jobs created directly as a result of participation in projects. The problem with such assessments, of which there are many examples, lies in their interpretation. These numbers capture only partial direct effects and omit indirect effects. Their limits should be understood, and the temptation to use them as justification for policies resisted.

The question of employment effects of technology policies will continue to preoccupy policy makers as long as job creation remains a problem. It is however important to be clear about what should be the objectives of different policies. In many technology programmes, employment objectives need not be directly identified. On the other hand, where such jobs impacts need to be identified, there is a need for more sophisticated approaches whereby information from surveys is validated by independent quantitative estimations and complemented by quantitative tools that capture the economy-wide effects (*i.e.* input-output techniques, macroeconometric modelling or general equilibrium approaches).

263. While first-generation evaluations were predominantly concerned with inputs, and following generations extended the examination of factors to various indicators of innovative outputs, best practice must now include an assessment of "soft factors" in the innovation process (intangible investments in skills and organisational practices, information, awareness, collaborative behaviour, etc.). These are increasingly recognised as of central importance for successful innovation and have been targeted by a growing number of programmes and policy measures. Best practice can be found in evaluations that use a "portfolio" approach rather than focusing on individual projects. Additionality cannot be appropriately measured by looking at individual projects, but has to take into account the portfolio of projects that firms pursue in order to judge the programme or policy with respect to how far it was able to change the "portfolio-choices" of the firm (for examples, see Fölster, 1991, as well as a pioneering study from New Zealand – Foundation for Research, Science and Technology, 1997). There is increasing demand for evaluations that analyse different programmes in order to compare the relative effectiveness of different policies using different instruments. Due to methodological problems, "good practice" has yet to evolve in this respect, and further development of evaluation methodologies is needed.

264. As regards the mix of evaluation methods, there are clear differences between countries in the faith they put in conclusions based on quantitative as opposed to qualitative techniques. There is, however, a growing awareness that no single best method exists. Different approaches are complementary rather than mutually exclusive and, to increase the credibility of evaluation results, a number of alternative methods should be used to consolidate the foundations for policy recommendations. The distinction is not clear-cut: quantitative techniques often produce mainly qualitative information. This mix must be tailored to the specific policy instrument (*e.g.* diffusion-oriented programmes, collaborative R&D programmes, etc.), the goal of the evaluation and the informational needs of the clients.

265. An interesting recent development in evaluation methodology concerns the use of econometric techniques based on longitudinal micro-level data, where the impacts of programmes are examined by comparing the performance characteristics of firms that are clients of government initiatives (such as extension services) with those of non-client firms (Box 5.5). The quality of results based on this approach is, however, conditional on the extent to which researchers can control for firm characteristics other than programme participation. Furthermore, this technique is only the first step in a full cost-benefit analysis: at its best it establishes the private benefits ensuing to firms as a result of the programme; justification for a programme needs to account for social benefits compared with total costs.

266. In a general sense, it is clear that the most rigorous evaluation schemes are constructed around social cost-benefit frameworks; however, such calculations can give a spurious sense of precision. Ideally, they should be combined with the qualitative information from user surveys, in-depth case studies and interviews to produce the variety of information needed by the different users of evaluations. Single-approach evaluations can be misleading, and placing too much emphasis on single quantitative estimations – while useful as a cross-check – might miss the essential qualitative effects of new initiatives. Furthermore, it is clear that quantitative techniques need to be further developed, especially with regard to the challenge of capturing the economic impacts of the "soft factors" of innovation (impact on learning, co-operative and innovative behaviour).

Table 5.2. **The evaluation "tool kit": pros and cons of different methodological approaches**

	Strengths	Weaknesses	Main areas of application	Cost
Peer-review methods	• Informed judgement, especially on quality of scientific quality • Can be systematised, checked and analysed to increase confidence in results • Relative simplicity	• Subjectivity of experts; lack of independence of experts • Only qualitative information • "Group think" within panels • Difficult to apply to commercially sensitive projects	• Evaluation of institutions • Support for pre-competitive research	• Low
Client follow-up and user surveys	• Questions can be tailored to interests of different stakeholders • Provide valuable feedback to programme managers	• No control group • Provide no way to validate information on cost and performance of measure	• Diffusion-oriented programmes • Consultancy and information services	• Expensive
Case studies	• Help understand complex processes • Provide detailed information about mechanisms through which programmes affect performance • Can induce substantial (individual) learning effects	• Highly dependent on evaluator's skill and experience • Generate little quantitative information • No control group • Rely on "success stories" • Hard to incorporate into routine monitoring • No way to generalise	• Consultancy and information services • Large-scale mission-oriented programmes	• High if done extensively
Technometrics, scientometrics, bibliometrics	• Objective output data of innovation projects • Standardised methodologies • Allow use of control group	• Measure only scientific and technological output, but not economic benefits	• The technological and scientific dimension of innovation output	• Moderate in general, but high if done extensively
Econometric studies	• Allow use of control group • Can utilise external existing data sources	• Impractical in many cases	• Financial support to industrial R&D • Diffusion-oriented programmes	• Moderate to high, depending on data availability
Cost-benefit analysis	• Incorporate all social benefits of programmes and accounts for opportunity costs of resources	• Difficult to collect all necessary information • Quantitative information often conceals qualitative aspects of programmes	• Large-scale mission-oriented programmes • Financial support to industrial R&D	• High (demanding data collection requirements and skill of evaluators)

Source: OECD Secretariat.

Box 5.5. **The use of micro-level data sets for evaluation purposes: the US approach**

An important methodological advance in the evaluation of technology programmes has been the development of micro-level data that allow information on firms participating in different government initiatives ("client firms") to be "matched" and confronted with information on their performance. In the United States, recent research has used "administrative" data collected during the delivery of services in the context of the Manufacturing Extension Partnership (MEP) together with longitudinal data on manufacturing establishments from the US Census Bureau (the Longitudinal Research Database) to determine whether observed changes in the performance of firms (*i.e.* growth in value-added per worker or plant survival rates) can be attributed to association with the MEP (Jarmin and Jensen, 1997).

The main justification for the use of micro-level data lies in the fact that the impact of programmes is at firm or plant level, making it sensible to examine the impact of these programmes at that level. Micro-level data allow researchers to explicitly recognise that programmes such as the MEP are addressed to heterogeneous populations and to compare performance of client plants with that of non-clients. They also allow to correct for selection bias (the fact that better-than-average plants seek out services such as MEP), as well as to take into account the competitive environment within which client firms operate, and in which the services provided are supposed to improve SME performance. This should help ensure that programme objectives are not at odds with those of the client SMEs.

Among the different evaluation methodologies that allow an examination of the impact of programmes (*e.g.* case studies, client surveys), econometric analyses based on such micro-level non-experimental data offer researchers and policy makers the best opportunity to assess the overall performance of programmes such as manufacturing extension. Building up databases that allow for such micro-level analysis will be an essential methodological tool for evaluation in countries wishing to better assess the impact of such programmes. Nevertheless, it should be noted that this type of approach only partly addresses the desirability of such policy initiatives. In addition to evaluating the impact of the policy, a full cost-benefit calculation is needed to form a judgement about the opportunity cost of the resources expended and the cost of potential distortions as a result of the policy.

267. The need for an approach which combines quantitative with qualitative information is underscored by the fact that programme management requires an analysis of the process and performance of different policy instruments. Given the high variance of returns in different technology projects, case studies are crucial in order to see which policies work and which do not. But, whatever the method used, the importance of a "counterfactual" in policy evaluation exercises is stressed. Much evaluation work ignores the broader context of programmes (competitive environment within which client plants and firms operate, history of the programme), in which the services provided are supposed to improve performance. It is important to have an understanding of this environment in order to optimally design, provide and evaluate programme services and to ensure that programme objectives are not at odds with those of clients.

Institutional setting and conduct of evaluations

268. Techniques aside, evaluation is very much a social process as it involves interaction of individuals, organisational beliefs, practices and routines. The institutional set-up within which programmes and policies are evaluated determines the nature, quality, relevance and effectiveness of evaluation. Hence the question arises whether there is such a thing as an "optimal" institutional set-up, transferable across countries. It would seem that while basic principles and challenges to evaluation are similar, the concrete practical arrangements of evaluation procedures are country-specific. However, from country comparisons one could conclude that the precise institutional framework for evaluation is of less importance than its functionality, making it possible to draw some common lessons on best practice.

269. One basic general lesson is that evaluations must take into account country specificities and build on the strengths and variety of national systems of innovation to develop systematic evaluation practices embedded in the policy-making process. This is especially important with respect to the implementation of results. From a practical point of view it is necessary to reconcile evaluation design with the varying needs of policy makers, funding agencies, providers and clients of a particular programme or policy. While in the most advanced countries evaluations are already standard tools in the policy process, in

others, an "evaluation culture" in the sense of a general awareness of the need for and a positive attitude towards regular evaluations, but including also the creation of a pool of knowledge and expertise with regard to evaluation practices, either needs to be created or could be much improved.

270. Another institutional prerequisite for valuable evaluations is the independence of the evaluators. Several institutional solutions exist in various countries (*e.g.* evaluations being carried out by the independent accounting offices of parliaments, the commissioning of evaluations to external consultants etc.). Increasingly, countries commission evaluations to international evaluators – especially in the European context. In some countries, the idea of a "code of conduct" for evaluations is advocated, comprising standards and basic requirements for those commissioning evaluations.

271. Even in countries where evaluations are carried out regularly, there is often an "implementation gap" in that results from evaluations are either not taken up at all or are taken up in a "localised form" (*i.e.* recommendations are only implemented if the institution evaluated can implement them on its own). The lack of a feedback mechanism is probably the most important single factor limiting the value of evaluations. In many countries, there is a pressing need to secure follow-up at the appropriate level of policy making. This can be achieved in various ways. Some countries have put a formal obligation on those responsible for policy making to react to the results of evaluations (see Box 5.6 for the example of the UK ROAME-F procedure). Others have a policy of exposing the results of evaluations to public discussion. A presumption in favour of publication of evaluation reports – although too much publicity might have its own drawbacks – is generally favourable for the development of an evaluation culture as well as to encourage policy implementation.

272. With respect to the practical conduct of evaluations, country experiences show that best results are obtained when evaluations are designed at the same time as the programme or policy to be evaluated. Early preparation is necessary to secure the collection and provision of the data needed in the course of the evaluation – especially where the use of micro-level data is essential for the estimation of the impacts. Best-practice examples include the build-up of databases that can be used for various evaluations of programmes and policies addressing the innovative behaviour of a large number of firms as in the United States. Such a "concurrent design" of both programme and evaluation procedure raises acceptance levels of the procedures and criteria by the persons and institutions involved.

273. Rather than being conducted on an ad hoc basis, evaluations need to be carried out regularly, subject to the condition that sufficient new results are available to test the rationale and effectiveness of the programme. There are substantial learning effects from frequent evaluations, both on the demand side for policy makers, programme managers and providers, as well as on the supply side for the professionals carrying out evaluations. The accumulated knowledge can be a valuable tool for policy making, as the practice in Nordic countries exemplifies. Frequent evaluations have been shown to have a lasting effect on the behaviour of the evaluated institutions and in many cases contributed *per se* to the improvement of routines and performance.

274. The design and choice of evaluation methods should reflect the different informational needs of the various actors involved (*e.g.* policy makers, programme managers, those people actually carrying out the programme, the clients of the programme). A well-designed evaluation has to take these different needs into account, while reconciling desired information needs with resource and information availability constraints. In some countries, valuable experience was gained in establishing multi-disciplinary evaluation teams to judge the scientific, economic, managerial and political dimensions of the programme or activity. Such a broad approach to evaluation, though desirable from a methodological point of view, has to be balanced with the resources available, and in practice will tend to be confined to large-scale programmes.

Box 5.6. **The UK ROAME-F model: evaluation and the policy-making process**

One of the most critical determinants of the success of evaluation is the extent to which it is embedded in the policy-making process. Even well-designed, well-run evaluations are of little use if their results are not picked up in redesigning or reforming existing and future policies. This understanding has led the United Kingdom Treasury to develop general guidelines for the management of support programmes. The Department for Trade and Industry and Department for Education and Employment have developed these further into the ROAME-F statement, which helps users to establish a rationale for policy, set objectives, monitor the process, evaluate the outcome and feed back the results into the design of future policies.

Rationale – making a case for undertaking an activity – involves justification in terms of the expected impact on economic performance or some other policy objective. Establishing an economic rationale involves identifying grounds for belief that an activity is likely to generate supply-side benefits (*e.g.* by increasing the efficiency of resource allocation, easing a supply constraint or promoting a generic technology). The specific sources of market failure that prevent firms from achieving these benefits in the absence of the policy have to be explained (*e.g.* public goods, externalities, inefficient market structures and entry barriers, information asymmetries or dynamic adjustment problems). A case should also be made that government actions can improve on imperfect market outcomes.

Objectives – making the aims of the initiative operational. This stage involves setting clear and measurable objectives that relate directly to the economic rationale and that allow the definition of a performance indicator that can be monitored during the life of a programme.

Appraisal – examines options available for delivery of the outputs of the initiative. It is intended to determine which set of options will best achieve the stated objectives. Appraisal techniques commonly used include cost-benefit analysis, cost-effectiveness analysis (comparing the costs of different ways of achieving similar outputs) and financial or commercial appraisal (applied when benefits can be measured as receipts from sales and where charges and costs represent payments for goods and services as inputs).

Monitoring – routine checking of progress against plan. Monitoring information should refer back to the scheme's stated objectives. It can relate to results (checking for the effect of the policy in terms of outputs, *i.e.* the effect on firms), and management (examining the extent to which the policy is being carried out as planned referring to input objectives). Monitoring differs from evaluation in that it does not address issues related to the validity of the rationale, additionality or wider effects of the scheme.

Evaluation – reviewing outcomes on the basis of an in-depth review over a number of years. This involves examining issues of effectiveness (achievement against stated objectives), with a quantification of the value added of the initiative based on data on higher sales, profits and incomes, as well as on costs incurred at market prices (distinguishing between economic costs and transfers). A focus on additionality (the change due to the policy as compared to what would have happened in its absence) and on potential crowding-out effects ensures that alternative uses of resources are taken into account. Issues of efficiency and programme management are also addressed, partly by comparing cost-benefit ratios of the initiative under evaluation with those in other cases, and partly by reviewing operational procedures.

Feedback – drawing on the lessons of evaluation for future initiatives. A presumption of publication of evaluation results and a requirement that the managers responsible for the policy initiatives respond to the evaluation are two practical ways to ensure some sort of feedback into the design of future initiatives.

275. Finally, in almost all countries evaluations have been used mainly for incremental changes (*i.e.* improving the design and administration of programmes), but rarely to guide more fundamental shifts and strategic re-orientations in technology and innovation policy. To empower evaluation for such a task, it would have to be embedded in a wider system of information gathering and preparation, linking it to technology foresight and technology assessment exercises. The role of the evaluator is also likely to change in such a setting. In bringing together various sources of information as inputs to a strategic policy formulation process, his/her role would be transformed from one of a "referee" to that of a "moderator" of the information-gathering process and a "coach" for the strategic policy decision-making process. With the growing need for comparing policies and programmes against each other and widening the scope of evaluation towards systemic and strategic aspects, this would seem to be a "best practice for the future".

276. This raises the question of how far evaluation can go. It is not a costless activity, and while there is a need for more and better evaluations, there can also be diminishing returns. The right balance

has to be found between the good practice of frequent evaluations of particular programmes, and the evaluation of new areas of government initiatives. While there is often a temptation to continue evaluating at regular intervals programmes for which evaluation methodologies are well established, the budgets available for evaluation would be better spent on addressing difficult evaluation issues in the newer areas of innovation and technology policies, such as collaborative research, public-private partnerships or diffusion programmes.

277. Furthermore, although welcoming an increased scope of evaluation techniques to produce a greater variety of information more reliably, there is a danger of stretching evaluation too far. Evaluation can help to guide informed choices, but it cannot substitute for a political decision-making process. Evaluations are not and cannot be decisive, partly because policy involves trade-offs and value judgements, and partly because evaluations are often simply not good enough due to uncertainty in the impact of many programmes. Many policy decisions are based on intuition and first principles; however it is important that, as far as possible, the correct rationale is given at the outset and that assumptions regarding market and systemic failures are tested empirically to determine their validity. Moreover there is a clear need for evaluations that go beyond individual programmes, and that instead compare the impacts of different spending initiatives and examine the appropriateness and efficiency of different policy tools in achieving a given objective.

5.5. Trends and challenges for the future development of evaluation practice

278. Despite the substantial efforts and progress made in evaluation in most countries, much remains to be done. In countries that are only now introducing elements of evaluation into their policy-making process, there is too much focus on efficiency reviews and too little on evaluating the economic impacts of technology and innovation policies and alternative means of achieving given objectives. And, even in countries with a longer experience in this area, evaluation practice often continues to be piecemeal, with insufficient attention paid to "softer" policies and systemic considerations. The single biggest weakness in most countries' evaluations seems to be the lack of an appropriate feedback framework.

279. From the discussion above, some broad trends and challenges emerge for the future development of evaluation practices. First is the challenge to establish or improve a country's "evaluation culture". Even with differing approaches and attitudes towards evaluation, there exists a possibility for mutual learning, including for those countries which have the most advanced methodologies and institutions. Second, there is a necessity to improve quantitative and qualitative methods to meet the challenges imposed by increased budgetary pressures, on the one hand, and the assessment of the impacts of more complex and systemic policies, on the other hand. Although efforts have been undertaken in this direction, substantial work remains to be done. Adequate training on evaluation techniques for civil servants and policy makers is important in this respect.

280. Finally, there is a need to assign an appropriate role for evaluation exercises in the policy-making process. This involves not only the establishment of feedback loops securing proper implementation of results – still absent in many countries, but also linking evaluation to other sources through which technology and innovation policy might be informed (such as technology forecasting or assessment). It also includes re-designing the role of evaluation and evaluators to reflect changing policy needs. Although these trends and principles are fairly common among countries, they need to be applied with an eye to the needs and specificities of the "national system of evaluation" in order to be accepted and properly implemented in the context of a specific country.

CHAPTER 6. MANAGING THE SCIENCE BASE

6.1. Introduction

281. The science base is a fundamental element of innovative dynamism. The focus of this chapter is to provide information to facilitate the search for best practice in the management of the science system from an innovation perspective.[35]

6.2. The relationship between science and innovation

How science contributes to innovation

282. As evoked in Chapter 2, the relationships linking science and innovation are complex and in no way direct. Two facts are worth recalling. First, innovation is clearly distinct from science, since it requires a series of actions, such as technical experimentation, market prospection and above all entrepreneurial initiative, which are different from scientific investigation. Second, until this century, technical change preceded scientific progress and owed little to it. On the other hand, the extraordinary expansion and success of the scientific enterprise has considerably modified the preconditions for innovation. The latter draws increasingly on advances in knowledge made by the science base, although no linear relationship exists between the two (as discussed below).

283. This trend seems to have accelerated in recent years: surveys show that inventive activity, as measured by patents, draws more and more upon basic science, notably publicly supported science (Chapter 2). These studies, carried out in the United States, show a threefold increase in publication citations in patents over the period 1987-94 (Narin *et al.*, 1997), and provide evidence of the increasing links between science and innovation. Although this trend needs to be confirmed by evidence from other countries, it sends a crucial message to governments, who have to efficiently support the science enterprise.

284. However, the contribution of science to innovation should be seen in a broad perspective going well beyond the role played by basic research as a source of new knowledge in innovation processes. The innovation climate in industry benefits from the problem-solving role played by the scientific

---

35. This chapter consolidates information from various sources, including OECD S&T statistics, studies and policy reviews, available government reports and articles published in the specialised literature. This work has also benefited from a mission to the Netherlands organised by the Dutch authorities in June 1997. An earlier draft was presented at the workshop held in Budapest on 26-27 September 1997 and further revised in light of discussions and contributions made at the workshop. It then benefited from further comments by Delegates to the OECD Group on the Science System.

community, the employment of a well-educated and creative science and engineering workforce, the transfer of advanced equipment, etc. (Science Policy Research Unit, 1996).

285. Sooner or later, all countries need to develop an efficient science base. The meaning of "efficient" will differ across countries. Smaller economies benefit from "natural" trade exchanges and from ideas and technological advances stemming from the R&D efforts of larger ones (National Bureau of Economic Research, 1995). Their ability to absorb outside R&D (whether embodied or not in products), depends to a great extent on their science base. In considering the remarkable performances accomplished by the Asian countries based on receptiveness to foreign technology and R&D with a broadly developed technical education, one might question the need for developing basic research capabilities. However, experience shows that such a situation cannot be maintained for long. As will be seen below, the Asian countries have now embarked on long-term efforts to expand their science bases, although their research efforts continue to be more technically oriented than those of the western world.

286. As noted above, innovation does not derive directly from science, even though it is increasingly nurtured by it. The knowledge required for innovation differs from that produced by science (Berkhout *et al.*, 1997). In the latter, knowledge is structured and produced in a fragmented way with little connection between disciplines and sub-disciplines, through a process of deepening and accumulation. Between scientific advance and innovations in the form of products or processes, knowledge is organised around technology areas of a generic or multi-application nature. Here, progress is based on a process of integrating separate elements. This is followed by dissemination, and/or further integration, of technology into different applications at the more detailed level of product development. These key aspects of the knowledge chain linking science and innovation are depicted in Figure 6.1 and Figure 6.2. They have important policy implications, notably as regards the design of research structures (in universities and elsewhere), the focus of research efforts in various S&T fields, and the science and engineering education which is required to train both knowledge integrators and disseminators.

Figure 6.1. **The complex interactions between scientific knowledge generation, technological research and product development**[1]

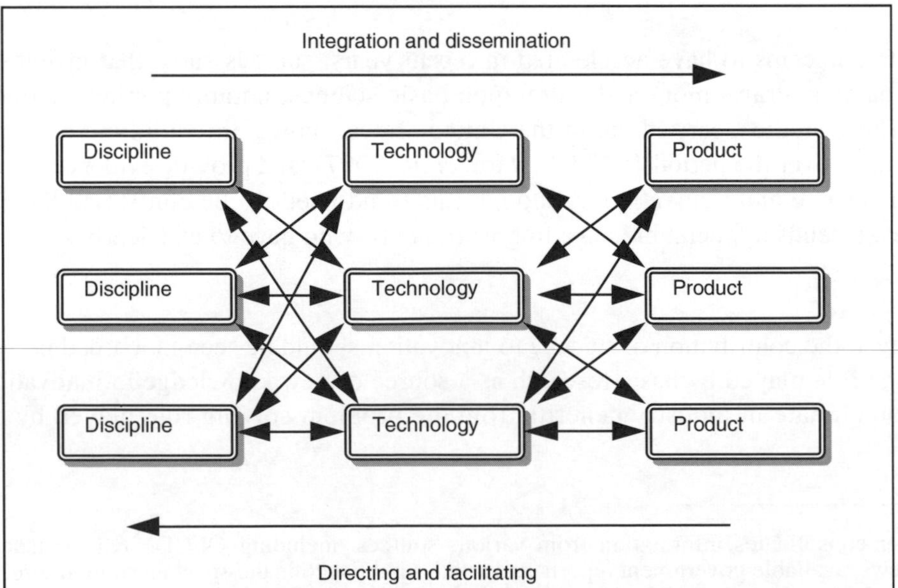

1. Discipline refers to one area of scientific knowledge.
Source: Berkhout *et al.* (1997).

287. Although the ways and means by which science and basic research contribute to innovation differ across sectors, some key features characterise climates conducive to fruitful science/innovation interactions (Science Policy Research Unit, 1996). There is a need for a high-quality science base in pursuit of excellence in research, and which is curiosity-driven or application-motivated. There is also a need for a dynamic industry with a strong R&D capability and a highly qualified science and engineering workforce, to enable the best use to be made of scientific advances. Finally, there is a need for an efficient interface between the academic and business worlds, facilitating the exchange of ideas and, to an even greater extent, of people since, as has been demonstrated by a number of studies (Science Policy Research Unit, 1996), people are the most important vector of knowledge.

Figure 6.2. **The interactive processes in knowledge generation and product development**

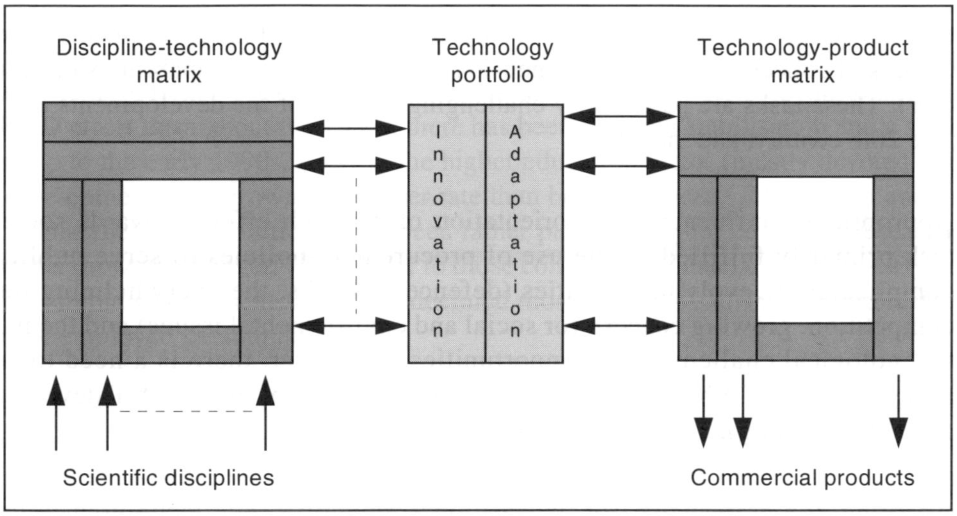

Source: Berkhout *et al.* (1997).

The role of government

288. Governments have two basic roles to play in developing a sound science base with a view to stimulating technological progress:

- *Providing appropriate financial support to scientific research*, notably the university and public research that depends primarily on government funding. This entails the provision of a sufficient volume of credit to sustain a long-term research effort (and related training activities) that cannot be financed by the private sector. It also entails finding the correct balance between sure and precarious resources to ensure fruitful interactions between the scientific world and the surrounding environment (a prerequisite for the development of innovative capabilities), as well as between mission-oriented support and non-oriented support to curiosity-driven research.

- *Improving the interfaces between science and industry:* the two sides differ in their rationales (the first being motivated by the advancement of knowledge, and the second by the quest for profits) as well as cultures (scientific and technological modes of investigation differ). Government has a role to play in stimulating communication between the two

several concurring factors to explain this trend. Firstly, core resources are generally obtained from general allocations given to universities for both research and education. The overall amount has often not been raised despite a significant increase in the numbers of students enrolled by universities as a result of the widespread process of democratisation and massification of higher education. A second factor is the growth of contract-based allocations for specific missions and/or a limited number of years. This policy seems to have been followed by science councils and related funding agencies in most OECD countries (Skoie, 1997).

296. One consequence of these trends is a significant increase in precarious positions for university researchers – a source of concern in more than one country (*e.g.* Belgium, France, the United Kingdom). It seems that serious problems appear when the ratio of sure (core) resources *vis-à-vis* precarious ones drops to under 50 per cent. Of course, this is a rough rule of thumb and important variations exist among university systems. It is well known, for instance, that engineering and medical faculties are able to attract much more external funding than other types of faculties.

297. In general, government laboratories have been more affected than universities by the reduction of government support. This has been accompanied by a trend towards privatisation in some countries and/or strong pressure on laboratories to become largely self-financing through the provision of services to industry, government agencies and local communities. This approach has certainly stimulated innovation, but it also has some drawbacks when pushed to excess; it disproportionally reduces the volume of research and related services of a collective nature provided to the economy (see recent OECD policy reviews).

298. The R&D effort which should have a "collective nature" in order to serve the needs of industry as a whole has always been a difficult issue for governments. The European countries used to support research associations as well as networks of "technical centres" partly funded by each trade on the basis of levies (tax on industry turnover). These mechanisms have been abandoned or neglected (receiving declining government support), without being replaced. The United States has a well-regarded organisation for agriculture research and extension services, but little for industry and the manufacturing sector. A few "generic technology centres" were initiated in the 1980s, particularly focused on advanced technology, such as Semiconductor Manufacturing Technology (SEMATECH) for semiconductor research. One of the limits of such centres is that they only benefit the consortium of (large) firms involved. In fact, it is only in Japan that research of a collective nature has been, and continues to be, developed on a significant scale. It takes place in the double network of national and prefectural laboratories, the first working mostly for large industry, the second for SMEs on a regional basis.

299. It is also important to consider the behaviour of industry regarding basic research. On the whole, and notably in the large scientific powers, the effort of industry in favour of basic research seems to have been roughly maintained, without suffering too much damage from the recent economic slowdowns. It seems, however, that in-house basic research efforts have been reduced. Meanwhile, the support of industry to university research has kept up its momentum in most countries, with important differences between countries (it is particularly significant in Canada, Germany and the United States).

300. This is apparently consistent with a general trend of industry outsourcing its basic research investment while reducing inner capacities in the enterprises themselves. There are concerns about a tendency towards "short-termism" of research projects developed by industry which goes hand in hand with a reduction of the life cycles of products in a climate of increasingly fierce global competition [see, for the United States, the survey carried out by the *R&D Magazine*, 1997, and for Europe, the R&D survey of European Industrial Research Management Association (EIRMA), 1997].

Countries' approaches to resource allocations

301. When facing a pressing need to prioritise or cut their support to R&D, countries adopt different behavioural patterns. The first pattern, characteristic of countries such as Australia, Canada, the United Kingdom and the United States, has been to significantly sharpen the allocation resource process: reinforcing selectivity, drastically reducing support to non-priority areas (such as defence), conditioning government support to matching business and voluntary sector funding, and increasing *ex post* evaluation efforts to ensure best value for money.

302. This process has stimulated the dynamism of the research enterprise. On the whole, the science base in all the countries concerned continues to demonstrate remarkable productivity, as can be attested by bibliometric indicators. Science-industry exchanges have also intensified, as seen in the data on patents and inventive activity which appear to call more and more on public science. At the same time, there are also adverse consequences.

303. The most important policy trend in the United States so far has been the drastic reduction of large-scale programmes in defence, space or energy which began in the late 1980s. It seems that the cut back in large government contracts has had a severe impact on university research, the exploitation of its results in very advanced systems and the creation of high-tech firms by academics – creations which in the past played a decisive role in the innovative dynamism of this country (Mowery, 1992). In view of the importance of US science and innovation for the whole world, these trends, if further pursued, could be troublesome. Meanwhile, considerable changes have also been noted in the US academic community which has adopted a very dynamic attitude towards collaboration with industry, government agencies and other actors.

304. In Canada, budget cuts have been even more drastic, creating a very difficult situation for the universities. In the United Kingdom, the tightening of the ex ante resource allocation process based on sharper peer review and reinforcement of quantitative evaluation criteria (such as publication rates) seems to convey a serious risk of excessive concentration of research in too few establishments. New Zealand has strongly pushed the approach of contract-based funding of the science base in an overall strong adhesion to the principles of the market economy. A bold restructuring of its policy has been implemented since the early 1980s, completely separating the policy orientation function from the funding function. The results, although positive on the whole, appear mitigated to the extent that this policy has induced a certain "short-sightedness" in projects developed by the research community. In addition, important segments have preferred to expatriate in search of safer research conditions (*Nature*, 1996).

305. The second main behavioural pattern, observed in most countries of Continental Europe, has been characterised by the maintaining, until recently, of the overall support to the science base, but with the persistence of serious rigidities preventing significant reallocations between departments, disciplines, institutions, etc. Some governments have reacted against these tendencies. Germany has recently decided to introduce more competition and selectivity in allocating resource to the set of public laboratories operating in fundamental as well as in more applied or technical research. The Netherlands has also increased the relative importance of the secondary money flow (contract-based finance) in the university system and in the government laboratory network and, notably, the major body constituted by the TNO has been obliged to increase its self-financing. Scandinavian countries, which used to suffer from a fragmentation of their resource allocation processes and research structures, have proceeded to reform their science councils and funding agencies: *e.g.* Iceland with the creation of a single research council and an innovation fund resulting from the merging of two sectoral funds; and Norway with the creation of a single research council out of the five sectoral ones.

306. The most significant initiative comes from Finland. In the context of a difficult economic and budgetary situation, the overall government effort is planned to increase by 25 per cent over the period 1997-99. A large portion of these funds will be earmarked for technology programmes and basic research in universities on a competitive basis. Some reallocation of resources among sectors is also taking place through an efficient incentive mechanism stimulating the different departments to fund R&D by matching funds from a central R&D budget. This effort takes place under the interdepartmental co-ordination of the S&T Policy Council, chaired by the Prime Minister, and with a broad view of the NIS and its constitutive "clusters" (Ormala, 1998).

307. In Asia, there has been a clear commitment to supporting the science base. In Japan, despite the slowdown of economic growth and severe budget problems, support to R&D, and particularly to basic research programmes and structures, has remained a clear priority. Government expenditure is planned to increase at a significant growth rate (5 per cent and more per year) in the context of long-term "visions". Similarly, in Korea, a vigorous effort has been made (OECD, 1996*c*), enabled by the rapid expansion of the government research laboratories and a significant increase in the means of the science funding agency [Korea Science and Engineering Foundation – KOSEF]. However, it seems unlikely that the country will continue along these lines in view of its current serious financial and industrial problems.

308. Significant changes have taken place in the less developed OECD countries and regions, thanks to international support. The southern European countries and Ireland have benefited from the impulse provided by the European Union. In particular, the "Structural Funds" have financed 50 per cent of infrastructure costs and facilitated the integration of these countries in the European research community. Similarly, Mexico's science effort has benefited from World Bank support. However, it should be emphasized that, in certain countries, linkages with local industrial needs are not always ensured.

309. In the former socialist countries, science, although highly regarded and well funded, was traditionally developed in a planned economy and in the context of a hierachised and compartmentalised innovation system. The higher education structures pursued limited research activities (with a few exceptions, as in Poland), while fundamental and applied research was the responsibility of Academies and their networks of institutes and branch institutes were in charge of industrial and technical research. Following the crash of the communist regimes, and the related economic recession, resources for research have been considerably reduced, leading to an important brain drain (both inside and outside the economies). Reforms have been implemented with a view to developing university research, but in more than one country they have met with resistance from the established institutions (*e.g.* the Academies have refused to give up their monopoly on research). Moreover the serious damage caused to the S&T capabilities formerly developed in branch institutes has not been yet compensated by the development of research in the private sector.

6.4. The science-industry interface

310. Governments have a long-lasting involvement in trying to improve industry-university relationships (see for instance, OECD, 1982), but their action in this domain has recently been amplified and diversified. Several types of initiatives, particularly widespread among OECD countries as a result of a common understanding of problems or imitation effects, will be mentioned below: the establishment of centres of excellence, co-operative R&D centres and science parks; R&D programmes and incentives. The persistent problems experienced by countries with similar socio-cultural backgrounds will be briefly evoked at the end of the section.

Centres and parks

311. Centres of excellence are becoming more widespread in a number of countries, initiated by significant government funding. The sums provided for each centre are in the range of US$300 000 to US$700 000, generally given for a period of three to five years with some matching funds required from industry, while using academic premises and personnel. More and more frequently, these centres take a virtual form, as research units without walls, associating several teams located at a distance from each other. The centres are generally focused on interdisciplinary fields which respond to generic technology needs and also serve as loci for training doctorate and "post doc" researchers. In most countries, these centres seem to be favourably evaluated and, in a large majority, received renewed funding following the initial period. For governments, they apparently constitute an efficient instrument of strong, selective support.

312. Co-operative R&D centres are generally set up for research of a more applied or technical nature, matching funding from industry. These centres have been particularly promoted in Australia, Canada and the United States where they fill a gap which would appear to be less felt in other countries, for instance those influenced by the German culture where there is a long tradition of such co-operation (the model being the Fraunhofer system). Once again, the evaluations are generally quite positive (extensive exercises have been conducted in Australia and the United States), to the extent that the funding is adequate, the industrial involvement serious and the topic well-defined. The joint industrial and academic work developed in these centres contributes to the establishment of a fruitful and durable climate of exchange of ideas and personnel.

313. Finally the concept of science parks has been very attractive to a number of countries, inspired by famous US examples. Unfortunately, it would appear that some of these initiatives have not fulfilled initial expectations, as measured in terms of creation of enterprises, jobs, etc. In fact, success depends on a series of factors including the provision of appropriate infrastructures such as business incubators and services (consulting, venture finance) located near an advanced university complex, a dynamic industry and even an international airport (although this factor may lose its importance with the development of ICTs). In addition, there is a need for a special "chemistry" between all the actors involved, which is not necessarily found in all cultures. From this viewpoint, Finland provides a series of a successful examples that deserve to be emulated and give an idea of the size of such parks when reaching a cruise regime in function of the size of the background localities (approximately 1 000 jobs created per 100 000 inhabitants for the most dynamic parks).

Programmes and incentives

314. Joint R&D programmes are either more focused on certain types of technology or, on the contrary, less focused, where government support is designed to respond to joint university/industry proposals. There have been few evaluations of such programmes, but those available and published in the literature recognise that these programmes have had the effect of orienting non-negligible groups of researchers towards fields of importance for the future and for industrial competitiveness. However, the evaluations tend to be more circumspect about the capacity of these programmes to generate real breakthrough discoveries or inventions, or at least critically push back the frontiers of knowledge, where they are only of moderate size (say, less than US$200 000 per year over a five-year period). On a smaller scale, they constitute more of a complementary support for the academic communities involved who can extend their networks (notably when programmes have an international nature or origin), while enterprises see such schemes as opportunities to keep an eye on evolving scientific disciplines or technology areas.

315. Particularly efficient have been the European Union's schemes developed through the successive Framework Programmes, and which have over the years created more than 150 000 science/industry links throughout western European countries, primarily benefiting universities and to a lesser extent government laboratories. On the industry side, participants are mainly large firms, with smaller firms experiencing difficulties in dealing with the heavy procedures involved in such multi-country and multi-institution programmes.

316. Special incentives have been developed to stimulate the collaboration of industry with surrounding university and government research. For instance, generous tax relief has been provided within broader schemes to stimulate R&D effort in industry, as in Australia (150 per cent tax relief) with some positive effects, although at a non-negligible cost for the budget (Lattimore, 1997). Ultimately, the cost was deemed to be too high and the scheme was terminated. Some countries partially subsidised the costs of research contracts with universities or government laboratories or the employment of university researchers on a fixed-term basis. Evaluations of the programmes introduced in France, Germany and the Netherlands were generally positive, but such incentives are generally aimed at increasing the receptive capability of SMEs rather than boosting their true innovative potential.

317. Among schemes praised for their efficiency are those which have facilitated the placement of young academics in enterprises, with a specific project task and under the close supervision of university professors. The Teaching Company Scheme (TCS) in the United Kingdom has been particularly appreciated and serves as model for a number of countries. Similarly, some countries have successfully developed new forms of industrial PhDs based on the placement of graduates in industry (*e.g.* Denmark).

Persisting concerns

318. Despite the broad dissemination throughout the OECD area of the above-mentioned schemes, science-industry linkages continue to suffer from structural difficulties or mismatches as they relate to the inner structures of research systems or to the broader regulatory framework.

319. For instance, a certain number of continental European countries have an excessively developed public research sector where scientific production does not fully meet the innovative needs of industry (OECD, 1997*j*). Measures taken to increase the interactions between the two sectors through the development of R&D contracts originating from the business sector are insufficient or have yet to produce the expected results. Several countries which used to have exemplary university/industry relationships, such as Switzerland and to a certain extent Germany, have experienced serious difficulties in coping with new technologies and need to re-invigorate these relationships.

320. Another major problem faced by science systems in continental Europe is the poor record of firm creations by scientists or innovators, notably in high-technology sectors. This stems from a number of factors, including the absence of a dynamic venture capital market, inadequate regulations concerning pension schemes and obstacles preventing academics from entering into business and returning to academia.

321. Some countries have attempted to financially support the creation of firms by scientists from university or government laboratories. Available evaluations (*e.g.* Austria) show that some positive results can be obtained at a reasonable cost. After several years, the firms created have had a modest innovative record, operating generally as providers of technology services, consulting or software. The French experience has shown that the establishment of quasi-public enterprises attached to large

government research structures presents obvious limits as a mechanism for spin-offs and technology commercialisation.

322. The Asian countries continue to suffer from a serious gap between university research and industry. In Japan, despite the progress made in the scientific effort, the lack of basic research funds in university has not facilitated the development of a large-scale advanced research sector attractive to industry (notably in high technology). Moreover, strict regulations on remuneration, transferability of pension schemes, etc., have hindered collaboration between academics and industry. Recent changes should improve the situation, but it will take years for practices and mentalities to adapt. Korea is experiencing the same problems and needs to modernise its institutional framework for university-industry collaboration.

323. Finally it is worthwhile mentioning a general problem throughout the OECD area regarding the status of researchers and their modes of evaluation. Generally, greatest attention is paid to peer assessments on the basis of pure scientific criteria as well as to publication records (preferably in mainstream journals and related citations). These criteria are obviously not very appropriate when considering more direct contributions to innovation, either through patenting, collaborations with industry, technology transfer, or even training of scientists and engineers to be further employed in industry. In most countries, there is an increasing awareness of the need to adjust evaluation and promotion procedures. However, progress is slow and none of the evaluation systems currently in place give precedence to innovation-related work (OECD, 1997*l*).

6.5. Structural issues

324. Having examined financial resource trends and measures concerning the industry-university interface, it is worthwhile to briefly discuss a few fundamental issues which derive from broad trends and problems that are characteristic of the end of this century: the orientation of the research effort, the internationalisation process and human resource aspects.

Orientation of research

325. Confronted with the need to cope with budget reductions, governments are facing serious problems in identifying priority research areas. In France, the United Kingdom and the United States, the "downsizing" of the defence objective has somewhat alleviated budget problems, but there is a need to identify new targets for support. As for other countries, the boosting of techno-industrial competitiveness is the major objective, requiring finely tuned programming through appropriate interaction with the business sector in selecting R&D projects. Under these circumstances, governments are forced to support fundamental research underlying notably generic technology developments, as well as to limit their support to pre-competitive R&D.

326. The structuring of technical change is complicated by the massive reduction of large-scale defence, space and energy programmes, and by the reluctance of governments to embark on significant programmes related to infrastructures in transport or telecommunications, with the exception of information highways (to a certain extent because related infrastructures are largely financed by the private sector). The only sector related to social needs that receives a significant level of support is health and medicine. Government support is playing an important role in the acceleration of innovation flows observed in this area in a number of countries.

327. The political and institutional framework proper to each country strongly influences the conditions in which priorities are formulated and translated into budget allocations. For instance the highly pluralistic

US political system allows a relatively good integration of national priorities in the R&D budget, but continuity and stability of the scientific effort are affected by the peculiar nature of the US government's budget process (*i.e.* it is difficult or even impossible to guarantee funding for more than one year at a time and virtually all government support for research comes from project-level grants).

328. Regarding the orientation of research efforts, the balance between institutional and contract-based resources is of primary importance. Within the latter, the balance between mission-oriented funding and non-oriented funding responding to research proposals is generally set on the basis of a competitive peer-review process. The institutional and non-mission-oriented part of university and public sector research involves between 50 and 70 per cent of total funding, with one-fifth to one-sixth of this sum being allocated through competitive and peer-review mechanisms. Although the variations across countries seem moderate, they may lead to significant differences in financing structures of research systems. In addition, scientists are not submitted to the same systems of incentives, with important consequences for the orientation, including the time horizon, of research efforts.

329. The choices of priorities among scientific disciplines are further complicated by the observed tendency towards saturation. Seriously declining returns on investment in many areas – dramatically illustrated by examples such as particle physics – have led a number of observers to point to the "end of science" (Horgan, 1996). The stimulation of interdisciplinary sciences today seems to be the best approach to "de-locking" or removing current saturations. At the same time, it should be noted that the development of computers has contributed to reduced research costs, notably with the use of computer simulation instead of "real world" experience. Similarly, current developments in information and telecommunication technologies and opportunities for joint use of large-scale instruments, as well as access to databases, digital libraries, etc., are altering research conditions. A number of parameters with conflicting effects need to be taken into consideration when planning investments in the scientific enterprise.

330. To help identify important fields in the medium and long term, a number of governments (*e.g.* France, Germany, Japan, the Netherlands, the United Kingdom) have developed foresight exercises focusing on technology as well as on science trends in relation to foreseeable economic and social needs (see OECD, 1995*a*, for a comparative overview). These foresight exercises involve, to a variable extent the science communities, and are more or less formalised in their methods (systematic questionnaires, etc.). They provide the communities involved (scientists, industrialists, etc.) with a better, commonly established, picture of future trends. Converging on broad areas for future research efforts, such exercises are confronted with the issue of feedback into the policy-making process and the further definition of priorities in budgets, programmes, etc.

331. The social sciences encounter specific difficulties in responding to the challenges with which modern societies are confronted (*e.g.* excessive urbanisation, societal disintegration). This derives from their status (which for a number of science policy makers is significantly lower than hard sciences), their structure and the lack of feedback into the policy-making processes in areas where they could usefully play a role. The problems encountered by human and social sciences have now become serious, giving rise to more or less bold proposals for change and restructuring (see, for instance, the report of the Gulbenkian Foundation, 1995). Nevertheless, change will not be easily implemented due to structural rigidities, prevalent ideologies, etc.

332. S&T developments have always raised important societal and ethical issues. However, the acceleration of S&T progress in the last few decades has created new challenges requiring a redefinition of the interactions between science and society. On one hand, the science communities are increasingly requested to provide an "objective expertise" – if not an immediate solution – to some of the dramatic problems appearing in modern societies (*e.g.* mad cow disease, the re-emergence of infectious diseases, the

effects of global climate change). On the other, representatives of societies or social groups are called upon to decide on ethical issues that result from the scientific enterprise itself (*e.g.* human cloning).

333. None of these situations are easy to deal with. When science is called upon to urgently provide a viewpoint, advice or solution, it is generally because a state of ignorance exists as a result of years of underinvestment in the scientific fields concerned. Warnings by the scientific communities are sometimes deliberately neglected by political bodies. The regulation of ethical problems associated with breakthroughs in research, notably in the medical field, are generally dealt with by permanent committees or ad hoc commissions once the issues arise. Once again, the earlier interactions are established between scientists, politicians and representatives of various social groups, the better equipped societies will be to deal with such issues.

Internationalisation and globalisation

334. The internationalisation of science is a long-lasting trend which has accelerated over the last ten years or so, as witnessed by bibliometric data (Okubo, 1996) that clearly show a strong rise in the number of joint publications between scientists from two or more countries in mainstream journals (Chapter 2). At the same time, there is also a process of "continentalisation" of science, once again shown by bibliometrics (Leclerc and Gagné, 1994), with a tendency towards increased collaboration within large regions (Europe, North America,[37] Asia). This results, in part, from government initiatives in relation to broader trends towards economical and political integration within broad world regions. The development of IT is likely to further stimulate the process of globalisation of science, although in ways that are not yet clear and that will differ across disciplines.

335. In parallel, as discussed in Chapter 3, we are witnessing a considerable acceleration of the globalisation of industrial research. Large (and small, dynamic) multinational firms tend to optimise at the world level the localisation of their laboratories. Traditionally, countries' innovative and technological developments drew extensively on national research inputs. This still tends to be the case, but it is likely that the globalisation of business industrial R&D will gradually modify this pattern.

336. To date, a number of governments have taken restrictive measures regarding the participation of foreign firms in their advanced centres and programmes. When they do authorise foreign enterprise participation, they apply discriminatory rules for the exploitation of patents and the further commercialisation of research results. Ongoing discussions on appropriate frameworks for international technology co-operation, as well as agreements related to the Agreement on Trade-related Aspects of Intellectual Property Rights (TRIPS), should help to get things moving in this area.

337. Good management of internationalisation trends is particularly crucial for the smaller economies. Iceland illustrates the point (OECD, 1993*a*). As it was not able to afford a full-scale university undergraduate programme until the 1970s, and only very recently set up a modest graduate programme, Iceland has traditionally sent university students abroad, thus securing access to world sources of knowledge. The fact that graduates show strong willingness to return when given the opportunity, and their visible contribution to the country's economic progress, indicates that this policy has worked well. It will be maintained even with the advent of a limited domestic graduate programme. Since the 1960s, Iceland has followed a policy of attracting foreign firms into its power-intensive

37. Throughout this publication, the terms *North America* and *North American countries* refer to the following: Canada, Mexico and the United States.

industrial sector, presently undergoing rapid growth. In the late 1980s and early 1990s, the domestic fishery industries started a major internationalisation programme with substantial investments in fisheries world-wide. In the 1990s the liberalisation of financial markets and emerging payoffs in knowledge-based innovations have begun to attract foreign risk capital (as exemplified by investments in gene-hunting venture firms which are already among the largest in this emerging field).

338. An important issue since the late 1980s has been the opening of the former socialist countries. This has had a considerable impact on the science communities of the OECD countries. Opportunities for new forms of collaboration giving entries into world class scientific competencies or structures (notably in Russia) now exist, but the other side of the coin is the migration of thousands of world-class scientists towards western laboratories and universities. The development of the Asian systems (especially in China) raises another type of challenge by reducing the migration process (in particular towards the United States), while creating new poles for international collaboration, so far mainly exploited by Japan and the United States. The European countries appear to be far more timid from this viewpoint.

339. Finally, international co-operation in science, megascience projects and programmes should be mentioned. In many fields, experimental research is becoming concentrated at a small number of "mega facilities". In addition to fields where this has traditionally been the case (*e.g.* high-energy physics, space-based astronomy), large facilities are assuming ever greater importance in condensed matter research and in the life sciences. In addition, some distributed research programmes (which consist of a large number of co-ordinated small and medium-sized efforts) are characterised by the same aggregate funding levels as those that are typical of large facility-based projects (*e.g.* research on genomes or climate change). The joint planning and implementation of large projects is complicated by the fact that most national and regional priority-setting and planning exercises are not co-ordinated on a global level, making it difficult to pull together the necessary financial and organisational resources. The OECD's Megascience Forum provides a venue, albeit on an experimental, non-permanent basis, where senior science policy officials can exchange information about priorities and plans, and begin early discussions on specific co-operative projects.

340. Despite the recognised need for collaborative efforts for solving dramatic common issues such as those related to climatic change, the implementation of significant initiatives in this area has met with considerable obstacles and delays. The absence of links between S&T and the conduct of foreign affairs, notably in larger geopolitical powers (see, for the United States, a recent critical viewpoint in *Science* by Watkins, 1997), would appear to be a major cause of the problems and inertia encountered. In addition, there are some world-scale issues that cannot be solved in the absence of the world-scale technological programmes that are being called for in some fora, as a means to boost growth and employment in large parts of the industrial world (Gaudin, 1997). The international frameworks for designing, implementing and structuring such S&T initiatives on the world scale do not yet exist.

Human resources

341. In a number of countries, mismatches exist between supply and demand for highly trained scientific personnel. This is due to the rapid development of certain disciplines requiring new qualifications not adequately provided by higher education systems. Reforms are therefore necessary in programme courses and studies. Some countries have taken important initiatives in this domain by creating centres of excellence (*e.g.* Australia, Canada, Sweden, the United Kingdom), research schools (the Netherlands) and innovative training programmes adapted to industry and career needs (Finland). In certain countries, the inadequacy of graduate and post graduate studies is dramatically illustrated by the number of PhDs who cannot find jobs and remain durably unemployed.

342. In this context, it is useful to mention the poor conditions and precarious employment experienced by young scientists in universities and government laboratories. As a result, large contingents of high-level researchers are "floating" in search of temporary positions in laboratories. This situation is not conducive to productive long-term research, which requires a climate of stability. In most OECD countries, the narrowness, if not absence, in the business sector (with the exception of North America), of a labour market for advanced scientists does nothing to facilitate their integration into the economy.

343. A grave problem affecting a number of countries is the ageing of the scientific workforce. Large contingents of scientists recruited some three decades ago are now approaching retirement age. In France, more than half of the science workforce will have to be replaced within the next ten years. Similar trends are noticeable in a number of European countries such as Belgium, the Netherlands and Sweden. In Canada and the United States, the traditional inflow of foreign students (mostly from Asia) has fallen significantly. Measures are being taken to smooth the retirement process and facilitate the recruitment of young people.

344. The problem is complicated by the fact that the young generation is showing a certain disinterest in science (OECD, 1997*m*). This is not generalised across all countries and does not concern all disciplines. While traditional fields such as physics or chemistry suffer from a noticeable lack of interest, there is an increasing interest in disciplines such as computer sciences. Action has been taken in some countries affected by the trend (*e.g.* Japan and the Nordic countries), from primary schools to universities. Surveys carried out in a number of countries indicate the need to implement significant changes in the curricula, selection and teaching processes at secondary school level to avoid discouraging those students who are not the brightest in maths and other abstract subjects and who tend to give up science studies. It is also important to make scientific careers attractive either through the incomes offered to researchers or the prestige associated with scientific research.

345. The issue of scientific creativity is of particular concern to Japan in its attempt to promote its science base to a world-class level. Having successfully provided its industries with high-quality human resources, especially in the field of engineering, the country now plans to develop a creative science labour force on a large scale. Teaching and learning conditions in universities, and in secondary and primary schools (which tend to stress memorisation and repetition rather than free thinking), seem to be the most important obstacles to the development of such creativity, and plans have been announced to remedy this situation (OECD, 1997*m*). It is also necessary to better balance research and teaching obligations in laboratories to enhance the relationships between professors and the researchers working under them. Increased funding for individual projects has been announced in support of this goal. A similar situation exists in Korea.

6.6. Main lessons

Ongoing changes and reform processes

346. The science enterprise seems to be at a turning point. Its funding, notably from governments, is becoming increasingly problematic. The targeting of research efforts has become more complex, while the support of national techno-industrial competitiveness constitutes the most important objective. Research for defence, space or energy projects has lost its priority status – especially in those countries which used to be pace-setters in the global R&D effort. Problems are being encountered with human resources: either with qualification mismatches or with shortages in the long term. The globalisation process makes the management of science systems more hazardous and difficult to monitor for national

governments, while world-scale problems such as climate change await solutions. Crucial ethical issues are emerging in relation to S&T developments.

347. In most countries, the question of structural reform is a difficult one. Governments are generally caught in one of two situations. Some are confronted with strong inertia or opposition to change by lobbies with contradictory or converging interests. Others go for easy solutions, such as cutting budgets and reducing support for long-term research efforts. In both cases, this raises problems which will, in the medium and long term, undermine the science base and the potential for innovation. There is no simple recipe for organising and implementing structural reform. Successful reforms generally require a crisis situation, facilitating drastic changes, a consensus-building process to prepare people for changes, strong leadership to conduct the changes and a very careful design of the new procedures, incentives or rules of the game.

348. The process of change is, in general, a gradual, adaptative one. Governments begin by tackling a first series of issues through selected financial and regulatory measures acceptable to the communities and political constituencies concerned. Then, after some years of application and in view of the results obtained, some corrective or additional actions are taken to complement or adjust the effects obtained by the first batch of measures. A second set of problems is identified, and adequate measures implemented. This continuous cycle normally requires a decade or so before significant results are visible.

349. The Netherlands illustrates such an evolution. A first series of actions was taken in the early 1990s to stimulate the basic components of the science base. Universities were pressed to finance a larger part of their research effort through competitive project funding from government agencies. Industry was encouraged to concentrate research teams in "research schools" and undertake evaluations of research structures, while government laboratories were pressed to self-finance more R&D. A foresight exercise was undertaken. Complementary measures are now being taken to "fine tune" the research school mechanism which was not sufficiently selective, money flow for universities will be further increased and decisions from foresight results will influence national R&D priorities. Meanwhile, new problems are emerging (in relation to the structural issues mentioned in Section 6.4 above): the orientation of research in the face of new societal demands characterised by strong participation of social groups; the internationalisation process for a country which has traditionally been very much involved in the global as well as the European economies and feels the need for further deepening this involvement (notably for cost-sharing and critical-mass concerns); and, finally, the human resource issue in view of the disinterest of youth for S&T studies and a too-narrow S&T curricula, both of which affect the competence and mobility of the scientific and technical labour force. A new batch of measures is envisaged, concretising a significant step forward, if not a quantum leap, for the policy-making process.

350. All countries are faced with similar tasks: applying general principles observed elsewhere, and carefully adapting these general principles to the national context through a thorough understanding of its specificities (paying particular attention to correcting identified weaknesses). These two points are developed in Table 6.1 and Table 6.2, showing selected country experiences.

Table 6.1. **Management of the science base: general principles and best practices**

Policy areas	General policy principles	Cases of best policy practices
	General organisation	
Science-policy and government structures	Incorporate science policy into central government decision-making and overall economic development strategy by appropriate mechanisms.	Finland with the Science and Technology Policy Council, Japan with the S&T Policy Council and the long-term plans, Canada with the co-ordinating role played by Industry Canada (Federal S&T and Industry Ministry).
Structure of the R&D effort (performing organisations)	Establish and maintain an appropriate structure in the R&D effort, with an adequate balance between industry, government and university.	Germany, the Netherlands, Switzerland, the United Kingdom, the United States.
	Funding of the science base	
Overall funding	Maintain or increase overall government support to university and public research with a long-term view.	Denmark, Finland, Iceland, Japan.
Funding of university research	Maintain and establish an adequate ratio between sure and precarious resources for university research at the overall level (around 70/30 per cent); at the institution level, maintain a minimum percentage of 50/50 between core and contract-based funding (on average).	Policies pursued at the national level by the Netherlands and Finland; at the institution level, see examples provided by well-performing universities in a number of countries, including Germany, Switzerland, the United Kingdom, the United States.
Funding of government laboratories	Maintain a minimal level of government research of collective interest and establish funding mechanisms accordingly.	Countries maintaining a strong network of government laboratories performing strategic research of industrial interest include Finland, Japan, Korea, Norway; core funding provided by government can exceed 50 per cent of laboratories' budget.
Management of funding schemes	Separate criteria for funding of basic research (excellence) and applied/technical research (relevance).	Most countries now follow such principles.
Financing of basic research in industry	Maintain a minimal level of effort by appropriate subsidies and tax incentives for in-house research.	To date, none of the OECD countries seem to have come up with incentives to prevent the drying up of in-house basic research in industry.
	Science/industry interfaces	
General framework	A climate favourable to academic/industry collaboration is characterised by: the absence of regulatory obstacles (regarding financial earnings, pension schemes, etc.); flexibility regarding teaching obligations; and autonomy in the development of new faculty structures (interdisciplinary).	Australia, Canada, Ireland, the United Kingdom and the United States present favourable climates with few obstacles. Climates favourable to institutional experiments can be found in the Nordic countries. Switzerland and Germany used to present excellent interactions in specific sectors, but these need to be reinvigorated.
Ad hoc centres	Centres of excellence (for basic research) and co-operative R&D centres (for more applied research), if properly funded and focused, have both proved to be efficient mechanisms for joint research work.	UK and Canadian schemes for centres of excellence, and Australian and US schemes for co-operative R&D. See also examples provided by Finland, Japan, Korea and Sweden.
Research programmes	If well-designed and generously funded (notably at the level of individual projects), such programmes can have a critical impact on S&T field concerned; if moderately funded, they can be instrumental in developing science/industry networks.	Significant programmes of the first type can be found in the United Kingdom (*e.g.* LINK) and in Japan (on specific technologies). There are many examples of the second type of programmes (see the European Union for complex, multi-country schemes).
Placement of scientists in industry	Placements can be promoted on an ad hoc basis with specific linkages with a given institution or professor, or through more general incentives.	The UK TCS and the Canadian Industrial Research Fellowship for the first type of programmes; and the French, Dutch and German incentives (paying part of the cost of employment of researchers by SMEs) for the second type of programme.

Source: OECD Secretariat.

Table 6.2. **Country experiences and issues**

	Strong points/good practices	Policy issues/structural weaknesses
Denmark	• Strong increase of R&D effort sustained over a long-term period • Very productive science base (as measured by number of publications per researcher) • Good network for R&D and technology diffusion in small industries	• Excessive spreading of resources due to an egalitarian approach • Lack of core money/institutional funding for university research • Insufficient institutional funding in government technological institutes
France	• Efficient science/technology/industry interactions in large-scale focused programmes (nuclear energy, aeronautics, space, transport) • Good theoretical research	• Excessive weight of public research structures and publicly supported research • Need for important renewal of the research workforce in the next decade and probable shortages to come • Insufficient university/industry interactions due notably to very limited mobility of scientists
Germany	• Well-organised R&D structures with good balance between the different components • Strong implication of regional governments in R&D funding and orientation • Good infrastructures and networks for diffusion of technical and tacit knowledge	• Difficulties with new technologies: need for multiple-target action including renewal of university/industry interactions, new incentives for industrial research, etc. • Some inertia in government laboratories (stimulated recently by increased competitive funding) • Lack of resources for university research (due to budgetary problems, notably limiting institutional funding absorbed by educational obligations)
Hungary	• Stabilisation of the decline of the R&D effort after sharp reduction in the post-communist period • Good academic research	• Slow development of university research (although now benefiting from increased resources) • Very poor development of research in industry and limited industry/university collaboration
Japan	• Good co-ordination at the government level in defining and budgeting the government R&D effort • Strong industrial research and well-developed government laboratories oriented towards industrial needs • Highly qualified personnel provided by universities	• University research still underfunded, despite significant recent efforts; regulatory obstacles to co operation with industry are being removed • Concerns about creativity of human resources (due to conditions of education and research climate) and potential shortages due to lack of interest of youth in S&T studies and careers
Mexico	• Good research infrastructures developed with international funding • Relatively well co-ordinated S&T policy by a central agency	• Excessive academic orientation of the research effort (due to researcher promotion system) • Good, but insufficient, contribution of government laboratories (due to personnel status and salaries)
Netherlands	• Relatively efficient research system (as measured by the ratio of outputs to expenses) • Government policy for increasing "second money flow" in university and facilitating concentration (in research schools)	• Problem with government sectoral research laboratories (lack of resources) • Need to adapt research system to mounting societal concerns in a consensus-based society • Human resources in S&T insufficiently developed; education system not sufficiently broad
United States	• Good balance between the different components of the overall R&D system • Excellent climate for university research and co-operation with industry • Well-spread development of university/industry co-operation schemes stimulated by government	• Good process for establishing R&D priorities reflecting national needs, but lack of continuity and consequently instability in support for research infrastructures; inadequate co-ordination among agencies, leading to risk of costly redundancy • Reduction of large-scale programmes (in defence, space, etc.) which used to be a major source of innovations • Reduction of in-house basic research effort in industry

Source: OECD Secretariat.

Applying general policy principles

351. The positioning of science and research policy in the overall government structure needs to be seriously reconsidered in most OECD countries in order to better integrate them into the overall government strategy, to facilitate interactions with other policies and to help maintain the overall science budget. The concern for integration is part of a general concern of innovation policy, and little progress seems to have been made in most countries. Budget co-ordination and the relationship with long-term government strategies require appropriate institutional mechanisms, which have been put in place in certain countries (*e.g.* Finland and Japan).

352. As regards the funding of the core of the science base (*i.e.* publicly supported research in the university sector), the maintenance of overall support is recommended. In most countries, a zero growth situation has been reached following a gradual decline since the early 1990s and there is a risk of deterioration of the science base if current trends continue. The ratio of precarious *vis-à-vis* sure resources (mostly provided by the institutional funding of universities) needs to be maintained at a reasonable level. Nevertheless, important differences exist among universities and faculties, depending on the disciplines in which they specialise; therefore, the ratio should be determined with appropriate flexibility.

353. In a number of countries, government laboratories continue to be a source of key efforts in basic research of technological interest. It is important that these laboratories continue to be appropriately funded by mechanisms that ensure an adequate diffusion – not only for the enterprises that collaborate directly with them, but also for the broader industries they may concern. Adequate financial mechanisms need to be (re)established for supporting research of collective interest.

354. Basic research efforts in industry are limited and even declining in a number of countries. To the extent that this trend continues, the receptiveness of the enterprise sector to scientific advance as well as the quality of its interactions with the science base will be seriously altered. Mechanisms need to be found by governments to stimulate the maintaining or (re)constitution of in-house basic research capabilities in industry.

355. Due to the cumulative nature of scientific knowledge creation, the institutional framework in which the science actors, and notably universities, operate has a tendency to grow rigid and resistant to change. A key challenge for policy makers is to design and implement mechanisms that allow stability to be coupled with enhanced flexibility and adaptability. In a number of countries universities should be given more autonomy, along with the adaptation of framework conditions, to more effectively initiate new forms of research, particularly of an interdisciplinary nature. As part of this agenda, policy should facilitate contacts with industry and encourage collaborative work based on a large amount of tacit and uncodified knowledge. Evaluation of disciplines, institutes and individuals needs to be adapted to go beyond simple criteria of scientific excellence to become properly integrated with all contributions to industrial, economic and social development. Co-operation with industry can be facilitated through regulatory reform. University and public researchers should be encouraged to move to industry, including through creating their own firms – an essential vector for innovation, especially in high-technology sectors.

356. Thus, there is scope for improvement in the relationship between science and society. At a time when societies are seriously re-considering their priorities, for instance pushing health and environment protection, preferences need to be formulated and channelled to decision makers in a way that allows for timely research efforts. Public participation in the formulation of research strategies is an important element of well-designed and stable science policies. Major breakthroughs in medicine and genetic engineering raise fundamental ethical issues that must be appropriately dealt with.

357. As regards human resources, a qualified scientific and engineering workforce is a primary condition for a dynamic and innovative climate. Education systems should be organised in such a way as to ensure adequate quantitative and qualitative flows of qualified scientists and engineers by timely actions, including at the primary and secondary school levels which play a decisive role in the future orientation of youth. This implies reforms of curricula and selection processes and well-targeted actions stimulating awareness in schools and through the media, museums, etc.

358. Finally, it is crucial that governments are better organised to face the internationalisation and globalisation trends that affect more or less directly the science enterprise. Three issues deserve particular attention: *(i)* the impacts of ICT on the organisation of the global research effort; *(ii)* the monitoring of potentially unfair exploitation of research efforts by other countries (especially when associated with free-riding behaviour); and *(iii)* the organisation of an international co-operative framework for large-scale projects of global significance such as climate change and sustainable development. Achieving these objectives requires a strategic repositioning of science policy by governments.

Reducing country-specific weaknesses

359. To be efficient, policies need to be based on a thorough analysis of each national context. Some key problems that need to be addressed in relation to the main socio-cultures in the OECD area can be identified. In general, the United Kingdom, the United States and other countries influenced by their science model, have shown flexibility and adaptation regarding the tightening and reallocating of government R&D budgets. However, excessive concentration of research efforts, as well as excessive conditioning of government support on performance-based criteria and/or matching funds from industry, leads to serious risks of durable alteration of the science base.

360. Continental European countries have so far been able to preserve their scientific base from major disturbances and budget cuts. Nevertheless, most countries will have to reorient and reallocate funding by increasing the amount of competitive funding. Moreover, measures should be taken to make more flexible and more supportive the institutional and regulatory frameworks in which universities reorganise their structures, scientists develop their initiatives including own enterprises, etc.

361. There are important variations in Western Europe. Countries influenced by the Latin culture with a large public research sector need to reduce mismatches with regard to industrial research and innovation expectations. Countries influenced by the German culture encounter difficulties in new technologies and need to adapt their university/industry interfaces. The Scandinavian countries,[38] committed to a consensus-based decision-making process, suffer from fragmentation and a certain conservatism in the resource allocation process. In the less advanced countries of Southern Europe (and in Mexico), a comprehensive effort is required to develop the research capability of industry and reduce the inward orientation of the academic community.

362. The eastern European countries in transition should make substantial efforts to re-invest progressively in their science bases. After the considerable reductions imposed by the recession and the transition process, there is an urgent need to pursue reforms to foster a functioning university research sector and build research capacity at the enterprise level.

38. Throughout this publication, the term *Scandinavian countries* refers to the following: Denmark, Iceland, Norway and Sweden.

363. Finally, while continuing the expansion of their science bases, the Asian countries need to further enlarge their investment in university research, increase project funding for university research teams, pursue measures for deregulating and removing obstacles to co-operative work with industry and further develop the internationalisation of their research systems by all means, including the attraction of foreign researchers and students. An effort is also necessary to stimulate the creativity of their scientific workforce, beginning in the primary and secondary school systems.

CHAPTER 7. FINANCIAL SUPPORT TO INDUSTRIAL R&D EFFORTS

7.1. Introduction

364. Financial incentives to industrial R&D performed by business firms are channelled through a myriad of support schemes. These can be grouped into two broad categories: indirect support in the form of tax incentives, which are generally the preferred support instrument where the objective is to reach all R&D-performing firms; and direct support, mainly grants, where governments wish to be more selective with respect to the type of R&D project or the technological area.

7.2. Tax incentives to industrial R&D

R&D tax treatment as a technology and innovation policy instrument

365. The innovation strategy of firms is influenced by the tax treatment of innovation-related investment – especially R&D. From a tax-policy perspective, R&D is only a mix of current expenditure (mainly wage costs which can be deducted from taxable income in the year they are incurred) and investment in equipment and machinery which must be depreciated. Over the last ten years in most OECD countries, tax reform has emphasized two main objectives: *(i)* simplicity, notably by reducing the number of tax exemptions; and *(ii)* greater neutrality regarding the impact on relative prices of production factors and costs of alternative business investment strategies. The fact that a number of countries have maintained, or even recently introduced in one case, exemptions in favour of R&D may appear paradoxical. An explanation is that tax incentives present unique advantages as a tool for stimulating R&D compared to other instruments of technology and innovation policy.

366. Tax concession is the more "market-friendly" form of government spending (as foregone revenues) to promote technological development and innovation. Private sector decision makers retain autonomy in deciding how to react to the diminution of the (after-tax) cost of R&D brought about by a tax incentive. The reliance on a pure price mechanism to stimulate private R&D, with no direct government involvement in the selection of "subsidised" projects, is specific to tax incentives. However, the drawback is that firms may find that a modest decrease in the cost of R&D does not justify undertaking more R&D, or may undertake additional R&D with satisfactory private return but low social return (*i.e.* few net social benefits). In addition, even if tax concessions entail generally lower administrative costs (for both government and recipient firms) than direct subsidisation programmes, like any form of government intervention involving public expenditure they have hidden costs since the lost revenues must be financed through additional taxation which may have distortionary impacts (Lattimore, 1997). Their effectiveness must therefore be carefully analysed on the basis of the collective experience of Member countries.

367. This section reviews the R&D tax schemes currently implemented in OECD countries, evaluates their effectiveness, identifies good practices in scheme design and formulates recommendations on how best to use R&D tax treatment as an instrument of technology and innovation policy.

R&D tax treatment in OECD countries

368. Governments can use one or a combination of the following tax measures to reduce the after-tax cost of business R&D:

- More rapid depreciation of investment in machinery, equipment, and even in some cases buildings, used for R&D activities.

- Full deductibility of current R&D expenditure from taxable income, which is a favourable tax treatment since such expenditure is in fact an investment yielding revenues over several years.

- Extra allowance which enables firms to deduct more than 100 per cent of their R&D expenditure from taxable income.

- Tax credit which allows firms to deduct a percentage of their R&D expenditure from their tax liabilities. Eligible R&D expenditure can be either the total amount of R&D performed (volume-based tax credit, also named flat rate tax credit) or the increase in R&D outlays over their amount in a preceding reference period (incremental tax credit).

Current practices

369. Tax treatment of R&D is reported for 25 OECD countries in Table 7.1. In all countries the tax system allows the accelerated depreciation of equipment used for R&D. All but one country, New Zealand, allow current business expenditure on R&D to be fully deducted in the year incurred, and seven extend this favourable tax treatment to non-current R&D expenditure. Ten Member countries provide additional tax incentives to R&D:

- Australia and Austria offer extra R&D depreciation allowances amounting respectively to 125 per cent (150 per cent until 1996) and 118 per cent of current R&D outlays.

- Eight countries provide R&D tax credits. Volume-based tax credits are found in Canada, Italy and the Netherlands (for SMEs); France and the United States offer incremental tax credits; Japan, Korea and Spain use both.

Tax incentive mechanisms differ further in their detailed features, with regard to:

- The eventual existence of a two-tier system involving both central (federal) and regional (provincial) tax incentives, as in Canada and the United States.

- The definition of eligible R&D expenditure. Most often both current expenditure and tangible investment costs are eligible but in Austria and the United States only current costs are eligible. In the Netherlands and the Province of Quebec, the tax credit is based on R&D-related labour compensation.

Table 7.1. **R&D tax treatment in OECD countries, 1996**

	Current expenditure	R&D depreciation rates & schemes		Tax credit		Other features		CITR[1]	B-index
		Machinery and equipment	Buildings	Level	Incre-mental	Special allowances	Credit taxable	1981-96	1981-96
	(per cent)	(number of years are approximate for a full depreciation)		(per cent)				(per cent)	
Australia	150[2]	3 years, straight-line	40 years, straight-line	. .	. .			46 - 36	1.01 - 0.76
Austria	118	5 years, straight-line[3]	25 years, straight-line[3]			12 per cent, machinery & equipment, bldg	No	62 - 34	0.93 - 0.93
Belgium									
SMEs	100	3 years, straight-line	20 years, straight-line[3]	. .	. .	18.5 per cent, machinery & equipment		48 - 40	1.01 - 1.01
Large firms						13.5 per cent, machinery & equipment		. . . .	1.01 - 1.01
Canada									
SMEs	100	100 per cent	4 years, declining balance[3]	35	. .		Yes	26 - 23	0.87 - 0.68
Large firms				20	. .			42 - 32	0.84 - 0.83
Denmark	100	100 per cent	100 per cent	. .	. .	25 per cent, current expenditure, machinery & equipment, bldg		40 - 34	1.00 - 0.87
Finland	100	30 per cent, declining balance[3]	20 per cent, declining balance[3]	. .	. .			49 - 28	1.02 - 1.01
France	100	5 years, straight-line or 40 per cent, declining balance	20 years, straight-line[3]	. .	50		No	50 - 33	1.02 - 0.92
Germany	100	30 per cent, declining balance[3]	25 years, straight-line[3]	. .	. .			63 - 57	1.04 - 1.05
Greece	100	100 per cent	12.5 years, straight-line[3]	. .	. .			n.a. - 35	n.a. - 1.01
Iceland	100	8 years, straight-line[3]	50 years, straight-line[3]	. .	. .			n.a. - 33	n.a. - 1.03
Ireland	100	100 per cent	100 per cent	. .	. .			10 - 10	1.00 - 1.00
Italy									
SMEs	100	10 years, straight-line	33 years, straight-line[3]	30	. .			36 - 53	1.03 - 0.41
Large firms				. .	. .			. . . .	1.03 - 1.05

	Current expenditure	R&D depreciation rates & schemes		Tax credit		Other features		CITR[1]	B-index
		Machinery and equipment	Buildings	Level	Incre-mental	Special allowances	Credit taxable	1981-96	1981-96
	(per cent)	(number of years are approximate for a full depreciation)		(per cent)				(per cent)	
Japan									
SMEs	100	Choice between 7 to 65 years, straight-line[3]	Choice between 3 to 25 years, straight-line[3]	6	. .	5 per cent for high-tech machinery & equipment	No	38 - 38	0.94 - 0.94
Large firms		or 1.6 to 14.2%, declining balance[3]	or 8.8 to 53.6% per cent, declining balance[3]	. .	20			55 - 51	1.02 - 1.02
Korea									
SMEs	100	22.6 per cent, declining balance[3]	5.6 per cent, declining balance[3]	10	25		No	38 - 30	1.03 - 0.83
Large firms				5	25				1.03 - 0.90
Mexico	100	3 years, straight-line	20 years, straight-line[3]	. .	. .			42 - 34	0.99 - 1.02
Netherlands									
SMEs	100	5 years, straight-line	25 years, straight-line	40	. .	18 per cent, machinery & equipment, bldg	No	48 - 37	1.01 - 0.89
Large firms				12.5		2 per cent (*idem*)		. . . .	1.01 - 0.90
New Zealand	. .	22 per cent, declining balance[3]	4 per cent, declining balance[3]	. .	. .			n.a. - 33	n.a. - 1.13
Norway	100	20 per cent, declining balance[3]	5 per cent, declining balance[3]	. .	. .			51 - 28	1.04 - 1.02
Portugal	100	3 years, straight-line	20 years, straight-line	. .	. .			35 - 36	1.02 - 1.02
Spain	100	100 per cent	10 years, straight-line	20	40		No	33 - 35	0.86 - 0.66
Sweden	100	30 per cent, declining balance[3]	25 years, straight-line	. .	. .			52 - 28	0.92 - 1.02
Switzerland	100	40 per cent, declining balance	8 per cent, declining balance	. .	. .			28 - 34	1.01 - 1.02
Turkey	100	100 per cent	100 per cent	. .	. .	Yes		n.a. - 25	n.a. - 1.00
United Kingdom	100	100 per cent	100 per cent	. .	. .			52 - 33	1.00 - 1.00
United States	100	5 years, modified accelerated cost-recovery system[3]	39 years, straight-line[3]	. .	20		Yes	46 - 35	0.82 - 0.93

Source: OECD Secretariat.

- The fiscal status of tax benefits. Tax concessions are taxable in Canada and the United States, but not in other countries.

- The existence and nature of a ceiling on tax benefits (fixed amount as in France or percentage of incremental eligible R&D as in the United States).

- The treatment of loss-making firms (*e.g.* provisions for carrying forward credits not used in the current fiscal year, or refundability of the tax credit).

370. Most importantly, the five countries that implement incremental tax credits (*i.e.* the reference amount of R&D against which eligible incremental R&D is calculated) define it differently. In France, Korea and Spain, the reference is the average R&D performed for the last two years. Japan defines it as the largest amount of R&D outlays incurred in any of the previous accounting years since 1966. In the United States, the incentive is proportional to the increase in R&D intensity (*i.e.* the share of R&D expenditure in gross receipts) rather than to the absolute increase in R&D expenditure. The reference is the product of a fixed-base percentage (the R&D intensity in the period 1984-88, with a ceiling of 16 per cent) and the average of total sales during the four preceding years. The actual base amount varies with firm sales performance since the period of reference.

371. Equally important are country differences in the degree of selectivity of tax incentives, *i.e.* whether they are used for giving more favourable or exclusive support to certain types of firms, technologies or R&D expenditure (*e.g.* basic research *vs.* development). Six countries grant special R&D tax treatment to SMEs, either through preferential rates within existing tax schemes (Belgium, Canada, Korea, the Netherlands) or through specific schemes (Italy and Japan). This is generally associated with reduced corporate income tax rates (CITRs) (except in the Netherlands). Denmark and Japan favour basic research and "priority technology areas". Some countries provide tax allowances for specific R&D-related expenditure: compensation of foreign researchers (Belgium, Province of Quebec in Canada, Sweden); qualifying employees involved in R&D work (the Netherlands); technology-intensive machinery and equipment (Japan).

Generosity of R&D tax treatment – an international comparison

372. Beyond the complexity and diversity of national R&D tax incentive schemes, it is interesting to compare how these schemes affect the after-tax cost of doing R&D, which is their common goal. The so-called "B index" is a synthetic quantitative indicator of the generosity of R&D tax treatment (Box 7.1). The underlying methodology is flexible and enables various types of tax treatment to be modelled in a comparable manner. Formally, the lower a country's B-index, the more generous its tax treatment of R&D outlays. A B-index equal to one means that corporate income tax is neutral *vis-à-vis* R&D investment, although other aspects of the tax system (*e.g.* the treatment of financial capital which is not captured by the B-index) may not be so.

373. OECD countries' B-indexes are reported in the last column of Table 7.1 for the years 1981 and 1996. The most generous countries in 1996 were (in descending order) Spain, Australia, Canada, Denmark, Korea, the Netherlands, France, Austria and the United States. The least generous R&D tax treatments are found in New Zealand, Germany, Iceland and Italy (for large firms).

Box 7.1. The B-index

The B-index is defined as the present value of before-tax income necessary to cover the initial cost of R&D investment and to pay the corporate income taxes, so that it becomes profitable to perform research activities. Algebraically, the B-index is equal to the after-tax cost of a US$1 expenditure on R&D divided by one, less the corporate income tax rate (CITR). The after-tax cost is the net cost of investing in R&D, taking into account all the available tax incentives.

$$B - index = \frac{(1-A)}{(1-\tau)}$$

Where τ = statutory corporate income tax rate; A = the net present discounted value of depreciation allowances, tax credits and special allowances on the R&D assets.

In a country with full write-off of current R&D expenditure and no R&D tax incentive scheme A=τ, and consequently B=1. ***The more favourable a country's tax treatment of R&D, the lower its B-index.*** The B-index is a unique tool for comparing the generosity of R&D tax treatment in different countries. However, its computation requires some simplifying assumptions and it should therefore be examined together with a set of other relevant policy indicators. Furthermore, its "synthetic" nature does not allow to distinguish the relative importance of the various policy tools it takes into account (*e.g.* depreciation allowances, special R&D allowances, tax credit, CITR).

B-indexes have been calculated under the assumption that the "representative firm" is taxable, so that it can enjoy the full benefit from tax allowance or credit. For incremental tax credits, calculation of the B-index implicitly assumes that R&D investment is fully eligible to the credit, and does not exceed the ceiling where there is one. Some detailed features of R&D tax schemes (*e.g.* refunding, carryback and carryforward of unused tax credit, or flowthrough mechanisms) are therefore not taken into account.

The effective impact of the R&D tax allowance or credit on the after-tax cost of R&D is influenced by the level of the CITR. An increase in the CITR reduces the B-index only in those countries with the most generous R&D tax treatment. If tax credits are taxable (as in Canada and the United States), the effect of the CITR on the B-index depends only on the level of depreciation allowance. If the latter is over 100 per cent for all the R&D expenditure, an increase in the CITR will reduce the B-index. For countries with less generous R&D tax treatment, the B-index is positively related to the CITR.

Source: *For further information, see Warda (1996).*

374. Important changes in R&D tax treatment, as reflected in the evolution of the B-index, have occurred in some countries over the last 15 years (Table 7.1). Australia, Denmark, France, Korea, the Netherlands and Spain have substantially increased their fiscal support to R&D. In Spain the rate of the volume-based tax credit increased from 10 to 15 per cent in 1984 and to 20 per cent in 1996. Moreover, an incremental tax credit of 30 per cent was introduced in 1992 and increased to 40 per cent in 1996. In Australia and Denmark, the reduction in the B-index is due to additional allowances from taxable income that increased eligible costs to 150 per cent (in 1985, back to 125 per cent in 1997) and 125 per cent (in 1995), respectively. The Netherlands introduced a volume-based tax credit of 12.5 per cent of labour costs in 1995, in addition to a special depreciation allowance of 2 per cent on material, equipment and building expenditure in place since 1990. Since 1983, France offers a 25 per cent incremental tax credit; the rate was increased to 50 per cent in 1985. In Korea, a mixed tax credit was implemented in 1988 [5 per cent of the level of R&D expenditure (10 per cent for SMEs) and 25 per cent of incremental R&D].

375. In contrast, firms in the United States, Sweden and to a lesser extent Italy (large firms) have experienced a deterioration of the tax treatment of their R&D activities, although the US tax system still ranks among the most generous for R&D. The increase of the B-index in the United States is mainly due to the lowering of the rate of the incremental tax credit from 25 to 20 per cent in 1987. It reflects also the fact that the credit is fully taxable since 1991. In Sweden, the B-index increased in 1983 with the abolition of the special 15.5 per cent allowance for current R&D expenditure. In Italy, the evolution

is explained by the increase in the CITR which worsened the fiscal treatment of investment in equipment and buildings devoted to R&D.

376. Over the last 15 years, there have been drastic reductions in the CITRs of most OECD countries, making the fiscal treatment of R&D activities more generous in countries with relatively low fiscal incentives for R&D (see Box 7.1 for technical explanations).

377. International comparisons must also take into account the relative role played by fiscal incentives compared with direct subsidies (Figure 7.1 and Figure 7.2). One could wonder whether these two instruments are used by governments as complements or as substitutes. Figure 7.1 shows that there is no clear cross-country pattern. Some countries favour fiscal incentives, with relatively weak subsidisation rates (Australia, Denmark, the Netherlands), whereas others rely more on direct financial support (Germany, Italy, Norway, Sweden, the United Kingdom). The remaining countries can be sub-divided into two groups. One comprises Canada, France, Spain and the United States, which provide generous fiscal incentives and high direct subsidies. A second group of countries, especially Japan and Switzerland, make below-average use of both instruments.

378. Between 1981 and 1996 a majority of countries increased the generosity of their R&D tax treatment (reducing the B-index) while reducing direct financial support to R&D – effectively substituting tax allowances for subsidies. Only Italy and Switzerland have done the reverse, although to a fairly limited extent. In a minority of countries, both types of incentives have evolved in the same direction (especially Spain, Sweden, the United States).

Figure 7.1. **Fiscal and direct support to business R&D, 1996**

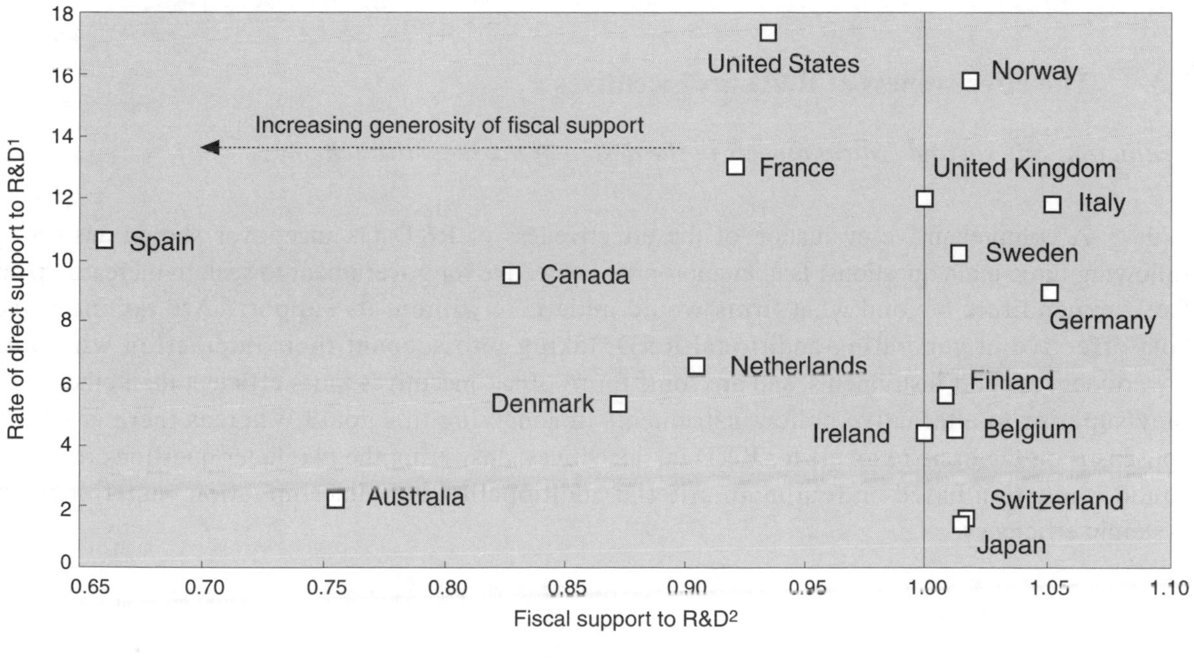

1. Measured as the percentage of business R&D financed by government.
2. Measured by the B-index, an indicator of the generosity of R&D tax treatment. The lower its value, the greater the generosity of R&D tax treatment.

Source: OECD Secretariat.

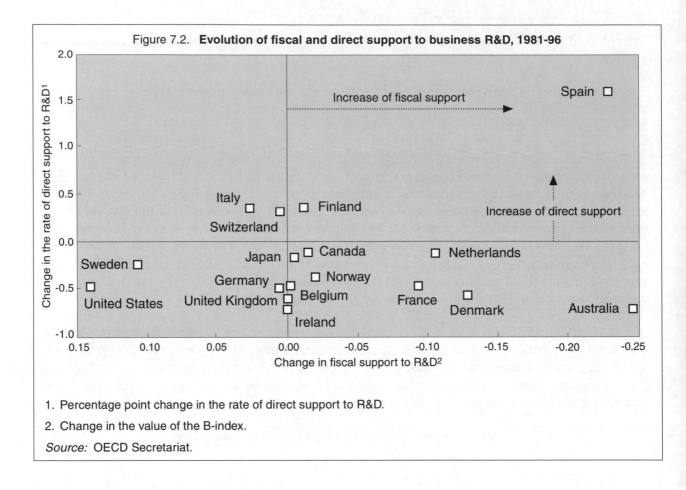

Figure 7.2. **Evolution of fiscal and direct support to business R&D, 1981-96**

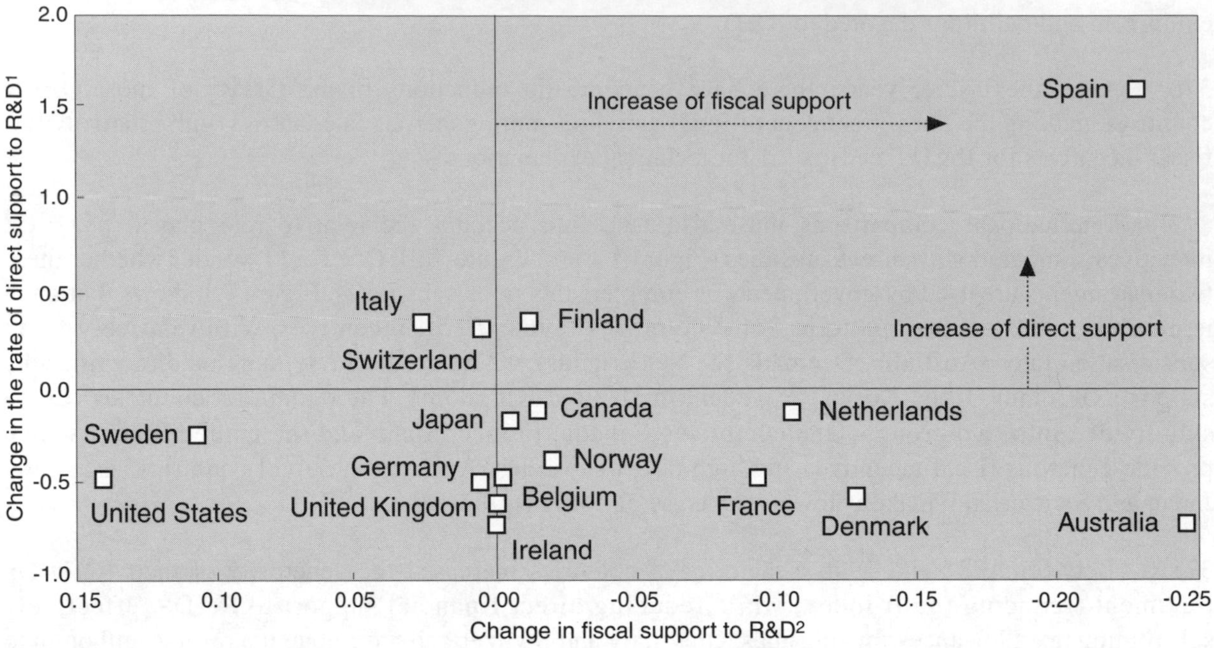

1. Percentage point change in the rate of direct support to R&D.

2. Change in the value of the B-index.

Source: OECD Secretariat.

7.3. The effectiveness of R&D tax incentives

Evaluation criteria and critical aspects in the design of tax incentive schemes

379. A comprehensive evaluation of the effectiveness of R&D tax incentives should answer the following three main questions: Is it an appropriate objective for government to seek to increase private R&D expenditure beyond what firms would undertake without its support? Are tax incentives cost-effective in generating additional R&D, taking into account their interaction with other government support instruments, and are some forms of tax incentives more efficient than others? Are they superior to alternative policy instruments in achieving this goal? Whereas there is a broad consensus on the basic rationale for R&D tax incentives, answering the two latter questions requires a sound evaluation based on four main criteria: additionality, non-discrimination, superiority and systemic efficiency.

Ensuring additionality

380. To what extent does a reduction in the cost of R&D induced by fiscal incentives stimulate firms' R&D investment? The technical answer to this question is that it depends on the "price elasticity" of R&D. If the R&D is weakly responsive to changes in its cost, there will be substitution of public funds to private ones ("crowding-out effect") instead of additional funds. This could be due to a lack of technological or market opportunities (Case 2 in Figure 7.3).

Figure 7.3. **Private and social returns: the effect of tax concessions**

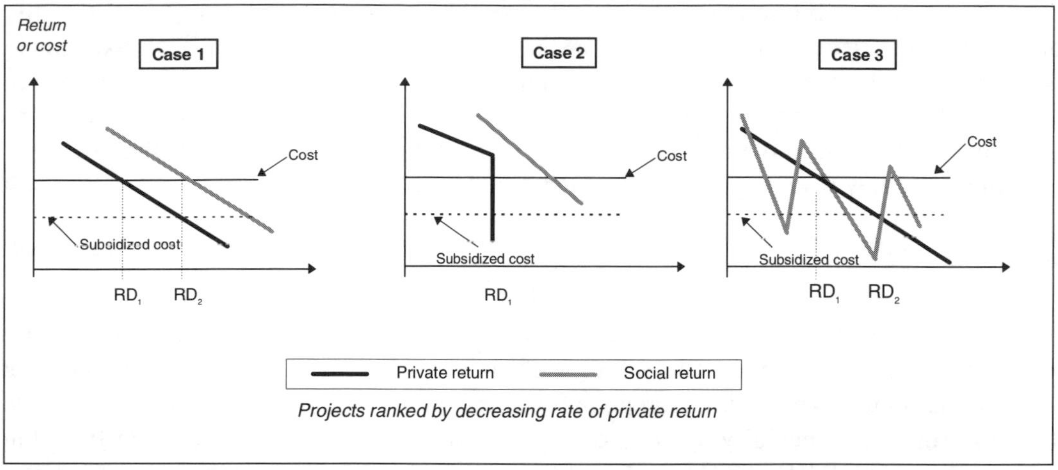

Source: OECD Secretariat.

381. How can maximum additionality be ensured? Tax concessions should define eligible expenditure in an unambiguous way so as not to encourage the "re-labelling" of non-R&D activities into R&D activities, although in practice this risk seems to be relatively small (Hall, 1996). More important is the choice of the tax inducement mechanism. With extra depreciation allowances, as well as volume-based tax credits, all R&D is subsidised although most might have been carried out in the absence of fiscal support. Incremental schemes reward "marginal" R&D only. They ensure that the cost incurred by government is compensated by an increase in R&D, as compared with a reference amount which is supposed to reflect the level of R&D that the firm would have performed anyway. As such, they minimise the amount of "subsidised" R&D that would have been undertaken even in the absence of support.

Avoiding discriminatory and distortive impacts

382. Whereas incremental tax credits seem to be a good practice with regard to the additionality criteria, they have the disadvantage of creating fiscal inequalities among firms performing equal amounts of R&D and of distorting R&D investment strategies. These drawbacks can be attenuated by careful design. Problems arise with respect to the definition of the reference amount of R&D against which the eligible incremental expenditure is calculated. A sliding reference base (as in France) aggravates the risk of lumpy investment behaviour (the firm will benefit from concentrating its effort, say, every odd year if the reference is the year before). A fixed reference base (as in the United States) is less distortive, although its relevance vanishes as time goes by. It is less effective in ensuring additionality unless, as in the United States, the reference is defined not as a level of R&D, but as the intensity of R&D efforts (R&D as a percentage of turnover). Such a solution does not favour fast-growing innovative firms (as would be the case with a reference fixed as an absolute amount of R&D), but this might be justified in countries where such firms already benefit from a supportive environment (*e.g.* dynamic venture capital market).

383. In principle, R&D tax concessions only benefit profitable firms. They are therefore less accessible in economic downturns, when more companies are loss-making, and are less beneficial for new firms which do not yet generate enough income. There are several solutions to this problem. Carryback and carryforward provisions (which allow loss-making firms to claim their unused tax

credits later, when they return to profitability) are the most consistent with the basic principles of a market-oriented general support scheme (they link benefits to medium-term economic viability), compared to cash reimbursement which addresses the specific needs of NTBFs, at the risk of supporting unviable firms. The solution of basing the exemption on less cyclical taxes than taxes on profits (as in the Netherlands) has the merit of simplicity by creating an immediate link between actual expenses and the tax exemption. Flowthrough mechanisms whereby unused tax credits are transferred to an eligible third party have proven to be subject to abuse and have been abolished in the two countries in which they were experimented (Australia, Canada).

Maximising social benefits

384. The fact that the possibility to design non-discriminatory R&D tax incentive schemes that ensure additionality exists is not sufficient to justify government intervention. Society as a whole must benefit from the public expenditure (foregone revenues) in the form of increased productivity, income and job opportunities, especially in firms other than those "subsidised", stemming from knowledge spillovers generated by R&D. The social benefits are likely to vary from one industry to another and to be limited when appropriability conditions are more favourable, due *inter alia* to good enforcement of IPRs and/or difficulties in imitation (*e.g.* the mechanical industry, pharmaceuticals). To some extent there is a trade-off between two contradictory objectives: minimising market distortions by granting equal treatment to all firms; and concentrating the benefits of tax incentives where the gap between private and social rates of return on R&D is the widest.

385. Tax concessions, in contrast with subsidies, leave a fair amount of freedom to the recipient on how to react in its R&D strategy. Firms undertake the most profitable projects first; those they decide to undertake thanks to tax concessions will have lower rates of private return. The question is therefore whether they will be those yielding the maximum social rate of return among all possible additional projects with a positive private return. This is the case in the situation depicted in Figure 7.3, Case 1. A general support measure such as a tax incentive is not well suited for maximising social benefits from additional private R&D when the relationship between private and social rates of return is that depicted in Figure 7.3, Case 3 (the ranking of projects according to the rate of private return is very different from their ranking in terms of social rate of return). Government has limited knowledge of such relationships. In practice, there are two ways of coping with the issue. The first is to restrict fiscal support to certain types of research, presumed to have a higher social return (basic, generic research). However, this is probably better achieved by targeted subsidies (see superiority criteria below). The second, sounder solution is to grant exclusive or preferential tax treatment to certain types of firms, *i.e.* SMEs, on the grounds that they may be more affected by market failures (appropriability problems, capital market failures) than other firms. However, it may be difficult to design a scheme that will meet the various needs of all types of SMEs, as illustrated by the relatively low participation rate in the Canadian scheme. In addition, such an approach should also be challenged by applying the superiority criteria, since there may be more efficient ways of correcting for market failures (Chapter 9).

Superiority and systemic efficiency

386. Comparing R&D tax concessions with alternative means of achieving the same goal, either through alternative use of public money or through non-financial means (*e.g.* perfecting market mechanisms through regulatory reform) is a challenging task. Different channels of financial support to R&D address different types of research activities. There is some overlap, which can be usefully examined only at national level. The same is true for the interactions between R&D tax treatment and the rest of the tax system.

387. In evaluation, there is a need to go beyond simply comparing the cost to government of R&D tax concessions with the amount of private R&D they generate. Even if the R&D generated is lower than the cost to government, the net social return of the scheme may be positive when one takes into account spillovers to other firms and customers, and the long-term effect on productivity, production and streams of corporate income taxes. A systemic approach needs also to integrate the international dimension of R&D activities: economic interdependencies and the internationalisation of R&D and innovation networks mean that the benefits of R&D tax incentives leak to other countries although, according to assessment work in Australia and the United States, such leakages are modest. There is also the risk of wasteful tax competition among Member countries in the hope of attracting R&D-intensive foreign investment. But, given the small size of these concessions, in subsidy-equivalent, compared to the direct subsidies and investment tax concessions granted in some cases to foreign investment, this is hardly a real issue.

The empirical evidence from assessment work

388. Severe methodological problems make it difficult to measure how close, and at what cost, tax incentives come to bridging the gap between private and social rates of return from R&D (for recent attempts to quantify private and social returns, see Bernstein, 1986). Policy makers are forced to fall back on seeking empirical answers to simpler questions. First, how is the cost of R&D affected by tax incentives? Second, how do firms respond to changes in R&D costs?

389. The first question can be answered in a direct way by calculating the impact of a tax incentive, along with other features of the tax system, on the return to R&D investment. This normative approach, as exemplified by the B-index, is useful to assess the potential inducement power of a tax scheme and to determine how it varies across firms, industries and countries. The second question can be addressed either at the microeconomic level ("anecdotal" analyses or firm surveys) or at the macroeconomic level (econometric analyses) (Mohnen, 1997).

Microeconomic approaches

390. "Anecdotal" studies compare private R&D expenditure before and after the introduction of a tax incentive scheme. In general, they suggest that firms are quite responsive to an improvement in R&D tax treatment (Cordes, 1989; Grégoire, 1995; Lebeau, 1996). However, they fail to properly isolate the own impact of tax treatment from that of other factors which influence R&D behaviour.

391. The few studies based on firm surveys reach more nuanced conclusions. Mansfield and Switzer (1985) found that the R&D induced by a volume-based tax incentive in 55 Canadian companies did not amount to more than 40 per cent of lost tax revenues. The Bureau of Industry Economics (1993) estimated this ratio at 60 to 100 per cent in the case of the Australian extra tax concession. But these results must be considered with care since survey studies might suffer from sample selection bias and are contingent to subjective answers by firm managers.

392. Econometric studies estimate both the price elasticity of R&D (*i.e.* the percentage increase in R&D induced by a percentage fall in the cost of undertaking it) and the additional amount of R&D generated by a marginal increase in foregone tax revenues (the "bang for a buck"). Early econometric studies (*e.g.* Bernstein and Nadiri, 1990) found a relatively low price elasticity of R&D (about 0.3), suggesting a modest potential inducement power of R&D tax incentives. The majority of more recent studies, using improved methodologies, are more optimistic, finding elasticities around unity. A comparison between Australia, Canada and the United States concludes that volume-based tax incentives do not generate much R&D beyond the tax expenditure incurred by government. The cost

effectiveness of incremental tax credit is "by construction" much greater (*e.g.* Hall found that US$1 of tax expenditure generates as much as US$2 of additional R&D).

393. There is only limited empirical evidence regarding aspects of the impact of R&D incentives other than their effectiveness in inducing additional R&D expenditure. Are the firms that benefit the most from tax incentives those that need them most? This is an important question given that the effective impact of tax incentives (especially incremental schemes) on R&D costs varies across firms and that many firms may be in a grey area with regard to eligibility criteria (especially small firms where R&D activities are occasional and not organised in a formal manner). Limited evidence suggests a rather negative answer (Dagenais *et al.*, forthcoming; Hall, 1996; Seyvet, 1996) and therefore point to the importance of designing schemes that minimise fiscal inequalities (*e.g.* carryforward and carryback provisions) and distortive impact on R&D investment behaviour – a clear drawback of incremental schemes with a sliding reference base year(s).

394. Available assessments have paid limited attention to the structural impact of tax incentives on national research and innovation systems. In Australia, however, the Bureau of Industrial Economics (BIE) concluded that the tax concession did not significantly encourage a greater number of firms to do R&D but was more influential in encouraging firms to use the existing research infrastructure. In France, on the contrary, the R&D tax credit is thought to have increased the number of R&D-performing SMEs (Seyvet, 1996). There is similarly scanty evidence on globalisation aspects, including the effect of R&D tax incentive schemes on international competition and on the location of R&D. First, regarding the capacity of national economies to absorb technology, the BIE found for Australia that whereas the R&D tax concession had little influence, compared to size of firm or foreign ownership, on the acquisition of foreign technology and know-how, there were significant leakages of its benefits to foreign countries. Second, R&D tax treatment may influence firms' location of R&D, but appears rarely to be a decisive factor (Hines, 1994; Bloom *et al.*, 1997). Are firms conducting R&D in countries which do not offer tax incentives (*e.g.* Germany, the United Kingdom) at a competitive disadvantage? There is no straightforward answer: the impact of R&D tax incentives on firms' competitiveness or countries' technological performance cannot be isolated from that of the other components of national innovation systems and framework conditions.

Macroeconomic approach

395. Quantitative analyses at the macroeconomic level are better suited than micro-level ones to inform policy makers on the economy-wide efficiency of fiscal support to R&D, taking into account other forms of government support. Extending the scope of earlier work (Bloom *et al.*, 1997), the OECD Secretariat has run a cross-country econometric test of the relationships between R&D tax treatment (B-index), government-funded R&D and business-funded R&D for a sample of 17 OECD countries over the period 1981-96. Box 7.2 summarises the methodology and empirical results from which three main lessons can be drawn.

396. First, both direct subsidies and tax concessions have a significant, although relatively weak, positive impact on private investment in R&D. On average, a 1 per cent decrease in the B-index – *i.e.* an improvement in R&D tax treatment – generates a 0.18 to 0.36 per cent increase in business R&D in the next years, the long-term impact being insignificant. At the aggregate level, international variations in R&D tax treatment cannot make a difference in technological performance. In contrast, the influence of direct subsidies is mainly felt in the long run. This confirms that the two forms of government support have different objectives and incentive mechanisms. Tax concessions encourage applied research with sufficient private return. Direct subsidies are granted to projects selected by government, taking a longer-term view on their social return.

Box 7.2. **Econometric estimates**

In order to quantify the impact of tax incentives and government-funded R&D on business-funded R&D, an error correction model (ECM) is used. Formally, R&D funded by business at time *t* is a function of three exogenous variables, plus various dummies and an adjustment process:

$$RP_{i,t} = f(RP_{i,t-1}, VA_{i,t}, RG_{i,t}, B_{i,t}, \varsigma, \tau_t, e_{i,t})$$

where *RP, RG, VA,* and *B* are respectively business-funded R&D, government-funded R&D performed by business (direct subsidies), value added and the B-index; the first three variables are deflated with the GDP deflator. The regressions are performed on a panel of 17 OECD countries, indexed by *i*, on the years 1981 to 1996, indexed by *t*. ζ and τ are an intercept and time dummies, respectively. The ECM specification allows for short-term and long-term adjustment processes of business-funded R&D to its various determinants. The parameters of interest are reported in the following table.

The determinants of business-funded R&D

	Value added	Direct subsidies	B-index
Short-term elasticities	1.26	0.06	-0.18
Long-term elasticities	2.50	0.24	0.00

ECM across 17 OECD, 1981-96, country and time dummies. SURE method.
All coeffcients are significant at a 1 per cent probability threshold.

Further results are found with respect to the stability of the R&D tax incentives and to the interactions with direct subsidies. The basic ECM has been constrained to allow for these interactions. This reduced dynamic model constrains the adjustment mechanism to be similar for all determinants of business R&D. The first row of the following table allows the private R&D elasticity of the B-index to vary with respect to the stability of the tax scheme in each country. INST indicates the instability of the scheme, calculated as the variance of the B-index over the period in each country. The second row allows for an interaction between the B-index and government-funded R&D. Additional regressions, run with country dummies (within estimates) to allow for country specificities, yield similar results.

Tax incentives – stability and interactions with government-funded R&D

	Value added	Direct subsidies	B-index	B-index INST	B-index direct subsidies	Adj. R2	D-W
Expected sign	+	+	-	?	?		
1. Stability of the tax scheme	1.50	0.08	-1.23	5.31		.414	2.04
2. Interaction with direct subsidies	1.50	0.08	-0.25		1.36	.423	1.97

Seventeen OECD countries, 1981-96. INST is an indicator of instability of the fiscal policy; all regressions include unreported intercept and time dummies. The econometric model is SURE.

Note: For more details, see Guellec and van Pottelsberghe (1998).

397. Second, at a certain level of government intervention, marginal changes in fiscal incentives and direct subsidies are likely to serve as substitutes. The higher the increase in subsidies, the weaker the impact of R&D tax concessions. Symmetrically, an improvement of R&D tax treatment reduces the stimulating effect of direct financial support. This demonstrates the need for better co-ordination in the design, implementation and evaluation of technology and innovation policy instruments.

398. Third, firms are more responsive to tax incentives in countries with relatively stable schemes. For the United States, Hall (1992) found an increasing effectiveness of R&D tax incentives over time. R&D is a sunk investment which is sensitive to uncertainty, including fiscal uncertainty, and the impact of tax incentives in this area will critically hinge on the extent to which firms envisage them as a long-standing feature of their environment (Coopers & Lybrand, 1998).

7.4. Policy implications and best practice in the design of tax incentives

399. Tax incentives are a potentially effective policy instrument to increase private R&D expenditure, although their inducement power is relatively modest and varies across countries, depending on other features of the tax system (especially corporate income tax) and on their industrial and technological specialisation (see Table 7.3 for country-specific policy conclusions). Since the efficiency of tax schemes declines with the level of direct subsidies to R&D (and vice versa), a policy to increase both, as in Spain, is unwarranted.

400. The detailed design of tax incentive schemes often makes the difference between efficient and wasteful fiscal support to R&D. Whereas generous volume-based tax allowances and credits can be justified as a tool for accelerating catching-up in terms of R&D intensity in some countries, their justification should be questioned at a later stage of technological development. Australia has recently reduced the rate of its extra depreciation allowance. Other countries offering generous tax incentives, such as Canada and Spain, should carefully evaluate their policies. Incremental tax credits are more cost-effective, provided that the reference base for calculating the eligible incremental R&D expenditure is defined so as to minimise distortive impact on investment behaviour (a fixed base, as in Japan or the United States, is better than a sliding one as in France). It is questionable why some countries, such as Korea and Spain, have both incremental and volume-based tax credits. Equal access to benefits by economically viable firms should be ensured by special provisions compensating for transitory differences in firms' profitability (Canada, France).

401. Selective volume-based tax incentives, concentrating benefits on certain types of research (*e.g.* basic research undertaken by firms as a follow-up to applied research projects) or firms (SMEs), can maximise net social benefits from a given amount of tax expenditure. However, the more selective the tax incentive scheme, the more acute the need to compare its effectiveness with that of alternative uses of public money, since many other policy instruments could achieve the same goal. For example, for NTBFs, preferential tax incentives are only justified as a tool to reach firms that would otherwise be missed by government-leveraged venture capital or direct support programmes. The very favourable treatment granted to SMEs by countries such as Canada and Italy should be re-examined from this perspective.

402. R&D tax incentives are more efficient when stable over time, allowing firms to plan more effectively their long-term investment strategy in a reliable fiscal environment. Legislative volatility and uncertainties, *e.g.* the suspension of the US tax credit scheme in 1996, reduces the effectiveness of fiscal support to R&D. This is not to deny the importance of regular evaluations: changes in the business environment of recipients may justify periodic fine-tuning of tax incentive schemes (*e.g.* the experience of Australia).

7.5. Direct financial support to industrial R&D

403. Direct financial support (usually in the form of grants) to industrial R&D is the common core instrument of many programmes with very different rationales or objectives. This section addresses those which are not covered by Chapter 6 (on managing university-industry interactions), Chapter 8 (on technology diffusion) and Chapter 9 (on technology-based firms). It focuses on policies whose main objective is to promote the development of advanced technology through targeted subsidisation of R&D costs or R&D public/private partnerships in selected areas.

Policy rationale and challenges

404. In specific areas of both high cost and uncertain technical and commercial outcomes, market failures can create gaps between private and social returns on R&D that are too wide to be corrected by tax incentives. In addition, defective linkages between industry and the public research sector may diminish both private and social returns on certain types of R&D and the size of some R&D undertakings may exceed the capabilities of single firms. There is thus a rationale for other forms of government intervention to ensure that investment efforts in technological development are in the long-term public interest and that private firms have incentives to expand their research agenda beyond that dictated by immediate market imperatives. IPR (to mitigate appropriability problems), R&D co-operation (to reduce risk and allow pooling of a critical mass of resources) and innovation-enhancing regulation or tax (to increase the cost of not innovating) are possible answers. Still, experience especially from the United States in the 1980s [*e.g.* Federal R&D Contractor Patent Rights, National Cooperative Research Act of 1984 (NCRA) Joint Research Ventures] suggests that they may not be sufficient (Scott and Martin, 1998; Office of Technology Policy, 1996).

405. Key questions which require constant attention concern whether governments can identify with sufficient accuracy the areas to which public support should be directed, how such support should be engineered to maximise social benefits without creating market distortions, and the role that public funding should play in the relevant support programmes or supporting institutions. Systemic aspects, along with the risk of government failure, come into play here.

Financial incentives as part of an overall technology policy strategy

406. Financial incentives to industrial R&D, which usually represent only a tiny fraction of overall S&T budgets, cannot be assessed without considering their role in the overall technology policy strategy. Ongoing changes in innovation and diffusion patterns (Chapter 2) challenge the two main traditional approaches to technology policy, mission orientation (*e.g.* France, the United Kingdom, the United States) or diffusion orientation (*e.g.* Germany and most smaller countries), as well as the more idiosyncratic Japanese strategy. They place heavy demand on governments of catch-up economies (*e.g.* Korea, Mexico), which must manage the transition from imitation to innovation, and of eastern European countries (*e.g.* the Czech Republic, Hungary, Poland) which must accelerate the transition from research-centred to innovation-driven technology policy.

407. Traditional mission-oriented policies – in areas like defence, aerospace and nuclear energy – were characterised by the concentration of resources in large-scale programmes, targeted predominantly at technical achievements, involving a small number of participants and managed through centralised administrative control. Such policies have lost their effectiveness given the characteristics of new technologies (ICTs, biotechnologies, new materials), the increased priority attached to some socio-economic goals (environment, health), and the more pressing social demand for

increased economic benefits from technological progress. Their economic benefits are questioned, especially as they crowd out limited financial and human resources for innovation.

408. To be effective, new-generation "mission-oriented" programmes (Soete and Arundel, 1993) need to adopt a systemic approach, providing a framework for a more market-driven and bottom-up definition of objectives and more decentralised implementation procedures. Emerging good policy practices (see Chapter 10 on policies concerning the "information society" and the environment) are characterised by: the articulation of missions according to the highest social return; the widespread diffusion of results in order to maximise economic benefits; the combination of the traditional instruments of mission-oriented policies (*e.g.* government procurement, funding of private pre-competitive research, establishment of mission-oriented research centres) with other instruments (market compatible subsidies, innovation-inducing regulation, etc.); appropriate co-ordination between the genuine policy purpose of the mission (*e.g.* sustainable development, improved quality of life for the elderly) with the other goals of innovation and technology policy (*e.g.* increased competitiveness); the involvement of all qualified partners, irrespective of their size and location within the NIS.

409. In a majority of Member countries direct financial support to industrial R&D is one of the instruments of a diffusion-oriented technology strategy (Chapter 8). Such a strategy was traditionally aimed at promoting a one-way transfer of knowledge from national or foreign research institutions to manufacturing, as well as interactive technological learning among firms in the same sector. Such an orientation is at odds with current trends towards more interactive modes of innovation based on multidisciplinary knowledge inputs. First, feedback loops from industry to research organisations have to be engineered, *e.g.* by making bridging institutions operate as two-way transfer mechanisms (Mowery, 1998). Second, greater flexibility than that allowed by a sectoral approach is warranted when linking sources and users of knowledge, as well as when filling gaps in the national knowledge base.

410. Overall, this points to a certain convergence of national technology policies towards two main overriding objectives: *(i)* to fill research gaps where this would yield the highest social return, instead of directing public support according to pre-defined sectoral or political priorities; and *(ii)* to improve linkages among all actors of innovation systems and provide these actors with market-compatible incentives.

Typology of support programmes and overview of current practices

411. Table 7.2 cross-classifies the objectives of support programmes and forms of government support, based on a partial inventory of programmes currently implemented in the OECD area (Table 7.4).

412. The first family of programmes comprises those aimed at supporting the development of advanced ("generic", "enabling", "fundamental") industrial technologies in undefined or loosely defined areas. Most provide government funding for research to single firms or consortia of industrial enterprises, on a cost-sharing basis. They often include participation by universities and research institutes, taking the form of full public/private partnerships, as distinct from traditional subsidisation schemes. Firms usually provide 50 per cent or more of matching finance. The criteria for project awards are foremost the technical excellence of the recipients and their proposals as well as their ability to contribute to technology developments of broad market significance. Such programmes are mainly found in the larger OECD countries [Advanced Technology Program (ATP) in the United States, Industrial Science and Technology Frontier Programme in Japan, *Sauts Technologiques* in France, BMBF R&D Support in Germany, LINK in the United Kingdom and Technology Partnerships in Canada) and at the European level (Framework Programme, EUREKA), although other countries (*e.g.* Australia and, very recently, Austria) have also implemented schemes to encourage public/private partnerships in the advancement of technological knowledge.

Table 7.2. **Typology of direct R&D support programmes**[1]

<table>
<tr><th rowspan="2" colspan="2">Policy objective</th><th colspan="3">Main form of government involvement</th></tr>
<tr><th>Provision of financial resources (regular or conditional grants, reimbursable or soft loans, equity)</th><th>Provision of infrastructural resources (regulatory or institutional framework conducive to research co-operation)</th><th>Provision of research facilities (e.g. scientists or instruments from universities and/or other public research organisations)</th></tr>
<tr><td rowspan="7">Develop "generic" or "enabling" industrial technologies</td><td rowspan="4">in broadly or non pre-defined areas</td><td>ATF (United States) TPC (Canada)</td><td>NCRA Joint R&D Ventures (United States)</td><td></td></tr>
<tr><td></td><td colspan="2">Cooperative Research Centre Grants (Australia)</td></tr>
<tr><td colspan="2">BMBF R&D support (Germany); Framework Programme and EUREKA (Europe)</td><td></td></tr>
<tr><td colspan="3">KIR (Austria); Sauts Technologiques (France); Industrial Science and Technology Frontier Programme (Japan); LINK (United Kingdom)</td></tr>
<tr><td rowspan="3">in specific sectors or technological areas</td><td>R&D Incentive Programme for ICTs (Canada)</td><td></td><td rowspan="2"></td></tr>
<tr><td colspan="2">FOTEK and MUP (Denmark); SEMATECH (United States)</td></tr>
<tr><td colspan="3">Grands Programmes (France); Business-Oriented Technological Co-operation (Netherlands); PNGV (United States)</td></tr>
<tr><td colspan="2">Promote R&D and innovation on a project basis, irrespective of sector and technological area</td><td>R&D Start (Australia); IPF (Austria); TEKES (Finland); Technology for Business Growth (New Zealand); Industrial R&D Programmes (Norway)</td><td></td><td></td></tr>
<tr><td rowspan="3">Enhance interactions between mission-related and industrial R&D to promote</td><td rowspan="2">industrial competitiveness</td><td colspan="2">Board for Space Activity (Sweden); SBIR (for SMEs) and CCDSP (Space) (United States)</td><td></td></tr>
<tr><td colspan="3">CRADAs (United States)</td></tr>
<tr><td>dual-use</td><td colspan="2">Dual-Use Application Programme (United States); Part of TPC (Canada)</td><td></td></tr>
</table>

1. For the full names of the acronyms used herein, please see the Glossary .

Source: OECD Secretariat.

413. The second family comprises programmes to support technological development in specific sectors or technological areas. They can be huge and play a central role in national technology policy, like the *Grands Programmes* in France, but generally have more modest budgets and objectives. Unlike advanced technology programmes which support pre-competitive research, they often target the commercial end of the innovation spectrum in areas deemed of strategic importance (*e.g.* SEMATECH in the United States). In several smaller countries their targets mirror the industrial specialisation (*e.g.* FOTEK for food industries in Denmark).

414. The third family is the domain of smaller countries and consists of schemes supporting R&D and innovation of commercial relevance on a project basis, often giving preferential treatment to SMEs.

415. The fourth family of programmes aims at enhancing interactions between business R&D and the public research sector, other than those concerning industry-university relationships, which are dealt with in Chapter 6. The most important [*e.g.* Cooperative Research and Development Agreements (CRADAs) and the Dual-Use Application Programme] are found in the United States, where they are assigned an important role in the new technology policy approach which emerged in the 1980s and matured in the 1990s.

The efficiency of direct financial support to R&D

Main lessons from experience

416. The variety of national programmes in terms of their size, objectives and design features, and the national specificity of their policy context makes an assessment based on common criteria and homogeneous information hardly feasible (for a review of evaluation methodologies and issues, see OECD, 1995*b*). Evidence from national assessment work is patchy, reflecting the lack of an evaluation culture in many Member countries (see Chapter 5). Moreover, many of the available evaluations were conducted by the sponsoring agencies themselves or through surveys of participating firms, making their conclusions partial if not biased. One can, however, draw some broad lessons from national experiences with direct financial support to R&D.

417. At an aggregate level direct financial support has been generally found to have a modest but positive effect on total business R&D expenditure, with corresponding social benefits in terms of additional growth in productivity and wealth. But this average may hide important differences in the effectiveness of the various components of such aggregate public funding of business R&D, especially the fraction corresponding to financial incentives to the business sector, as opposed to procurement and contracts. Some evaluations at the programme level add important qualifications, which can be summarised as follows:

- Public support enlarges the scale and quickens the pace of R&D, but only rarely reorients existing research themes of recipient firms. There are on this point striking convergent conclusions by studies on the impacts of programmes as different as Industrial Consortia in Japan (Sakakibara, 1997), Framework Programmes of the European Union (de Montgolfier and Husson, 1995; Larédo and Callon, 1990), Innovation and Technology Fund (ITF) in Austria (Polt *et al.*, 1994), and ATP in the United States (Link, 1998).

- There is some trade-off between increasing additionality and ensuring greater economic impacts (Hervik, 1997), and the right balance is always difficult to achieve, especially when support is directed at near-market research (commercial relevance is often secured at the expense of additionality, a criticism often addressed to, *e.g.* EUREKA). The long-term and diffused nature of benefits from programmes to support pre-competitive research create uncertainties in evaluating their benefits, but there is evidence that programmes which attempt to influence too much the research agenda of firms fall short of expectations in terms of their commercial outcomes (*e.g.* Industrial Science and Technology Frontier Programme and Key Technology Centers in Japan).

- Additionality has another, "behavioural", dimension. Programmes that give preference to consortia of firms and invite the participation of universities and research institutes yield a wider range of benefits than those funding single companies. Even if they do not directly induce firms to push their investigations much beyond their own research agenda, they indirectly contribute to expanding the research frontier over the longer term by encouraging research synergies and by creating lasting linkages within national innovation systems (Metcalfe and Georghiou, 1998).

- Matching fund requirements as well as competition among applicants for funding increase the efficiency of programmes and reduce the risk that they attract only second-level research projects and less-qualified research teams (OECD, 1997*n*).

- Many programmes to promote R&D and innovation on a project basis, with often preferential treatment of small firms, have had mixed results (*e.g.* the lack of additionality of some NUTEK schemes has been criticised in Sweden), explaining recent efforts to streamline or reform them (*e.g.* the new Start Innovation programme in Australia and the reshuffling of ITF in Austria). A general issue is the appropriateness of the current scope and design of such programmes when support to the development of market mechanisms for innovation financing (venture capital) becomes an increasingly attractive alternative (Chapter 9).

Enhancing the efficiency of support policies

Public/private partnership; a new policy paradigm

418. The classical market failure rationale has inspired traditional R&D subsidisation policies. The recognition of the need to also address systemic failures and accumulated evidence on the risk of government failures in traditional R&D subsidisation policies are giving birth to a new paradigm of technology policy. In this emerging paradigm, public/private partnership (P/PP) is the main institutional framework within which public funding of industrial R&D is delivered (Office of Technology Policy, 1996).

419. P/PPs organise the co-operation between the public sector (*e.g.* government agencies or laboratories, universities) and the private sector (usually firm consortia) in undertaking joint projects (research, development of S&T infrastructure, human resource development) in areas where they have mutual interests but lack capabilities and incentives to act efficiently alone. Partners provide several types of resources in addition to finance (*e.g.* research facilities, qualified personnel). In comparison with traditional spin-off policies, P/PPs ensure a higher-quality contribution by the private sector to government mission-oriented R&D and open new avenues for commercial spillovers from public research. In comparison with traditional R&D subsidisation policies, P/PPs are characterised by a more competitive selection of private participants, increased influence from the private sector on project selection and management, as well as by greater leverage of public funding on private resources. P/PPs have the potential to improve the articulation between mission-oriented and market-oriented R&D to the benefit of both.

420. Over the past ten years, a growing number of policy initiatives or reforms testify to efforts to implement this new approach to direct public support to industrial R&D, *e.g.* ATP and CRADAs in the

United States and, more recently, Co-operative Research Centre Grants in Australia, KIR *(Kompetenzzentren – Impulsprogramme – Regierungsinitiativen)* in Austria, and the Proposal-based Creative R&D Promotion Programme in Japan. Many other programmes incorporate some of the features of P/PPs (*e.g.* LINK in the United Kingdom, the 5th Framework Programme in the European Union), since P/PP is not a "revolution" in policy making but rather the conceptual crystallisation and systematisation of main lessons learned from good and bad policy practices. As such it represents both a useful generic institutional framework to support innovation at the national level and a benchmarking and learning tool at the international level (Chapter 4).

Optimising public financing in P/PPs

421. An unresolved issue in existing P/PPs is the articulation between selection and funding mechanisms, the latter remaining relatively crude, in contrast with the increasing sophistication of market financing tools (*e.g.* venture capital). Institutional and contractual arrangements in a P/PP must ensure that: *(i)* the best projects, from a convergent social and private perspective, will be chosen; *(ii)* the best private partners will be selected; *(iii)* an optimal sharing of costs, risks and rewards among private and public partners will be found, avoiding unnecessary government expenditure; and *(iv)* opportunistic behaviour will be discouraged and all partners will invest the necessary quality and quantity of resources. This cannot be done in sequence and it is of utmost importance that the incentive structure underlying the P/PP be compatible with all these objectives. While financial arrangements are of critical importance, the share and form of delivery of public funding are usually defined according to administrative criteria and do not give the government and the recipients the right incentives to make the best use of public money (they do not meet the requirements of an "incentive subsidy", according to the concept forged by Fölster, 1988). Box 7.3 gives an example of a possible bidding mechanism, to illustrate why and how improved financial arrangements in P/PPs could enhance the efficiency of public support to R&D.

422. The new technology paradigm challenges the managerial capabilities of government. There is a growing discrepancy between the hierarchised organisation of the public sector providing inadequate performance incentives and an increasingly network-based and flexible organisation of the private sector oriented towards maximising returns on investment. To become a reliable partner of the private sector, government must change the way it operates and the nature of its contribution within P/PPs, not only in terms of finance, but also by increasing its speed of operation and by developing new competencies. Whereas the objective of lowering administrative costs of public programmes remains valid, this should not be pursued by reducing the quality of public inputs in P/PPs, since the management of P/PPs is often more demanding than that of conventional subsidisation policies.

International aspects

423. Promotion of R&D is both an area of competition where governments seek to enhance national competitiveness (raising issues about transparency and rules of the game) and an area of collaboration where governments join efforts to reach critical mass in producing international public goods that are needed to address global concerns (raising issues about obstacles to co-operation).

Box 7.3. **Optimal design of public funding in R&D P/PPs: the example of a three-part bidding mechanism**

An optimally designed financing mechanism must help: *(i)* ensure an efficient selection of private partners, taking into account that the private sector knows more than the government about the investment characteristics of the R&D projects, including expected streams of returns and risk; *(ii)* secure the desired amount and quality of R&D at least cost to the government; and *(iii)* avoid opportunistic behaviour by either the government or the private partners.

Broad principles for a bidding mechanism

As part of its policy to correct market failures causing underinvestment in R&D, the government announces that it will provide an up-front payment of *F* to support project(s) in a specific or more broadly defined field, to be conducted by the winning bidder(s) in an auction to determine the private partner(s) for the public-private partnership. Further, the government pledges to provide a periodic flow of funds *c* throughout the project's life to support the flow costs of the R&D project. Interested firms then bid for the right to be the private partner(s) in the project (programme) by submitting a three-part bid:

- for how much they will pay the government up-front;
- on the periodic flow payment during the life of the R&D project;
- on the royalty rate that they would pay the government on the innovation produced by the public-private partnership and licensed (perhaps exclusively) to the private partner(s).

This bidding mechanism would have the potential of leveraging public funding optimally for the following reasons:

- The company that can (or at least thinks it can) produce the best results at least cost will gain more value from its participation in the government programme and therefore will bid higher and win.
- The government's investment cost [the present value of *(i)* the up-front investment, minus the up-front bid, and *(ii)* the flow cost minus the periodic flow payment] will be minimised since the firm with the best capabilities for producing the research at lowest cost will submit the highest bid for the up-front payment and the periodic flow payment. The government's net costs will be reduced further by the royalty payments it will receive. Those royalty payments, however, serve other specific roles in the mechanism design.
- The royalty payments are the contingent payment option that mitigates the effects of uncertainty by tying the actual payment by the private firm(s) to the government to the actual performance of the R&D investment and the innovation it produces. This contingent payment mechanism increases the willingness of private firms to bid, increases the winning bid and reduces the expected cost to the government.
- The royalty payments reduce the likelihood of opportunistic behaviour on the part of the government, especially when public support – not only funds but also the energy and talents of the government's employees of public laboratories and technology policy departments – is needed for many fiscal years. The government's equity position in the project is a way to ensure the credibility of the public support.
- The likelihood of opportunistic behaviour by the private investors is lessened because they will have invested up-front and periodic payments, and good-faith behaviour will be required to protect that investment and to retain the prospect of sharing the project's earnings.

Detailed design and scope for application

Details remain to be developed before applying this mechanism to actual public-private partnership programmes. This includes the type of auction, the use of a reservation price, etc. The bidding mechanism would seem particularly well suited for programmes to correct market failure stemming from transaction costs in financial markets. In some cases the bidding mechanism could involve private venture-capital market supervision of the public investments in early-stage firms or joint ventures. In principle it could also be considered in any situation where the type of market failure suggests a policy solution based on subsidies.

Source: Scott and Martin (1998).

R&D subsidies and international trade

424. International R&D spillovers, especially trade in high-technology products and foreign investment, are an increasingly important source of world economic growth. Correcting for market failures at national level through programmes to support industrial R&D should be done without distorting international competition and weakening the multilateral trade system. Public debate on trade and technology usually focuses on the special case of R&D-intensive industries with few market players and strong direct or indirect (through defence budget) government involvement such as aircraft and civilian space (*e.g.* Airbus). This debate often mixes two different questions, namely that of the historical role of government in the creation of new industries, and that of defining fair trade practices in industries which share part of their costly knowledge base with the defence sector and whose clients are responsive to political marketing.

425. A more general issue, concerning a broader range of sectors and technologies, is whether support to R&D should be subjected to the same multilateral disciplines as other subsidies to private firms, or whether the public-good character of some R&D results justifies a more lenient treatment. The outcomes of the last Uruguay Round tilt towards the latter by considering as non-actionable: "assistance for research activities conducted by firms or by higher education or research establishments on a contract basis with firms if: the assistance covers not more than 75 per cent of the costs of industrial research or 50 per cent of the cost of pre-competitive development activities, and provided that such assistance is limited exclusively to expenditure incurred directly as a result of the research activity" (World Trade Organization, 1994).

426. This international agreement has been criticised for the vagueness of its basic concepts (industrial research or pre-competitive development) which could encourage "techno-nationalism" and corresponding wasteful government expenditure in a negative-sum game. But this underestimates the inherent limitations of a political compromise and, even more, the difficulties of operationalising sharper concepts given international differences in the institutional arrangements for government involvement (*e.g.* the notion of pre-competitive research is not the same in the Japanese Industry Consortia as in the French *Grands Programmes* or the US Advanced Technology Program).

427. Finally, it is important to realise that imposing hard economic efficiency requirements on technology programmes at national level contributes to securing their innocuity for international competition. In particular, the higher the additionality of government support to R&D, the lower the risk of harmful effects on competition at both national and international levels.

Foreign access to national technology programmes

428. The impact of R&D subsidies on international competition depends also on the extent of foreign participation in national technology programmes. The formulation and implementation of technology and innovation policies in economies that are more closely linked creates a fundamental tension between the need for governments to be accountable to national citizens for the economic benefits of such programmes, and the growing reliance by national firms on foreign partners, foreign markets and foreign suppliers (Mowery, 1997). There is a trade-off between promoting national R&D capabilities and obtaining economies of scale in, and access to, foreign and international programmes – especially for smaller countries and certain types of technology. Foreign access to government-funded programmes for R&D remains a controversial issue that confronts governments with a dilemma. On the one hand, many programmes have the explicit objective to increase "national competitiveness". On the other hand, governments must recognise that national technology programmes should engage the best

private partners, irrespective of their country of origin. Internationalisation of innovation networks makes it increasingly difficult to prevent benefits from public investment in R&D from spilling across borders. In addition, too-restrictive practices (*e.g.* the strict application of reciprocity requirements) would entail an underexploitation of the potential contribution to P/PPs of firms from small countries in which the implementation of support programmes in some areas exceeds national capabilities.

429. The rules and practice regarding foreign participation in publicly supported research are generally not very transparent (OECD, 1997*o*). They tend to differ from country to country and from programme to programme, reflecting the variable incidence of national security considerations but also the lack of national or multilateral policy guidelines or the difficulties in implementing or interpreting existing ones, especially with regard to economic performance requirements and reciprocal or comparable treatment provisions. Overall, the vast majority of national programmes are open to domiciled foreign firms and only less that one-tenth have no restrictions on the geographic location or ownership of firms, the remainder being strictly reserved to national firms (OECD, 1996*d*).

430. In the United States, access by foreign companies is determined by each funding and managing agency. For example, in the case of the ATP, the decision is taken on a case-by-case basis. Currently, around 10 per cent of ATP projects involve foreign-owned companies. Participation in CRADAs is limited to domestic and domiciled foreign firms, and federal agencies must also consider reciprocity or comparable treatment conditions. Around 10 per cent of the 500 CRADAs managed by the National Institute of Standards and Technology (NIST) include subsidiaries of foreign firms. The Japanese government has not adopted any explicit general policy on foreign participation in government-funded R&D and technology programmes, and implicit rules governing individual programmes differ depending on their objectives. Whereas some past MITI projects, such as the Very Large-Scale Integrated Circuit Project, were closed to foreign firm participation, in recent years access by foreign researchers and participation by foreign firms in a number of government-funded research programmes has improved. In Europe, the participation of domiciled foreign companies is actively encouraged in the smaller countries (*e.g.* Ireland) and generally unrestricted in others, although some countries (*e.g.* Germany, the Netherlands, the United Kingdom) apply specific rules relating to exploitation of research results. For non-domiciled foreign companies, rules governing access, finance and exploitation of results are rarely specified and vary widely across countries and programmes. The EU research activities, such as those carried out within the context of the Framework Programmes, are in principle open to domiciled foreign firms, with some restrictions in practice.

431. In summary, international discrepancies in the access of foreign firms to government-funded research programmes have been reduced, especially following positive initiatives in Japan. Rules (*e.g.* reciprocity requirements or conditions regarding exploitation of research results) and practice differ as much from programme to programme as from country to country. Their lack of transparency remains the major obstacle preventing national technology programmes being used to their full potential as a tool for international technology co-operation.

International technology co-operation

432. Other obstacles to international technology co-operation stem from legal or regulatory differences (IPRs, competition law, standards). There is scope for improving the regulatory framework for transborder co-operation among private enterprises, especially in the area of IPR. Despite progress in harmonization under the aegis of the World Intellectual Property Organization (WIPO) and the World Trade Organization (WTO) (TRIPS Agreement), the lack of predictability in intellectual property standards, enforcement and litigation still hampers firms' global operations, particularly in new technology fields (OECD, 1997*p*).

433. Government can also act more directly, by sponsoring collaborative research programmes. In basic science, and more recently in mission-oriented R&D, the need for such initiatives is clearly recognised; the escalating cost of equipment (*e.g.* Megascience projects, the Space Station) and the rise of global concerns (*e.g.* climatology, environment) encourage governments to pool resources. In more applied and nearer-to-market research activities, multilateral collaboration is a recent and still limited phenomenon: governments find it difficult to delineate areas in which joint investments to produce tcchnological knowledge as an international public good would be justified for motives other than the promotion of national or regional competitiveness. In fact, the most important programmes are found at the European level (*e.g.* Framework Programme and EUREKA) and there are few examples of truly global initiatives (*e.g.* Intelligent Manufacturing Systems sponsored by Japan).

Table 7.3. **Best practices and recommendations for tax support to R&D**

Policy choice		Practices	Evaluation	Best practices and recommendations	Country specificity
Whether or not to use tax incentives for promoting R&D		Two-thirds of total OECD business R&D expenditure benefit from tax incentives. Among the largest R&D performers, only Germany and the United Kingdom do not offer such incentives.	Tax incentives are cost-effective in increasing private R&D, but their inducement power is moderate and contingent to the level of corporate income tax. Their superiority over alternative uses of government resources is clear only with regard to across-the-board (non-selective) subsidies. The overall effectiveness of tax incentives depends also on their interaction with other financial support policies. At an aggregate level, it tends to increase (decrease) with the decrease (increase) of R&D subsidies.	For an R&D fiscal measure to induce substantial and worthwhile R&D at low cost to taxpayers, there must be high spillovers from the modest amount of induced R&D to generate net benefits. This is unlikely to be the case in countries where R&D activities are relatively less diversified and more concentrated in large firms operating in sectors where appropriability problems are less severe (*e.g.* oligopolistic industries).	Industry structure and technological specialisation of countries have an impact on the efficiency of R&D tax incentives. Country-specific interactions with the rest of the tax system may reduce/enhance the incentive power of the R&D tax scheme.
If yes, choose between:	Volume-based scheme	Australia, Austria, Canada, Netherlands, Spain, Japan (special schemes for SMEs)	The most generous form of tax incentives (*c.f.* the lowest B-indexes in Table 7.1). Appropriate instruments as part of a catching-up strategy in terms of R&D intensity, include raising R&D content of foreign investment. An effective inducement is achieved at high cost. Low additionality on average translates into substantial dissipation of the concession as transfer payments to firms and significant leakages to foreign countries.	The generosity of the scheme can be reduced as countries catch up (Australia has reduced the extra tax allowance from 150 per cent to 125 per cent). The generosity of support can be limited for large firms and eligible expenditure defined in a restrictive way (Netherlands). A switch to an incremental mechanism always needs to be given careful consideration.	Specificities of the tax system may reduce the feasibility of implementing an incremental scheme.
	Incremental scheme	France, Japan (general scheme), Spain, Korea, United States	More cost-effective (higher additionality) than volume-based schemes in increasing R&D. However, the effective rate of support varies considerably across industries and firms and the choice of the reference base for calculating eligible incremental R&D raises difficult problems. A major challenge is to mitigate the distortive impact on firms' R&D investment strategy ("lumpy investment behaviour") when the base is a sliding one.	A fixed reference base (Japan, United States) is preferable to a sliding one. An incentive proportionate to the intensification of R&D efforts (as a percentage of turnover, *e.g.* United States) is more cost-effective than one proportionate to the increase of R&D expenditure, unless the target is to favour fast-growing young SMEs.	

Policy choice	Practices	Evaluation	Best practices and recommendations	Country specificity
Deal with loss-making firms (avoid unwarranted exclusion of some firms from the benefits of the scheme)	Three major solutions have been experimented: carryback and carryforward provisions (*e.g.* United States and Canada for large firms), cash reimbursement (*e.g.* France and Canada for SMEs), base the exemption on less cyclical taxes than taxes on profit (Netherlands).	Carryback and carryforward provisions are the most consistent with the basic principles of a market-oriented general support scheme (*i.e.* they link benefits to medium-term economic viability), compared to cash reimbursement which addresses the specific needs of NTBFs. The Dutch solution has the merit of simplicity by creating an immediate link between actual expenses and the tax exemption.	Carryback and carryforward provisions are best suited for general support schemes.	
Target or grant favourable treatment to certain types of research, sector or firm	Six countries (Belgium, Canada, Italy, Japan, Korea, the Netherlands) have selective tax credit schemes favouring small firms. Ceiling on benefits of general schemes can make them more generous to smaller firms (*e.g.* in France). Denmark and Japan favour basic research and "priority technology areas".	Preferential treatment of SMEs might be justified on the grounds that small firms are more affected than large ones by liquidity constraints stemming from capital market failures. However, it is difficult to design a scheme which will meet the various needs of all types of SMEs, as illustrated by a relatively low participation rate in Canada. Specific, targeted policy tools (for which tax incentives cannot substitute efficiently) exist to provide capital to start-ups as well as to promote specific technologies or basic research.	The own value of R&D tax incentives should be carefully examined at a time when alternative forms of support strategy are becoming more credible (promotion of venture capital).	The quality of the financial and infrastructural environment of SMEs varies greatly, from good in the United States to relatively poor in many other countries. R&D tax incentives can be seen to some extent as a transitory remedy which may become less effective as the business environment improves.

Source: OECD Secretariat.

Table 7.4. **Direct support to industrial R&D in OECD countries – selected examples of programmes**

Country	Programme	Target (beneficiaries and participants)	Financing instrument (order of magnitude)
	Targeted technology programmes (Fund development of generic technologies or support technological development in specific industries)		
Australia	Co-operative Research Centre Grants	Long-term research (no direct funding to specific companies which benefit from access to CRCs' R&D facilities in exchange of compensatory resources)	Grant (A$ 150 million)
	National Space Program	Space technologies	Grant (A$ 1 million)
Austria	ITF (planned to be replaced by KIR)	ICT, technology transfer, biotechnology, advanced manufacturing, etc.	Mixed (volume of financial support: Sch 250 million)
	Competence Centre Programme	Support the establishment of competence centres	Grant (Sch 200 million)
	Christian Doppler Laboratories	Medium-term industrial basic research (links university research and industry research groups)	Grant (Sch 16 million)
Canada	Technology Partnerships Canada (TPC)	Environmental technologies, generic technologies (*e.g.* new materials), ICTs, aerospace and defence technologies (including dual-use)	n.a.
	R&D Incentive Programme	ICTs	Grant (C$ 2 million)
	Microelectronics and Systems Development Programme	Systems development	Grant (C$ 2 million)
	Microelectronics Sector Campaign	Microelectronic technologies	Reimbursable grant (C$ 1 million)
Denmark	FOTEK	Food industries	Grant (DKr 100 million)
	MUP	New materials	Grant (DKr 50 million)
	Support to industrial and space research	Suppliers to the European Space Agency (ESA)	Grant (DKr 100 million)
	CFC (Chloro Fluorocarbon) Programme	Environmental technologies	Grant (DKr 20 million)
Finland	Promotion of Energy Research	R&D projects for energy investment	Grant (MK 20 million)
France	*Grands programmes civils*	Space, aircraft, nuclear and telecommunications	(Accounts for about 70 per cent of total publicly financed business civilian R&D)
	Grand Projets innovants	Large-scale innovation projects	n.a.
	Sauts technologiques	Projects to demonstrate industrial feasibility of products or processes based on new technologies	Grant (n.a.)
	Bioavenir, PREDIT (until 1994)	Biotechnologies and transport	Grant (n.a.)
	Support to R&D in electronics industries	Two actions focus on SMEs (Logic and Puce)	Reimbursable grant (FF 2 000 million)

Country	Programme	Target (beneficiaries and participants)	Financing instrument (order of magnitude)
Germany	Direct project promotion in selected areas (BMBF)	R&D in 12 main fields, especially ICT, energy, ground transport, aeronautical, space, materials, chemicals, environmental technologies	Grant (DM 750 million)
Iceland	Support to R&D in selected areas	Aquaculture, computer vision, extremophile biotechnology	Mixed (of which IKr 30 million in grants)
Ireland	PATS	Advanced technologies	n.a.
Japan	Industrial Science and Technology Frontier Programme (NEDO)	Fundamental industrial technologies, *e.g.* superconductivity, micromachine (joint industry consortia with, more recently, universities)	Grant (Y 25 billion)
	Key Technology Centre	High-risk research, *e.g.* opto-electronics, operating systems for future generation computers (consortia of technology-based smaller firms)	Mixed (Y 25 billion)
	Exploratory Research for Advanced Technology (ERATO)	Multi-disciplinary and cross-institutional research (joint industry, laboratory and university teams of researchers)	n.a.
	Proposal-based Creative R&D Promotion Programme	Targeted at new industries (new initiative, 1996)	Mixed (total budget = Y 5 000 million)
	Global Environment and Recycling Technologies	Environmental technologies	Grant (Y 20 billion)
	Joint International Development of Civil Aircraft	Aircraft industry	Grant (Y 10 billion)
	Other sectoral R&D promotion schemes	Specific sectors (energy, shipbuilding, software, etc.)	n.a.
Netherlands	Business-oriented Technological Co-operation (BTS)	Biotechnology, environmental, materials and ITs	Grant (Gld 100 million)
	Environmental Incentive Scheme	Environmental technologies	Grant (Gld 10 million)
Portugal	R&D Incentives of INETI	Biotechnology, microelectronics, information, materials, and prototype construction technologies	Grant (Esc 6 million)
Sweden	NUTEK Centres of excellence	Firms and universities	n.a.
	NUTEK Energy Research	Private firms get only 15 per cent of public funds	Grant (Skr 5 million)
	Specific R&D Projects	Large & risky projects (*de facto* few firms in the aircraft industry)	Conditional loan (Skr 500 million)
Switzerland	Grant to the Electronics and Micro-Engineering Centre	Around 10 per cent of total budget is allocated to research projects	n.a.

Country	Programme	Target (beneficiaries and participants)	Financing instrument (order of magnitude)
United Kingdom	LINK	Pre-competitive R&D (business sector and higher education institutes)	Grant (30 million)
	Advanced Technology Programme	Pre-competitive innovative R&D (preferential treatment for firms with less than 500 employees)	Grant (2 million)
	Civil Aircraft Research and Demonstration (CARAD)	Aircraft industry	Grant (20 million)
United States	ATP	Pre-competitive R&D (single firms, joint industry consortia, universities and public labs)	Grant (US$ 500 million)
	CRADAs	Promote co-operative research between firms and federal laboratories	Grant (US$ 900 million)
	Technology Reinvestment Project (TRP)	Promote R&D for dual use	Grant (US$ 1 500 million)
	SEMATECH	Semiconductor manufacturing technologies (joint industry consortia)	Grant (US$ 90 million)
	Centers for the Commercial Development of the Space Program (CCDSP)	Commercialisation of the space programme	Grant (US$ 20 million)
	Textile/Clothing Technology Corporation [TC]2 and American Textile Partnership (AMTEX)	Textile industry	Grant (US$ 10 million)
	Partnership for a New Generation of Vehicles (PNGV)	First-tier suppliers of the car industry, universities, public labs	n.a.
	High Performance Computing and Communications Program (HPCCP)	Involves 12 federal agencies	Grant (US$ 800 million)
	Department of Energy (DOE) R&D support programmes	Technologies for energy production, conversion and use	Grant (US$ 350 million)
Pan-European initiatives	EU Framework Programme	Targeted at pre-competitive research (by joint industry consortia, universities and/or research institutes) in several fields, especially ICT (28 per cent of total funding) and industrial and material technologies (14 per cent of total funding)	The 4th Framework Programme (1994-98) is funded at a level of ECU 13 billion.
	EUREKA	Targeted at near-market research in ICT, robotics, medical and biotechnology, new materials, environmental technologies, energy, lasers and transport (65 per cent of participants are firms, 15 per cent are research institutes and 15 per cent are universities)	n.a.

Country	Programme	Target (beneficiaries and participants)	Financing instrument (order of magnitude)
General R&D and innovation promotion schemes (support industrial R&D or innovation-related investment on a project basis)			
Australia	R&D Start Programme	Projects with a clear commercial focus and high potential rates of return	Grant (A$ 50 million)
Austria	Industrial Research Promotion Fund	R&D projects with relevance for Austrian industry	Mixed (total value is Sch 1.6 billion, of which Sch 600 million of grants)
Belgium	Support to basic industrial research	Regional managing structure and focus (Brussels)	Grant (BF 150 million)
	Promotion of industrial and technological R&D	Regional managing structure and focus (Flanders)	Mixed (n.a.)
	Technological Promotion Contracts	Regional managing structure and focus (Walloon)	Reimbursable grant (BF 1 500 million)
Canada	Sector campaign	Innovation projects	Grant (C$ 25 million)
	Industrial Research Assistance Program (IRAP)	R&D (focus on SMEs)	Grant (C$ 80 million)
Finland	Grants and soft loans for industrial R&D (TEKES)	High-level R&D projects	Grant (Mk 300 million) and conditional loan (Mk 200 million)
Iceland	Technology Fund	R&D	Grant (IKr 200 million)
	Innovation Fund	Innovation by SMEs	Grant (IKr 100 million)
Ireland	Promotion of new or improved industrial processes and products	R&D (preferential treatment for SMEs)	Grant (Ir 10 million)
New Zealand	Technology for Business Growth	R&D (preferential treatment for SMEs)	Grant (NZ$ 5 million)
Norway	Industrial R&D programmes	R&D (preferential treatment for basic industrial research and SMEs)	Grant (NKr 300 million)
	Industrial R&D projects	High-R&D-intensive projects (preferential treatment for basic industrial research and SMEs)	Grant (NKr 50 million)
Portugal	Technological Infrastructures (PEDIP)	R&D and innovation (fewer than 100 projects annually)	Grant (n.a.)
Switzerland	Encouragement of applied research	Firms and other research institutions	Grant (SF 30 million)

Source: OECD Secretariat.

CHAPTER 8. TECHNOLOGY DIFFUSION POLICIES AND INITIATIVES

8.1. Introduction

434. It is widely recognised that the impact of technology on the economy strongly hinges on its diffusion across the public and private sectors and between and within firms, both large and small. In a knowledge-based and globalised economy where national borders matter less, even for small, domestic-oriented firms, the ability to access and exploit technology and know-how is essential for improving firm performance. It is also important for the realisation of the economy-wide effects of technological progress, including productivity growth as well as job creation. The growth of the service sector, which has a relatively low R&D intensity as measured by existing indicators but is now the main user of technology and source of jobs, illustrates the importance of diffusion.

435. Despite the increase in foreign investment and trade flows as well as the advancement in ICTs during the 1980s and 1990s, significant obstacles to diffusion persist within and between OECD countries. This applies at several levels: the macro level of framework conditions; the meso level of firm networks; and the micro level of the single firm. This chapter assesses the role and evolution of technology diffusion policies, especially discrete programmes/initiatives, with a view to identifying general best policy principles and practices.

8.2. From technology transfer to diffusing knowledge

436. Diffusion policy requires an understanding of how knowledge is generated, how it flows and how it relates to innovation, productivity and job creation. In the past, technology was defined as the knowledge embodied in capital equipment, intermediate goods and services or disembodied in patents, licences and design. This view ignored the knowledge embodied in people and in organisational structures. The NIS framework of analysis, discussed in Chapter 2, provides empirical support for diffusion as a multi-dimensional and multi-directional process whereby technology, including "tacit" or uncodified know-how, spreads from the original innovator to other users. This process involves a range of private and public actors including networks of small and large firms, suppliers, customers, subcontractors, public research (*e.g.* universities, laboratories) as well as bridging institutions (*e.g.* technology transfer centres, applied research centres). There is also a marked international aspect, as FDI and trade represent the major channels for flows of technology and know-how.

437. As discussed in previous chapters, there is traditionally a distinction and perceived trade-off between knowledge creation and diffusion. Although this remains valid in part, in many cases this perspective is becoming artificial and irrelevant as the two processes are increasingly interdependent. For the firm, adopting a technology requires the same kinds of skills as creating one – opportunity identification, options assessment, technical development and integration into the firm's organisational

structure and production processes. Indeed, innovation often consists in rearranging existing technologies in new ways, so that even innovators are technology receivers. Many innovations such as the personal computer (PC) emanated from a few radical innovations in the first half of this century (*e.g.* the transistor), while others such as wireless communications and fuel-efficient cars have built on innovations going back to the l9th century (*e.g.* radio, propulsion engine). The basic principles behind magnetic storage of data existed long before the transistor – but there was no demand and hence no prospect of returns from innovation. What brought these inventions to fruition were incentives that reward innovation (Romer, 1997).

438. Of course, the absolute or relative importance of either knowledge creation or diffusion is not the same in every sector (Pavitt, 1984). Some innovations, such as those embodied in equipment and software, are more easily diffused than others, depending on the extent to which the underlying knowledge is codifiable or tacit and the degree of appropriability (*e.g.* via patents) as well as on the role of structural (*e.g.* regulations) and macroeconomic polices. Patents have been very valuable in manufacturing industries like pharmaceuticals and electronics, but are of less significance in other areas where secrecy and tacit knowledge may be more important (which can have the effect of limiting diffusion). Indeed, while knowledge which can be codified is formal and systematic and can be easily shared and diffused, tacit knowledge consists of behavioural and social patterns, intuitive learning skills, beliefs and perspectives that cannot be easily articulated and hence diffused.

439. ICTs have accelerated the diffusion of codifiable knowledge by lowering prices and transaction costs, but the tacit and imperfectly codified elements of technology often require human and organisational interactions which are not cost-free and are highly localised, especially in advanced/emerging technologies. As discussed in earlier chapters (Chapter 2 and Chapter 4), there is no clear-cut relationship between, on the one hand, this improved circulation of knowledge and increased competition and, on the other hand, the incentives for innovation.

440. Again, as discussed in Chapter 1, firm-level evidence demonstrates a link between technology, productivity and employment. Even in traditional industries such as textiles and automobile manufacturing, technology together with organisational change has renewed competitiveness in OECD countries. On the other hand, the Schumpeterian process of creative destruction is not without short-term costs. Although technological change and market demand have stimulated innovation and the diffusion of new products and processes, contributing to significant job creation, especially in sectors such as retailing, engineering design, financial and business services, employment in mature industries has continued its structural decline and many OECD countries experience continuously high structural unemployment.

8.3. Evolving roles for technology diffusion initiatives

441. Public intervention can be justified when product markets do not adequately reward the diffusion of technologies that are socially desirable (positive externalities). Examples include the diffusion of environmentally sustainable products and processes or energy-reducing innovations. Furthermore, despite the increase in (codified) knowledge, asymmetric information concerning technological or market opportunities commonly drives a wedge between the private rate of return from technology uptake and the cost of capital and skilled labour for investing in technology. Internal obstacles in firms, stemming from weak organisational, managerial or human capital abilities, can further impede their capacity to evaluate, absorb and exploit technology. This is particularly the case for SMEs which, at the same time, are relatively dependent on external sources of know-how.

442. Because private providers of information (*e.g.* technical consulting) will only seek out users if they can profit in some way, there may be a welfare loss arising from market disincentives to service firms which, for instance, are small or located in isolated regions On the supply side, governments may improve the quantity or quality of available information by subsidising the acquisition of technology and transfer services or supporting the distribution of technical information via public information networks and databases. On the demand side, governments may subsidise or broker consulting services to help firms identify and address management and organisational obstacles to the effective use of technology.

443. The fact that knowledge is not created and exchanged purely in markets further underlines that market mechanisms alone do not cater for optimal diffusion of technology. In this area, policy intervention thus cannot be limited to correcting for market failures, but needs to incorporate government and systemic failures. The former may arise from policies that discourage adjustment to competition and technological change (*e.g.* subsidies or trade barriers in sectors such as textiles, steel, shipbuilding), barriers to inward FDI, or public procurement that is biased towards large firms. The latter may arise when public institutions lack the links and incentives to co-operate with (smaller) firms in commercialising and diffusing technology.

444. Special policy issues arise with respect to job creation. Diffusion of technology is particularly important for broad-based productivity growth, entry into new markets, start-up by new firms and general economic expansion which can create new jobs. At the same time, given labour market rigidities and structural unemployment associated with skill mismatch, the impact on net job creation will strongly hinge on the extent to which diffusion of technology is accompanied by upskilling. Conversely, upskilling is important for the absorptive ability of firms. Technology diffusion policies, insofar as they can help firms and workers adjust to technological change, serve to cushion the process of creative destruction. Together with effective labour market and education policies, diffusion measures that support training in new technologies and promote flows of both tacit and codified knowledge can help to address the problems associated with skill-biased technological change.

445. On this basis, the thrust of diffusion policy has evolved on two levels: *(i)* maximising the efficiency of specific diffusion programmes; and *(ii)* improving the framework of institutions and connections that firms use to innovate, and which influence the overall interplay between innovation and diffusion. Until recently, policies mostly focused on the first level because of the priority given to market failures that result in barriers to technology diffusion. Thus, the prime concern of diffusion policies was to increase the speed with which specific technologies were employed in the economy, mainly in manufacturing, through fairly direct measures such as subsidies and the direct provision of information. Recognition of structural impacts on innovation and diffusion has broadened the scope for policy making, and diffusion policy increasingly addresses the "facilitating structures", including the science-industry interface, firm networks or access to information. At the level of the firm, which is the prime concern of this chapter, interest in technology is viewed in the context of building broadly defined innovative capabilities – the ability to identify, assess and adapt necessary technologies and the ability to successfully innovate in the market-place.

8.4. Levels of policy intervention

The importance of framework conditions

446. While firms themselves must take the lead in developing their internal capacities, governments have a role to play in providing a favourable climate in which firms can reap the benefits from national and international sources of technology. Macroeconomic policies and framework conditions influence the preconditions for diffusion, with implications for targeted diffusion policies which aim to raise

innovation and performance in specific industries and firms by influencing the supply of and demand for technology and know-how. Lower real interest rates and price stability can positively affect productivity growth through the response of capital-intensive production. This growth can potentially be sustained in the longer term if innovations are widely diffused. Macroeconomic instability, as demonstrated by past experience in OECD countries or by the crises of 1997-98 in Asia, imposes higher costs on the enterprise sector and raises the uncertainty and risk associated with investments in new technologies.

447. Structural policies are equally important. The functioning of product markets and competition has a major impact on innovation as well as diffusion. Regulatory reform, which improves market compatibility and signalling of societal needs, is of great importance for spurring technology diffusion while avoiding lock-in to inferior or outdated technologies (OECD, 1996*e*). This is especially true in new growth industries such as multimedia, environmental, biotechnologies and energy technologies (Chapter 10). Inconsistent IPR requirements may hinder technology development, while lack of predictability in standards, enforcement and litigation can impede diffusion. A key challenge for policy is to provide incentives for innovators (*i.e.* allow for private returns) while minimising barriers to diffusion (*i.e.* raising social returns).

8.5. Targeted technology diffusion initiatives

448. Technology policies to promote diffusion can be broadly classified in accordance with an emphasis on five types of knowledge flows: *(i)* interactions among enterprises, primarily joint research activities and other technical collaborations; *(ii)* interactions among enterprises, universities and public research institutes, including joint research, co-patenting, co-publications and more informal linkages; *(iii)* other innovation-supporting institutional interactions, such as innovation funding, technical training, research and engineering facilities, market services, etc.; *(iv)* technology transfer, including industry adoption of new technologies and diffusion through capital equipment; *(v)* personnel mobility to and from universities and industry and between firms. Over the past decades, targeted diffusion policies have focused mainly on the fourth category, providing subsidies for technology adoption, demonstration schemes, manufacturing extension services and technical consulting. Less attention has been paid to knowledge flows such as managerial or marketing skills, technical expertise, skilled research personnel and network interactions between firms.

449. In the 1970s and early 1980s public support was mainly supply-led and biased in favour of manufacturing, the rationale being that technology-intensive manufacturing firms have higher employment and productivity growth than manufacturing as a whole. OECD countries established technology data banks, licensing and transfer agencies and manufacturing extension service centres – modelled on earlier initiatives to modernise the agricultural sector – to promote the adoption of specific technologies such as microelectronics and computer-aided design and computer-aided manufacturing (CAD/CAM) systems. While experience with supply-driven programmes has been mixed, survey evidence in Austria, Norway, Sweden and the United Kingdom has shown that many of the obstacles to diffusion were internal to the firm and stemmed from deficiencies in labour skills and in organisational and managerial capacities (OECD, 1997*q*).

450. In recent years, greater attention has been paid to addressing these "internal" obstacles to technology diffusion by developing the "absorptive capacity" of firms. Contrary to common assumptions, the diffusion of technology does tend to require sunk costs on the part of adopters. Since the 1980s, several OECD countries have set up technology demonstration programmes, technology brokerage services and business advisory services as well as networking schemes. Another trend is the

provision of training and human capital development in smaller firms to help enhance absorptive capacity (*e.g.* in Denmark, Sweden, the United Kingdom). Improving the ability of workers to keep pace with technical change not only facilitates diffusion but could also have positive effects on the mismatch caused by skill-biased technological change, speeding up the reallocation of labour.

Table 8.1. **Typology of technology diffusion programmes/initiatives**

	Goal	Programme types	Objectives
Level 1	Improve the adoption and adaptation of specific technologies	Technology-specific	Diffuse a specific technology to a wide number of firms and sectors.
		Institution-specific	Promote technology transfer from specific institutions.
		Sector-specific	Diffuse technology to a particular industrial sector.
		Demonstration	Demonstrate the practical implementation of technologies.
Level 2	Improve the general technology receptor capacity of firms	Technical assistance	Assist firms in diagnosing technology needs and in problem solving.
		Information networks	Access to information on technology sources, etc.
		Assistance for small-scale R&D projects	Build capacity for autonomous technology development.
Level 3	Build the innovation capacity of firms	Sector-wide technology road maps	Systematic planning for future strategic technology investments.
		Diagnostic tools	Assist firms to develop innovation oriented management (includes organisational change).
		Benchmarking	Transmit best practice from elsewhere.
		University/industry collaboration	Upgrade the knowledge base of the firm.

Source: OECD (1997*q*).

451. Table 8.1 illustrates the transition of diffusion policies from the one-way transfer of public research results and capital equipment (Level 1 goal in Table 8.1) to policies that recognise diffusion and innovation as interdependent processes. At the second level, these policies seek to improve the general technology receptor capacity of firms through instruments such as technical assistance and manufacturing extension services. On the third level are policies/initiatives for building the overall innovative capacity of firms, including the use of sector road maps, diagnostics and benchmarking tools which can help firms develop and implement a more strategic uptake of technology.

Absorptive and innovative capacity

452. Broadly speaking, innovative capacity requires absorptive capacity, creativity in new products and modes of organisation, management ability and entrepreneurial risk-taking (Chabbal, 1995). A distinction should be made between individual and organisational-based abilities; the former refer to formal

technical, financial and managerial skills but also to creativity and interpersonal skills, while the latter include in-house or outsourcing of R&D, a high-trust environment and networking/co-operation with other firms. The mutually strengthening relationship between technology and upskilling applies to both individual and organisational-based capacities (Chapter 11). Wage premiums have been recorded for employees who use modern technology relatively intensively (Krueger, 1993; Entorf and Kramarz, 1995; Johnson *et al.*, 1995). Doms *et al.* (1997) found that plants using sophisticated equipment employ more highly skilled employees.

453. Innovation surveys in several OECD countries have sought to classify and measure absorptive and innovative capacities in firms. A general finding is that underdeveloped absorptive and innovative capabilities make it difficult for firms to identify and correctly gauge opportunities and risks. Company decisions on whether or not to adopt technology, invest in workers' skills, undertake organisational change or innovate in some form, will then discriminate against taking advantage of external technologies and know-how. The implications are that OECD government diffusion policies, although they have attempted to counter past reliance on supply-side measures with ways for improving firms' access to knowledge, have only partially addressed obstacles to technology diffusion. Effective support for diffusion must explicitly consider building the absorptive capacities of firms, in particular the knowledge and skills embodied in individuals and organisational structures.

Intermediary and bridging institutions

454. A main vehicle through which OECD countries promote technology diffusion, either generally or via specific programmes, is intermediary institutions which operate at the pre-competitive stage of technological development and/or at the interface between industry and the public research base. Pre-competitive refers to non-proprietary R&D. The intermediary institutions act as "producers", "users" and "carriers" of knowledge. Well-known examples include the Steinbeis Foundation and the Fraunhofer Society Institutes in Germany. In France the *Centres de Recherche Techniques* (CRTs), mainly sectoral based, and the *Centres Régionaux d'Innovation et Transfert Technologiques* (CRITTs) and *Technopoles* are the main intermediaries between public research and industry. In the United Kingdom, the same applies to the Research Councils, while the Business Links network and various schemes provide direct services to firms. In Denmark, the networks of Technological Service Institutes (GTS) and Technological Information Centres (TICs) similarly operate at the interface between public sources of knowledge and industry needs. In Japan, subsequent to regulatory reform in the area of academia-industry co-operation, the planned Technology Licensing Organisations (TLOs) are expected to promote technology transfer from universities to industry. Public-private intermediaries such as science and technology parks, technology incubators and technology transfer agencies also play an important role. Many intermediary institutions play a brokerage role such as the Dutch Innovation Centres Network (ICNN), Australia's Technology Access Programme (TAP) which includes technology counsellors for small firms or the United Kingdom's Business Links network of technology counsellors. Non-governmental intermediary institutions such as trade unions or industrial associations also provide support for technology transfer, management or human capital development.

8.6. Country differences in policy challenges and diffusion strategies

455. Despite these commonalities, the potential benefits of diffusion policies depend on the specific issues and national innovation systems which characterise different economies. Extending the typology proposed by Ergas (1987) which categorises countries as either diffusion- or mission-oriented, the diffusion trajectories of OECD countries may be broadly grouped into four categories: *(i)* mission- or defence-oriented (France, the United Kingdom, the United States); *(ii)* diffusion-oriented (Austria,

Germany, Italy, Japan, Korea, Sweden, Switzerland; *(iii)* resource-based (Australia, Canada, Denmark, Finland, Norway); and *(iv)* multinational-based (Ireland, Mexico). These categories are not hermetic and countries differ in their diffusion policy challenges and responses. In smaller economies, promoting inward FDI and trade has represented a traditional solution to accessing knowledge and technology from abroad, with imports, for example, accounting for up to 50 per cent of acquired technology in countries such as Canada or the Netherlands. FDI flows between large countries (*e.g.* Japan, the United Kingdom, the United States) have been motivated by access to markets and technological expertise in specific areas. The increased globalisation of R&D has become an important vehicle for diffusing technology, especially in Belgium, Ireland, the Netherlands and the Nordic countries.

456. International co-operation, particularly in the context of EU research programmes, has helped countries such as Spain, Italy and the Netherlands to access and diffuse technologies in fields such as aerospace (Amable *et al.*, 1997). Since joining the European Union, Spain has striven to develop its research capacity and promote technology uptake in manufacturing processes and products. While the low level of business-performed R&D reflects the underdeveloped tradition of research within Spanish firms (Ayala, 1995), it likely understates the amount of technology that is acquired by these industries from suppliers of capital equipment and machinery including imports. Survey evidence suggests that European integration has incited Spanish firms, including SMEs, to adopt a strategy of product differentiation and increased participation in other domestic firms (*e.g.* distribution networks) in order to maintain competitiveness. The transfer to private shareholders of Spain's large state-owned industries in the banking, telecommunication and utilities sectors should further stimulate competition and diffusion.

457. In the United States, federal investments in defence-oriented technologies combined with government research contracting and procurement were the main engines for diffusing technology until the end of the Cold War. This fostered the clustering of technology development and diffusion around geographic regions with strong university research capabilities (*e.g.* California, Massachusetts, New York, Texas) which, together with ample risk capital and an entrepreneurial environment, generated high exports and job growth. However, traditional sectors and other states have displayed a strongly varying ability to benefit. Since the mid-1980s, the federal government has promoted transfers of technology from federal labs to industry with limited success. Increasingly efforts focus on public-private partnerships, especially involving smaller firms, as evidenced by the increase in the number of state-level manufacturing extension centres.

458. In France, technology diffusion has traditionally been organised around a mission-oriented technology policy dominated by large technology programmes and government procurement (*e.g.* aerospace, electronics, telecommunications and nuclear energy). This has benefited large firms but has tended to exclude SMEs. In the 1980s, this challenge spurred various types of institutions [*e.g. Agence Nationale pour la Valorisation de la Recherche* (ANVAR)] and programmes targeting SMEs and specific sectors and regions, including schemes to enhance innovation management and training. In the 1990s, policies have continued to move away from large programmes towards diffusion, but surveys suggest that greater efforts are needed to promote the diffusion of organisational innovations in firms in addition to that of process and product technologies. The United Kingdom, where the evaluation of technology and innovation policies is increasingly institutionalised, undertook reforms in the early 1990s to reduce overlaps in its infrastructure for diffusion. While the United Kingdom has strong university-industry linkages for large firms and leading SMEs, low levels of technical competence in most small firms have been an obstacle to diffusion. Targeted policies increasingly promote organisational change and human capital development in small firms, including flows of tacit knowledge.

459. Among diffusion-oriented counties, Japan and Korea have focused on channelling foreign technology to production in high-technology electronics (*i.e.* semiconductors) and high-value-added

consumer products, but university-industry links have traditionally been weak. In Japan strong R&D capabilities in domestic firms combined with large co-operative research programmes and a network of locally supported extension centres diffusing advanced technologies helped Japanese industry adapt and exploit foreign technologies in the post-war period. Japan is currently reforming regulations governing technology transfer from universities to industry to improve licensing arrangements and foster greater mobility of research personnel. In contrast, while the large industrial conglomerates (*chaebols*) in Korea play a major role in acquiring technology, the lack of emphasis on adaptation and weak competition among firms in domestic markets mean that diffusion is limited. In the 1980s, as Korea encountered greater difficulties in acquiring foreign technologies, restrictions on inward foreign investment were relaxed and S&T policies have increasingly focused on diffusion, particularly among SMEs.

460. Austria, Germany and Switzerland (but also certain regions of Italy) have concentrated on diffusing domestic technology in manufacturing such as electrical, machinery, quality precision equipment and chemicals. In Germany a comprehensive technology diffusion infrastructure was built over several decades, especially in states such as Baden-Württemberg. Because of specialisation and the emphasis on the one-way transfer of technology to medium-sized manufacturing firms, however, it appears that this infrastructure has been less successful in helping diffuse technologies from emerging sectors (ICT, biotechnology), especially among smaller firms. Until the mid-1990s capital and regulatory obstacles to firm creation were seen as important barriers to technology diffusion, but reforms have recently been implemented. Following the restructuring of the research infrastructure in the new *Länder*, Germany's current diffusion strategy is based on strengthening networking among small firms and applied technology centres. Several new federal programmes aim to fill gaps in the institutions and markets for technology, especially at the regional level. Increasingly, mixed funding requirements and competition are being promoted in federal technology development and diffusion initiatives.

461. In resource-based countries, the predominance of firms with low levels of R&D led to a strategy based on technology imports of capital equipment, but with little diffusion to other sectors. Efforts to enhance diffusion have focused on supporting the emergence of new sectors (*e.g.* telecommunications in Finland, software in Canada), especially through university-industry partnerships. In Finland, for example, recent support for diffusion seeks to address problems arising from the lack of linkages between new technology-based clusters and traditional resource-intensive sectors. To this end, Finland's national network of technology development centres was recently reorganised around universities to create "competence" centres with links to firms. In Denmark, which did not undertake an active policy towards diffusion until the 1970s, industry successfully incorporated technology in its production processes, gaining a comparative advantage in traditionally low-tech sectors such as the food and wood sectors. Recent efforts have concentrated on improving the coherence of technology diffusion infrastructure and creating a favourable environment for business expansion around existing "clusters" rather than supporting specific sun-rise industries.

462. Sweden has long supported diffusion through technology institutes and the links between large customer firms and small suppliers. Targeted policies to diffuse technology have built on these relations as in the case of advanced manufacturing technology (AMT) schemes which focused on the supply-chains surrounding large firms such as Volvo and Saab-Scania (Bessant, 1995). However, the complexity and rapid pace of technological change has made it difficult for the science base to keep up. Indeed, the concentration of R&D efforts in very large firms reflects the dualism of the Swedish economy, with a dynamic multinational sector and a stagnant small-business sector. Increasing international specialisation has led to reduced dependence by the large firms on their domestic suppliers, limiting the sources of technology and know-how for small Swedish firms. Since the late 1980s there has also been a rapid internationalisation of R&D by Swedish-based multinational firms, while the involvement of skilled

foreign researchers in home R&D has been hampered by high indirect labour costs and personal income taxes. The policy focus has been on industry participation in university research as well as on raising mobility of R&D staff from universities to industry within Sweden.

463. Small catch-up economies such as Ireland, Mexico and to a lesser extent Greece, have relied on multinationals for diffusion. In Ireland and Mexico, however, there has been a partial trend towards "dual economies", with outward- and export-oriented sectors rapidly adopting technology while small domestic firms without links to foreign or national sources of technology are excluded. Policy towards technology diffusion in Ireland has become more active, benefiting from EU support and low market barriers due to EU Membership. Mexico, on the other hand, is characterised by a more science- than technology-based strategy, which has led to the concentration of scientific and technological capabilities around a few regional poles (*e.g.* Monterrey, Mexico City), while the export processing zones (*maquiladoras*) are dependent on foreign technology with few spillovers to domestic firms. The atomised structure of SMEs in Mexico, but also in Greece, inhibits diffusion. In addition to building own R&D capacity, technology policies focus on building partnerships and stimulating firm networks to enhance knowledge flows.

464. In the Czech Republic, Hungary, Poland and the Russian Federation, a main policy challenge is to facilitate the absorption of foreign know-how but also to exploit the stock of technologies from the national science system. Here too, countries differ. Hungary has acquired foreign technology associated with high levels of inward FDI, but slow changes to management structures in newly privatised firms and weak competition in product markets act as a break to broader diffusion. In Poland, inflows of technology and foreign investment have been highly uneven as entire regions and sectors, especially the agricultural sector, have been largely excluded. In several transition economies, low rates of capital replacement are an obstacle to technology diffusion. The technology transfer infrastructure remains fragmented (*e.g.* lack of bridging institutions), although efforts, drawing on international experience, are underway to address this in both the Czech Republic and Hungary. In the Russian Federation, inadequate IPR protection and macroeconomic instability hinder technological co-operation and the diffusion of scientific knowledge.

465. Ultimately, the technology diffusion strategies of OECD countries over the past decades shape to some extent current policy challenges (Table 8.2). It is against this background that the next section assesses targeted measures for promoting technology diffusion in OECD countries.

8.7. Assessing targeted policy initiatives: evidence from OECD countries

Improving the adoption and transfer of specific technologies

466. Encouraging the transfer of technology from the public research base to the business sector is a common policy challenge, and OECD countries maintain a myriad of policy instruments and institutions which can be grouped under the term "technology-diffusion infrastructure". This includes grants/subsidies, technology (transfer) centres, technology extension services, patent offices, university technology transfer offices, bridging institutions, networking schemes, etc. Grants are increasingly oriented towards sharing responsibility with participating firms through matching or in-kind support, partnerships or by requiring incremental investment and time-specific outcomes such as product quality improvements. These schemes, however, often require an element of subjective judgement in selecting technologies and participating firms. They are also subject to the vagaries of fiscal pressures and policy priorities. Finally, they may inadvertently help firms that already invest in innovation (including R&D) rather than those lacking an investment tradition, especially smaller firms. Evidence from innovation surveys suggests that prior in-house investment in innovation is associated with the likelihood of participating in such schemes.

Table 8.2. **Country strategies for technology diffusion**

	Macro level/framework conditions	Meso level of firms networks/ institutional infrastructure	Micro level of the firm/specific programmes
Australia	• Sustain improvements in R&D and lower trade barriers to encourage diffusion	• Consolidate technology diffusion structures and link them to government research agencies • Improve the university-industry interface via co-operative research centres	• Emphasize personnel mobility and tacit knowledge flows in targeted programmes • Increase efforts to evaluate specific programmes and disseminate best practice in technology adoption/ management to industry
Austria	• Attract FDI • Liberalise infrastructure sectors	• Enhance networking between technology transfer structures (*e.g.* science parks, co-operative research centres) and firms • Improve industry-university co-operation	• Make innovation management services (*e.g.* MINT-type schemes) more demand-driven
Canada	• Strengthen competition in product and service markets	• Build-up public information infrastructure • Encourage networking of existing competence centres	• Minimise subsidies in scope and repayment
Denmark	• Improve coherence between various administrative bodies and the national research centres	• Build up firm networks to facilitate diffusion • Strengthen commitment to bridging institutions (*e.g.* technology services institutes, GTS)	• Improve effectiveness of advisory services • Enhance mobility between research (universities) and advisory services (GTS)
Finland	• Integrate technology diffusion policy and broad economic policies	• Strengthen research training and development of "centres of excellence" around universities • Strengthen co-operation among large and small firms	• Encourage measures which raise absorptive capacity in firms • Improve marketing and targeting of technology transfer structures (*e.g.* technology "clinics")
France	• Liberalise infrastructure sectors (*e.g.* telecommunications, energy, rail services)	• Diffuse and apply research results via contractualisation policy between industry and large research establishments	• Diffuse generic technologies: electronic components, advanced materials, ICTs to SMEs • Incorporate training and human capital development within diffusion schemes
Germany	• Strengthen product market competition • Reduce regulatory/capital market barriers to firm creation • Integrate and upgrade the S&T infrastructure of the new *Länder*	• Improve the established technology diffusion infrastructure (both regionally and nationally), especially through the promotion of firm networks	• Introduce competition among firms and regions in tenders of specific co-operative programmes
Hungary	• Improve competitiveness • Rebuild R&D capacity with emphasis on cross-disciplinary research	• Build a technology transfer infrastructure for SMEs (*e.g.* the Zoltan Bay Foundation, S&T parks, innovation centres)	• Improve production process and product qualities in firms by diffusing existing technologies
Japan	• Increase support of basic research • Improve regulatory framework for industry-university collaboration	• Improve R&D co-operation among firms (*e.g.* integrating research across firms rather than separately)	• Integrate evaluation in innovation policies • Encourage mobility of university researchers • Encourage joint funding for technology development/ diffusion

	Macro level/framework conditions	Meso level of firms networks/ institutional infrastructure	Micro level of the firm/specific programmes
Korea	• Increase support for basic research • Improve corporate governance structures of large conglomerates (*chaebols*)	• Strengthen the role of bridging institutions • Build information infrastructure for SMEs	• Adapt best policy practices from diffusion initiatives in other countries (*e.g.* AMT, technology centres)
Netherlands	• Strengthen domestic competition in goods and service markets • Limit regulatory burden on firms, especially SMEs	• Increase the leverage of applied research institutes (TNOs) via partnerships with companies (small and large) • Exploit synergies between firms/research institutes using cluster-based policies	• Encourage technology awareness schemes and advisory services for SMEs • Promote mobility of technology specialists
Norway	• Strengthen domestic competition policy	• Promote cluster-based policies which support innovation in traditional sectors (*e.g.* fisheries, oil)	• Stimulate innovation in small firms with strong demand-driven public measures
Poland	• Promote FDI • Encourage restructuring in industrial sectors (*e.g.* coal, fuel, transport) and privatisation	• Build legal and institutional systems for innovation • Strengthen links between R&D institutes and industry • Support diffusion at regional level	• Promote diffusion in the agricultural sector through technical advisory centres • Diffuse technologies in mature industries (*e.g.* food processing) • Support ecologically-oriented technologies • Promote quality certification among SMEs
Spain	• Privatise state banking, telecom and utilities firms • Enhance domestic competition	• Decentralise and regionalise technology diffusion schemes • Support diffusion of public-research through innovation and technology centres	• Promote technology in the production process (*e.g.* textiles) • Promote schemes which encourage quality management including training
Sweden	• Liberalise external trade regime and globalisation of Swedish industry • Enhance domestic competition and strengthen structural change to facilitate firm creation	• Strengthen firm networks • Improve P/PPs involving government institutes and industry	• Encourage the outward mobility of research personnel from universities to industry • Strengthen inward mobility and mobility of skilled workers between sectors and firms
United Kingdom	• Give priority to reforming product markets • Reduce overlap in technology diffusion infrastructure	• Target public/private partnership schemes to promote industry-public research collaboration (*e.g.* biotechnology) for development and diffusion • Use technology foresight to encourage industry-led diffusion strategies	• Support broad, geographically based schemes for SMEs which link technology and training • Maintain specific technology-cluster diffusion initiatives (*e.g.* ICT)
United States	• Decentralise policies for technology diffusion • Make capital markets more effective	• Emphasize P/PPs in technology development programmes • Facilitate technology transfer from federal labs	• Strengthen market-based technology and business advisory services to SMEs • Tailor technology support to firm needs

Source: OECD Secretariat.

467. Supply-side initiatives remain an important component of technology diffusion policies. They are, however, becoming more customer-oriented and integrating many "softer" technology supports. Technology support to manufacturing, for example, has moved away from simple subsidisation and the choosing of "winning" technologies to a more demand-driven approach. In the United States, the Manufacturing Extension Partnership (MEP) network of state-level extension centres focuses on helping small firms in mainly traditional sectors exploit "appropriate" technologies. Several evaluations of the MEP network have shown positive effects in terms of sales, productivity and increased use of technology (Shapira, 1995; US General Accounting Office, 1996).[39] A survey of participating firms revealed that 70 per cent considered that the technical consulting services provided by MEP centres and their intermediaries were either unavailable in the market or were complementary to existing services (National Institute of Standards and Technology, 1996). One of the keys to the MEPs' success has been the development of a local base and access to a local innovation network including links to private consultants and industrial associations.

468. In Canada, where the concentration of R&D and innovative activity has been associated with lower rates of technology diffusion, supply-driven government R&D programmes such as the Canadian Space Agency's Space Station Programme (CSSP) have made the commercialisation of public research an explicit objective. Through its industry-led contracts the CSSP has successfully helped firms, including SMEs, develop and commercialise the application of dual-use space technologies in areas as diverse as agriculture, automation and toxic waste management. Similarly, in Korea, evaluations of the highly advanced national (HAN) technology development projects involving co-operation between industry and government-supported research institutes (GRIs) found that industry participation in programme design from the outset was instrumental in successful technology transfer and commercialisation (Park *et al.*, 1996).

469. Evaluations of Canada's Industrial Research Assistance Program (IRAP) to assist mainly manufacturing firms in technology uptake found that a local presence and networking were important factors in increasing the technical capacity of participating firms (National Research Council of Canada, 1990). In Japan, studies of the *kohsetsushi*, a network of mainly locally funded technological assistance centres, found that while long-term support was a factor in institutional and staffing stability, this reduced incentives for managers to raise outside financing. Recent changes aim to fill gaps in the technological skill level of researchers and the capacities of the centres to improve manufacturing processes and foster advanced product developments in SMEs. In Korea, as in Japan and the United States, a main factor in the ability of manufacturing extension centres to help firms is effective and up-to-date training of consultants. Evaluations from Finland's Technology Clinics (TEKES), a network of centres that matches SMEs with universities/research centres to solve specific technological problems, showed that while participating firms increased R&D spending and use of external technology, active marketing of the centres' services could improve the targeting of firms. A related issue is that of institutional competition; university/research institutes may prefer to participate in larger government programmes than in the small projects brokered by the clinics.

470. In Germany, evaluations of AMT programmes targeting CAD/CAM and computer-integrated manufacturing (CIM) technologies found that the more advanced the diffusion and development of a technology, the greater the likelihood of limited impact and the larger the free-rider effect. On the other hand, targeting the diffusion of very underdeveloped technologies in the market-place raises the risk

39. A 1994 study showed that firms involved with MEP centres were six times more likely to plan technical improvements than non-participating firms (National Institute of Standards and Technology, 1996).

and problems associated with its initial diffusion. The policy implication is that the timing matters in targeting specific technologies. Another important finding from similar programmes in Germany was the lack of sufficient and ongoing training in the diffusion process. The recent follow-up programme, Production 2000, represented a shift in the German government's diffusion strategy for manufacturing insofar as it sought to integrate the development and application of technology with education and training. In Germany, but also in other countries, it is increasingly acknowledged that technology diffusion policies cannot merely support new research results and their experimental application. Particularly for the contribution to overall job creation in economies plagued by problems of upskilling, diffusion policies need to be conducive to training and upgrading of individual as well as organisational skills, although, as noted above, there has been limited progress in this area. The means and incentives for upgrading skills are crucially influenced by a range of conditions, including taxes and wage structures, on which government, the social partners, firms and workers all have a bearing.

471. Like AMTs, the diffusion of ICTs continues to receive strong public support in Austria, Japan, the Nordic countries, the United States and through EU programmes. Increased flows made possible by ICT and lower prices have made information more easily available to SMEs. Yet experience suggests that while the disadvantages of small scale have been reduced, they have not been eliminated; evidence shows that smaller firms continue to encounter barriers in access and demand for ICT. This is more acute in countries which have been slower in removing regulatory and product market barriers in telecommunications and other network-based industries (Chapter 10). Regulatory burdens on SMEs, biased public procurement, lack of access to capital and other obstacles contribute to making sure that smaller firms remain ICT outsiders.

472. On the supply side, ICT diffusion programmes have been oriented towards infrastructure building such as creating public information networks to help SMEs access technical and market knowledge. Austria's Electronic Data Interchange (EDI) initiative aims to increase the competitiveness of SMEs by helping them reach the critical mass for exploiting EDI. The Strategis initiative in Canada seeks to capitalise on new ICTs for improving the information infrastructure of SMEs. Mexico's Information System on Technological Services (SISTEC) Internet network acts as a bridge between businesses and technology and service providers. The UK Supernet network matches SMEs with technical centres for assistance with product or process problems. The success of such schemes depends on keeping information accurate and up-to-date together with trouble-shooting expertise. Turkey's National Information and Telematics Services, an information network, aims to promote diffusion and knowledge flows. At the level of the European Union, the Community Research and Development Information Service (CORDIS) is an electronic network linking potential technology users with technology service providers.

473. With regard to the transfer of technology from public laboratories to firms, efforts in the United States have been strengthened although the outcomes are difficult to measure. One of the main factors limiting such initiatives has been a mismatch in the mission of federal labs and the needs of industry, including firms without past collaboration experience (Mowery, 1995). In Europe, evaluations of similar transfer efforts have shown that the inflexibility of centralised administration and funding structures results in a poor match with industrial needs, limiting success. One of the lessons has been that the effectiveness of transfer is enhanced by a certain level of managerial independence for individuals, units or structures responsible for stimulating the transfer of technology to industry. Transfer initiatives characterised by longer-term relationships with firms were more successful than single projects. Providing a broad range of technology diffusion services was shown to be a positive factor in meeting the needs of individual firms. Successful marketing approaches for attracting industrial partners are also important but there are limits as firms may be wary of sharing information with other firms, particularly in terms of product development (European Commission, 1996*b*). The

1996 innovation survey in Germany, for example, found that firm co-operation with public research or universities depended on the size and sector of firms, with smaller firms and those in competitive markets less likely to participate (Licht and Stahl, 1997).

474. Mature industries such as steel, textiles, shoe-making, shipbuilding, wood products and food processing industries are main targets of diffusion programmes. Efforts are generally devoted to subsidising technology costs in these sectors, especially for small firms, or to promoting collaborative R&D projects. For the textiles sector, evidence suggests that the weak success of large technology development and diffusion programmes in the United States, Japan and Europe was due to a lack of responsiveness to market trends towards quality, higher design content and rapid response. Such programmes focused on technologies based on mass production principles (OECD, 1998*b*). In Spain, efforts to diffuse computer-aided technologies to leather cutting in the shoe industry met with similar difficulties. In response, the Technological Footwear Institute (INESCOP), an applied technology centre, and local shoe manufacture associations worked together to apply water jet cutting technology to the cutting of leather for shoe-making firms. The implication is that using input from industry to tailor diffusion schemes to the specific needs of firms is a key factor in diffusing technology and stimulating incremental innovation.

Improving the general technological receptiveness of firms

475. Demonstration and technical assistance schemes are among the most common types of initiatives for improving the technical receptiveness of firms. Evaluations of technical assistance programmes in several OECD countries, however, have shown that while there are positive impacts on the technical capability, sales, costs and employment of participant firms, there are limits to economy-wide effects. Pure technical assistance programmes are generally limited in scope and isolated from other public and private technology-related programmes. Their industry coverage may be restricted and programmes not sufficiently demand-driven. Difficulties have been encountered in keeping the programmes technically up-to-date.

476. In Mexico the Compite Programme aims to increase productivity in small manufacturing firms by identifying problems and solutions along the firm's production line (*e.g.* inventories, response time, production flows). Providing effective technical assistance requires a precise assessment of firms' problems and needs – sometimes firms are seeking solutions to very specific technical problems. Programme success depends on quality consultants and expertise and requires the active participation of the firms' management or the entrepreneur. Improving awareness of programme benefits among potential participants is another challenge to achieving greater impact. Austria's *TechnoKonatakte* is a demonstration programme based on company visit schemes in Germany, Spain and the United Kingdom to raise awareness of technology transfer.

477. A main trend in improving the technological receptiveness of firms is promoting P/PPs as a way to share costs and ensure that technology diffusion is industry-driven. Norway's TEFT Programme incites SMEs, especially those with low or medium R&D capabilities, to collaborate with technological research institutes. Led by a corps of ten geographically-based technology attachés, firms receive an analysis of their position and recommendations for projects where the research institutes could provide collaborative support. A main difficulty inherent in such schemes is selecting the appropriate type of firm with a minimum level of applied research capabilities.

Building the innovative capacity of firms

478. Many recent diffusion programmes such as consulting schemes seek to stimulate firms, especially SMEs, to develop and implement a more strategic upgrade path for themselves. The rationale for these schemes rests upon the information asymmetries between small firms and private consultants and the high risk and uncertainty involved for firms with scarce resources. Government support helps lower the risk for firms and stimulate private demand for innovation and management competencies. Experience with Norway's Business Development Using New Technology (BUNT) programme which provided funding and training for industrial development consultants to help firms develop a strategy for technology use, showed that organisational change must be a precursor to the introduction and efficient use of new technology. A main strength of the BUNT approach is the effective training of consultants and the use of continuous (external) evaluations.

479. Evidence from a similar cost-sharing consulting scheme in Austria, the Managing Integration of New Technology (MINT) programme, which provides comprehensive management consultancy services to SMEs, indicates that in addition to trained staff, effective support requires the active participation of management. Changing the management culture is one of the aims of the European Commission's Euromanagement scheme, which through a network of consultants diffuses best practices in innovation management tools to SMEs in areas such as certification, quality and research. Programmes that provide such business support services are most effective when they fill a gap in the market or institutional infrastructure. In Sweden, the ALMI network of consultants provides business and technology advice to small firms in regions, including remote areas where private services are unavailable. However, there are limits to demand-side policies. The Dutch ICNN, whose consultants act as intermediaries between firms and private and public sources of technology and know-how, aims to stimulate awareness of technology among entrepreneurs/managers, without generating dependence on public support. In some cases, however, only businesses that were already planning to invest in a given area would do so because of the public incentives.

480. Benchmarking is another policy instrument used to strengthen the innovative capacity of firms. Such schemes include France's ANVAR Diagnosis programme, the UK Benchmarking Index – a national benchmarking service for SMEs, and the US Benchmarking Performance Service that serves companies through the US MEP centres. At the European Union level, the new Innovation Programme, building on the experience of the former Strategic Programme for Innovation and Technology Transfer (SPRINT), aims at "fostering an innovation culture" through *inter alia* the Innovation Management Techniques (IMT) programme. While methodologies differ, a main requirement for success is the involvement of well-trained consultants who can gain the trust of managers and thus increase the probability that recommendations are implemented (European Commission, 1996*c*).

481. Measures to promote innovative capacity in firms through flows of tacit knowledge are gaining ground in OECD countries. Initially ad hoc and often detached from other diffusion and innovation policies, they are increasingly being integrated in Denmark, Sweden and the United Kingdom. As technology brings about rapid change in organisational structures and in the workplace, there is a tendency for tasks to change continuously, increasing the need for lifelong learning within the firm. Mobility of scientists and technical staff is one way to increase the abilities of firms to enhance absorptive capacity. The Dutch Specialists in SMEs Scheme (*Kennisdragers in het Midden-en Kleinbedrijf* – KIM) to promote technology personnel in SMEs has been quite successful. Germany has two main schemes targeting R&D personnel in SMEs: the Ministry of Economics provides wage subsidies for R&D workers to firms in the eastern *Länder*; while the Research Ministry provides funding to cover the costs of additional R&D personnel. Evaluations of these programmes found they

had a significant impact on the hiring of additional personnel, but failed to adjust for the quality of R&D staff (Kuntze and Hornchild, 1995).

482. Norway's SME Competence Scheme helps small firms increase their level of competence by recruiting newly qualified graduates or graduates with some experience. The initial results have been intangible but positive, changing the attitudes of participating firms towards graduates and increasing co-operation between small firms and educational institutions. Evaluations of the UK TCS, which places post-graduates in a semi-academic or company-based environment for two years, not only found significant effects on jobs, firm turnover, exports and R&D spending, but also intangible benefits such as increased co-operation with industry and making academic courses more relevant to industry needs.[40] The challenge faced by such schemes is to reduce the risk of dead-weight (*i.e.* the risk of subsidising firms which would have sought outside help even in the absence of the subsidy). The TCS aims to minimise this risk by targeting the smallest firms.

8.8. General best-practice principles in technology diffusion programmes

483. At the level of specific initiatives/programmes, the experience of OECD countries provides examples of successful and less successful policy practices (OECD, 1997*q*). Understanding what does not work is just as important as understanding what does work. At the general level, technology diffusion programmes involve multiple stakeholders, complicating implementation. Programmes, if they are to be comprehensive, must often involve alliances and cross-sectoral networks as well as institutional investments and business incentives. Technology diffusion services generally have to be delivered locally. Conflicts may arise between local and national levels of government over management practices and programme goals. There is also a risk that diffusion strategies developed in, or targeted to, particular regions might preclude involvement by firms and institutions from other regions within the same country. As public agencies pursue more market-oriented approaches to delivering diffusion services and place greater reliance on private service providers, there may also be clashes between management styles and objectives.

484. Effective technology diffusion takes time and money and can be difficult to measure and evaluate. It also requires operational flexibility to meet diverse and emerging company needs. These are elements that traditional government decision-making and budgeting systems do not easily accommodate. Questions arise as to the appropriate target and scope of technology diffusion programmes. Firms which already have advanced capabilities may be targeted but may have least need of support. Governments should avoid prescribing uses of technology; promoting technologies that are generic and in early stages of development is likely to produce more social benefits than promoting specialised technologies (Lipsey and Carlaw, 1998). The problems in targeting firms may well reflect weaknesses in evaluation systems as to what types of diffusion policies, projects or services are more (or less) effective, for which clients.

485. General principles for best policy practice in targeted diffusion programmes are set out in Box 8.1. Beyond identifying what works in a given programme, however, transferring good practice requires distinguishing the general from the specific. Practices and methods need to be understood and mapped within their institutional contexts: what works in one context may do so as part of a broader set of explicit

40. A recent independent evaluation in 1995 found that £1 million of TCS support generates the following net cumulative additional activity: 58 jobs; £3.6 million value added; £3.0 million exports; £13.3 million turnover; £1.5 million capital expenditure; and £0.2 million R&D expenditure.

and implicit arrangements and may not easily be transferred to other national innovation systems, even if they face similar policy challenges. Adaptation and interpretation is generally necessary. Indeed, this is analogous to the process of technology diffusion itself, which requires learning and sunk costs on the part of adopters.

Box 8.1. **Best-practice principles for targeted diffusion programmes**

Policy context

- *Integrate technology diffusion at various levels of policy making, including macro and structural policies.*
- *Establish coherence between the scope of the general diffusion policy challenge and the specificity of the policy instrument.*

Rationale and objectives

- *Look beyond market failure.* Identifying clear market failures in technology diffusion remains important but government and systemic failures may also justify policy action.
- *Define objectives and mission from the outset while integrating evaluation tools to ensure regular monitoring and feedback into policy design.*
- *Anticipate the indirect impacts of other measures (e.g. tax support for R&D) as well as potential displacement effects.*

Design and delivery of programmes/initiatives

- *Consider how to transfer and licence technology from the outset.*
- *Ensure quality control of technology diffusion service providers,* through, for example, merit-based competition and external review.
- *Ensure sufficient geographic proximity.* This requires significant programme scale and coverage.
- *Build on existing resources.* Channelling programmes through existing structures and linking different types of institutions (*e.g.* SME service providers and patent offices).
- *Create an appetite for change among firms, but avoid dependency.*
- *Promote organisational development and change.*
- *Maintain close links with industry groups and associations.* Such groups not only help tailor programmes to firm needs but are instrumental in sharing and diffusing best practices among firms.
- *Ensure stability and sustainability.*
- *Build on evaluations of programmes.* Tailor evaluations to user needs and enhance the effectiveness of evaluations for benchmarking programmes.

Responding to new challenges and innovating with regard to diffusion policy tools

- *Link technology foresight to diffusion strategies.* Public-private technology foresight exercises for identifying new technologies can help policy makers develop new or adjust existing instruments to facilitate their sustainable diffusion.
- *Enhance responsiveness of policies to societal goals.* Environmental challenges (*e.g.* global climate warming) and demographic trends (*e.g.* ageing populations) will place greater pressure on social and market demands for technology. Diffusion policies play a role in responding to societal demands in areas such as health (*e.g.* diffusing tele-medicine) and education (*e.g.* ICT as a tool for lifelong learning) as well as in industry (environmentally benign manufacturing).
- *Share experience and diffuse best practices.* Governments have a role in promoting the diffusion of best policy practices within the institutional infrastructure for diffusion and among firms, including firm networks, industry associations, etc.

Source: OECD Secretariat

8.9. Main lessons and implications for diffusion policy

486. Three main implications arise from the assessment by OECD countries of targeted technology diffusion policies as they have evolved over the past decades. First, there are common challenges but also differences in the perception of the barriers to diffusion and in the priorities of governments. Second, while past patterns of scientific and technological specialisation continue to shape policy responses, there

are significant indications of convergence among OECD countries. The trend, for example, towards reducing financial support for technology uptake implies a trade-off in favour of soft support such as technology consulting services and a recognition that technology is more than just R&D embodied in capital equipment. Both demand- and supply-side measures are increasingly user-driven.

487. Third, the diversity of targeted technology diffusion initiatives in OECD countries suggests that countries pursue their own distinctive combination of policies and programmes, or "diffusion mix", which operates at the macro, meso and micro levels of the economy. The characteristics of this mix reflect not only specific national innovation systems, but also different challenges with respect to economic performance and job creation. The federal systems of government in Germany, the United States and to a lesser extent Belgium and Canada where diffusion policies are highly decentralised, account for an institutional set-up which is quite different from that of countries where policies are more centralised. Although effective technology diffusion policies thus require varying instruments, there are still a number of general lessons that countries can learn from each others' experience.

488. Most OECD countries maintain diffusion promotion measures which target manufacturing. The experiences of Switzerland and Austria on the importance of tacit knowledge flows in AMT schemes can help other countries planning similar schemes. Similarly elements of the MEP centres, such as external funding and close contact with industry associations, are useful for countries contemplating similar centres. Korea's Small and Medium Industry Promotion Corporation (SMIPC), a manufacturing extension scheme, has drawn on good practice in other countries and integrated soft supports such as technology consulting and training in support for product quality and production processes in manufacturing. The innovation management schemes for SMEs such as the BUNT in Norway were successfully adapted and transferred to Austria and other European countries with EU support. Many of the recent diffusion-oriented institutions (*e.g.* technology agencies, science and technology parks, incubators, etc.) and targeted programmes of the central and eastern European economies have been modelled on diffusion policies in other OECD countries. But the scale of some challenges (*e.g.* a large, fragmented agricultural sector in Poland, weak enforcement of IPRs) suggests that such efforts will take time and require structural reforms.

489. The assessment of targeted measures also reveals that the rationale for policy intervention is broadly similar despite local, regional or national specificities. In most countries, notably Australia, the United Kingdom and the United States, market failure continues to drive the bulk of technology diffusion policy initiatives. While policy makers, especially in Austria and the Nordic countries, increasingly acknowledge the importance of systemic failure, there appears to be a "policy lag" and many programmes do not take into account firms' interactions with the surrounding infrastructure. For example, while some SMEs are highly technical, most have little (internal) technical capacity. Consequently programmes for improving technology transfer from universities to SMEs could be inappropriate in regions with little critical mass. At the same time, technology diffusion is more than a problem of access to R&D-intensive machinery or patents, and many governments maintain schemes to raise the management capabilities of small firms. Several countries, not least Austria, Denmark, Finland, the Netherlands and Norway, encourage the further diffusion of know-how around existing clusters, many of which are low-technology but highly innovative. Germany recently conducted a "competition" whereby regions sought support for biotechnology research, not solely on the basis of firm-level competence, but also on the basis of strengths in the surrounding research institutes, universities, banks and the local regulatory environment. This initiative explicitly acknowledged the advantages for support to technology development and diffusion that can flow from local structural coherence.

Importance and limits of evaluations

490. Technology diffusion initiatives are particularly challenging for evaluators, not least because of the multiplicity of objectives involved and the myriad of indirect effects on both targeted and non-targeted firms/organisations. Technology diffusion initiatives, because they simultaneously operate at the macro, meso and micro levels are highly contextual to the institutional framework and market environments in which they operate. In addition, the majority of evaluations of technology diffusion schemes are concerned primarily with efficiency in a narrow sense (Arvantis and Hollenstein, 1997). Intangible and difficult to measure impacts such as encouraging a "culture of entrepreneurship" among academics participating in technology transfer schemes or increasing university "awareness" of industry needs are perhaps as important for society, in the longer term, as the productivity gains of some participating firms. The existence of multiple stakeholders, while important as an external review mechanism, may also give rise to conflict in terms of the objectives of evaluations. Programme managers may be more interested in programme services and delivery than in broader economic impacts, while policy makers seek to observe broad outcomes such as employment and productivity effects. Firms' decisions, based on enhancing profitability, may go against underlying policy objectives, as in the adoption of technology that may be labour-saving rather than labour-enhancing, at least in the short term (Jarmin and Jensen, 1997). Still, evaluations play a critical role in improving the effectiveness of technology diffusion programmes and identifying good practices. Qualitative or "soft" techniques such as those used in the Nordic countries and Switzerland are potentially useful in assessing new types of diffusion instruments (*e.g.* networking initiatives).

8.10. Conclusions

491. This chapter has reviewed the diffusion efforts of OECD countries and identified best-practice principles and policies based on the assessment of discrete policy instruments. Best practices can help improve the effectiveness of existing policies and maximise private and social returns from technology. They cannot, however, substitute for public and private investments in R&D and innovation. Moreover, in formulating and designing diffusion policies, OECD countries must take account of broader framework conditions. First, conditions allowing for FDI and trade in technology embedded in goods and services have a major bearing on the opportunities of more narrowly defined diffusion programmes. Structural reforms in product and labour product markets, if not appropriately designed, may contribute to distorting market incentives for innovation and diffusion, limiting the overall effectiveness of targeted programmes. The extent to which labour market conditions, taxes, etc., provide incentives to upgrade labour-force skills crucially influences how, and to what extent, diffusion policies can help to raise absorptive capacity as well as generate economy-wide employment effects.

492. Summing up, technology diffusion is an important policy area for OECD governments and countries have taken policy action at several levels to broaden diffusion (Table 8.3). The majority of OECD countries have lowered barriers to FDI and trade; several have given high priority to strengthening competition in product markets (Canada, Germany, the Netherlands, Sweden, the United Kingdom), allowing faster reallocation of labour and speeding diffusion. The central and eastern European countries and Korea have relaxed restrictions on FDI, but further action for strengthening domestic competition is warranted. Australia, Finland, the Netherlands and the United Kingdom have consolidated the institutional infrastructure for diffusion to reduce overlap, while in France the roles of multiple regional structures could be better delineated. Denmark has taken steps to make technology service institutes more responsive to firms' needs, while Spain is strengthening existing technology transfer institutions (*e.g.* patent offices, technology centres). P/PPs are not new in the area of technology diffusion and are increasingly favoured in Australia, Canada, the United Kingdom, the

United States; they are being broadened in Germany where most technical centres remain heavily dependent on public support. Australia, Canada the United States and to a lesser extent France have integrated diffusion more explicitly in large technology development projects, often with a focus on SMEs. Austria, Germany, Korea, Switzerland and the United States have integrated "soft supports" such as training, into diffusion schemes for AMTs. In Switzerland, despite high innovativeness in traditional sectors and a strong research base, the diffusion of emerging technologies in industry remains weak. Service firms continue to receive little attention in most countries, except in the context of schemes to promote the diffusion of ICTs in SMEs.

Table 8.3. **Summary of best policy practices to improve and broaden technology diffusion policies**

Areas	Best policy practices and country examples
Strengthening links between firms and the public research infrastructure	Enhance role of intermediary institutions (*e.g.* patent offices, technological institutes, science parks) (Australia, Austria, Denmark, Korea, Spain).
	Integrate "soft supports" in technology transfer of process and product technologies (Austria, Germany, Korea, Switzerland, United States).
	Institutionalise evaluation in diffusion policy initiatives (Australia, Canada, Germany, United Kingdom, United States).
	Integrate technology diffusion in large technology development projects (Australia, Canada, United States).
Building up network capacities among firms	Promote effective partnerships in technology commercialisation (Australia, Canada, Germany, United Kingdom, United States).
	Promote access by small firms to the information structure (Canada, France, Netherlands, United Kingdom, United States).
	Maximise diffusion around clusters of firms, including between suppliers-users (Austria, Finland, Netherlands, Norway, Sweden).
	Stimulate competition and co-operation in joint collaborative research projects (France, Germany, Japan, United Kingdom, United States).
Building up the internal absorptive and innovative capacities of firms	Promote organisational change and training in small firms (Austria, Denmark, Norway, United Kingdom).
	Enhance effectiveness of innovation management schemes (Austria, Ireland, Netherlands, Norway, United Kingdom).
	Encourage personnel movements between industry-public sector, especially SMEs (Australia, Sweden, United Kingdom).

Source: OECD Secretariat.

493. Promoting diffusion between large and small firms remains a key issue in a number of countries, including Finland and Sweden but also in Ireland, where small, domestically oriented firms have weak linkages to large, highly internationalised or foreign firms. Tools for the diffusion of non-R&D sources of knowledge such as innovation management skills, etc., via cost-sharing consulting schemes, are particularly developed in Austria, the Netherlands, the Nordic countries and the United Kingdom but less so in Southern Europe. Mobility of research personnel between industry and the public sector, often with an emphasis on SMEs, is being promoted in Australia, the Netherlands, Sweden and the United Kingdom, and needs to be strengthened in France and Japan where institutional barriers limit mobility. A large number of countries conduct technology foresight exercises; in the Netherlands and the United Kingdom they are used to design and improve technology diffusion

programmes. At the international level, the European Commission has undertaken efforts to facilitate the diffusion of technical information and best practice in technology transfer, especially among SMEs. There is a need, however, to encourage synergies between national and international diffusion schemes. Finally, the evaluation of targeted diffusion initiatives – although institutionalised in Australia, Canada, Germany, the United Kingdom and the United States – remains a weak area in most OECD countries.

CHAPTER 9. PROMOTING NEW TECHNOLOGY-BASED FIRMS

9.1. Introduction

494. The contribution of small firms to economic development and job creation has gained in interest in recent years. Young, high-growth SMEs typically account for a sizeable share of overall employment growth (Birch, 1994). Economists have reopened the debate on the role of business start-ups and the size distribution of firms in determining sectoral and overall economic performance, and on whether some market and systemic failures disproportionately affect small firms. Governments have generally increased the priority attached to policies directed towards SMEs, with a growing focus on the promotion of innovation.

495. This reassessment is partly dictated by budgetary constraints but there are other more important reasons. First, there are uncertainties about the impacts of the many national or sub-national support programmes and measures that have accumulated over time. Second, policies must take into account the challenges and opportunities that new technologies and globalisation raise for small firms. Third, an increased emphasis of SME policies on the promotion of innovation makes more acute the need to find the right balance between measures addressing generic problems related to size or newness and more targeted approaches to he specific problems of particular types of SMEs.

496. In many OECD Member countries, governments consider that new technology-based firms (NTBFs) deserve special attention on the assumption that they play an important role in the early commercialisation of new knowledge and, more generally, in facilitating growth-enhancing structural change in product markets (creation of niches) and creating opportunities for labour upskilling and mobility. The following questions are addressed in this chapter: Do NTBFs make a distinctive positive contribution to innovation, economic development, and job creation? Does their creation and initial growth face specific obstacles? How could governments best lower such obstacles?

9.2. The importance of NTBFs in a knowledge-based economy

497. Many studies confirm that a subset of SMEs make a particularly important direct and indirect contribution to knowledge generation, technology diffusion, productivity gains and job and wealth creation. Whereas it is generally agreed that such enterprises, often called "new technology-based firms", are younger and more innovative in developing or using new technologies than the average firm, there is no precise definition common to all authors and all countries.

498. Some empirical studies utilise industry-based classifications of "high-technology", allowing easy international comparisons, while others use firm-based classifications which have the advantage of recognising that some firms in "medium-" or "low-technology" industries are more innovative in developing new technologies than some firms in "high-technology" industries. Definitions of "technology-based" and "innovative" also vary. The criteria of technological sophistication can be

R&D intensity (*e.g.* R&D expenditure as a percentage of sales) or the percentage of workers that are "skilled" or "educated", and sometimes include some measure of productivity growth. The criteria of "innovativeness" is usually the proven capability of the firm to introduce new products or processes, but other firm characteristics or performance can also be taken into account. This chapter draws on studies based on these different definitions of "new technology-based firms" or "young, small innovative firms" with a view to identifying common policy-relevant findings.

The role of NTBFs in innovation systems

499. Schumpeter argued that new firms are indispensable "agents of technological change", not only because they open new routes for the commercialisation of knowledge, but also because their competitive pressure prompts incumbent firms to become more innovative. Recent economic research has expanded this argument and brought substantial evidence that NTBFs fulfil an increasingly important role in a knowledge-based economy, both directly as generators of new products and services and indirectly as catalysts in improving knowledge interactions within national innovation systems.

NTBFs complement large firms in renewing and widening the technological base of economic expansion

500. NTBFs often bring entirely new products to market, enhancing productivity, quality and choice. There are several well-known "revolutionary" inventions by start-up firms, including: the FM radio (Armstrong), the microwave oven (Raytheon), the microcomputer (Altair and Apple) and the microprocessor (Intel). Almeida and Kogut (1997) observe that "semiconductor start-ups continue to drive new design technologies, [while] larger firms dominate in the manufacture of integrated circuits and the development of more mature segments of the industry". The US National Academy of Engineering (1995) underlines the key role played by NTBFs in the creation and early growth of technically dynamic and fragmented markets (*e.g.* advance displays and visual systems, implantable surgical and medical devices, and environmental testing services).

501. This is not a new phenomenon. A start-up by Edison gave birth to the incandescent lamp in 1878, and Klepper and Simons (1996) recall that the technological base of the automobile, automobile tire, television and penicillin product markets in the United States was initially established through the creation of a number of firms (for example, there were almost 400 automobile manufacturers in 1910 and 80 firms in 1925, compared to only 10 in the 1960s when the industry reached maturity). However, recent trends in innovation modes and surrounding framework conditions have changed the traditional division of labour between and co-operation among different actors of innovation processes to the benefit of small, flexible and entrepreneurial teams, while facilitating their institutionalisation as independent firms (*e.g.* ICTs, venture capital).

502. Large and small firms possess different advantages in innovating, reflecting different profiles of risk/reward ratios. Large firms have greater financial, technological and production resources and easier access to distribution networks. They are also more likely to have the market power that helps appropriate economic returns from innovative activity, and are generally able to reduce the risk of R&D by diversifying across projects. But large firms often have vested interests (*i.e.* high sunk costs) in existing technological trajectories and are reluctant to invest in areas remote from their core competencies, especially when markets are not large enough to allow the rapid amortisation of overhead costs.

503. Small, innovative and new technology-based firms, conversely, specialise in innovative activities which do not require large R&D expenditure but benefit from entrepreneurial dynamism, internal flexibility, responsiveness to changing circumstances and technological expertise in highly specialised fields (Rothwell and Dodgson, 1993). Their advantage lies where "advances in technology

accumulate upon a myriad of detailed inventions involving individual components, materials and fabrication techniques ... [and where the] ... sales possibilities for making such narrow, detailed advances are often too modest to interest giant corporations" (Scherer, 1984). Broadly speaking, small firms tend to innovate in response to customer needs; their innovations are commonly more demand-pulled than those of large firms.

504. Such differences in innovation style are reflected in R&D and patenting patterns (Baldwin, 1997). Large firms rely more on R&D performed on an ongoing basis, whereas smaller firms build their innovation capabilities through external linkages, especially with suppliers and clients. For small firms, being first in the market is relatively more important than other means of protecting their innovations, both because they lack legal and managerial resources to maintain specialists in IPR, but also because they tend to pioneer new applications of advanced technologies in market niches rather than develop entirely new products or processes.

NTBFs improve knowledge interactions within national innovation systems

505. In addition to serving different markets, NTBFs are complementary to large firms in their way of interacting with other actors of innovation systems. This is evidenced by their participation in inter-firm knowledge flows, their involvement in partnerships and the importance of spin-offs (the creation of a new firm by the personnel of an existing firm) and spin-outs (the creation of a new firm by the personnel of a public research organisation or university) (Box 9.1).

506. NTBFs perform a special function within innovation networks as bridging institutions that close the information gap between large knowledge organisations and firms in traditional industries. For example, a Finnish survey[41] found that the adaptive focus of NTBFs makes them efficient agents of technology and knowledge diffusion across sectors (Autio and Yli-Renko, 1997). A large proportion of Finnish NTBFs reported that their most important contribution to clients was to help them adopt and adapt new technologies and know-how, and that their most important customers were in low-technology industries (30 per cent of the sample served the forest cluster).

507. Spin-offs from large firms, as well as partnerships between small firms, large firms and public research organisations, are gaining in importance because they are efficient ways of refining the division of labour within innovation systems to the benefit of all. The success of NTBFs often depends on close relationships with large firms to secure access to managerial, financial and technical resources and marketing channels. Partnering with NTBFs, or informal privileged relationships with spin-off firms, gives large firms the possibility to reconcile the need to explore other opportunities at low risk and to offer value-added characteristics to their products, without straying from their core production. These benefits are enhanced by globalisation since spin-offs or contractual arrangements with NTBFs can offer a viable alternative to direct investment or acquisition as an internationalisation strategy.

The contribution of NTBFs to employment and productivity growth

508. In addition to their contribution to innovation and technology diffusion, other factors have raised the perceived importance of small, innovative and new technology-based firms. There are many examples,

41. 150 experts were asked to name the most promising technology-based growth companies – "one which based its business idea on innovatively exploiting advanced technological knowledge in its industry." They also had to be: independent, entrepreneurial (owned by an entrepreneur/group of entrepreneurs), and employ less than 500 workers.

particularly in the United States, of NTBFs achieving phenomenal rates of growth (*e.g.* Intel, Microsoft), providing wealth to the founders, direct jobs for employees and stimulating the economic development of their region, thereby leading to sizeable indirect job and wealth creation. By contrast, the quasi absence of such "success stories" seems a characteristic feature of the recent economic history of most OECD countries, where employment growth has been lagging and unemployment rising. This section assesses the extent to which new and/or small technology-based/innovative firms have contributed to growth in turnover, productivity and employment, and how this contribution has differed across countries, drawing on a number of empirical studies on start-up, survival and growth rates (see overview of results and references in Table 9.1).

Box 9.1. **Partnerships, spin-outs and spin-offs – examples from Canada and Belgium**

Telecommunications in Canada: large and small firm partnerships

The advantages of a large firm partnering with small firms are illustrated by the case of Newbridge Networks. The company, founded in 1986, has grown at a rapid rate, now employing 7 000 people world-wide and grossing almost C$ 1 billion in revenue. The company makes network switches, often responding to specific customer requests. Producing highly customised options for small markets would not be advantageous for such a large company. Hence, it seeks out small or new leading-edge companies with the capabilities to provide the options. It "partners" with small companies, providing them with financial resources to meet the demands for the specific options and "labelling" them (they become a "Newbridge Company"). Thus, Newbridge benefits by improving customer satisfaction without having to stray from its core production. The partnering small company benefits through access to financing and a large customer base.

Biotechnology in Belgium: spin-outs and partnerships

Segers (1993) cites the importance of a spin-out, and reviews how important partnering has been in its growth. Plant Genetic Systems (PGS) was a spin-out from the genetic engineering laboratories of the universities of Gent and Leuven, founded in 1983. In an early phase, the high cost of development and lack of standard products resulted in losses. Through a series of co-marketing licences, joint ventures and product development agreements with large companies, the company has been able to commercialise its products by obtaining footholds in associated market niches. It has been able to move from being a technology-driven company based on a research idea, to a market-driven manufacturing and research company. The large firms with which it has partnered have been able to benefit from PGS' development of leading-edge products without having to invest directly in risky product development.

Start-up of technology-based firms

509. Inferences on the rate of start-ups of NTBFs can be drawn from information on the proportion of start-ups that are technology-based or innovative, in combination with data on start-up activity in general. A first group of studies provides estimates using industry classification of start-ups at the time of creation, for example: in the United States only 7 per cent of start-ups in 1977 and 1978 were in "highly innovative industries" and, in France, about 9 per cent of manufacturing start-ups are "high-tech".[42] In addition, there is evidence that in the United Kingdom and the United States, high-tech start-ups are concentrated in the service sector, including the software industry.

510. An alternative way of measuring the extent of high-technology start-up activity is to survey firms after their start-up, and determine the share engaged in technology-intensive or innovative activity. A Dutch study has found that "techno-starters" account for about 10 per cent of manufacturing start-ups. However, if the "techno-starter" definition is restricted to firms introducing entirely new products, this percentage falls to between 5 and 7.5 per cent. About 30 per cent of German start-ups are "innovative" in a "broad sense", but only 7 per cent offer new technical solutions, and 6 per cent new products.

42. High-tech industries are: pharmaceuticals, office machinery, computers and other equipment, electrical machinery, radio, television and communication equipment and instruments.

Table 9.1. **Start-up, survival and growth of small innovative and new technology-based firms**[1]

Stage	Findings	Studies
Start-up	Only a small percentage (5-10) of start-ups are technology-based.	United States (Kirchhoff, 1995), France (APRODI, quoted by de Lind van Wijngaarden, 1995), United Kingdom (Storey and Tether, 1996; de Lind van Wijngaarden, 1995), Netherlands (Braaksma, 1995)
	While about 7 per cent of German start-ups offer new technical solutions and 6 per cent offer new products, 30 per cent are innovative in a "wider sense".	Hunsdiek, 1987 (quoted by de Lind van Wijngaarden, 1995)
	High-technology start-ups are more common in services and software than in manufacturing.	United Kingdom (Storey and Tether, 1996; de Lind van Wijngaarden, 1995), United States (National Science Board, 1996)
	Start-up rates across all firms are highest in the United States, lowest in Japan, and varied throughout Europe.	EIM Small Business Research and Consultancy, 1995
Survival	High-technology firms have higher survival rates than do average start-ups.	United Kingdom (Westhead and Storey, 1994; Garnsey and Cannon Brooks, 1993), Italy (Malerba *et al.*, 1995), West Germany (Nerlinger, 1995), Germany (Bruederl *et al.*, 1993), France (Mustar, 1995)
	In one study of Austrian firms, technology-based SMEs have a higher failure rate than average SMEs.	Parger, 1995
	In terms of their survival rates, start-ups in high-technology sectors do not differ from firms in other sectors.	United States (Kirchhoff, 1995)
	Firms that derive from incubators have higher than average survival rates.	United States, Australia, France, the Netherlands and the EU (NBIA, 1995; Gardner and Kenyon, 1994; APCE, 1997; EBN, 1996)
Employment growth	Start-ups in high-technology industries grow more rapidly than do other start-ups.	United States (Kirchhoff, 1995)
	Firms started by scientists achieve higher growth rates than do other firms.	Mustar, 1995
	NTBFs in the United Kingdom have higher growth rates than "comparable" firms in other sectors.	Westhead and Storey, 1994; Garnsey and Cannon Brooks, 1993
	In Canada, more-innovative SMEs are more successful than less-innovative SMEs.	Baldwin and Johnson, 1996
	Technically oriented, design-intensive discrete parts small manufacturers in Turin (Italy) grow faster than other firms.	Calderini and Swann, 1996
	Small R&D-performing firms grow more rapidly than non-R&D-performing small firms in France, Japan and the United States.	Motohashi, 1998
	In Finland, growth in NTBFs is most rapid among the smallest firms, the youngest firms and firms located in the high-technology sectors.	Lumme, 1995

Stage	Findings	Studies
Productivity growth	Technically oriented, non-design intensive discrete parts small manufacturers in Turin (Italy) grow faster than other firms.	Calderini and Swann, 1996
	In France, small R&D-performing firms experience faster growth than non-R&D-performing small firms.	Motohashi, 1998
	In the United States, small R&D-performing firms experience slower growth than non-R&D-performing small firms.	Motohashi, 1998
	In Japan, small R&D-performing firms experience the same growth as non-R&D-performing small firms.	Motohashi, 1998
Aggregate effects	Employment in technology-based SMEs is increasing more rapidly than SME employment in other industries.	Austria, Finland, France, western Germany, Greece, Ireland, Italy, Norway, Spain, Sweden and the United Kingdom (Tether and Storey, forthcoming)
	Employment gains in technology-based industries are superior to those in non-technology-based industries in small firms, but are inferior in micro-sized units.	As above
	In Sweden, employment gains in technology-based industries are inferior to those in non-technology-based SMEs.	As above

1. For the full names of the acronyms used herein, please see the Glossary .

Source: OECD Secretariat.

511. The rate of high-tech start-ups is conditioned by the overall rate of start-up activity, which is highest in the United States and lowest in Japan (EIM Small Business Research and Consultancy, 1995).[43] The average for Europe falls between, with substantial differences across countries. Start-up rates in France, Germany, Portugal, Iceland, Ireland, Spain and the United Kingdom are close to those in the United States, while they are much lower in the other European countries.

Survival of NTBFs

512. The creation of technology-based firms has both a direct and an indirect impact on the economy; indirectly by spurring innovative activity among incumbents through competitive pressure and because they act as agents of technology diffusion, and directly depending on the length of time firms survive and the rate at which they grow. High-technology firms have higher survival rates than do average start-ups in France, Germany, Italy and the United Kingdom. Conversely, Austrian technology-based SMEs have a higher failure rate than do SMEs on average, although this average survival rate is exceptionally high (76 per cent over six years). Start-ups in "highly innovative industries" in the United States were not found to be more likely to survive than other start-ups. Evidence on the NTBFs which emanate from incubators is more consistent since their survival rates are higher than average in all countries for which evidence exists, namely Australia, France, the Netherlands, the United States and the European Union.

43. These conclusions are drawn from a special study that was conducted by EIM Small Business Research and Consultancy to adjust birth rates across countries for differences in definitions, so as to make comparisons possible.

Employment growth in NTBFs

513. Recent years have seen a multiplication of studies on the growth of both small, innovative and new technology-based firms. Although based on different definitions (*e.g.* NTBFs created by scientists in France, start-ups in "highly innovative industries" in the United States, NTBFs in the United Kingdom) and covering different periods, they converge on the conclusion that new innovative firms grow faster than other start-ups and SMEs.

514. Some studies have examined whether relatively higher growth is observed among small, innovative or technology-based firms, as opposed to just new ones. Small, R&D performing firms experienced superior growth in employment compared with non-R&D performing firms in France, Japan and the United States (Motohashi, 1998). Other research relates employment creation to innovativeness, on the understanding that the latter is underestimated for small firms if only R&D performance is considered. In Canada "more-innovative firms" enjoyed higher growth in their share of industry sales, assets, employment and profits, than did "less-innovative firms". A German innovation survey demonstrates that small innovative firms without formal R&D activities have better employment prospects than larger ones characterised by R&D-intensive innovation (Table 9.2).

Table 9.2. **Employment performance of innovative firms in Germany**

1995, percentage – Mannheim Innovation Panel

	Non-innovative firms	Firms without R&D	Firms with R&D without R&D department	Firms with R&D department
Exporting firms	28.9	42.5	63.4	83.7
Average export rate	6.3	9.5	17.7	29.1
Firms expecting an increase in sales	38.7	51.1	49.7	47.4
Firms expecting increased competition	67.2	77.8	85.6	87.6
Firms expecting to increase employment	20.6	26.4	22.0	18.1

Source: German NIS reports, 1997.

515. According to a Finnish study (Lumme, 1995), not only are small, innovative and new technology-based firms more likely to create jobs at a faster rate than other firms, but the newer and the smaller they are, the more rapid their growth. Specifically, firms less than ten years old accounted for 40 per cent of employment among the firms sampled, but were expected to account for about 70 per cent of potential new jobs in the 1993 to 1998 period. Another Finnish survey of 1 445 firms provides an interesting assessment of the variable contribution of different types of NTBFs to job creation: application innovators (applying existing technology in an established market), market innovators (developing new product concepts), technology innovators (introducing new technologies into existing markets) and paradigm innovators (introducing new product concepts based on a new technology). It concludes that firms developing entirely new product concepts (*i.e.* market and paradigm innovators) are expected to achieve the strongest rates of growth in sales and employment (Autio and Lumme, 1995; Table 9.3).

Table 9.3. **Employment performance of NTBFs in Finland**[1]
Percentage

	Expected annual growth					
	Sales			Employment		
	1993-94	1993-95	1993-98	1993-94	1993-95	1993-98
Application innovators	20.0	21.3	16.2	5.5	8.8	8.4
Market innovators	57.9	51.0	33.0	44.4	35.3	20.7
Technology innovators	26.7	25.4	22.0	5.7	14.1	14.9
Paradigm innovators	66.7	57.4	35.9	25.0	33.0	24.6

1. Estimates for a sample of 392 new firms.

Source: Autio and Lumme (1995).

516. Calderini and Swann (1996) have shed light on the association of technology development with employment *vs.* productivity growth. In a detailed study of 650 small and medium-sized discrete-part manufacturers in Turin, Italy, they examine the relationship between product and technological complexity and performance. Firms that were both technologically complex and design-intensive exhibited the strongest employment growth. Conversely, firms that were technologically complex but not design-intensive did not experience superior employment creation, but enjoyed the highest productivity gains among all clusters. Hence, technological complexity alone was associated with strong productivity-led growth in output. In combination with design-intensive activity, it was also associated with strong employment growth, further indicating a close connection between upgrading of skills and job creation.

517. In conclusion, it is important to stress that, while technology-based firms do indeed exhibit faster average employment growth rates than firms in other sectors, there is little evidence of European firms exhibiting an aggregate growth performance comparable in any way to that reported in the United States (Tether and Storey, forthcoming).

Aggregate effects

518. A key question is whether the superior employment and growth performance of a tiny group of firms is significant enough at the aggregate level to justify policy attention. Using longitudinal data pertaining to a cohort of new firms (with less than 100 employees) in 1977 and 1978, Kirchhoff (1995) demonstrates that start-ups are a significant source of job creation. Over one in five jobs created in the United States in the 1978 to 1984 period derived from firms with less than 100 employees that started in 1977 or 1978. Table 9.4 demonstrates that the bulk of job creations came from the non-high-tech sectors, where the greatest number of start-ups occurred. However, firms in high-innovation industries created proportionately more jobs, due to their higher growth.

519. In order to assess how pervasive the aggregate contribution of small technology-based firms is to employment across countries, Tether and Storey (forthcoming) have carried out a detailed study of the changes in employment levels from the early 1980s to the early 1990s, by firm size among firms in technology-based and other industries. They found that employment in technology-based industries increased in most of the 14 European countries studied. Increases in employment were more prevalent in

micro, small and medium-sized units than in large firms, and were more consistent in the service than in the manufacturing sector, although employment gains (or minimisation of losses) in technology-based industries have been superior to those in other industries in each of the size classes in most countries.

Table 9.4. **Entry, survival and growth (1978-84) among start-ups in 1977 and 1978 in the United States**
Percentage

Industry type	Entrants	Survivors	Aggregate growth for survivor cohort	Aggregate growth for entire cohort	Cohort employment (1984)
High innovation	7.2	36.8	169.2	13.9	9.7
Low innovation	34.4	37.1	67.4	-31.5	30.6
Other	58.4	39.4	68.5	-25.5	59.7

Source: Kirchhoff (1995).

Summary

520. Both small, innovative and new technology-based firms play a key and exclusive role in innovation systems and are important generators of jobs. The innovation and job creation of NTBFs will, in some cases, be at the expense of other less efficient firms, yielding productivity gains but not always net job creation. The process of "creative destruction", while inherent to economic development, is unfortunately difficult to model and quantify on the basis of available information. Moreover, while small, innovative and new firms generate a significant share of new jobs, less- or non-innovative firms, by their sheer number, have a greater aggregate impact on employment. Given their ability to couple innovation with upgrading of labour skills, however, NTBFs are particularly likely to spur economy-wide employment gains in a context of labour market rigidity and skill mismatch.

9.3. Obstacles to the creation and growth of NTBFs

521. The distinctive performance of small, innovative and new technology-based firms in the face of increasing global competition and pervasive unemployment explains their interest for policy makers. This section reviews the results of the most recent empirical research on the main factors that limit the willingness or ability of individuals to start and grow innovative new businesses, with a view to identifying those obstacles that can be overcome by government policies.

522. Market failures (*e.g.* in the field of financing), systemic failures (*i.e.* conflicting incentives of different actors of innovation systems or lack of a critical mass of actors to justify market initiatives) and government failures (*e.g.* regulatory obstacles to entrepreneurship, dissuasive tax systems, unwarranted product market regulations), combine with cultural factors (*e.g.* risk aversion) to explain why the potential of NTBFs is unevenly realised in the OECD area.

523. The "entrepreneurial culture" that prevails in each country, *i.e.* social appreciation of commercial success, as well as the stigma associated with failure, conditions the likelihood of individuals investing their talents outside existing organisations. The lack of an entrepreneurial culture is often cited as the main explanation for the scarcity of rapidly growing NTBFs in Europe and Japan relative to the United States. Entrepreneurial culture is deeply rooted in education systems and social values. It is also shaped by a collective experience of achievements (*i.e.* the cumulative impact of success stories on psycho-social attitudes) which, in turn, depends on overcoming a number of obstacles that governments can lower in the short to medium term.

524. Such obstacles diminish the opportunities available to entrepreneurial individuals and reduce the possibilities for successfully exploiting them. Innovation surveys and studies of NTBFs reveal that in most countries, the creation and growth of innovative firms is severely constrained by difficulties in accessing key resources (*e.g.* finance, technical knowledge, market information, human resources, managerial know-how) and markets. In addition, framework conditions often mean that expected rewards are not proportionate to risks or raise both costs and risks to dissuasive levels.

525. In reviewing these obstacles, it is important to keep in mind that the main difference between the United States, where NTBFs prosper most, and other OECD countries is not the rate and chance of survival of start-ups, but rather the compound probability that they occur in technologically progressive activities and that a significant proportion of them will enjoy sustained fast growth in rapidly expanding niche markets. Therefore, from a policy perspective, it is of the utmost importance not to be concerned exclusively with conditions for firm creation and entrepreneurship in general, but to identify the specific factors which restrain the number of valuable entrepreneurial technology-based projects, raise obstacles to their transformation into business start-ups, and weaken subsequent market selection processes to the detriment of firms with high growth potential.

Inadequate financing

526. Among these factors, the most frequently cited is inadequate access to external finance, compounded in some cases by the reluctance of entrepreneurs to share control with outside providers of equity finance. Firm surveys and studies provide ample evidence that small firms experience difficulties in financing innovation (*e.g.* Niedersächsisches Institut für Wirtschaftsforschung *et al.*, 1996), and that financing can be an issue at several stages of the life of an NTBF (Figure 9.1). First, lack of seed financing is an endemic issue – particularly in Europe and Japan. Second, weak financing at the start-up stage compromises later development ("NTBFs well funded at start-up tend to be more successful commercially than those that are poorly funded or must fund themselves primarily through growth in their own retained earnings", Utterback *et al.*, 1988). Third, some years after their creation, NTBFs are usually at a strategic cross-roads: should they remain relatively small or should they initiate a sustained high-growth trajectory involving a new wave of investments that might prove difficult to finance without adequately developed venture capital markets?

Figure 9.1. **Financing the life cycle of a growing firm in the United States**

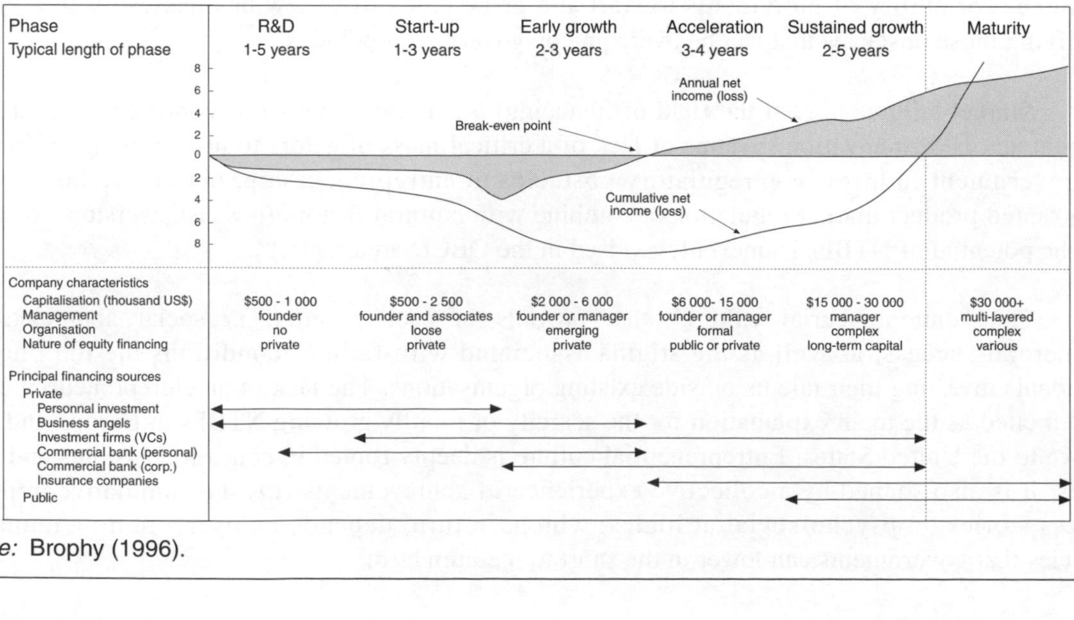

Source: Brophy (1996).

527. Venture capital plays a unique role among financing channels for NTBFs since it is the most value-adding and growth-enhancing market selection mechanism. Surveys of venture-backed companies in Canada confirm the experiences of those in the United States (Table 9.5), demonstrating that venture-backed firms outperform other firms, in terms of growth, employment creation and R&D. For example, their total employment grew by 30 per cent a year between 1989 and 1994, while total employment in the economy grew by only 3 per cent, and that of the largest 100 companies declined by 1 per cent over the same period (OECD, 1996*f*).

Table 9.5. **Employment growth in venture capital backed firms in the United States, 1994**[1]

	Scientists, engineers, managers in labour force	Average R&D per employee	Average equity/assets	Average annual job growth rate, 1989-93
	Per cent	US$	Per cent	US$
Venture-capital-backed firms	59	16 000	90	25
Fortune 500	15	8 000	30	3

1. Based on a survey which compared 1 800 of the largest firms in business at least five years.

Source: VentureOne, for the US National Venture Capital Association, 1995.

528. Venture capital is provided by both specialised financial firms acting as intermediaries between primary sources of finance and NTBFs (formal venture capital) and "business angels" (usually wealthy individuals experienced in both business and finance who invest directly in NTBFs). At the earliest stages in their lives, a large proportion of NTBFs requires equity financing in excess of what founders can afford, funding that venture capital funds are reluctant to provide, especially when firms are located outside regionally concentrated clusters. According to estimates, in the United States, business angels invest annually in NTBFs almost twice as much as do venture capital funds. The financing potential by business angels in OECD countries remains largely untapped; this is true even in such countries as the United States, Canada and the United Kingdom where this source of risk capital is more abundant than average (OECD, 1996*f*).

529. Formal venture capital is at very different stages of maturity across the OECD area. In a vast majority of countries its underdevelopment constitutes a major weakness of the innovation system. It is best established in the United States, where it took off in the early 1970s, and where the amount of capital invested annually exceeds the overall venture capital investment effort in Europe (Table 9.6). In addition, there are important differences in the orientation of venture capital flows, which are attracted more towards NTBFs in the United States than in other countries. Japanese venture capital firms are mostly subsidiaries of financial institutions which provide financing mainly in the form of loans to established firms. Interests represent almost half of venture capital firms' income, and almost two-thirds of the funded firms were established more than ten years ago, compared to less than 20 per cent in the United States.

530. The unique breadth and depth of the American venture capital industry is explained by a combination of mutually reinforcing factors which enable to manage higher levels of risk, and thus enjoy higher returns on investment in a wider range of entrepreneurial activities. These factors include more attractive and numerous innovative projects reflecting a strong science-industry interface, greater availability and variety of the primary sources of funds (*e.g.* pension funds), efficient exit mechanisms, especially NASDAQ, and highly developed market and financial information systems and specialised business services.

Table 9.6. **Venture capital in the United States and Europe, 1996**

	United States				Europe[1]			
	Number of deals	Per cent	US$ million raised	Per cent	Number of deals	Per cent	ECU million raised	Per cent
Stage of investment								
Seed/start-up	383	17	1 134.0	12	941	18	441	7
Expansion	1 697	76	6 372.5	68	2 624	51	2 650	39
Acquisition/buy-out	160	7	1 905.8	20	1 100	21	3 007	45
Replacement	6	0	7.7	0	516	10	653	10
Industry								
Computer-related	815	36	3 003.9	32	512	11	337	5
Communications	303	14	1 325.3	14	197	4	298	4
Consumer-related	160	7	1 256.9	13	777	17	1 231	18
Medical/health	350	16	1 191.1	13	250	5	242	4
Biotechnology	174	8	645.1	7	266	6	181	3
Semiconductors & other electronics	94	4	475.5	5	286	6	272	4
Business services	74	3	392.4	4	114	2	806	12
Industrial products	88	4	373.0	4	1 042	22	1 372	20
Manufacturing	16	1	266.6	3	456	10	655	10
Finance, insurance, real estate	116	5	198.3	2	114	2	431	6
Energy	18	1	161.2	2	67	1	74	1
Construction	14	1	84.6	1	165	4	255	4
Agriculture, forestry	5	0	28.5	0	64	1	107	2
Transportation	14	1	18.3	0	127	3	197	3
Utilities	1	0		0		0		0
Other	1	0		0	252	5	250	4
Total	**2 243**		**9 420.7**		**4 689**		**6 708**	

1. Includes private equity investment other than free venture capital, such as management buy-outs (MBOs).

Source: EVCA, 1996 and 1997, *Annual Venture Economics Review*.

531. The importance of specialised business services is often underestimated. A dynamic venture capital industry cannot develop well in the absence of sufficient transparency of information on markets, investment sources and opportunities, technologies, etc., and without the capabilities to exploit it. Research houses that perform such functions and well-trained human resources are common in the United States. Elsewhere, the financial sector faces greater difficulties in processing the information necessary to evaluate risky ventures in rapidly evolving areas. For example, European investment banks are concerned "about their ability to recruit and integrate techno-economic analysts, particularly when financial experience, technological knowledge and an understanding of commercial realities have to be combined with a knowledge of foreign languages" (European Commission, 1997*c*).

532. The huge difference between the United States and most other countries with regard to the role of venture capital (including business angels) in financing NTBFs is well illustrated. Table 9.7 contrasts France with the United States.

Table 9.7. **External financing of NTBFs in France and the United States**
1996

	United States		France	
	US$ million	Per cent	FF million	Per cent
Total annual investment	17 500	100	6 600	100
Of which: self financing	7 500	43	5 000	75
Total external financing	11 000	100	1 600	100
Venture capital	10 000	91	400	25
Public support	1 000	9	1 200	75

Source: Chabbal (1997).

Lack of information, human resources and managerial competencies

533. The energy spent in overcoming obstacles to financing and the cultural inclination of many founders of NTBFs with a scientific or technical background frequently lead to the neglect of the "marketing side" of successful innovation (*i.e.* learning about customer requirements, adapting products accordingly, and disseminating information about the company's products). The quality of marketing depends on the amount, quality, cost and accessibility of information on markets, which are not entirely satisfactory outside North America – especially in those countries lagging in the diffusion of new ICTs such as the Internet.

534. While the creation of NTBFs hinges on qualified entrepreneurs, their subsequent contribution to job creation is constrained by the availability of skilled managers and workers, as well as by disincentives for upskilling. Besides entrepreneurial culture, a major factor limiting the formation of NTBFs is regulation prohibiting or complicating spin-off or spin-out initiatives from large firms, universities or public research organisations or limiting the possibilities to provide powerful enough incentives for high qualified staff (*e.g.* stock options). A shortage of skilled workers is a barrier to innovation in many countries (*e.g.* Licht *et al.*, 1997; Baldwin and DaPont, 1996), reflecting in part delays in adapting education and training systems to the new requirements of a knowledge-based economy. Enterprises, like NTBFs, at the forefront of technology development, adoption, diffusion and learning are particularly affected. In most countries, the shortage of skilled workers is also due to the lack of mobility of qualified workers (for whom the perceived risk of leaving secure jobs to join risky ventures is greater when total job opportunities are fewer). In addition, in a majority of European countries, some labour market regulations had the detrimental effect of raising the risks associated with firm growth while also, together with high marginal tax rates, impeding incentives for upskilling (Union of Industrial and Employers' Confederations of Europe, 1995).

535. From their very inception, some NTBFs are condemned to a short life span because of a defective business plan. Many others will not achieve a sustained growth trajectory because of the absence of a corporate governance structure sustaining adjustment to changing conditions. The success of NTBFs requires superior governance and management capabilities involving a comprehensive understanding of product technology, manufacturing technology, market research, financial planning,

accounting, legal aspects, contracts and networking, as well as a supportive environment of relevant business services. Again, a well-functioning labour market helps to facilitate the mobility of experienced managers, allowing new ventures to benefit from the experience gained in existing ones. An entrepreneurial climate and the availability of skilled venture capitalists, further help to marry skilled management, corporate governance and external resource contributions. Still, remaining imperfections in information and corporate governance systems provide a rationale for government action to help spur management and innovation capabilities. Governments can supplement or catalyse private initiatives in three ways: the public provision of innovation management tools or benchmarking services (*e.g.* the Benchmarking Index in the United Kingdom); promotion of the development, diffusion and adoption of management know-how (*e.g.* the Benchmarking Performance Service of the Manufacturing Extension Partnership programme in the United States, the Austrian MINT and the Norwegian FRAM programmes); development of "infrastructure" for the correction of information imperfections in the market of business services (*e.g.* Strategis in Canada). Evaluation of existing policies to promote innovation management capabilities (*e.g.* in the context of the Innovation Programme of the European Union or of the OECD project on national innovation systems) demonstrates that there is large scope for improved policy responses in this area, pointing especially to the need for founding them on an improved understanding of innovation processes in small firms and better tailoring them to specific types of firms and stages in innovation capability building.

Barriers to market entry and other regulatory obstacles

536. Regulatory barriers to market entry and lenient competition policy hamper the creation and growth of NTBFs. They are particularly detrimental when other factors (*e.g.* currency and language barriers and the absence of a truly single market in Europe) already inhibit the development of a "critical mass in the functions necessary to get companies growing" (Lumme, 1995). High registration costs have dissuaded new firm start-ups in many European countries. Entrepreneurs learn from failure if, as in the United States, bankruptcy regulations do not make starting again too difficult. Differences in environmental and health regulations across countries have implications for start-up opportunities in certain industries such as biotechnology. Finally, cost and delays in obtaining IPRs affect the likelihood that new ideas will be commercialised, especially by NTBFs which often innovate in response to short windows of opportunity. Predatory strategies by large companies exacerbate such problems. A related aspect is that risks of high judicial costs can impede market access, serving as a deterrent for entry by some foreign NTBFs in the United States. Overall, the "regulatory burden" shouldered by entrepreneurs is heavier in Europe and Japan than in the United States (Union of Industrial and Employers' Confederations of Europe, 1995).

Lack of integration within national and global innovation networks

537. NTBFs seldom succeed in isolation from other actors of innovation systems, and participation in innovation networks helps alleviate the obstacles discussed above. A French study demonstrates that firms lacking extensive contacts achieved significantly lower survival and growth rates (Mustar, 1995). Whereas opportunities for partnering with large enterprises tend to be firm- rather than country-specific, this is not the case for other types of external linkages, especially with venture capital firms or business angels supplying not only capital but also managerial, financial, human resource, marketing, and sometimes even operational, advice and support. This is also true for science parks, technology incubators and technology centres which offer integrated services to NTBFs as well as platforms for co-operation with a variety of actors (witness the superior survival rates observed among firms originating from incubators). Finally, government technology and innovation policy (*e.g.* procurement, R&D contracts, financial support to R&D) contributes to a variable extent to catalysing or supplementing these network

relationships. Here, there is room for improvement especially in countries where government has traditionally emphasized mission-oriented technology policies through programmes involving co-operation between public research organisations and large firms, with few openings to smaller private partners (*e.g.* France, Japan, the United Kingdom and the United States).

538. In sum, the successful American experience in realising the potential contribution of NTBFs to economic growth and job creation is explained by the simultaneous occurrence of a strong entrepreneurial culture, an accessible large pool of knowledge, a differentiated set of highly interactive and regionally concentrated innovation networks, the availability of relevant information and financing, framework conditions conducive to growth and rewarding success in accordance with prevailing social values, and the availability of qualified labour (OECD, 1997*r*). These conditions cannot be replicated in every OECD country – especially those pertaining to social and cultural values – but lessons can be drawn. In the following section the report reviews relevant fields of policy action and identifies promising approaches and measures, emphasizing those which facilitate the financing of NTBFs.

9.4. Promoting NTBFs: best policy practice

539. The need for concomitant initiatives in a number of fields falling within different realms of government policy requires policy makers to co-ordinate their actions within a clear-cut strategy (Figure 9.2). Such a strategy needs clarification in a number of countries, where increased awareness has often led to unrelated actions by administrations competing to enter a politically visible area, or even to the temptation to simply re-label traditional SME policies. Several countries (France, Germany, the United Kingdom) have individually or collectively (in the context of the European Union) devoted considerable efforts to achieving a coherent view of the issues involved and to determining priority lines of action. Beyond the specifically national emphasis, a common wisdom is emerging.

540. The overriding principle is that, in addition to securing appropriate framework conditions for entrepreneurship, government should: *(i)* focus direct support on the early stages of innovative ventures where market failures are so pervasive as to justify intervention even in the most favoured countries (*e.g.* small risky investments targeted by the SBIC programme in the United States); and *(ii)* strengthen market selection processes at all stages, in particular by promoting the development of the private venture capital industry (including relevant specialised financial market segments). It is also important to improve access by new firms to information, technical knowledge bases and innovation networks, including through their increased participation in public S&T programmes.

541. Three main types of framework conditions affect the start-up and development of NTBFs: *(i)* conditions for market entry, as influenced by competition policy and economic growth; *(ii)* the risk-reward system, as influenced by tax policies or bankruptcy laws; and *(iii)* labour market functioning and the education system. A discussion of most of the policies shaping these conditions falls outside the scope of this report, but it is important to stress here that market liberalisation and regulatory reform, as advocated by the OECD in other parts of its work on employment/unemployment, are preconditions for increasing the opportunities for NTBF creation and growth. Government regulations and charges associated with business start-up and continued operation should also be considered. Even if they seem to be less important than other factors in explaining international differences in NTBF performance, their simplification is a good practice and has been the objective of recent initiatives in several countries (Austria, Belgium, France, Germany, Greece, Ireland, Italy) (OECD, 1997*s*).

Figure 9.2. **Promoting NTBFs – the overall policy framework**

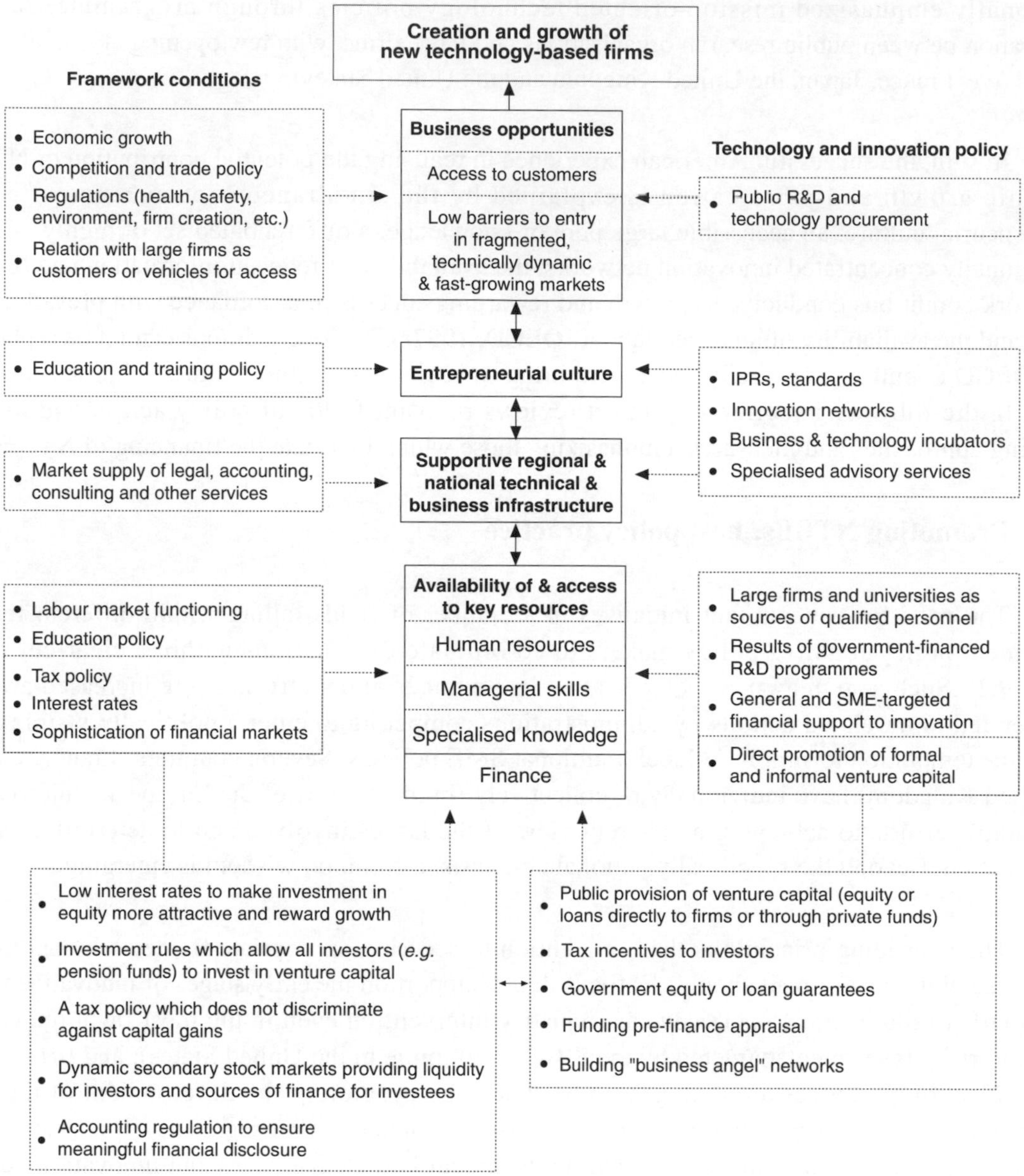

Source: OECD Secretariat.

The contribution of technology and innovation policy

542. Almost all the technology and innovation policies discussed elsewhere in this report have an impact on NTBFs. R&D tax incentives benefit R&D-intensive NTBFs, although Chapter 7 casts doubt on their effectiveness as selective support instruments. As reviewed in Chapter 6, best-practice policies to secure funding of basic research and to promote university/industry relationships increase the likelihood of entrepreneurial spin-outs. However, it is in the area of technology diffusion (covered by Chapter 8) that the main contributions of technology and innovation policy to the creation and growth of NTBFs are to be expected.

543. In placing greater emphasis on innovation in their SME policies, Member countries are confronted with the heterogeneity of the population of small innovative firms in general, and the specific needs of NTBFs in particular. Technology incubators have been a popular response (OECD, 1997*t*). They combine the usual function of business incubators, providing ready access to a package of services that help nurture new firms, with that of organising close linkages with providers of resources of special importance to NTBFs (scientific and technical expertise or venture capital). Lessons from countries with the most experience (France, Germany, the United Kingdom, the United States) are fairly positive, and in all countries, incubated firms exhibit higher survival rates. However, policy expectations as to the role of technology incubators in the overall process of NTBF creation should be realistic; nowhere are they close to becoming a magic "fast-breed reactor" of technological entrepreneurship. Their efficiency in playing a limited but useful role is greater when they are located within dynamic knowledge-intensive clusters comprising a wide range of activities. On the contrary, they display disappointing performance when insufficiently linked to sources of venture financing; witness the experience of Denmark or Japan.

544. Less specifically designed for NTBFs, but of great importance to them, are policies to improve the access of SMEs to information, large-scale public S&T programmes and high-skilled labour, and to strengthen incentives for upskilling. North America leads in the first area, reflecting both its advance in the use of new ICTs and its rich pool of information and information brokers. The Strategis programme of Industry Canada, and the Small Business Administration (SBA) information services of the United States, are good practices which show that government has to correct information imperfections even in the most advanced market economies. International co-operation could magnify the benefits of national programmes. In particular, initiatives to connect Internet-based government-sponsored services would be of great value.

545. Measures to assist small firms in taking on qualified individuals are widespread, especially in Europe – *e.g.* Germany (*Kooperation*), France [*Convention Industrielle de Formation par la Recherche* (CIFRE), *Convention de Recherche pour les Techniciens Supérieurs* (CORTECHS), *Aide au Recrutement des Cadres* (ARC), *Aide au Recrutement pour l'Innovation* (ARI)], the Netherlands [Innovation Fund for Technology and Vocational Education (*Wet Bevordering Speur- en Ontwikkelingswerk* – WBSO), Specialists in SMEs Scheme (KIM) and PROMOTIE], and the United Kingdom [Teaching Company Scheme (TCS)]. Generally, they do not specifically target NTBFs, but aim at increasing the technical and managerial capabilities of a larger number of existing SMEs. In some countries, *e.g.* France, they have evolved into a complex support system, the impact of which is now unclear. As a general rule, before introducing or when evaluating such programmes, it would be wise to consider the possibility that regulatory or tax reforms might provide a better alternative, or a necessary condition, *e.g.* facilitating personnel mobility between industry and public research organisations. In the European setting, addressing such issues is vital to enabling greater economy-wide employment effects of NTBFs.

546. The fact that the creation and growth of NTBFs in the United States are financed primarily by private investors does not mean that government technology and innovation policy is of little importance for their success (Acs, 1997). For example, even if the share of small firms in federal R&D expenditure is only about one-third of their share in private R&D expenditure (around 10 per cent), "the number of small firms receiving 20 per cent or more of their total R&D finance from government sources is nearly ten times larger in the United States than in the United Kingdom or France" (Acs and Audretsch, 1993). The Small Business Innovation Research (SBIR) programme in fact requires all federal departments with R&D budgets to set aside a portion of their budget for small firms. In France it has been found (Mustar, 1995) that some NTBFs have derived benefits not only from national programmes targeting small firms (*e.g.* ANVAR), but also from large-scale international technology programmes (EU Framework Programme, EUREKA). However, the access of small firms to

large-scale programmes remains an issue, especially in countries where the over-concentration of government support on large firms is not mitigated by a dynamic process of entrepreneurial spin-offs.

Financing NTBFs – government promotion of venture capital

547. The financing of NTBFs provides a textbook example of the meaning and practical policy implications of the notions of market, government and systemic failures. The factors leading to market failures in financing small (*e.g.* transaction and monitoring costs), new (*e.g.* lack of a track record) and technology-based (high technical and commercial risks) firms are well established by economic theory and need no further examination. It is now better understood that venture capital is a radical innovation in both financial engineering and corporate governance which makes possible innovations that would not have been financed in its absence due to both market failures and government failures in "picking winners". Its creation and development in the United States demonstrates that, when propitious conditions prevail in the NIS, the market can be creative in finding solutions to some of its own shortcomings. By contrast, in other countries, systemic failures have prevented venture capital from emerging as a new market tool and have hampered its early adoption and development as a best-practice tool for innovation financing and selection of new firms with high-growth potential.

548. Actions to remove bottlenecks on the demand side of venture finance are necessary, but not sufficient. Governments must also act on the supply side and contribute to building efficient mechanisms for supply/demand interactions. In recent years, a growing number of initiatives have been implemented throughout the OECD area (OECD, 1997*s*). Table 9.8 provides an overview of these initiatives, points to the main lessons to be drawn and identifies best practices. The main findings can be summarised as follows.

549. Programmes to bridge gaps in finance through the public provision of equity investment (directly to NTBFs or through private venture capital funds) are justified as a "pump-priming" device in countries where the private venture industry is nascent or lacks a critical mass. Successful programmes are those which do not crowd out, but instead build on private initiative (public money should as a rule be provided on a matching basis), and leave management responsibility to experienced private venture capitalists [*e.g.* Innovation Investment Fund (IIF) in Australia, Participation Company for New Technology-Based Firms (PMTSs) in the Netherlands]. Ultimately, they can be phased out when private venture capital reaches maturity (*e.g.* *Yozma* in Israel). Permanent government involvement should seek only to compensate endemic market failures affecting early-stage small investments [*e.g.* seed funding by ITF in Austria, Finnish National Fund for Research and Development (SITRA) in Finland and Small Business Investment Companies (SBICs) in the United States]. Support to pre-finance appraisal can be a useful component (*e.g.* Technology Rating programme in the Netherlands). Sound financial foundations for a NTBF cannot be created by subsidies granted on a project basis or by government loans, which are not the most appropriate form of government support to venture capital funds, as demonstrated by the experience of the SBIC programme in the United States.

Table 9.8. **Government promotion of venture capital – policy approaches, instruments and best practices**[1]

Approach	Instruments and current practices	Evaluation	Best practices and recommendations	Country specificity
Supply capital directly to fill financing gaps	**Government equity investment** Government venture capital fund(s), sometimes managed by the private sector, directly invest in firms (GIMV in early period in Belgium; part of BDB operations in Canada; Forbairt programme in Ireland; Yozma in Israel from 1993 to 1996; FIN1 in Sweden). Public investment is made in private venture capital firms (part of BDB operations in Canada; TESI and regional SITRA and Kera funds in Finland). Hybrid funds created by government blend public and private money (Innovation Investment Fund in Australia; GIMV in recent period in Belgium; BJTU and its successor BTU in Germany; PMTSs in the Netherlands; SEP in Scotland; Atle and BURE in Sweden; SBICs from 1992 in the United States; part of EIF operations at the European Union level).	Experience with government equity investment is mixed. It is justified as a "pump-priming" device in countries where private venture industry lacks a critical mass or as a complement to private venture capital and individual business angels if properly targeted at early-stage small investments. Experience, especially with the first generation of programmes in the 1980s and early 1990s, demonstrates that there are several pitfalls to be avoided by careful design of schemes, especially: crowding out private initiative by driving returns down when growth in the supply of funds outpaces that of viable projects; direct involvement of government in the investment process leading to investment decisions more inspired by a "picking winners" approach than by market-friendly selection criteria; investments shifting towards lower-risk later stages (*e.g.* Atle and Bure in Sweden).	There are three ways to ensure maximum additionality of government intervention: First, by directing programmes to those categories of firms and investments that are most affected by financial market failures, especially small and early-stage (seed and start-up) investments in technology-based firms. Second, by attracting an increasing participation of private investment (as a rule, governments funds should be offered on a matching basis). It is crucial to build on rather than compete with private sector initiatives. Programmes should be phased out once private venture capital industry reaches maturity (*e.g.* the privatisation of Yozma in Israel). Government should closely monitor programmes but delegate management responsibility to high-quality venture capitalists from the private sector. Third, demand for and return on venture capital can be increased by measures which spur greater management and innovation capabilities within firms.	Degree of development of the venture capital market, and magnitude and structure of demand of venture funding, as influenced by country size, industrial specialisation and other characteristics of national innovation systems.

Approach	Instruments and current practices	Evaluation	Best practices and recommendations	Country specificity
Supply capital directly to fill financing gaps	**Government loans or subsidies** Government provides debt financing or subsidies to venture capital firms, new technology-based firms, or SMEs undertaking innovation projects (often in the form of conditional loans) (IPF in Austria; *VoeskstFonden* in Denmark; Kera and TEKES in Finland; ANVAR and ATOUT in France; KfW and ERP in Germany; TOK in the Netherlands; ALMI, FINB2 and NUTEK in Sweden; SBICs until mid-1990s, and SBIR in the United States).	Sound financial foundations for an NTBF cannot be created by subsidies granted on a project basis or through loans, which are also not the most appropriate form of government support to venture capital funds, as demonstrated by the experience of SBIC in the United States (it induced SBICs to concentrate their investments in later-stage firms which could generate cash, explaining the shift of SBICs funding to equity in 1992). In fact, most schemes providing loans support innovation projects by established small firms rather than technology-based firm creation or accelerating growth.	Government loan schemes to support innovation projects should be designed to take account of the specific characteristics of NTBFs. In particular, a differed repayment schedule might be necessary given that they have often a negative cash flow. Also, one should avoid worsening the debt to equity ratio of firms which tend to be financially fragile (conditional loans – to be reimbursed only in case of success – are a good solution, but concomitant investment in equity should also be facilitated where possible, for example through improved co-ordination with relevant venture capital public programme).	Government loans are generally not stand-alone policy instruments but elements of broader technology and innovation policies.
Provide incentives to lower costs and increase rewards for investors	**Tax incentives to investors:** ● in venture capital funds (MICs until 1991, and PDFs since 1992 in Australia; LSVCC in Canada; FCPI in France; BES in Ireland; VCT in the United Kingdom); ● to investors in NTBFs (BES in Ireland; BES until 1993, and EIS in the United Kingdom); ● to individuals or groups which loan to young firms (Netherlands).	Tax incentives are an increasingly popular instrument to motivate greater investment in NTBFs, directly through venture capital funds. However, early experience in the United Kingdom with the BES scheme has shown that reconciling the objective of attracting a maximum amount of liquidity with that of channelling it to NTBFs may raise difficulties, especially when using front-end tax incentives alone. The cost effectiveness of tax incentives is also dependent on general characteristics of the tax system, especially the fiscal treatment of personal income in the highest tax brackets and of capital gains.	The eligibility criteria should be as tight as possible in order to avoid programmes being abused for tax evasion purposes, missing their main target, achieving it at too-high a cost, or creating unfair competition between supported venture funds and others (problem raised in the case of LSVCC in Canada). Good practice examples include the recent revision of the eligibility criteria for VCT in the United Kingdom. Some combination of front-end (giving a reward proportional to the amount invested) and back-end tax incentives (giving a reward proportional to capital gains, *i.e.* to the success of NTBFs) is better than exclusive use of the latter. Good practice examples include the recently introduced French FCPI and EIS in the United Kingdom.	Variable size and nature of gaps in supply/demand of venture financing and differences in overall tax system.

Approach	Instruments and current practices	Evaluation	Best practices and recommendations	Country specificity
Offer guarantees to lower risks for investors	Equity guarantee (FGG in Austria; *Udviklingsselskaber* in Denmark; FGB in Finland). Loan guarantee (one of the most widely used instrument, although not always targeted at NTBFs. Examples include: SBLA in Canada; SOFARIS in France; part of operations of BJTU until 1994 in Germany; VEC in Japan; BBMKB in the Netherlands; SPGM in Portugal; LGS in the United Kingdom; GBLP in the United States).	Equity guarantee against losses is a rare form of government intervention. It has the legitimate objective of mitigating the negative consequences of investors' risk aversion but may have perverse effects, including: distorting project selection criteria; discouraging venture capitalists from making their best efforts to help all firms in their portfolio survive. Loan guarantee (see remarks on loan above).	Equity guarantee is an approach that can hardly be recommended on the basis of past (*e.g.* the PPM scheme in the Netherlands, discontinued in 1995) or current experiences. If implemented, an equity guarantee scheme should include provisions that minimise potential drawbacks. For example, in the Danish scheme the guarantee works only for firms in which the venture capital investor has a seat on the board.	Same as for government equity investment
Remove regulatory obstacles to investment in NTBFs	Following the pioneering example of the United States (the ERISA legislation in the late 1970s allowed pension funds to invest in venture capital funds), several countries have recently made regulatory changes to ease the flow of "patient capital" towards NTBFs (*e.g.* Australia, Ireland, Finland, Italy) or are considering such changes (*e.g.* France, Japan).	ERISA was a necessary but not sufficient condition for the take off of venture capital in the United States.	Increasing the supply of "patient capital" and, more generally, diversifying the sources of funds of venture capital is good practice, provided that concomitant actions ensure parallel expansion of demand for venture funding.	Financial market structures and pension systems
Create exit mechanisms for investors	**Secondary stock markets** (Finance in Time in Austria, *Nouveau Marché* in France, *Neue Markt* in Germany, EASDAQ and EURO.NM pan-European initiatives; JASDAQ and regulatory reforms of OTC market in Japan). **Equity guarantees against illiquidity** (government plays the role of "exit of the last resort") (BTU in Bavaria, Germany, under consideration in several other countries, including France, at national or regional level).	American NASDAQ serves as an exit mechanism for venture capitalists throughout the world (*e.g.* booming Israeli NTBF sector), but at some cost, including the risk of "entrepreneurial drain", and of providing weaker impulsion to the development of the related financial service sector outside the United States. Building efficient secondary markets in Europe or Asia must take into account the need for critical mass and for concomitant development of a specialised competitive intermediary sector (*i.e.* dealers, analysts, etc.). Equity guarantee against illiquidity is an interesting solution when IPOs on secondary markets are not feasible and when market for trade sales lacks critical mass.	With regard to secondary stock markets, no best practice example exists other than the American NASDAQ. Experience with guarantee of exit is still very limited but current experiments should be carefully monitored (*e.g.* BTU in Germany).	Structures and regulations of existing stock markets.

Approach	Instruments and current practices	Evaluation	Best practices and recommendations	Country specificity
Build business-angel networks	Government encourages the creation; operates and/or supports the operation of networks that match demand and supply of informal venture capital (many examples mostly in Canada, the United Kingdom, the United States and, to a lesser extent, in Scandinavian countries; more recent RFI experiment in France and forthcoming BMBF initiative in Germany).	Success of networking initiatives depends on sufficient funding of marketing efforts in order to build a critical mass of investors and entrepreneurs and to establish credibility, and is doubtful in areas remote from high concentrations of population, venture capital and "high-tech" firms.	A bottom-up approach should build on P/PPs at local and regional level, with central government possibly providing financial support to operation, helping the interregional dissemination of good practices, and ensuring the interconnection of local networks (*e.g.* the SBA-sponsored Internet-based ACE-net in the United States). Extending the scope of networks to include all the main public and private actors of innovation financing can be valuable in countries where the need to increase the leverage of public financing is the most pressing (*e.g.* RFI in France).	Country size; existence of regional clusters of knowledge-intensive activities; and degree of decentralisation of government policy.

1. For the full names of the acronyms used herein, please see the Glossary .

Source: OECD Secretariat.

550. To encourage investors in NTBFs or in venture capital funds, tax incentives to lower their costs and increase their rewards should generally be preferred to government guarantees that lower their risks. However, the criteria for eligibility for tax incentive schemes should be tight in order to avoid tax evasion, and should not create unfair competition between supported venture funds and others. In addition, some combination of front-end (giving a reward proportional to the amount invested) and back-end (giving a reward proportional to capital gains, *i.e.* to the success of NTBFs) tax incentives is better than exclusive use of the latter [*e.g.* the recently introduced French *Fonds Commun de Placement Innovation* (FCPI) and Enterprise Investment Scheme (EIS) in the United Kingdom]. The experience of the United States [the Employment Retirement Income Security Act (ERISA) legislation which in the 1970s relaxed the regulation on investment by pension funds] demonstrates that removing regulatory obstacles can have a large positive impact on the availability of venture capital, provided that other conditions ensure parallel expansion of the demand for venture funding. Positive steps in this direction have been observed recently in a number of countries (Australia, Finland, Ireland, Italy).

551. The existence of a stock market which encourages initial public offerings (IPOs) is crucial for the development of venture capital (by allowing investors to realise their capital gains and reinvest them in other projects) and fast-growing NTBFs (allowing them to raise additional capital at competitive prices). The American NASDAQ serves as an exit mechanism for venture capitalists throughout the world (*e.g.* the booming Israeli NTBF sector), but at some cost, with the risk of "entrepreneurial drain" and of providing weaker impulsion to the development of the related financial services sector outside the United States. The building of efficient secondary markets in Europe (*e.g. Nouveau Marché* in France, *Neue Markt* in Germany and EURO.NM (*Réseau Européen des Nouveaux Marchés*) and EASDAQ at the European level) or Asia (*e.g.* JASDAQ) must take into account the need for critical mass and for concomitant development of a specialised competitive intermediary sector (*i.e.* dealers, analysts, etc.). There may be a need to establish other types of exit mechanisms when IPOs on secondary markets are not feasible and when the market for trade sales is too narrow [*e.g.* Venture Capital for Young High Technology Firms (*Beteiligungskapital für Junge Technologieunternehmen* – BTU) government guarantees in Germany]. This could help develop business angel investment, which can also be encouraged through government help in building networks by providing channels of communication between angels and entrepreneurs seeking finance, possibly including other providers of venture funding, as in Canada, the Scandinavian countries, the United Kingdom, the United States, and, more recently, in France.

CHAPTER 10. FACILITATING GROWTH IN NEW DEMAND

10.1. Introduction

552. The development and exploitation of new technology is determined not only from the supply side; demand also plays a key role. A number of issues arise in this context, including lack of information on the part of customers regarding options for new processes or products, and the presence of regulations which stifle the take-up of such opportunities. On the other hand, regulations or other policy actions may be needed for the articulation of potential consumer demand. Demand-related policies with implications for innovation and technology diffusion reflect a move by governments away from a directive mode of picking technological "winners" towards fostering market mechanisms which can generate new areas of economic growth and job creation. Ways are being sought by which demand and supply for innovative products can be broadened to reach, and be motivated by, wider markets, and thus be rendered more economically autonomous of ongoing government support.

553. The focus here is on Internet-based multimedia services and environmental goods and services. In these two areas, a range of new goods and services have a potential application in industry or at the home so extensive that they may provide a basis for new economic growth and job creation. The lessons that can be drawn from best policy practice in a number of OECD countries in these two areas are compared and contrasted in this chapter. Table 10.6 and Table 10.7 present conclusions at the country level, while more general lessons are presented in the final section.

10.2. Internet-based multimedia services

The policy challenge: demand and supply for Internet-based services

554. To date, new network-based services have developed in two ways: first, through public/private sector co-operation in R&D in advanced, high-capacity communication technologies (such as for the Internet); and, second, through competition in the provision of communication infrastructures. There is a growing appreciation, however, of the need for policies which can complement these supply-side measures by encouraging demand among businesses and consumers. This appreciation derives from the realisation that, despite their potentially widespread impact, take-up of network-based services may be retarded by lack of awareness (and experience) in their use, regulatory complexities in their utilisation, and high prices for services and the equipment and software needed to access them. While it is recognised that the private sector must lead the development of demand, it is also recognised that positive externalities and economies of scale may bring down costs only once greater demand exists – and that government can play an important role in stimulating the use and diffusion of innovative forms of demand for new services.

555. The network-based delivery of specific services to businesses, government and final consumers involves a complex structure of demand and supply relations. A series of networked and

stand-alone components connect business-to-business or business-to-government along an extended chain of supply and demand prior to final consumption. If the contribution of Internet-based services to overall economic productivity, growth and job creation is to be fully realised, this entire chain needs to be restructured through the development of network-based production and delivery. Two issues are particularly pertinent for government policy in this respect. First, new Internet-based services often overlap traditional national media definitions by agglomerating content in a highly focused manner, facilitating market growth and the development of new, local enterprises through economies of scope. Second, the often international development and availability of Internet-based services means that demand which is currently restricted by national regulatory and physical limits can potentially be dramatically expanded, increasing market growth through enhanced economies of scale. Reform of national regulatory demarcations can thus remove barriers to the efficient provision of inputs along the extended chain of supply and demand, enhancing the potential for growth of business, government and consumer demand in different market sectors.

556. However, identifying the generators and levels of supply and demand for Internet-based services is not simple: *(i)* the network technologies characteristically used on the Internet mean that communications can be very indirect; *(ii)* computer connections to the network may be used by a varying number of users at one and the same time; and *(iii)* users can be service providers – no registration requirement exists for Internet-based content providers in OECD countries. Instead, it is necessary to apply indirect indicators of: *(i)* penetration and use of ICTs (*e.g.* PCs, modems and network-servers) by individuals, socio-economic groups or institutions in the household, business and government sectors; *(ii)* growth in general Internet traffic; and *(iii)* subscriptions to general and sector-specific service providers. Such data can help to disclose factors influencing demand for Internet-based services in general as well as specific network-based services.

557. Although governments are adopting more or less explicit policies for fostering demand for Internet-based services, it should be stressed that such policies are still at an experimental stage; this also applies to the evaluation of such approaches. As a result, it is often only possible to make broad policy assessments in this chapter. Table 10.6 sums up the position of the major OECD countries in relation to some key policy areas. These are divided into, first, infrastructure and equipment market liberalisation; and, second, sector-specific policy initiatives in business and government markets. The rationale for these policies is outlined below.

Infrastructure and equipment market liberalisation

558. Advances in basic networking technologies and architecture have been vital for articulating demand for Internet services. Co-operation on a not-for-profit basis between the public and private sectors has been (and continues to be) essential in establishing such advances, as for instance in the case of the Internet in the United States and the Minitel in France. The key area of technological development today is, however, not just in basic networking but also in applications and architectures where development needs to be of a broader and more commercial nature. Thus, while the underlying network technologies were developed during the 1960s and 1970s by the US military and major universities in co-operation with private sector network operators and computing companies, the take-off in popularity of the Internet coincided with the development of user-friendly navigation tools for the World Wide Web (WWW), such as Mosaic and Netscape Communications Corporation's Navigator browser. Further commercial development of applications' technologies and architectures will (and already are) expand(ing) opportunities even more. Ongoing government/private sector co-operation in basic physical network technologies and architectures will continue to be valuable within such a context, but its essential location will move further upstream. The Internet2 programme in

the United States, the Next Generation Internet projects in Japan and the Advanced Communications Technologies and Services (ACTS) programme of the European Union are examples of programmes between governments and industry for the development of such technologies.

559. Commercial trade-offs between different capabilities and investments are crucial in determining the success or failure of particular applications' technologies and architectures. Policies for stimulating demand and supply will need to support competitive markets which allow different means of delivery to demonstrate their relevance and effectiveness for users. OECD countries have made significant progress towards achieving this goal. But some still effectively block competition between different forms of Internet delivery, such as, for instance, between public switched telecommunication and cable television networks. Commercialisation and competition have been essential to the low costs and prices of Internet service provision. Small-scale Internet Content Providers (ICPs) can set up a Web page for little more than the cost of a PC with a modem and a subscription to space on the server of an Internet Access Provider (IAP). IAPs have been forced to keep down costs and prices because of the low barriers to market entry and unregulated nature of the Internet network market. The critical role of competition is apparent in the remarkable growth of the Internet since controls were relaxed in the early 1990s over who could interconnect with the existing networks and the first commercial IAPs (previously operating as non-profit providers of Internet connections) began offering links to commercial enterprises and residential users. Differences in competition-related factors seem to explain major variations in the advance of the Internet:

- Consumer access charges to the Internet are lowest in countries where network competition has been liberalised. In 1995, the average price for leased line access to the Internet in countries with monopoly telecommunication infrastructures was 44 per cent more expensive than in countries with competitive provision of infrastructures.

- The penetration of Internet hosts is five times greater in competitive than in monopoly markets.

- On average, IAPs' prices for "dial-up services" were nearly three times less expensive in countries with infrastructure competition than in those with monopoly markets in 1995 (OECD, 1996*g*).

560. In many instances, strengthening demand for Internet-based services will require governments to actively promote competitive conditions in network markets. The agenda includes various measures to prevent large public telecommunication operators from manoeuvring so as to restrict market entry.

561. Demand for and usage of ICTs such as computers and modems crucially influence demand for Internet-based services as well. Variations in ICT penetration can to some extent be explained by differences in equipment prices across countries. Relative prices are, of course, affected by exchange rate fluctuations, but manufacturers and distributors can maintain higher mark-ups in countries where competition is restricted. Governments can increase potential demand for Internet-based services through measures which increase competition in terminal equipment markets. Although OECD governments have formally liberalised equipment markets, the wide variance in equipment prices between North America, Europe and Asia suggests that distribution arrangements in many cases maintain excessive consumer prices. The WTO International Technology Agreement for reductions in existing tariffs on ICTs by 2000 should help lower prices and thus increase penetration, but marketing regulations will need to be monitored in order to ensure that its provisions are fully effective.

562. Based upon increasingly cheap and easy access to the Internet, mass markets have started to emerge for general Internet-based services where programming of content occurs. America Online (AOL), the largest Internet-based general service provider, had around 10 million members world-wide by the end of 1997, up from less than half a million in 1993. There were almost 1 million subscribers in Germany, 200 000 in the United Kingdom, 100 000 in the rest of Europe, and 100 000 in Canada (*Financial Times*, 1997*a;* 1997*b;* 1997*c*). T-Online, a branch of Deutsche Telekom, had 1.4 million members (*Financial Times*, 1997*b;* 1997*d*), while in Japan, Nifty, a subsidiary of Fujitsu, reached 2.39 million members in May 1997 compared to 1 million in April 1995.[44]

563. This is a fragile mass market, however, and differences in subscriber demand have led to a commercial focus on more specific service markets. While AOL has succeeded in building a business on the basis of general consumer demand in the major OECD economies, other providers (such as CompuServe, Prodigy and Apple e-World) have been bought out by rivals or more specialised providers. Providers of general services for businesses (*e.g.* Reuters) have had to upgrade dedicated services for business, technical and professional demand as Internet-based competitors have entered at the lower end of the market for specialised business and consumer markets. Few general or specialised Internet-based service companies can as yet be considered truly profitable, as subscriber numbers have not yet proved to represent real or sustained economic demand. As a result, the content specific to particular types of service will become the key criterion determining demand for Internet-based services; as the technological sophistication and capability of networks grow, audio-visual content will be a key distinguishing feature of such services' content.

564. Existing markets for audio-visual content are huge. World-wide sales of pre-recorded music reached almost US$40 billion in 1995, a growth rate of 9.9 per cent over the year, while for the OECD countries it was around US$34 billion (International Federation of the Phonographic Industry, 1996). Gross box office revenues for motion pictures in Europe, North America, Australia and Japan during 1994 were lower, at just over US$11 billion,[45] while broadcasting revenues for the OECD countries reached approximately US$123 billion (OECD, 1997*u*). Significant job creation already occurs in audio-visual media: the motion picture industry in the United States has created over a quarter of a million jobs since 1985, according to the Motion Picture Association of America, with most of these being in production or distribution and video sales. The smaller independent production companies are as important as the major studios. According to a report for the American Film Marketing Association (AFMA), in 1994 independent productions generated more than one-third of all jobs in the industry. In Los Angeles County alone, independent productions directly employed about 131 000 people across all sectors of the motion picture industry, with a total payroll of more than US$2.1 billion. Nation-wide, independents had a payroll of nearly US$2.5 billion in 1993, or 29 per cent of the industry total of about US$8.3 billion. Jobs in the independent film industry totalled some 148 000, almost 36 per cent of the employees of the film industry (Arthur Anderson Economic Consulting, 1995). In Europe and Canada, too, employment has grown in the audio-visual and related sectors.[46]

44. See Niftyserve Website at <http://www.niftyserve.or.jp/corp/data/htm>, and <http://www.niftyserve.or.jp/corp/index.htm>.

45. OECD analysis, adapted from information provided by the European Commission and Industry Canada.

46. Note that the European figures compared to those for the United States include all audio-visual activities. This makes comparison tricky, but is relevant insofar as a large proportion of content production in Europe is carried out by broadcasters, whereas in the United States there was a legal barrier preventing broadcasters from producing content.

565. Future growth and job creation in audio-visual content will largely be based on the convergence of the media sector with computer software development industries – another sector of high growth, job creation, wages and skills. As digital networks expand, demand for customised services and goods will develop rapidly. In Canada, for instance, the computer service industry provided 99 000 jobs in 1994, a remarkable 20 000 increase over the previous year; earnings of employees in the industry (average annual salary US$47 000) were substantially higher than the average US$38 000 for the Canadian economy. According to the *New York Times* (1997), roughly 50 000 jobs were created in Silicon Valley in 1996, while average real wages grew 5.1 per cent after accounting for inflation – more than five times the national average. Average annual earnings among software companies came to US$78 400 in 1995 (*New York Times*, 1997). Digitisation of television networks (with between 200 and 500 channels) will increase demand for new multimedia content, while the Internet will provide an important channel for the development of interactive new multimedia content.

566. The move towards network-based (particularly Internet) services will reduce employment in physical delivery systems and retail sales channels for traditional stand-alone media such as printed text and CD-ROMs, which require heavy investment in manufacturing plant, shops and physical distribution systems.[47] However, network-based distribution of content is expected to increase demand for staff in technical, creative and management/administration and direct marketing positions (DJC Research *et al.*, 1995). As digital technologies contribute greater value to audio-visual production and distribution, demand will increase among traditional media and new multimedia companies for employees with computer authoring and networking skills. Total new media employment in the New York metropolitan area (New Jersey and Connecticut) was estimated by Coopers & Lybrand at 71 500 workers in 1994, up from 28 500 in 1992, and was expected to increase by 39 000 employees from 1996 to 1998. This compared with 17 000 television-industry workers, and fewer than 14 000 in book publishing. The average New York area annual pay for new media employees was US$31 421. The size of the new media industry in the New York metropolitan area had more than doubled in a year to an estimated US 3.8 billion-a-year business. The other leading centre in the United States, San Francisco, had over 2 200 new media companies employing 62 000 workers. By 1994, the broadly defined "copyright industries" (media and computer software publishing) were estimated to contribute 5.72 per cent of GDP (US$385.2 billion) and to have created almost 6 million jobs (or 4.81 per cent of the total workforce) in the United States (Siwek and Mosteller, 1996).

567. As distribution channels proliferate within the context of increasing infrastructure liberalisation, a wide variety of services will be needed to prevent capacity underutilisation and unprofitable investments. Liberalisation of network and equipment markets on the supply side therefore needs to be complemented by policy measures which address content development – particularly audio-visual content – for different service markets on the demand side.

47. *Encyclopaedia Britannica Inc.*, for instance, has moved to electronic and direct mail sales only. As part of this move, Britannica has laid off 140 sales representatives in the United States and Canada and disbanded a similar sales network of 300 independent sales contractors. Britannica has moved distribution to CD-ROM and the Internet, and increased on-line, television and direct mail advertising (*New York Times*, 1996; *Wall Street Journal*, 1996). See also DJC Research *et al.*, 1995.

10.3. Sector-specific policy practices

568. As infrastructure liberalisation increases and transport costs continue to decline, the number and type of Internet-based services can be expected to multiply. Penetration of ICTs has grown rapidly in businesses in many if not all OECD countries, with household demand lagging somewhat behind, except in a few cases. In Australia, for instance, 1.9 million computers were used in households in February 1994, compared to 1.6 million regularly used in non-agricultural business in June 1994 (Australian Bureau of Statistics, 1996*a*; 1996*b*). In the United States, household demand for PCs has recently exceeded business demand. Computers with modems (*i.e.* with access to services on the Internet) represent between 15 to 30 per cent of the total, but have been increasing rapidly in the last few years.[48] Within these broad categories, demand varies considerably between different socio-economic groups as well as market segments (OECD, 1997*b*). Policies for stimulating demand for Internet-based services through national regulatory reform will therefore often target both general and sector-specific conditions. The remainder of this section analyses the socio-economic characteristics of demand in business, household and government markets, and considers the policy practices that could usefully be adopted by governments in each of these areas.

Policy practices for business markets

569. Business-to-business services cover a broad range of industries. While ICTs are used in both manufacturing and service industries, penetration remains low in agriculture and construction. Employees in finance and insurance services make greatest use of ICTs, generally followed by public administration workers. Workers in real estate and business activities, utilities and mining also tend to make higher than average use of these technologies.[49] Usage of ICTs in businesses has until recently outpaced use in the home and in educational institutions.

570. Business-to-business services are the largest and fastest growing area of demand for Internet-based content. While still at an infant stage of product development, the value of business-to-business transactions is already much larger than that of business-to-consumer transactions (some estimates suggest a factor of 9 to 1), with projections for future growth ranging from US$50 billion to US$500 billion by the year 2000.

571. Firms in the retailing and manufacturing sectors have long used proprietary networks and applications for internal delivery and information purposes, and some (particularly financial information) service companies have also found demand sufficiently rewarding to justify investing in high-capacity infrastructure for delivery of products to customers. Internet technologies are increasingly being implemented in such systems (known as intranets and extranets); intranet spending by companies in 1996 has been estimated at between US$4 billion and US$6 billion, with projections of four-fold growth by the year 2000.[50]

---

48. Between 1994 and 1995, for instance, the percentage of computers with modems in Canada jumped from 33.7 to 41.9 per cent. See Dickinson and Sciadas (1996).

49. The measure of ICT usage compared to total employment in an industry differs from computerisation by industry: that is, the percentage of businesses with computers compared to total businesses. In Australia, for example, almost 50 per cent of businesses have computers. Those in the electricity, gas, and water supply industry have the highest penetration, 86 per cent. The finance and insurance industry comes fourth by this measure, with a computer penetration of 71 per cent – after communication services and property industries, as well as the business services industry, which includes the computer services industry itself.

50. See <http://www.tpn.geis.com>.

572. The private sector is also rapidly developing the Internet as a general medium of exchange to increase competition, reduce costs and increase productivity in demand and supply relations. At one level, individual firms in specific industries are developing services to link new suppliers and customers. For instance, General Electric, which did more business-to-business electronic commerce in 1996 than all individual business-to-consumer activities combined, has announced its intention to move all its procurement – which is valued at US$5 billion – onto the Internet by the year 2000 (*Financial Times*, 1997*e*). Japan's leading electronics manufacturer, NEC Corporation, has also announced its intention to use the Internet for 90 per cent of its procurement activities, valued at US$17.3 billion per year (Nakamoto, 1997). At the industry level, Apparel Exchange has since 1994 offered an on-line sourcing service to more than 26 000 textile companies (*Financial Times*, 1997*e*; 1997*f*). At a more general level, services such as Industry.Net in the United States provide users with a list of 36 000 suppliers of different kinds of industrial goods.

573. A number of OECD governments have established programmes to try to stimulate the development of business-to-business services. The European Union, for instance, has projects under the European Strategic Programme for Research and Development in Information Technologies (ESPRIT) and ACTS programmes which aim to support the evolution of business organisations towards the electronic management of their commercial activities with suppliers and other business customers. As regards stimulating demand for general business-to-business services, there is little that governments can do directly, other than supporting industry initiatives. The United Kingdom has recognised this with its UK Trade project, which is intended to become a comprehensive electronic market-place, where a range of goods and services can be offered and transactions completed. The aim is to have 250 000 companies participating within five years; the project itself is run by the company ICL, with a £450 000 grant from the UK Department of Trade and Industry and information from trade associations (*Financial Times*, 1997*e*).

574. Governments also need to address social factors affecting demand for ICTs and Internet-based services in industry. The widest disparities in computer use, for instance, relate to educational attainment. In Finland in 1996, 79 per cent of women and 84 per cent of men with a tertiary education were using ICTs at work. The values drop to 57 and 54 per cent respectively for those having only upper secondary education, and 41 and 37 per cent for primary or lower secondary education. Similarly, differences in occupations account for large variations in the use of computers at work. Use is greatest in high-skill occupations such as administrative, managerial and professional workers, but also in lower-skilled ones such as clerks and salespeople. In Canada in 1994, 95 per cent of scientists and engineers, as well as 22 per cent of those involved in manufacturing/processing activities, 20 per cent of those employed in primary activities and 15 per cent of service workers were using computers, the average for all occupations being 48 per cent. In France in 1993, the values ranged from 6.5 per cent for elementary occupations to 54 per cent for technicians and associate professionals and 70.5 per cent for legislators, senior officials, managers and professionals. Policies for education and training in computing and Internet-based applications skills need to be developed in general, but those which address the upskilling of workers can particularly help to foster more broad-based demand.

575. The use of computers also varies with the age and gender of workers. The plot of use against age reveals inverted U-curves for all countries corresponding to low use for young workers (less than 30 years old), the highest use for workers between 30-45 years, and rapidly declining use thereafter. In four of the five countries for which data are available (except Sweden) women use computers more frequently than do men. Most of this difference can be explained by different participation rates in industries and different occupational distributions: women's employment is higher than men's in industries and occupations where computers are more prevalent. Data from the United States show that within occupations, however,

differences are no longer significant except for primary occupations and services (where use by men is significantly higher) and transportation and communications (where the opposite is true). In Finland in 1996, women had higher usage rates than men in service occupations, technical and humanistic work, and, to a lesser extent, industrial work. Again, these factors suggest that broad-based educational and training policies are needed to stimulate demand for Internet-based services.

576. Broad-based policies are also needed to encourage the development of Internet-based services and demand among SMEs. SMEs are often the seedbeds of innovative digitised content for large media companies who outsource component production for a range of printed and audio-visual products in a number of sectors (film, education, advertising), and may increasingly be able to deliver such content to broad audiences via the Internet as easily as large enterprises. It is quite possible that the traditionally heavy capital investments and personnel costs required for audio-visual production (in particular), and the subsequently large economies of scale needed to achieve adequate returns, may no longer be as vital to successful product and market development as in the past. Governments may encourage this potential through supporting extra-industry networks – for example, through private sector co-operation with local government bodies or universities in the development of new services. Relaxation of foreign investment and import quotas in the media sector could also encourage links between domestic SMEs and foreign enterprises based upon innovative, but perhaps temporary, Internet-based production and distribution partnerships. The growth of business-to-business Internet-based service markets may thus create a potential development path (by decreasing unit costs through increasing economies of scale) for business-to-consumer services.

577. The need for such policies will, however, depend on the degree of openness of network-based services. This, in turn, is influenced by the relationship between large firms and their SME suppliers and distributors, and on the level of competition this allows at various points along the chain of demand and supply. Large companies may not consider product development worthwhile until markets of sufficient size have developed, while SMEs may develop products for niche markets because they are satisfied with smaller returns (although they may also be faced with greater costs of capital). In the new digital environment, however, the rate of return from economies of scope increasingly produces relatively greater aggregate wealth generation than that from economies of scale. One of the benefits of digital technologies in general is their ability to reduce corporate overheads and more efficiently tie together production and distribution systems. However, regulations securing open access and competition are important to counteract lock-in of SME content into specific networks.

578. The situation will very much depend on the degree to which competition exists for the delivery of: *(i)* the same Internet service content within telephone, satellite, cable and terrestrial over-the-air television networks; *(ii)* the same content between these different media (OECD, 1996*h;* 1993*b*). Eventually, competition is likely to increase in the provision of services' content irrespective of the technological delivery platform, but the actual level of market development varies across countries. To the extent that competition exists at different levels of the production and distribution chain (such as now seems extensive in the United States), there is little need for regulatory constraints on vertical integration among companies. To the extent that competition is limited at various points along the chain (as is currently the case in many other OECD countries), utilisation of competition and antitrust policies can speed up market access and substitution. Market size also makes a difference; small countries may have much to gain from regional or multilateral harmonization of regulations and standards. The G7 has established a pilot project linking national efforts to the international dimensions of SME use of Internet-based services.

579. Similar approaches may be required in the development of network-based audio-visual markets. As large studios generally outsource special effects' work, or form close partnerships with the SMEs involved, close inter-working of computer firms and film producers is necessary in order for technological spin-offs to occur. The rapid evolution of "Silicon Valley" IT start-up companies has been dependent upon close inter-working with venture capitalists, legal and personnel specialists with a deep knowledge of sectoral conditions and technological developments (and who can provide a "peer-review" for product development and commercial strategies) (*Financial Times*, 1996*b*). Governments can help to foster such professional-industry inter-working, while allowing it to remain open and dynamic as a form of vertical integration.

580. A key question concerns the institutional frameworks that can enable governments to successfully implement such policy practices. OECD governments have in the past sought to achieve consensus on audio-visual policies through a range of independent or semi-independent institutions which, while having a broad political mandate, regulate markets free from day-to-day political influence.[51] Despite the increased number and variety of network-based services, the multi-faceted nature of demand for Internet-based services suggests that effective policy in this area will need to assess and act upon developments within a broad context of market, sectoral, social and technological evolution. Managing this task will depend on the ability to co-ordinate measures in different areas, which may require reform in governance, for instance, by clarifying responsibilities within governments. The development of "information society" programmes which co-ordinate a multiplicity of actors in large-scale technology initiatives such as the EU Framework Programme, has demonstrated the value of a comprehensive approach. The US National Information Infrastructure initiative also represents a systemic policy orientation. Australia provides an example of a country where policy co-ordination has traditionally been relatively weak, although this may be rectified by the recent appointment of a single Minister. Such institutional frameworks are also important for extending the development of business-to-business Internet-based services to consumer and other markets.

Policy practices for consumer (household) markets

581. Business-to-consumer markets were initially thought to be the area of greatest potential demand for Internet-based services. Despite less than favourable general economic conditions, the share of households equipped with computers and other ICTs grew significantly in a number of OECD countries between the early and mid-1990s. Supported by substantial price reductions and an increasing number of applications, household computer penetration in 1994-95 reached 26 per cent in the United States, 25 per cent in Germany, 20 per cent in the United Kingdom, 23 per cent in Australia, 16 per cent in Japan and 14 per cent in France.

582. Home PCs are used for a variety of purposes, including games, educational activities, word-processing, record-keeping and work-related activities. Desk-top publishing, newsletter creation, working at home, and network-based services such as electronic mail, connecting to bulletin boards, databases and a computer at work have gained importance in recent years. The largest segment of Internet-based household services is for intangible products that can be delivered directly to consumers

51. For instance, the Australian Broadcasting Authority (ABA) and Australian Film Commission; the Canadian Radio and Telecommunications Commission (CRTC), Canadian Film Commission and Canadian Council; the French *Conseil Supérieur de l'Audiovisuel* (CSA) and *Centre National de la Cinématographie* (CNC); the UK Independent Television Commission, Office of Telecommunications (OFTEL), British Film Commission and British Council; the US Federal Communications Commission and National Foundation for the Arts and Humanities.

over the network. Entertainment, including "adult" entertainment, online games, music and video, is the largest single product sold to consumers (OECD, 1997*v*). Forrester Research estimates that adult entertainment alone accounts for 10 per cent of all 1996 business-to-consumer electronic commerce (US$50 million), just behind computer products and travel. "Pay-for-play" online games generated a slightly lesser amount. Jupiter Communications predicts that Internet-based music sales will increase to US$186 million by 2000. The situation in broader retailing services varies, although projections of future demand are high. To date, the main tangible products sold electronically have been computers, clothing and food/drink, generating about US$120 million, 90 million and 40 million, respectively, in 1996. Many of these categories are dominated by traditional retailers that have established Internet-based operations. For other consumer services, demand still appears feeble.

583. Notwithstanding high growth overall, demand for ICTs varies greatly according to socio-economic characteristics of households.

- *Income*: This is the most important single differentiating factor. In Australia and Canada, for instance, for every US$10 000 increase in income, the likelihood of a household owning a computer increases by 7 per cent.

- *Age and family type*: Demand is highest in households where the head is between 35-44 and 45-54 years old. This is partly due to the presence of children and teenagers, the most avid computer users, but is also linked to high overall income levels, particularly for those in the 45-54 age bracket.

- *Labour force characteristics such as employment status, occupation*: Homes where the householder is self-employed exhibit the highest level of demand for PCs and modems, while those where the householder is unemployed exhibit the lowest. Workers in white-collar occupations (whether highly skilled or less skilled) are more likely than blue-collar workers to have home PCs. Usage increases with level of education.

- *Location of households*: In all income brackets, urban households typically exhibit higher demand than rural ones, with penetration rates in urban areas typically varying between 33 and 17 per cent of households/individuals, compared to between 24 and 11 per cent in rural areas. The difference by residential location is even more pronounced for households that have a modem. In Canada, for example, twice as many urban as rural households have a modem (13 per cent *vs.* 6.5 per cent).

584. While households already in possession of PCs and modems may be viewed as informed customers, and their usage of Internet as a question beyond the concern of policy makers, there is scope for demand-related policy in regard to those households which do not yet own a computer/modem. While the principal reasons for not having a computer and/or a modem include lack of interest as well as cost, home computing still represents a significant investment for many households. For households without a PC, public libraries and other community centres may constitute points of access to the Internet, underlining the importance of social and educational policies for the development of demand for Internet-based services. In addition, low-cost network computers (NCs) and television set-top boxes will facilitate growth in domestic demand if combined with low communication costs and user-friendly services, depending on the degree of competition in network and terminal equipment markets. The range of variables influencing demand for business-to-consumer services indicates, again, that a mix of policies needs to be developed in an integrated and comprehensive manner. A major use of PCs in homes is for educational purposes, and the use of ICTs at school, work and the home is highest among those who use them on a daily basis in all three locations. Internet-based educational services could

play a special role in generating household open-mindedness to and interest in other types of services. Again, this underlines the value of developing broad-based policy practices within coherent and comprehensive institutional frameworks.

585. There is no rationale for governments to directly stimulate demand for a broad range of business-to-consumer Internet services reducing costs. The focus should be on maintaining competitive conditions in the supply of business-to-business Internet services, reducing costs across the extended chain of supply and demand and thus the costs of delivery to the final consumer. Policies should further focus on providing a comprehensive framework for the development of Internet-based services in business, consumer and government markets. Such an extension is already occurring in equity trading, where electronic business-to-business trading systems implemented in stock exchanges have in some countries led to the development of Internet-based consumer services for stock price information and trading. Just a few years ago businesses would have been confined on a proprietary basis by groups such as Reuters. Indirectly, governments can facilitate consumer demand for such services by allowing small-scale buying and selling of shares on stock markets (currently forbidden in a number of OECD countries). In addition, governments can work with industry to establish common standards for trading and consumer protection in electronic commerce transactions. In Japan, for instance, MITI and 240 private firms are working on a standard contract enumerating the rights and duties of merchants and customers of Internet-based virtual malls.

Policy practices for government (education) markets

586. Governments can also stimulate the growth of demand for Internet-based business and consumer services by developing their use in business-to-government sectors. A wide range of business-to-government services could become Internet-based. Financial and banking service markets, for instance, can be stimulated through the online payment of and for government services. By the year 2000, the United States will require that all social security payments be made online, requiring all recipients to have bank accounts and banks to develop online access.

587. Education services play a special role in expanding possibilities for wider economic and social demand for Internet-based services. As we have seen, educational achievement is a major factor in determining demand for ICTs in both household and business markets. Computer literacy is essential in a growing number of professional, clerical, sales and administrative jobs, and individuals retraining for these activities will increasingly need ICTs. Schools constitute an important source of computer training for household users in OECD countries, but PCs are also increasingly being used for self-education in the home. In Australia, for instance, just over 1 million persons with household PCs (out of an installed base of 3.9 million) indicated use of "mainly educational products" in February 1996 (Australian Bureau of Statistics, 1996*b*). In addition, education in ICTs is growing in business or in business-sponsored institutions: in Finland, for example, 13 per cent of all employees receive training in ICTs from employers or in employer-supported courses (Statistics Finland, 1997). The development of content for educational applications thus provides a key means by which governments can expand growth possibilities in business and household markets.

588. Education offers opportunities for new demand to and from household and business sector markets through technological spillovers, in ways analogous to the spillovers offered by the development of advanced audio-visual content in business-to-business services considered above. Educational institutions have long been used as test-beds for ICTs by private sector groups such as Apple Computers, and provide a basis for product development for broader professional, consumer or business markets through providing people with experience in using and developing new services and applications. In comparison with business-to-business markets, education markets are more

homogenous, as public sector bodies constitute the largest source of demand for educational services in OECD countries. Compared to household markets, though, the development of demand for Internet-based services in schools and other educational institutions may be relatively cheaply stimulated by governments, as fewer connections are needed to give access to a large number of individuals. As a result, a number of OECD governments have begun connecting, or have stated their intention to connect, schools and other educational institutions to the Internet for administrative, educational, professional development and community building purposes.

589. The basis for such networking has to some extent already been laid. The use of PCs in educational institutions has risen considerably in many OECD countries since the early 1980s. US surveys, show that children's access to computers at school rose from 28 per cent in 1984 to over 60 per cent in 1993 (OECD, 1997*b*). Widely available software tools, such as text processors, spreadsheets, electronic mail and network browsers, which were developed for commercial markets, have found educational applications. Dedicated educational software, providing structured sources of information and opportunities for practice, has also become more available in recent years. Such software is sometimes housed on central servers linking 15-30 networked computers, although these are as yet in a minority to stand-alone PCs.

590. Studies on the use of Internet-based (and other network-based) services have found that, in general, network-based services enable educational institutions to offer a more diverse curricula and reduce their dependency on local teaching resources. They have the potential to reach populations that have traditionally been under-served and to reduce the separation between school and the home and between school and work. Network communications can provide post-training support to teachers and enable access to new ideas, master teachers and other professionals beyond their school setting, in both formal and informal courses and enrichment activities. This more direct, more flexible education is particularly valuable for adult education and training where work is performed at many sites or in remote areas. On-site training and skill upgrading are cheaper and more efficient than transporting employees to distant training sites. While the Internet is at present mainly restricted to text, data and graphic communications, it will increasingly provide access to a large and growing list of interactive audio-visual services. Educational services hold promise for the development of richer, higher capacity content.

591. In addition to these issues, three factors with implications for broad-based policy practices for demand and supply of Internet-based educational services can be noted. First, while PC penetration and Internet access in schools is increasing in OECD countries, penetration of network servers is much lower, so that experience of networking is less widespread. Policies for the wiring of educational institutions need to focus on the implementation and development of networking technologies, including very advanced technologies and architectures which can be extended from higher educational institutions to schools. The United States is leading the way in developing such practices: the Internet2 programme, which aims to develop collaboration among over 100 US universities, private companies and federal agencies for next-generation Internet technology and applications, already involves over 50 institutions. Members have committed up to US$50 million per year in new funding for the project, and it is expected that they will receive federal funding in the form of competitively awarded grants from the NSF and other federal agencies. More than half a dozen companies have pledged over US$5 million in cash and in-kind donations to the project. Internet2 will share its discoveries with others in the education community.

592. Second, even with such networking capabilities, there is still a challenge for educational services to develop Internet applications and content appropriate for children, and also services' content with a specifically pedagogical orientation. There is evidence that enthusiasm for such activities is high. In Japan, for example, the government initially expected few applications for a project to develop

Internet-based services, as the Internet was still relatively unknown and involved advanced server and client technologies which were considered to be unfamiliar in schools. In the event, however, 1 543 schools applied, with many proposing advanced applications. Policies are needed to bring together not just traditional educational groups, but also those traditional and new media groups from both the public and private sectors with experience in network-based content and applications, in order to develop engaging educational services. France, where the Ministry of Education is working with the private sector software company I-Card to develop a service-specific intelligent chip Internet charge card, provides an example. Given their traditional public service goals and audience profiles, public broadcasters [such as the British Broadcasting Corporation (BBC) in the United Kingdom and the Public Broadcasting Service (PBS) in the United States] can be expected to take a leading role in the development of educational content.

593. Third, while stimulation of demand for Internet-based education services might seem relatively straightforward as governments are the largest consumers of such services, much of this government consumption is actually determined at a sub-national level.[52] The most advanced government policies aimed at developing demand for educational services will tend to involve novel combinations and contributions from educational professionals and institutions, local government authorities and the private sector. A number of public/private sector pilot projects in the United Kingdom and United States have revealed significant demand for Internet-based educational services from children from economically and educationally deprived communities, once given the basic means to use and develop these services. At another level, a joint private (Japanese and foreign investors)/public sector grouping has begun the Asia-Pacific Interactive Communication NETwork (APICNET), which offers Japanese-based international educationally oriented Internet access and service development support.[53] Governments have a role to play in facilitating the development of such partnerships in education.

Comprehensive frameworks for Internet content markets

594. With declining communication costs, services' content has become the key factor for new economic growth and job creation in network-based services. With each new generation of ICTs, ever-more-advanced multimedia and interactive services become possible, providing for market expansion from business-to-business (or business-to-government) services where margins are high to business-to-consumer services where margins are lower but volume potentially greater. However, as distribution channels proliferate, and as networks are able to carry a wider variety of services, inadequate institutional and regulatory frameworks are associated with increasing regulatory costs or opportunity costs. For the migration to a fully digital environment, covering enhanced audio-visual and new multimedia and interactive services, broad-based policy measures are the best form of protection against systemic market failures arising from mismatches between supply and demand for Internet-based services.

595. There is a need to rationalise, simplify and reduce regulatory constraints, and to promote industry self-regulation of content. At present, OECD countries are generally moving towards policies which are more consistent with market-driven development of new distribution channels. Digitisation and the dissolution of technological distinctions between voice, data and audio-visual networks and traffic challenge the practicality of distinct regulatory frameworks for individual media services and for

52. In terms of research and comparative analysis, the almost inherently local and parochial nature of pre-university education certainly complicates matters. For the OECD Secretariat, for instance: most countries' Web pages are in local languages, with little substantive information in English.

53. For information on the project, their Website can be found at <http://www.apic.or.jp>.

regulating and promoting audio-visual content production. The German government has taken the broadest approach towards meeting this challenge with its proposed Multimedia Law; the Australian Broadcasting Authority (ABA) has formulated a more limited but nonetheless comprehensive framework based on rating and licensing regulations for industry-developed measures for online service content; the US Telecommunications Act of 1996 takes a comprehensive communications approach, but provides no framework for content.[54] In some instances governments are constrained by constitutional obligations in the degree to which they can utilise single policy approaches (such as competition policy). As a result, different approaches to the challenge are being developed. Some governments have appointed senior politicians with single responsibility for guiding and co-ordinating policy in the area (Australia, European Commission). Others have established broad standing task forces (Canada, United States) – sometimes alongside the creation of single regulatory agencies responsible for television and telecommunications (Australia, Canada, Italy, Japan, the United Kingdom, the United States). But market convergence is in its infancy, and in many cases the early stage of Internet development means that best policy practices are those able to combine effective responses to systemic issues with an ability to keep arrangements flexible and open to future developments.

10.4. Supply and demand for environmental goods and services

596. As in the case of Internet-based services, the diffusion and application of new environmental products is determined by a complex structure of demand and supply relations. Demand for environmental protection, and thus for environmental products and processes, enables growth in the supplying industry (demand pull), while the development of the environmental goods and services supply industry enables enterprises to better integrate cleaner technologies and environmental practices in production (supply push).

597. Demand for environmental products and processes strongly depends on governments' commitment to environmental protection. In the absence of such commitment, many environmental effects take the form of externalities, *i.e.* costs and benefits which are neglected in the market-place. At the same time, by influencing the legislative processes, modifying buying patterns and constituting third-party and citizen suits, the public is exerting growing pressure for the development of an environmentally friendly society and economy. This results from: the impact of expanding economic activities on the environment; increased appreciation and ability to pay for a cleaner environment linked to higher incomes;[55] better education of the general public; and better information on environmental impacts.[56]

598. The last few years have witnessed a greater emphasis by firms on pollution prevention strategies and strategic environmental planning, driving new technological developments and opening up new markets. Enterprises operating in traditional sectors create or adapt products and processes

54. The original act contained the Communications Decency Act (CDA), which of course did address content issues, although in a limited manner. In any case, the relevant parts of the CDA were struck down by the Supreme Court on constitutional grounds.

55. It is generally reasonable to view tastes and preferences as similar, irrespective of income. In other words, poor people may not really be different from rich people. What differs is income and, hence, the ability to sacrifice material goods for a sound environment (Stigler and Becker, 1997).

56. Beginning in the late 1970s, most OECD governments for the first time became subjected to major public mobilisation in this area, targeting health problems caused by air and water pollution as well as resource conservation and waste recovery and management. For example, the discovery in 1978 that buildings in Love Channel in New York were constructed on an old leaking hazard waste disposal, urged the government to establish the Superfund toxic waste clean-up programme. In Japan, the strong public reaction to widespread respiratory problems, caused by a petrochemical complex at Yakkaichi in the early 1970s, led to the first air pollution control act.

initially to improve environmental performance and fulfil environmental regulations, and then to increase competitiveness and develop a new business. Although there is a shortage of cross-country evidence, studies in some countries point to a positive impact of environmental technologies on the competitiveness of firms and industries in general, with potentially widespread productivity and employment effects (Repetto *et al.*, 1996; Porter and van der Linde, 1995).

599. In general, the adoption of "green design" or environmental auditing by enterprises is associated with organisation opportunities, capabilities and processes. Enterprises which engage in regular or continuous evaluation or modification of their product or process design will have greater opportunities to recognise competitive advantages (*e.g.* improved product quality, reduced costs, etc.), born from integrating environmental considerations into product and process design (Atlas and Florida, 1997). Firm size, financial resources, skilled personnel and the opportunity to reduce long-term costs will further spur the adoption of "green design".

600. However, environmental regulation and customers' preferences strongly influence companies' behaviour with regard to environmental performance. Analysis of factors prompting 750 Canadian enterprises to include environmental protection in their plans identified environmental regulation in a broad sense as the most important factor, although customers were also found to have influenced the choice. Studies analysing factors affecting the behaviour of European companies with respect to the environment similarly found that both regulation and consumer preferences had played a role (Rimmer, 1995; Madhurst, 1995).

601. Although business communities sometimes complain about environmental legislation, in practice, there is little evidence of plant closures or job losses due to environmental regulation. For example, one study (Management Information Services, 1993), indicated that during 1988, US employers attributed only 0.1 per cent of all layoffs to compliance with environmental regulations.

602. On the contrary, the introduction of environmental regulations has been found to have a positive impact on employment in OECD countries (OECD, 1996*i*), albeit other factors are generally more decisive for industrial performance. In the United States, as of 1992 environmental regulation has been estimated to support 3.96 million jobs, or 3.7 per cent of total employment (Management Information Services, 1993). In Europe, as of 1994 1.5 million jobs can be classified as environment-related (Eurostat, 1997) (Table 10.1).

603. The most visible and quantifiable, but more narrow, positive effects in terms of growth and job creation are related to the environment industry. This industry contributes to environmental innovation and macroeconomic growth in general, as well as to productivity and job creation by encouraging, supporting and re-vitalising the market-oriented socio-economic networks which underlie technological dynamism and market development. The definition comprises activities which produce goods and services to measure, prevent, limit, minimise or correct environmental damage to water, air and soil, as well as problems related to waste, noise and ecosystems. The industry includes both end-of-pipe equipment and cleaner technologies, products and services which reduce environmental risk and minimise pollution and resource use (OECD, 1996*j*).

604. In many OECD countries, the environmental industry has displayed very high growth over the last 20 years. In Germany, which has the largest environmental market in the European Union, growth in the sector amounted to 6.3 per cent per year between 1980 and 1993. In Austria, the rate was about 14 per cent over the same period. In the United States, growth was close to 6 per cent between 1990-92, with 16 per cent in the segment of environmental engineering and construction. Forecasts point to even higher growth rates in the future: in the OECD as a whole, 10 per cent growth has been predicted for the period 1998 to 2000.

Table 10.1. **Environment related employment, 1994**[1]

	Total environment employment – direct and indirect (in thousands)	Total employment (per cent)	Direct employment (Eurostat) (in thousands)	Total employment (per cent)	Direct employment (EBI) (in thousands)	Total employment (per cent)
Australia	. .	. .	11.0	0.2	29.1	0.4
Austria	52.3	1.4	41.5	1.1	9.3	0.2
Belgium	26.1	0.7	15.5	0.4	17.1	0.5
Canada	. .	. .	123	0.9	56.4	0.4
Denmark	22.3	0.9	15.9	0.6	11.5	0.5
Finland	21.2	1	13.6	0.7	8.1	0.4
France	322.6	1.5	200.9	0.9	102.4	0.5
Germany	447.8	1.2	316.5	0.9	212.1	0.6
Greece	8	0.8	5.1	0.1	9.4	0.2
Iceland	. .	. .	. .	. .	0.4	0.3
Ireland	12.5	0.9	8.7	0.7	2.7	0.2
Italy	165.6	0.8	100.6	0.5	57.5	0.3
Japan	. .	. .	. .	. .	323.6	0.5
Luxembourg	1.8	0.9	1.6	0.8	0.8	0.4
Mexico	. .	. .	. .	. .	10.0	0.03
Netherlands	107.4	1.6	88.7	1.3	32.9	0.5
New Zealand	. .	. .	. .	. .	3.1	0.2
Norway	. .	. .	. .	0.4	8.7	0.4
Portugal	24.8	0.6	17.1	0.3	6.9	0.2
Spain	52.8	0.4	37.6	1	43.7	0.4
Sweden	72.6	1.8	40.7	. .	16.4	0.4
Switzerland	. .	. .	. .	. .	12.9	0.3
Turkey	. .	. .	. .	. .	7.3	0.04
United Kingdom	195.5	1.0	140.3	0.5	109.4	0.4
United States	. .	. .	. .	. .	855.2	0.7

1. Total environment employment includes direct environment employment plus the indirect employment, calculated on the basis of the Harmonized Econometric Research for Modelling Economic Systems (HERMES) macroeconomic model. Eurostat and Environmental Business International (EBI) direct environment employment estimates differ according to methods used, although they are based on the OECD/Eurostat definition which includes the core group and some of the non-core group. Eurostat data are based on the estimated levels of capital and operating environmental expenditure, while EBI data are based on comprehensive primary data on the environment industry for the United States, which are scaled against known environmental industry, economic and development statistics in all other countries.
2. Canada Statistic Environment Industry preliminary data for 1995.

Source: Eurostat Working Papers, 1997, "An Estimate of Eco-Industries in the European Union for 1994". Interim results by EBI, 1995 for OECD Secretariat.

605. Employment in the environmental sector is estimated to have grown by 10 per cent in the United States between 1990 and 1995, and by 3 per cent in Canada and Japan (OECD, 1996*j*). A recent survey in Australia showed that one-half of environmental goods and service enterprises had expanded employment by more than 20 per cent in the period from 1988 to 1993. The interim OECD/Eurostat classification and definition (OECD, 1996*k*) of the environment industry (a conservative, narrow definition, which includes mainly the core group of the environment industry and part of cleaner technologies and products) found it to employ about 1 per cent of the total OECD labour force (Table 10.1), with half recorded as manufacturing (including construction) and half as services.

606. In the OECD area as a whole, most employment is in solid waste management (45 per cent) and in waste water management (25 per cent). On average, job opportunities tend to be more high-skill than in other industries, as evidenced by data from Australia and Germany, with an emphasis on high-skilled white-collar occupations (above 50 per cent), but also with a sizeable element of low-skilled blue-collar occupations (20-30 per cent). In Canada, it has been estimated that the distribution of new employees will be as follows: 50 per cent technicians/technologists; 25 per cent undergraduate degrees; 25 per cent post graduate degrees. If this pattern holds true for other Member countries, future shortfalls are widely predicted in the supply of required professional and technical staff (OECD, 1996*j*).

607. Growth in the environment industry will be highly dependent on technological innovation to efficiently adapt goods and services to new regulatory and customer requirements, on supply and upgrading of skilled labour, and on the international adoption of environmental regulations and standards. It has been suggested that 50 per cent of the environmental goods that will be used in 2010 have not yet been invented. Demand for environmental products is gradually moving away from "end-of-pipe" solutions towards product substitution and process modification. This reflects the quest for more efficient means to reduce environmental burdens coupled with the move by firms towards "cleaner production with greater value added".

10.5. Policy assessment

608. Policies can amplify the positive effects of environmental innovation by:

- facilitating development of the demand for environmental goods and services through environmental regulations which are designed to improve current and future environmental performance;
- promoting the environmental goods and service industry through support for environmental R&D, financial support, export incentives, etc., as either general incentives for all industry or specific incentives for the environment industry.

609. To date, no systematic evaluation is available to assess the overall effectiveness of different environmental or industrial regulatory systems in creating demand for environmental goods and services, or in supporting the environment industry, but there are variables which can be used to indicate policy performance. These include approaches to environmental regulation, environmental expenditure and environmental R&D, both private and public. The following section provides some analysis of these variables.

Approaches to environmental regulation

610. Environmental regulation, while aiming to improve environmental performance, should allow scope for evaluating and encouraging the diffusion of new and cleaner technologies. In the last

20 years, OECD countries have used two policy approaches to environmental protection: the "command-and-control" approach, based on pollution abatement and control (PAC) principles and focused on local pollution issues; and, more recently, the "market-based" approach based on the Polluter Pays Principle (OECD, 1986*a*).

611. Both approaches can present short-comings in boosting development and diffusion of cleaner technologies if policies are too complicated or uncertain; present gaps; or are too or insufficiently specific (OECD, 1995*c*). In the light of these and other considerations,[57] some OECD governments (Austria, Canada, Czech Republic, Denmark, Iceland, Japan, Mexico, Netherlands, Norway, Portugal, Spain, Sweden, Turkey, United Kingdom, United States, European Union) have undertaken a number of reforms aimed at correcting deficiencies in existing regulations.

612. Success in these reforms has depended on their ability to support, or act in concert with, the development of demand. The following have been crucial in this respect:

- the extent to which there has been an integrated approach with other policies (*e.g.* agriculture, industrial or innovation policy);
- the extent to which there has been effective signalling to economic actors about environmental performance and potential technological innovation;
- reduced uncertainty concerning the value of environmental innovation, related to an increased probability that it will eventually be costly for products and processes not to integrate environmental concerns;
- pressures for innovation and the diffusion and absorption of new technologies, coming from competitors, customers, rising prices of raw materials or the abolishment of distorting subsidies;
- inclusion from the outset of a cushion to reduce initial compliance costs, but which will be abolished once new technologies are in place.

613. In the process of reform, it has been recognised that market-oriented instruments, by modifying behaviour through more or less explicit internalisation of what used to be external effects, are more effective in stimulating demand for environmental products as they assure a higher level of flexibility and certitude. They are also more efficient in modifying consumer preferences and life styles, which have the most far-reaching and long-term effects in stimulating demand for environmental products (OECD, 1998*c*).

614. Such measures include charges and taxes; grants and subsidies; mechanisms to create markets, such as emission permit trading systems, in combination with fines for non-compliance. Other measures, which include feedback mechanisms, improved monitoring systems and procedures (*i.e.* self-monitoring and the use of direct measurement for small discharges); voluntary agreements

57. Targeted deficiencies in regulatory systems have concerned (OECD, 1997*w*):

- regulatory burdens for companies and increasing difficulties in achieving adequate and efficient enforcement as interrelations among firms and countries become more complex;
- disproportionately increasing marginal cost to reduce emitted pollutants;
- poor co-ordination in the environmental media;
- emphasis on "react and cure" pollution crises instead of anticipating and preventing pollution.

with industry (*e.g.* eco-label); environmental auditing procedures [Environmental Management System (EMS), Life-Cycle Analysis, etc.]; fuller information and wider publicity and environmental education, have been introduced to obtain a wider diffusion of environmental practices and raise environmental awareness in the public. A certain pattern can be discerned across OECD countries in the timing and emphasis given to various policy areas, as illustrated by Table 10.2. For instance, a number of countries have sought a co-ordinated policy approach over the last five years, but only New Zealand is currently giving priority to this aspect. Special emphasis is today placed on changing consumption and production patterns, public information and R&D (OECD, 1997*x*).

615. On the whole, those countries with a market-compatible approach have generally been able to combine it with relatively strict enforcement of environmental regulations (*e.g.* Germany, Japan, the Netherlands, the Scandinavian countries, the United States). These are the countries that display the most rapid technological innovation and have the most advanced markets in this area (OECD, 1997*x*) in that they have reduced the uncertainty and inconsistency which inhibit the development of demand. Nevertheless, command-and-control regulations are the most common type of legislation in most OECD countries. In many cases, new products or applications have not been implemented because prevailing regulations prescribe certain technologies or product properties and because of inconsistencies in regulations.

616. Canada, the Netherlands, the Scandinavian countries and the United States have recognised the importance of having a body responsible for enhancing the co-ordination and integration of environmental protection with other policies, although their efforts remain somewhat patchy and are not completely effective. Nevertheless, these countries, along with Germany and Japan, have sought to take a decisive step towards environmental policies which both aims at explicit goals and at putting in place incentive structures combining a mixture of regulatory and market-based instruments that leave a high degree of flexibility as to their implementation. As a result, they presently benefit from better structured demand for environmental products, more competitive environmental technologies and a better developed environmental industry compared to other OECD countries. Between 1992-97, the Czech Republic, Hungary and Poland radically reformed their environmental policy along the above lines. In a few years, it will be interesting to evaluate their effectiveness in creating and structuring environmental demand.

617. However, most, if not all, OECD countries continue to pursue policies contradictory to the goals of greening demand. While environmental regulators focus on eco-efficiency in general, energy, transport and agricultural policies still include extensive subsidies effectively stimulating pollution or resource waste. Energy subsidies are especially distorting in Italy and the United States (OECD, 1997*x*). Transport systems in Europe largely favour road and air transport, while rail and water transport is impeded by contradictory national planning and regulation. In agriculture, New Zealand is the only country to have implemented reform by comprehensively removing subsidies on fertilisers and pesticides, and vetting all agricultural policy for harmful environmental impacts.

618. Policies will also have greater impact if they are co-ordinated, and possibly harmonized, at the international level, as contradictory legislative frameworks in different countries are counterproductive. International trade liberalisation of markets for environmental goods and services underpins the expansion of markets and thereby higher growth, given the presence of conditions which allow for the internalisation of environmental impacts. International agreements, such as the Montreal Protocol, provide important impetus in areas where emissions are global in nature. Harmonization of national environmental standards on a regional basis, as in the European Union, can provide far more leverage than national measures on firm behaviour.

Table 10.2. **Environmental policy and instruments in OECD countries**

	Co-ordinated policy approach	Compliance and enforcement	Changing consumption and production patterns	Environmental expenditure	Environmental expenditure for R&D	Economic instruments (*e.g.* taxes and charges)	Voluntary agreement	Public information education and participation
Canada	●		●●	●	●●	●	●●	●
Mexico	●		●●	●	●●	●●	●	●
New Zealand	●●			●	●	●	●	●●
United States	●		●	●	●●	●	●●	●
Austria			●●	●	●	●	●	●●
France		problems with	●	●	●	●	●	●●
Germany	●		●●		●●		●	
Netherlands	●		●	●	●●	●	●	●
Finland	●		●●		●	●		
Norway	●			●		●		●
Sweden	●		●●	●	●●	●	●	●●
Japan	●		●	●	●●	●	●●	●●
Korea	●		●●	●	●	●	●	●●
Czech Republic	●	problems with	●●	●		●		●
Hungary	●	problems with	●●	●		●		●
Italy		problems with		●	●	●		
Poland	●	problems with	●●	●		●		●
Portugal				●[1]	●[1]	●		
Spain		problems with		●[1]	●[1]	●	●	●

● means country has established initiatives in the area.

●● means country is currently putting special emphasis on the area.

1. They are supported by the European Union with regional and cohesion funds.

Source: OECD Environmental Performance Reviews.

Size and structure of environmental expenditure

619. The size and structure of pollution abatement and control expenditure reflect differences in regulatory approaches and environmental markets (Table 10.3). In general, expenditure for environmental goods and services in most OECD countries represents between 1 and 2 per cent of GDP, depending on national environmental regulatory systems. The Netherlands and Switzerland display particularly high figures. However, there is considerable variation in the contribution of the public, business and household sectors. In Canada, Germany, the Scandinavian countries and the United States, environmental public awareness is such that consumers are willing to pay for cleaner products (Table 10.3). The evidence suggests a similarity in the trends and composition of private and public expenditure across Germany, Japan and the United States (Table 10.4). Generally, however, the public sector remains the major player on the demand side, with more than 50 per cent of the total. Direct household environmental expenditure remains insignificant in most countries (*e.g.* 1 per cent in Portugal). In Australia and Germany, the private and business sectors are equally committed to environmental protection. The United States is the only country in which demand for environmental goods and services derives principally from the business sector.

620. In the period between 1985 and 1992, the structure of demand for environmental goods and services changed very slightly. In most countries, the business sector increased demand for environmental goods and services, while public or household sector demand decreased. This is consistent with the introduction of market-oriented policies and their more effective internalising of environmental externalities, as well as an increasing commitment to environmental protection within the business sector, where the increase in the demand for environmental goods and services goes beyond government requirements.

621. During the same period, public environmental expenditure remained constant or increased slightly while public deficits decreased, indicating that countries have given priority to this area. Some OECD countries (*e.g.* Poland), have put in place an environmental fund or a deposit/refund system to use revenues from environmental taxes to finance environmental initiatives both in the form of environmental projects (*e.g.* waste disposal systems, environmental investment by enterprises) and in the form of loans to environmental goods and service suppliers.

622. The composition of environmental expenditure has changed over the same period. Public expenditure, which in the early 1980s mainly financed environmental infrastructure (*e.g.* sewage, waste and waste water treatment plants), at present more widely supports diffusion of innovative environmental technologies (*e.g.* through demonstration projects) and projects which have a larger – although less direct – impact on demand for environmental goods and services. For instance, the Netherlands and the Scandinavian countries are now focusing on changing consumption and production patterns, and financial support is directed to improving public environmental awareness (environmental information and education) and to diffusing cleaner technologies (accelerating depreciation of environment investment, subsidies to environmental R&D). Other countries (Canada, Denmark, Germany, Japan, Korea, the Netherlands, Switzerland, the United States) have sought to institute mechanisms to ensure that public procurement takes environmental effects into account, thereby broadening the presence of environmentally conscious demand in the economy (OECD, 1997*y*).

Table 10.3. **Pollution abatement and control expenditure as a percentage of GDP[1, 2]**

	1985	1987	1988	1989	1990	1991	1992
Public and private sectors (unless otherwise noted)							
Australia	..	..	..	..	0.6	0.7	..
Austria[3]	..	1.8	1.7	..	2.0[4]	2.1[4]	..
Canada				0.9			
Finland[5]	..	..	..	..	..	..	1.4
France	0.9	1.0	1.2	1.2	1.2	1.2	1.2
Germany[6]	1.5	1.6	1.6	1.6	1.6	1.6	1.5
Italy[7]	..	..	..	0.9	..	..	..
Japan[8]	1.0	1.1	1.1	1.1	1.1	..	..
Korea	..	..	..	..	..	..	1.5
Mexico	..	..	..	..	..	..	0.8
Netherlands	1.4	1.5	..	1.4	1.7	1.8	1.9
Norway[9]	..	..	..	..	1.2	..	..
Portugal[10]	..	..	0.5	0.5	0.8	0.7	..
Sweden[11]	0.2[12]	..	0.4[12]	..	..	1.2	..
Switzerland[13]	..	..	..	..	..	..	2.1
United Kingdom	1.3				1.4		
United States	1.4	1.4	1.4	1.4	1.5	1.5	1.6
Public and private sectors (including private households)							
Australia	..	..	..	..	..	0.9	..
Austria[3]	1.0	1.8	1.8	..	2.1[4]	2.2[4]	..
France	1.0	1.1	1.3	1.3	1.3	1.3	1.3
Korea	..	..	..	..	..	..	1.5
Netherlands	1.5	1.5	..	1.5	1.8	1.9	2.0
Portugal	..	..	0.5	0.5	..	..	..
Switzerland[13]	..	..	..	..	..	..	2.1
United Kingdom	..	..	..	..	1.5	..	..
United States	1.7	1.7	1.7	1.6	1.7	1.6	1.7

1. Changes in PAC expenditure shares must be reviewed with care, as they may also increase because of improved sectoral coverage and data availability.
2. Based on the abater principle (expenditure 1). For some countries this includes receipts from by products.
3. Estimates made to remove double counting of waste water and waste fees. Figures include street cleaning.
4. Definitions and methodology used are different from and are not comparable with other data. The OECD Secretariat estimate for public/private sector PAC expenditure is 1.7 per cent of GDP.
5. Public and private sectors: includes an estimate for public sector PAC expenditure.
6. Data cover western Germany only.
7. Public sector. Partial figure for 1988, thus 1988 and 1989 data are not comparable.
8. Partial figure. Data on business sector current expenditure not available.
9. Secretariat estimate.
10. Only investment expenditure is included in the business sector data.
11. Public and private sectors: 1985 and 1988 business sector data only.
12. Public sector: 1987 data refer to 1986.
13. Business and household sectors: 1992 data refer to 1993.

Source: OECD Secretariat.

Table 10.4. **Environmental expenditure by the public, business and household sectors**
Percentage

	Public sector			Business sector			Private households		
	1985	1990	1992	1985	1990	1992	1985	1990	1992
United States	32	38	39	50	52	53	18	10	8
France	68	65	65	23	26	26	9	9	9
Germany	50	52	56	50	48	44	. .	. .	. .
Netherlands	69	57	58	30	37	37	1	6	5
Portugal	76	95	90	23	5	10	1	. .	. .
Australia	52	43	. .	48	57	. .	. .	. .	. .
Japan	88	90	. .	12	10	. .	. .	. .	. .
Korea	. .	. .	49	. .	. .	44	. .	. .	7

Source: OECD Secretariat.

623. In countries such as Canada, Germany, the Scandinavian countries and the United States, environmental public awareness is high and consumers are exerting pressure for better environmentally friendly products and processes. This consumer attitude has forced industry to adopt greener practices in the 1990s, as witnessed by the use of both eco-labels, which seem to have gained wide credibility (*e.g.* the Nordic Swan label is found on 100 products in the Nordic market), and eco-audits within industry. For example, estimates indicate that by 1995, 50 to 60 per cent of Swedish industry was conducting environmental audits (using EMS) and investing in waste minimisation projects, boosting demand for environmental products and fostering the development of the environment industry.

Environmental R&D

624. Support to environmental R&D has been important in stimulating demand for environmental goods and services and the environment industry in general. The private sector will rarely make the necessary investment for developing and incorporating environmental processes and products into existing systems unless there are proven benefits.

625. This is especially true for a new environmental technology where, compared with conventional technologies, profit margins are often uncertain and not easily quantifiable (OECD, 1998*c*). Major innovations in the environmental field are often complicated by imperfect information, changing technological opportunities and organisational inertia. There is thus a rationale for governments to assist in the development, demonstration and dissemination of environmental products and processes, and to encourage capacity building and public awareness.

626. In general, environmental regulatory reform aiming to promote environmental R&D should improve the flexibility of command-and-control instruments by shifting away from technology specifications, monitoring systems and requirements, and encouraging alternative compliance methods. The greatest potential for far-reaching innovation may reside with new approaches such as producer responsibility, information disclosure and environmental management systems, which can encourage the redesign of products and process through life-cycle analysis of ecological impacts.

627. Most significantly, environmental policy instruments may best stimulate innovation when used in combination, and when they take into account the industry-specific and even firm-specific context.

This may require improved interactions between environmental policy and technology policy, where the latter could offer insights from R&D funding mechanisms, technology foresight exercises, innovation system models and P/PP schemes (OECD, 1997*z*).

628. Both environmental and industrial policy have contributed to the promotion of environmental R&D through direct financial support. In most OECD countries, support in this area increased from 1-2 per cent of total government R&D appropriation in the early 1980s to 3-4 per cent at the end of the decade (Table 10.5). Although these increases appear to have levelled off as of the mid-1990s, government expenditure in aggregate totals around US$2.5 billion per year for all OECD countries.

Table 10.5. **Government budget appropriations for environmental R&D**
Percentage of total GBAORD

	1981	1992	1993	1994	1995	1996
Australia	2.7	3.0	2.9	2.7	..	..
Austria	0.4	2.2	3.2	2.9	2.4	2.1
Belgium	2.8	1.7	1.5	1.5	1.5	2.5
Canada	1.2	2.4	2.6	2.7	2.5	..
Denmark	1.8	4.5	4.5	4.5	4.1	..
Finland	0.9	3.1	3.0	2.4	2.5	..
France	0.5	1.1	1.3	1.4	1.9	..
Germany	1.8	3.7	3.8	3.7	3.5	..
Greece	3.1	1.9	4.1	3.3	3.2	..
Iceland	..	1.7	3.5	3.8	3.9	4.0
Ireland	0.4	0.6	0.7	1.3	1.3	..
Italy	1.8	2.2	2.4	2.4	2.4	..
Japan	..	0.5	0.5	0.5	0.6	0.6
Mexico	..	0.4	1.7	1.7	..	..
Netherlands	..	3.5	4.6	4.4	3.7	3.5
New Zealand	..	2.6	2.7	..	..	..
Norway	3.6	3.3	3.0	2.6	2.6	..
Portugual	..	2.9	2.5	1.7	..	..
Spain	0.7	1.9	2.3	2.4	2.6	2.7
Sweden	1.8	3.6	3.4	3.8	2.3	..
United Kingdom	1.2	1.4	2	2.3	2.1	..
United States	0.8	0.1	0.7	0.8	0.8	..

Source: OECD Secretariat.

629. Some countries, such as Canada which directs 25 per cent of new R&D funding to environmental technology, or Korea which needs to upgrade its products to international environmental standards, have put a great deal of effort into co-ordinating and developing systems to direct R&D towards environmental technology. Industry and the private sector is actively responding to these incentives (Lanjouw and Mody, 1995).

10.6. Best practices to stimulate supply and demand for environmental goods and services

630. The development of markets for environmental goods and services strongly depends on government commitment to environmental protection. In most OECD countries, the demand for environmental goods and services has progressed through similar phases: increased environmental awareness; development of national environmental policies and regulations; institutional capacity building (*e.g.* the establishment of agencies or ministries responsible for environmental protection); environmental expenditure plans by either the public or the private sector and, most recently, strategic action by private companies to exploit cleaner products and processes as a sales argument.

631. Evidence shows that policy reforms can facilitate the diffusion of new environmental products and processes to the extent that:

- Environmental policy is co-ordinated with other policies, *e.g.* industrial, innovation, agriculture (Canada, Denmark, the Netherlands, New Zealand, Norway, Sweden).
- Environmental policy has clear and explicit goals, enforcing a shift from command-and-control instruments which include technology specification, to more flexible measures like market incentives, *e.g.* emission trading or voluntary agreements. Environmental policy should avoid prescribing solutions, leaving it to the interplay between businesses and between firms and customers to engineer innovation and technology diffusion. This approach will encourage the redesign of products and process through life-cycle analysis of ecological impacts (Canada, Denmark, Finland, Germany, the Netherlands, Norway, Poland, Sweden, the United States).
- Governments directly support the demand and the supply of environmental R&D through both direct financial support to environmental R&D and private/public joint demonstration projects to illustrate the applicability of clean products and processes (Canada, Korea).
- Policies involve the general public. This approach has the most far-reaching effects: if consumer life styles change and demand for cleaner products becomes the norm as clean products are identified, then manufacturers must adapt to meet this demand (*e.g.* greening of public procurement introduced by Canada, Germany, Iceland, Japan, Korea, the Netherlands, Sweden, the United States).
- Environmental instruments are internationally harmonized (*e.g.* taxes on CO_2) (Table 10.7).

10.7. Conclusions

632. The two new growth industries considered in this chapter share some important characteristics for technology and innovation policy:

- both are areas of rapid innovation and growth;
- both are the source of considerable externalities (in terms of their impacts on other industries as well as on consumers); and
- in both, the articulation of demand and the creation of markets depends crucially on policy (government procurement, regulation-induced demand, provision of legal frameworks, etc.).

633. To be successful, policies in both these areas have to be "systemic". They have to integrate and co-ordinate different policy targets (*e.g.* the goals of environmental and technology policy or the need to encourage the positive social impact of Internet-based services) and different policy areas (reflected in dispersed political competences), as well as different instruments targeting both the supply and demand sides. They have to create and shape appropriate institutions for these markets, especially the bodies to set, implement and supervise standards and competition policy – which involves both de-regulation and re-regulation. In the absence of such "institution building" there is the evident risk of systemic failure in both areas.

634. Also, examples from both areas show that policies – rather than trying to pick winners or winning technological solutions – act best when strengthening the incentives for innovation and removing barriers. Policy is confronted with the need to develop a balanced mix of regulatory and market-incentive-based instruments which effectively correspond to and articulate consumer demand while leaving a high degree of flexibility as to their implementation. The contribution of these industries to macroeconomic growth, productivity and job creation will be optimised to the extent that they encourage, support and re-vitalise the market-oriented socio-economic networks which underlie their technological dynamism and market development.

635. Policy in both areas is beginning to recognise these necessities: a number of comprehensive policy initiatives aim at establishing the "information society" and attempt to address the need for policy co-ordination, creation of institutions and balancing of social goals with technological development. In the same vein, governments are increasingly designing integrated environmental policies which can be considered as a step in the direction of designing "systemic" technology and innovation policies.

636. Finally, in both areas, policies will have greater impact if co-ordinated at the international level. International trade and investment liberalisation typically facilitate the expansion of markets. In Internet-based services, international agreement by governments on framework conditions for electronic commerce in areas such as consumer protection and privacy will facilitate growth in trade, investment by companies and demand by households. In environmental goods and services, free circulation needs to be coupled with, for instance, harmonization of standards (*e.g.* at the European level) or more internationally accepted systems for information or certification relating to environmental performance. Compared to purely national measures, international co-ordination will allow better articulation of demand and will facilitate technology transfers.

Table 10.6. **Summary of best policy practices for supporting Internet-based services**

Best policy practice	Applicability	Country specific
Infrastructure competition (cable television, PSTN, satellite)	General policy	*High:* Australia, Canada, Finland, Japan, Netherlands, New Zealand, Sweden, United Kingdom, United States *Medium:* Austria, France, Germany *Low:* Belgium, Greece, Italy, Mexico, Spain
Overall policy co-ordination	General policy	*Standing task force:* Canada, United States *Single minister:* Australia, European Commission *Single broadcast/telecoms regulator:* Canada, United States
Competition and antitrust policy	General policy and sectoral (business markets)	*High development:* Australia, United Kingdom, United States *Medium development:* Canada, Germany *Low development:* France, Italy, Japan, Mexico
Industry clearing houses and self-regulation	General policy and sectoral (business markets), public/ private co-operation	Australia, Canada, Japan, United Kingdom, United States
Wiring schools	Sector specific, public/ private co-operation	Australia, Canada, France, Finland, Germany, Japan, Norway, Sweden, United Kingdom, United States
Education content development	Sector specific, public/ private co-operation	Sweden, United Kingdom, United States
Advanced network projects	Sector specific, public/ private co-operation	United States (Internet2 programme), Japan (Next Generation Internet projects), European Union (ACTS programme)

Source: OECD Secretariat.

Table 10.7. **Summary of best policy practices to encourage demand for environmental goods and services**

Areas	Best policy practices
Co-ordinated policy approach	Interministerial co-ordination (Denmark, Netherlands, Norway, Sweden) Council/Commission on Sustainable Development (Canada, United States) National Environmental Plans (Austria)
General regulatory framework	Environmental policies with explicit and clear goals Incentive structures which combine a balanced mix of regulatory and market based instruments and which effectively correspond to and articulate consumer demand, while leaving high degree of flexibility as to their implementation (Canada, Denmark, Finland, Germany, Netherlands, Norway, Poland, Sweden, United States) Coherence with other policy measures (*e.g.* subsidies to transport, energy and agriculture and other fiscal instruments)(New Zealand)
Economic instruments	Properly designed and implemented Internationally co-ordinated (*e.g.* CO_2 taxes) (Scandinavian countries)
Voluntary agreement	Traditionally, when there is public/private co-operation or limited capacity to introduce new taxes and regulation (France, Germany, Netherlands) Clearly targeted (Belgium, Denmark, France, Germany, Netherlands) The agreement specifies a reliable baseline against which improvements will be measured (most countries) External control, evaluation and transparency are provided (Belgium, France, Germany, Netherlands)
Environmental R&D	Stricter environmental regulation stimulates technological innovation (Austria, Germany, Scandinavian countries, United States) Promotion and direct support for environmental R&D (Austria, Canada, Germany, Iceland, Japan, Korea, Netherlands, Sweden, United States)
Changing consumption and production patterns	Greening of public procurement (Canada, Denmark, France, Germany, Japan, Sweden, Switzerland, United States) Increasing public awareness and participation through education and information (Canada, Finland, France, Japan, Korea, Mexico, Netherlands, New Zealand, Spain)

Source: OECD Secretariat.

CHAPTER 11. HIGH-PERFORMANCE WORKPLACES AND INTANGIBLE INVESTMENT

11.1. Organisation, skills and technology

637. The productivity and job gains associated with new technologies are best realised when firms make complementary investments in organisational change and upskilling. However, there is no static single model of firm organisation and firm strategy which automatically brings benefits. Firms adopt different strategies to improve performance in response to competitive pressures. These range from product innovation, improvements in quality and variety, customisation and upgrading of customer service, where employee skills and organisation are of key importance, to strategies based on price, product standardisation and varying the quantity of labour input. There is a continuum of firm strategies across these possibilities, with a variety of more or less flexible forms of organisation.

638. In this chapter, the focus is on a set of strategies and organisational forms based on innovation, high skills, organisational flexibility and trust, often termed "high-performance work practices". These practices are typically based on employee commitment and less use of contingent (part-time, temporary) employees. However, in some settings individual firms have adopted mixed strategies, with a core group of high-skill employees and a quantitatively variable peripheral workforce. More generally, part-time and temporary working have increased in many OECD countries. The following therefore includes consideration of ways of enhancing the skills and conditions of peripheral workers so that they can be involved more productively in the high-performance workplace, thus enhancing overall employment performance.

639. A series of recent surveys shows that the flexibility associated with high-performance workplaces has positive impacts on firm and establishment performance, particularly in association with technology and more highly skilled workers (OECD, 1998*d*). These large-scale cross-sectoral surveys of the characteristics and benefits of "high-skill, high-trust" work practices supplement and extend the plethora of case studies. High-performance workplaces are strongly associated with:

- higher labour productivity, better wage performance (due to the premium placed on skilled workers), and satisfactory unit cost performance due to enhanced productivity and improved quality of outputs, particularly when a range of organisational innovations are adopted (based on high skills, high levels of training, distributed responsibilities, innovative pay systems and, often, quality-based practices);

- higher sales – as better organised, more efficient firms create markets and capture market share, customer satisfaction is greater due to better product quality and improved customer relations, and the financial performance of firms adopting these organisational strategies is often better;

- positive employment performance (particularly when high-performance work practices are associated with technology adoption) in conjunction with higher labour productivity due to improved enterprise performance, and lower staff turnover due to better working conditions and higher wages.

640. Furthermore, there is evidence that firms and establishments adopting new organisational structures have stronger and more productive external linkages with their customers and suppliers of inputs and services (OECD, 1996*b*). Overall, high-performance workplaces are based on two distinct sets of features: new ways of organising work to effectively exploit technology; and a greater premium placed on building and using intangible assets, most importantly technology and human resources.

641. However, the evidence shows that the ability to adopt new organisational structures, or adequately invest in intangibles, varies widely across firms, sectors and countries, with important effects on output, productivity and employment. Taking into account the positive effects of adoption of high-skill, high-trust forms of organisation, countries need to ensure that favourable conditions exist for firm-level experimentation with, and adoption of, new forms of organisation. The challenges are to identify required changes in policies and incentive structures in order to remove barriers to experimentation and adoption of organisational innovations. Furthermore, market failures and/or systemic failures lead to underinvestment in intangible assets, raising the question of what is needed to strengthen the incentives for firms to invest in these assets.

642. While these issues are more or less common to OECD countries, there are considerable differences in terms of uptake of high-performance workplaces as well as in the policies which impact on them. This chapter builds on previous OECD work characterising and mapping high-performance workplaces, discusses recent initiatives to measure and report on intangibles, and analyses how country policies create a more or less favourable framework for the adoption of new forms of work organisation and investments in intangible assets. It highlights best practices, and draws lessons on the impediments, barriers or distorting conditions that countries must address as a priority.

Characteristics of high-performance workplaces[58]

643. The high-performance workplace is a loosely-defined "model" based on "high skill" and "high trust". Jobs are more complex, with more tasks and greater interdependence and communication among workers, firms, their customers and suppliers. Organisations are often simpler, as responsibilities shift to operators or autonomous work teams or are pushed out to suppliers. This is in marked contrast to earlier work organisation, based on simplifying tasks and jobs and organising them in complex hierarchies. There are many ways of organising work within these boundaries and no simple "one size fits all" prescription of organisational attributes, as they encompass such concepts as "total quality management", "quality circles", "continuous improvement", "autonomous team work", and participatory decision making combined with such human resource management practices as continuous training and innovative pay systems that reward ideas and skills. Furthermore, it is the mutually reinforcing nature of these bundles of practices taken together that produces the positive

58. Work on high-performance workplaces has been undertaken by Directorate for Science, Technology and Industry (DSTI) and the Directorate for Education, Employment, Labour and Social Affairs (DEELSA), in the projects Technological and Organisational Change and Labour Demand/Flexible Enterprise: Human Resource Implications. Work on intangible investment is being undertaken in collaboration with DEELSA. This work was reviewed in an International Conference, Ottawa, December 1996, published in Government of Canada and OECD (1997).

results outlined above (Newton, 1996). Many of the stylised examples of new organisational forms have been built on structures and strategies developed in Japan and Sweden, principally in automobile assembly and similar industries, in conditions of tight labour markets. As the original models have been widely studied, adapted and adopted, Japanese and Swedish firms have themselves adopted some of the features of work organisation found in other countries. More than fixed ideas about single organisational "models", the key is flexibility and experimentation.

644. The broad idea underlying the new ways of organising work is that firms and organisations can achieve their objectives by using the innovative abilities of individuals more effectively, *i.e.* employing more highly skilled people and encouraging them to use their abilities more fully. To achieve these aims, minimum qualification requirements have risen, and greater emphasis has been put on continuous learning and training, coupled with stronger incentives for upgrading skills to improve performance. The new work organisation has some or all of the following features:

- marked specialisation of enterprises or business units (focus on "core" activities);
- horizontal inter-firm links for subcontracting (purchase of components or services that are part of the final product) or outsourcing (purchasing supporting business services, transport, cleaning, cafeteria or other ancillary services);
- effective use of technology;
- increasingly flattened hierarchies in which greater importance is accorded to horizontal communication and horizontal links, with less importance attached to vertical or hierarchical ones;
- information is gathered at more levels and channelled less hierarchically;
- authority to act is less dependent on hierarchical models of authority;
- employees are better trained and more responsive;
- multi-skilling and job rotation increase, blurring differences between traditional work activities;
- small, self-managing or autonomous work groups are common and take more responsibility.

645. These organisational features, their combination and importance, will vary according to the national setting, the sector and the size of firm or establishment. In the past, different forms of labour flexibility and adjustment in the workplace have been loosely grouped into two extremes – "functional" and "numerical" flexibility. Many of the characteristics of the new innovative forms of organisation described above are associated with "functional" flexibility, although they may be combined with elements of "numerical" flexibility. Furthermore, there are major differences between firm adjustment strategies adopted in countries which can be described as having "market-driven" approaches compared to those with more consensual ones. Some of the stylised features of these approaches are summarised in Box 11.1.

Box 11.1. **Differences across countries in firm-level adaptability and flexibility: "market-driven" *versus* "consensual" approaches**

Two different kinds of flexibility are described in the literature on strategies for using labour at the firm level. Functional flexibility involves high-skill, collaborative approaches to work based on high quality labour inputs, often made up of a "core" group of long-tenured, educated and trained employees. Common features are shifting job design and job boundaries away from traditional narrow ones, mobility across tasks, multi-skilling and wide-skilling, extensive training and retraining. Autonomous self-managed multi-functional teamwork is often associated with this kind of flexibility. Numerical flexibility usually involves changing quantities of labour input. These include numbers of employees, hours of work, use of more peripheral part-time and temporary employees, and making use of liberal provisions on hiring and dismissals, usually in countries with lower hiring and firing costs.

There is also another dimension to adjustment. Internal flexibility is within the enterprise or the existing contract structure of the enterprise. External flexibility involves interaction in markets outside the firm, usually requiring changes in the nature and type of contracts. There is much overlap between internal and functional flexibility, and external and numerical flexibility. The country groupings that follow correspond to different patterns of institutional and policy arrangements, that, in turn, influence the way firms adjust and adopt different kinds of flexibility. They also correspond to wider patterns of adjustment.

Broadly, firms in Austria, Belgium, France, Germany, the Netherlands, the Nordic countries and Switzerland have adopted functional/internal strategies, based on long-term skill-based contracts between enterprises and workers, with education and training systems often investing heavily in building a deep skill base and high levels of individual competence. This can be described as an economy-wide consensual (or "relations-based") approach, typified by extensive negotiation among a broad range of stakeholders to reach consensus, with restricted capital markets, and concentration and cross-holdings of capital ownership in banks and corporations. Collective bargaining is conducted through consultation at the broad industry level.

Japanese firms have also adopted functional/internal forms of flexibility, but overall adjustment is more centred at the firm level. As in Europe, more restricted capital markets and concentration of capital ownership have often led firms to focus on achieving objectives such as market share and technology development rather than short-term financial performance. Labour adaptability is achieved through broadly-based general education and highly developed human resource development within enterprises. Workplace negotiations are based to a large extent on firm-level arrangements, and overall it may be described as a firm-based consensual approach.

In contrast, in countries where firm strategies can be described as more market-driven (Australia, Canada, New Zealand, the United Kingdom, the United States), firms have adopted numerical/external strategies based on use of external markets to adjust to change. Influenced by the relatively liberal structure of factor and/or product markets, and an economic environment which encourages entrepreneurship and risk-taking, firms have followed a variety of strategies to achieve adaptability and manage risk, while maximising shareholder value and satisfying other short-term financial criteria. Flexibility has often been based on enterprises being able to add to and shed fixed assets through take-over and divestment strategies, and have recourse to well-developed labour markets external to firms, hire workers with required skills and dismiss those whose qualifications are no longer needed.

More heterogeneous approaches to firm-level adaptability and flexibility can be distinguished in "intermediate" or "catch-up" countries (Greece, Ireland, Italy, Portugal, Spain, Turkey). Firms are usually less technologically advanced and fewer have adopted new models of organisation, although foreign multinationals often use advanced organisational strategies. Firms operate in more traditional institutional settings, which are often more rigid than in the "market-driven" approach. These settings may steer firms to adjust labour supply internally, even though firm adjustment is constrained by poor worker qualifications. Participation in regular education is below the OECD average, firm training effort low. These countries generally have average or below-average rates of union membership, but high levels of collective bargaining coverage. Regarding the group of new OECD Member countries, firm-level adjustment strategies are still evolving. Firms could be expected in part to adjust in the same way as in neighbouring countries: Czech Republic, Hungary and Poland similarly to northern European adjustment strategies; Korean firms along the lines of firm-level consensual approaches; and Mexican firms with elements of Canadian and US strategies. But recent institutional changes, economic upheaval and new laws have rapidly altered the institutional environment for firm-level adjustment, or introduced entirely new elements. Furthermore, these countries are in the "catch-up" group, and policy frameworks and prescriptions must take account of these factors.

(continued on next page)

(continued)

There have been recent shifts in the broad patterns described above. Countries that have typically greater recourse to external markets and strategies based on numerical flexibility have shown greater interest in making more functional and internal adjustments within the firm. Interest in the "high-performance enterprise" and in best practice in countries such as Australia, Canada, the United Kingdom and the United States is largely about how to build functional flexibility and improve the quality of labour and other inputs. In the European setting, the shift has been towards greater use of numerical flexibility and external functional adjustments as product and factor markets are liberalised. Examples are the increases in Italian self-employed, growing levels of short-term employment in countries such as France, signs of increased outsourcing in German manufacturing, and the growth in temporary job agencies where they are allowed. This has paralleled major restructuring efforts in many firms and industries, as greater competition, initially from Japanese firms and subsequently from North American ones, has led European firms to rapidly adopt quality and efficiency practices such as "just-in-time", "total quality management", etc., to improve competitiveness (for more detail, see OECD, 1986*b*; 1989; 1996*b*).

Organising for innovation

646. There are also differences across countries in the organisation of innovation (OECD, 1992). The United States' approaches were characterised as extensions of the "Taylorist" organisation of the factory floor. This stressed deep, but narrow, technical specialisation, separation of functions and local functional responsibility. In large US and European automobile firms, a separate research organisation interacted with product development, with minimal interaction with manufacturing and distribution. In contrast, large Japanese manufacturing enterprises appeared to integrate and overlap research with all phases of product development, manufacturing and distribution. Innovative ideas were encouraged from customers and employees, with major aims being to improve design for manufacturability and to reduce the time to market. The overlapping approach required effective information transfer, feedback and dialogue, using cross-functional task forces.

647. Under pressure from efficient Japanese industrial innovation techniques, large firms in the United States, followed by European firms, have increased efficiency of central corporate activities, including technology functions. This has been part of a strategy to become more market-responsive and to maximise shareholder value. R&D is organised on a centre-of-excellence model, and human resource implementation is decentralised. The optimum size of central functions is often seen as several hundred people (Boston Consulting Group, 1996). Team-based approaches have proliferated. Detailed surveys in Germany show that R&D and creative management tasks are often organised in high-level autonomous work teams, particularly in technical and business services and other producer services (Kleinschmidt and Pekruhl, 1994). This suggests that approaches seen to give Japanese organisation the edge were adopted widely in R&D and technology areas, at least in other consensual-based countries such as Germany. In the meantime, Japanese organisation of innovation has also been undergoing change. In the 1990s, cost reductions have come increasingly from lean product design and simplification of incremental innovations (Fujimoto, 1998).

648. Turning specifically to SMEs, there is growing evidence that innovative small firms have many of the organisational characteristics of large firms, emphasizing human resource development and developing intensive networks with other firms. In contrast to large firms, however, they rely on customers and market information rather than R&D departments for innovative ideas. Speed to market is critical for protecting intellectual property, and relatively little attention is paid to patents (Chapter 9; OECD, 1996*b*; OECD, 1997*aa*). Organisational barriers to innovation vary markedly: in several countries, including the United Kingdom and the United States, there is excess demand for skilled labour. Firms in northern European countries appear to have greatest problems translating technological advance into marketable products and entering non-traditional markets. "Catch-up" countries show

weaknesses in the scientific, technological, financial and business services infrastructure which inhibit innovation and productivity growth. These patterns reflect broad differences across countries in entrepreneurship, firm start-up and growth. Ireland, the United Kingdom and the United States generate many innovative new and small firms which experience turbulence in surviving. In contrast, start-up rates and growth of firms are lower in some northern European countries (*e.g.* Finland and Sweden, but not Germany) and Japan (Chapter 9).

649. There is no single best way to organise innovation, either for large or small firms. Flat organisational structures and streamlined business processes improve efficiency in delivering products, but other flexible approaches are also evolving (Tidd *et al.*, 1997). Organisation and the efficiencies derived from it will differ across countries, sectors and firms. The broad approach to policy is to improve education and the preconditions for skill development and, where necessary, remove barriers or provide stronger incentives for experimentation and adoption of new ways of organising innovation.

The incidence of high-performance workplaces

650. By the mid-1990s, the high-performance workplace model is estimated to have been adopted by about a quarter of all enterprises in the OECD area. The level of adoption appears fairly similar across countries, suggesting common competitive conditions and similarities of practices. An increasing number of countries are carrying out large cross-sectoral surveys of various aspects of organisational change; but coverage is generally better in manufacturing than for services, and definitions of the new work organisation vary (Vickery and Wurzburg, 1998). Adoption appears to be somewhat higher in the United States and northern European countries – up to one-half of responding establishments or firms. However, the responses depend partly on the kind of organisational changes being surveyed, and whether change is defined as using a range of different techniques to suit firm circumstances, or whether stand-alone individual characteristics of organisational change are considered (OECD, 1996*b*).

651. The only multi-country cross-sector survey (of direct employee participation in organisational change) shows that firms in northern Europe were more likely to adopt bundles of initiatives for organisational change. Workplaces in industry, construction and services in France, Italy, Portugal and Spain were less likely to be involved. On the other hand, workplaces in Denmark, Germany, the Netherlands and the United Kingdom have high levels of organisational change initiatives, with or without direct employee participation. Ireland and Sweden fell between these two groups. Thus there is a distinct north-south divide, with extensive workplace change in northern Europe, less in the south (European Foundation for the Improvement of Living and Working Conditions, 1997). In this survey, the principle motives given for organisational change were to improve productivity and performance, and the prime force driving them was increased competition.

652. Most of the surveys show that new kinds of organisation have been widely adopted in manufacturing. Assembly industries, notably automobile producers, have been much-studied and are often thought to typify the new kinds of organisation, emphasizing quality and flexibility, reducing capital use, and shifting from vertical integration to horizontal supply arrangements, with external suppliers increasingly responsible for development of components. In services, change has been most pronounced in financial services and other tradeable and business services facing mounting competition. However, the extent of change by sector depends on what is being measured. The European survey found manufacturing to be lagging public and private services in the use of direct

participation – one indicator of organisational change (European Foundation for the Improvement of Living and Working Conditions, 1997).

653. Finally, size counts: large firms and multinational firms are more likely to adopt new organisational forms than smaller ones. Small firms may in fact not need to adopt formal kinds of organisational innovations, simply because their more flexible structure means that these are *de facto* part of their operations. However most surveys show that large and medium-sized firms are more capable of adopting new flexible forms of organisation and may also draw greater productivity gains and other benefits from adoption (OECD, 1996*b*, Chapter 6; Lund and Gjerding, 1996; Ministry of Labour, 1996).

654. The broader impacts of firm-level organisational and technological change and adoption of the high-performance workplace, on employment, for example, depend not only on firm size and sector, but most importantly on the national institutional and economic setting. Policy approaches to workplace adjustment aiming at improving enterprise efficiency and contributing to overall growth, productivity improvement and employment, are discussed below.

Approaches to best policy practice

655. A number of impediments to the diffusion of organisational change limit the effectiveness of change. The nature and seriousness of these institutional barriers vary across countries. Notions of "systemic" approaches to policy (Chapter 2) depend on the broad set of national institutions, infrastructures and incentives which are explicitly or implicitly in place.

656. Approaches to adaptability and flexibility can be grouped into: *(i)* a "market-driven" approach in the English-speaking group of countries – Australia, Canada, New Zealand, the United Kingdom and the United States; *(ii)* a more consensual or relations-based approach in northern Europe; *(iii)* a firm-based consensual approach in the Japanese model; and *(iv)* a heterogeneous set of approaches in "intermediate" or "catch-up" countries (Box 11.1). This broad categorisation is useful to simplify discussion of policy design and country-specific "best-practice" policy recommendations. Policy responses broadly need to combine the experimentation and flexibility that are part of the numerical/external strategies common in "market-driven" settings, with the longer-term skill formation and abilities to diffuse and adopt innovations that are part of firm functional/internal strategies common in consensual settings.

657. Policies to improve the adoption and impacts of high-performance workplaces are discussed below in five broad groups: *(i)* encouraging innovation; *(ii)* accelerating diffusion of organisational innovations; *(iii)* raising skills; *(iv)* encouraging labour-related flexibility; and *(v)* co-ordinating and delivering policy. Different aspects of the policy framework and policy initiatives fostering adoption of high-performance work practices are shown in Table 11.1. These show relative national strengths, corresponding to: policies to provide information on organisational strategies (usually but not always focused on SMEs); initiatives to improve skill formation (incentives/levies to encourage firm-based training, and vocational training); indicators of incentives to improve employee performance (profit-sharing); and indicators of flexible working practices and part-time employment as measures of labour flexibility.

Table 11.1. **Fostering high-performance workplaces: current policy practice**

	Consultancy/ information for SMEs	Incentives for firm-based training	Vocational training	Incentives for employee effort[1]	Flexible work	Collective bargaining/level	Co-ordinated policy approach[2]
Canada	•		Reform efforts	•	Liberalised/part-time work common	Enterprise/plant	•
United States	•		Reform efforts	•	Liberalised/part-time work common	Enterprise/plant	
Australia	•		Reform efforts		Liberalised/part-time work common	Enterprise/plant & sector	
New Zealand			Reform efforts		Liberalised/part-time work common	Enterprise/plant	
United Kingdom	•		Reform efforts	•	Liberalised/part-time work common	Enterprise/plant & sector	•
Austria	•		■ Reform efforts			Centralised	
Belgium	•	•	■			Centralised	
France	•	•	■ Reform efforts	•	Liberalised	Sector	
Germany	•		■	•		Sector	
Netherlands	•	•	■ Reform efforts	•	Part-time work common	Enterprise/plant & sector	
Switzerland	•		■ Reform efforts		Part-time work common	Sector	
Denmark	•	•	■		Part-time work common	Sector	•
Finland	•		■ Reform efforts		Liberalised	Centralised	•
Iceland	•		■ Reform efforts		Part-time work common		
Norway	•		■ Reform efforts		Part-time work common	Centralised	•
Sweden	•		■		Part-time work common	Sector	
Japan	•		Reform efforts	•	Part-time work common	Enterprise/plant	
Italy		•	Reform efforts	•	Liberalised	Sector	
Ireland	•	•	Reform efforts		Liberalised		•
Mexico				•	Part-time work common		
Portugal	•	•	Reform efforts			Sector	
Spain	•	•	Reform efforts		Liberalised	Sector	
Turkey					Part-time work common		
Hungary		•					

• means country has policy/practice at national level; ■ indicates a strong vocational training system.

1. Profit-sharing moderately common.
2. Policy areas co-ordinated to foster development and spread of high-performance workplaces, *e.g.* Industry, Science, Education, Labour Ministries/Departments co-ordinating. In a few countries (*e.g.* the United Kingdom), many of these functions are in one department.

Source: Consultancy/information from Table 11.3 and Chapter 8; incentives for firm-based training, Secretariat compilation; vocational training reform from OECD (1997*a*, and 1997*e*); incentives for employee effort from OECD (1995*d*); flexible work liberalisation from OECD (1997*a*); part-time work from OECD (1997*c*); collective bargaining levels from OECD (1997*c*).

Table 11.2. **Strategies for flexibility in organisational innovation and diffusion**

General models and countries	Firm behaviour	Implications for organisational Innovation and diffusion systems
Market-driven approach (high-skill)[1] (Canada, United States)	Short-term strategies, due to liberalised capital, labour markets, product markets, dispersed profit-maximising ownership. Technology part of core strategy, prone to cuts in downturns. Flexibility, innovation through: take-over, divestiture in active stock markets; dynamic capital markets (Canada less); fluid labour markets for trained, skilled workers. Experimentation, adoption of high-performance work practices in large firms, extensive outsourcing of inputs and services.	System bolstered by relatively large share of business R&D expenditure financed by government and well-developed government research infrastructure (defence, energy, health). *Need to:* increase relevance of government-supported technology programmes; strengthen incentive framework for intangibles to shift investment strategies to long-term; expand adoption of best practice in small firms.
Market-driven approach (low-skill) (Australia, New Zealand, United Kingdom)	Main features as above, but capital markets more risk-averse. Firm strategies and industrial performance constrained by industrial structure, particularly in rural, extractive, traditional industries.	Well-established government/university research infrastructure, often weakly linked with business. *Need to:* increase long-term resources going to technological development.
Consensual approach (Austria, Belgium, France, Germany, Netherlands, Nordic countries, Switzerland)	Long-term orientation due to concentrated capital ownership, regulated labour and product markets, consensual decision making. Flexibility constrained by these factors in traditional, medium-technology industries; less acquisition and divestiture of technological assets; capital markets more risk-averse; slow growth of NTBFs.	Flexibility facilitated by government support for: applied research; diffusion infrastructure (chambers of commerce, business associations, technology institutes); high status of engineering and industrial occupations. *Need to:* encourage experimentation, adoption of technologies/innovations; enhance external market flexibility, including mergers and acquisitions, outsourcing; extend firm-level bargaining/strategy setting; remove barriers to start-up and growth of firms in innovative areas.
Firm-based consensual approach (Japan)	Long-term orientation due to concentrated capital ownership, regulated product markets, focus on market share, employees, customers. Technological innovation increasingly complementing efficient high-quality production. Flexibility constrained by low labour mobility, scarce venture capital, slow growth of NTBFs.	Flexibility facilitated by government support for: co-operative applied research; best practice diffusion networks (prefecture, local levels), but networks being disrupted by globalisation of large firms. *Need to:* remove impediments to start up and growth of firms in innovative areas; enhance external markets and incentives to use technological, business and human resources outside large industrial groups; increase use of external specialists
Intermediate catch-up countries (Greece, Ireland, Italy, Mexico, Portugal, Spain, Turkey)	Short-term orientation, fragmented industrial structures concentrated in traditional industries. Technology generation low, shortages of trained personnel, conservative capital markets.	Some diffusion, best practice intermediary organisations. *Need to:* increase technology development efforts, improve links between business/university/technology institutions; expand demand business infrastructure for SMEs to improve quality, skills, management capabilities.

1. For the distinction between "high-" and "low-skill" market-driven approaches, see Table 11.4.

Source: OECD Secretariat.

Table 11.3. **Government policies and programmes to foster firm-level organisational innovation**

	Model of firm adjustment: market-driven
Canada	Sector Competitiveness Framework: government guidance on strategic issues. Canada Business Service Centres: one-stop access to government services for SMEs. Business Networks Demonstration Project: establishment of 30 new SME business networks. Several federal/provincial programmes have helped finance consultancy, including the Advanced Manufacturing Technology Application Program (AMTAP). Technology Outreach Programme supports start-up of technology diffusion centres. IRAP network for SME technical and business assistance. Modernisation of Canada Labour Code: to encourage greater labour-management co-operation.
United States	Manufacturing Extension Partnership: network of non-profit extension centres providing services including assessment of business practices. State economic development programmes provide technological and business development services and associated job-related training and re-training. Department of Labor's Employment and Training Administration initiatives to introduce new technologies and best-practice work systems. The former Office of the American Workplace focused on best practices.
Australia	AusIndustry Business Networks Program: promotes networking among SMEs in procurement, production, distribution, R&D and marketing. National Industry Extension Service (federal-state initiative) supported strategic upgrading services to small firms (<100 employees), including benchmarking, human resources.
New Zealand	Business Development Programme for SMEs includes improving business skills, business appraisal services. SME direct grants for strategy, innovation, R&D implementation and, particularly, technology management. Technology for Business Growth Scheme aims to change management practices and attitudes through "learning-by-doing".
United Kingdom	Managing in the '90s spreads best practice across business functions. Enterprise Initiative Consultancy Scheme and Diagnostic and Consultancy Service provide subsidised consultancy to improve business performance. Business Links delivers business and innovation support services. Sponsorship Programme encourages partnerships in key industrial sectors to address competitiveness.

	Model of firm adjustment: consensual
Austria	From 1994 development of a "cluster-oriented policy" supporting horizontal, vertical, diagonal links between suppliers and customers, large and small firms, manufacturers and service providers at local level. Institute for the Promotion of the Economy (WIFI) provides management consultancy services for SMEs. Techno-Counselling Programme advises firms on management and organisational issues. Integrated Production Innovation Programme provides training in technology-orientated management. SME programmes (loans and grants from *BURGES Förderungsbank*, state governments and institutions) promote intangible and tangible investment, restructuring, business improvement, etc.
Belgium	Brussels-Technopol programme for information networks among enterprises and research bodies. SME consultancy and training services, and regional assistance for intangible investments.
France	Regional advisory services [*e.g.* Regional Fund for Consultancy Support (FRAC), and technology transfer (FRATT)]. Programmes for automation [*e.g.* Agency for Development of Automated Production (ADEPA)].
Germany	Programmes to assist SMEs with rationalisation and modernisation (*e.g.* ERP programmes of the KfW, *Länder* programmes), productivity improvement projects (*Länder*), technology and business consulting services (*Länder*, local chambers of industry and commerce, etc.), promotion of NTBFs (BMBF), support for intermediary institutions and technology consultancy centres (*Länder*).
Netherlands	*Knowledge in Action* White Paper outlined paths to enhance the knowledge intensity of the Dutch economy, including more efficient use of new technologies.
Switzerland	Enterprise Revitalisation Programme. Government has reformed public management and sheltered sectors to make public employees more accountable to agency objectives and clients.
Denmark	Knowledge and quality promotion programmes, network-formation programmes, to improve organisational efficiency. Professional Boards of experienced executives to extend management expertise.
Finland	Regional business service offices provide SME development and training programmes below market price.
Iceland	Market Qualification Programme provides information, innovation and employment counselling to small firms. Various other consultancy programmes. Labour laws reviewed to promote stability, responsibility of contracting parties, extend trade union member influence. *ALMI Företagspartner AB* supports R&D, work environment innovation.
Norway	Norwegian Industrial and Regional Development Fund supports competency raising, restructuring projects, etc. Specialised regional consulting services provide subsidised business-development planning services.
Sweden	A number of ongoing mechanisms provide support to innovative and risky industrial projects (Industry and New Business Fund – project finance, Regional Development Funds – development capital), NUTEK public advisory system, consulting services.

Model of firm adjustment: firm-based consensual	
Japan	SME management training under Temporary Law Concerning Measures for the Promotion of Creative Small and Medium Enterprises. Employment Adjustment Subsidy Scheme assists workers made redundant by technology or structural change. Numerous tax concessions and other incentives at central and prefecture level support structural reform, organisational modernisation, adoption of modern business methods. Comprehensive system of ongoing assistance (guidance) and financial incentives (subsidised loans) to SMEs at prefecture level to upgrade management, improve subcontracting, technological capabilities, etc.
Intermediate "catch-up" countries	
Greece	Operational Programme for Industry to improve product quality, product and process innovation, flexible production and environmentally safe methods and products. EU SME initiatives to modernise business, develop trade and distribution networks, improve education and training.
Ireland	State-backed institutions provide support to domestic firms (SMEs) to improve technology and business competence.
Italy	Support for machinery investment (*e.g.* machine tools, advanced equipment) and associated costs.
Mexico	Studies and Advisory Programme [*Nacional Financiera/Comision Nacional Bancaria y de Valores* (NAFIN/CNB)] provides subsidised loans to improve investment and competitiveness. Technological Development, Modernisation Programme (NAFIN/CNB) and Fund for R&D for Technological Modernisation [*Consejo Nacional de Ciencia y Tecnología* (CONACYT)] provide subsidised loans to improve production processes.
Portugal	Business Strategies Incentive Programme (SINPEDIP) supports business and investment evaluations, strategic analysis and quality promotion. Business Assistance Information System provides administrative information to help firms modernise. Government backed institutions, Institute for the Support of SMEs and Investment (IAPMEI) for SMEs and the National Institute for Engineering and Industrial Technology (INETI) for technology, support subsidised modernisation and counselling services.
Spain	Programmes focusing on encouraging co-operation among firms and expanding the use of information services have been developed, and organisation management is a priority in the ATYCA Initiative (*Iniciativa de Apoyo a la Tecnologia, la Seguridad y la Calidad Industrial*) for technological innovation (Ministry of Industry and Energy). Plan for Technical Industrial Qualification supports SME training of managers and technicians, reinforces non-profit training institutions and assists external training for managers and technicians.

Source: OECD Secretariat from various sources.

Table 11.4. **Strategies for flexibility in skill development**[1]

General models and countries	Firm behaviour	Implications for skill development systems
Market-driven approach (high-skill) (Canada, United States)	Flexibility achieved through acquisition of skills in well-developed external labour markets. Flexibility enhanced through human resource development of functionally flexible core employees, acquisition of competences by outsourcing of firm functions.	Functional flexibility facilitated by relatively high levels of formal qualifications, large numbers with post-secondary technical training. *Need to:* further reduce early school leaving; enhance capacity for basic skills remediation for adults with low-level initial qualifications; reinforce and expand vocational, technical training to reduce large numbers with low academic or vocational qualifications.
Market-driven approach (low-skill) (Australia, New Zealand, United Kingdom)	Flexibility achieved and enhanced as above. Flexibility constrained by: occupational and craft orientation of training and industrial relations; scarcity of highly skilled workers with intermediate qualifications; large numbers with insufficient academic or vocational qualifications.	*Need to:* further reduce early school leaving; enhance capacity for basic skills remediation for adults with low-level initial qualifications; reinforce and expand vocational, technical training; ensure balance between technical/scientific and other tertiary education.
Consensual approach (Austria, Belgium, France, Germany, Netherlands, Nordic countries, Switzerland)	Functional flexibility based on negotiated redefinition of tasks within firms and sectors; facilitated by industrial relations systems based on industrial sector or occupational groupings (white-, blue-collar). Flexibility being enhanced by shift towards greater use of numerical flexibility through easier hiring and firing, and greater flexibility in working-time arrangements.	Functional flexibility facilitated by widespread vocational training providing deep skills base (Austria, Germany, Switzerland). *Need to:* further reduce early school leaving; enhance basic skills remediation for adults with low-level initial qualifications; broaden content of vocational and technical training and expand tertiary capacity; enhance mobility between vocational/technical and academic studies.

General models and countries	Firm behaviour	Implications for skill development systems
Firm-based consensual approach (Japan)	Functional flexibility based on high levels of human resource development and flexible shift of workers between occupations and tasks. Facilitated by company-based unions. Some shift towards greater numerical flexibility through easier hiring, firing, early retirement (narrower use of lifetime employment). Less use of firm-based training as main source of new skills and know-how, greater use of hiring people with requisite vocational qualifications.	Functional flexibility facilitated by high-level initial qualifications providing a deep base for occupation and task-specific firm training. *Need to:* strengthen and expand vocational and technical education at the secondary level; facilitate mobility between vocational/technical studies and academic studies at the tertiary level; enhance capacity for further training outside firms.
Intermediate catch-up countries (Greece, Ireland, Italy, Mexico, Portugal, Spain, Turkey)	Flexibility constrained by shortages of highly trained personnel, higher-level human resources, business skills.	*Need to:* sustain increases in upper secondary completion rates; address balance between academic and vocational studies; encourage participation in higher education balanced between academic and technical/vocational studies; raise low levels of initial qualifications of most workers and expand adult training capacity; expand low level and limited pool of highly qualified and scientific personnel.

1. Canada and the United States have relatively higher shares of the adult population with a university level education, and lower shares with less than an upper secondary education compared with Australia, New Zealand and the United Kingdom.

Source: OECD Secretariat; OECD (1997), *Education at a Glance: OECD Indicators 1997*, Table A2.1.

11.2. Encouraging innovation

658. The development and adoption of high-performance workplaces and practices are examples of social and organisational innovation. Policy strengths and weaknesses across countries are very similar to those discussed in Chapter 9 in regard to the start-up and growth of new technology-based firms. Broadly following the adjustment patterns outlined in Box 11.1, these are:

- Experimentation and innovation with new work practices may be easier in countries where business regulations are relatively straightforward, and there is liberal product and labour market regulation. The ease with which firms can start up is an indicator of a pro-entrepreneurial approach which encourages business experimentation, including with work organisation. The United States is usually seen as leading in these areas, and there has been a great deal of policy interest in emulating some aspects of its framework. The United Kingdom and an increasing number of continental European countries have very respectable rates of new firm formation. On the other hand, there are major weaknesses in start-ups in Finland, Sweden and Japan.

- Ease of financing new ideas may also contribute to experimentation and adoption of new ways of organising work. Capital markets to finance new ideas have worked much better in the United States than elsewhere. In northern Europe and Japan, more relations-based investment has favoured established enterprises over new ones. In Japan and Korea, rather than searching more widely for new firms to invest in, banks have tended to retain investment within narrow conglomerate groups, encouraging incremental innovation but hindering more radical breakthrough.

11.3. Accelerating diffusion of organisational innovations

659. Despite growing evidence of the importance of organisational change and the impact of "high-skill, high-trust" work practices on firm productivity and performance, policies directly aimed at diffusing firm-level best practice are not widespread. Reasons include the fact that it is difficult to define the characteristics of these work practices and strategies, that it is up to employers and workers to implement change, and that most countries lack a broad policy approach to the new challenges confronting businesses. Furthermore, human resource issues are not typically part of industry policies, while education and training and labour market policies have tended to ignore firm and industry dynamics, focusing on formal compulsory education, and external labour markets and unemployment, respectively. However, shifts in the economic environment are challenging firm structure and performance, and there is a potentially important role for policies which enhance the transition to new conditions. The growing importance of small firms and their low levels of training and investment in intangibles need to be taken into account. Finally, policies need to focus on human resources and human capital accumulation for long-term economic development.

660. Government intervention may be justified if there are market failures in the adoption of high-skill, high-trust strategies and structures. Firm performance could be improved by better information flows on organisational change, management strategies, quality improvement, "benchmarking", through, for example, demonstration activities, identification and exchange of information on best practices, or activities which lead to continuous improvement and upgrading at the firm level.

661. Policies to diffuse best practice in organisational innovation and human resource development often consist in a broadening and re-orientation of established policies for technology diffusion. They have major differences, however. The focus is no longer on technology push, but rather on implementing systems of continuous improvement in firms across the whole range of firm functions, including organisation, quality, marketing, internal and external networks, but most importantly including more attention to skills and encouraging employee initiative. This places great demand on delivery mechanisms (consultancy quality assurance is increasingly important), and better articulation with education and training programmes. To be effective, programmes to promote organisational change and upskilling need to have a broad, but manageable, scope, be correctly targeted, raise awareness, ensure programme uptake and have appropriate programme flexibility. Delivery is usually more efficient if it uses existing "demand-driven" institutions and infrastructures.

662. Overall, diffusion policies vary across countries (Table 11.2, Table 11.3 and Chapter 8):

- The availability of information on the benefits and costs of adopting organisational innovations is important for diffusion. Private sector mechanisms are likely to be good in "market-driven" countries, due to an extensive private sector consulting and information industry. However, there are problems with quality assurance and a focus on large-firm issues on the supply side which restricts opportunities for small-firm uptake, while the demand side has limited capabilities to select and absorb information. Government mechanisms are more developed in consensual countries which, on the other hand, may face difficulties in upgrading their services, attracting staff in new areas and keeping abreast of rapid changes in organisational strategies (*e.g.* the *Kohsetsushi* network in Japan, OECD, 1995*e*).

- In market-driven countries, the focus on short-term productivity and profitability may undermine long-term investment in human resources, organisation and technology, and the diffusion infrastructure may equally not be adapted to fostering long-term continuous improvements in firms. Consensual countries benefit from stronger infrastructure of supporting institutions, intermediaries, industry associations, unions, etc., all of which support diffusion and effective adoption. However, there are rigidities in some consensual countries, and traditional institutions providing business support need to become more demand-driven and pay more attention to new issues and challenges (*e.g.* the German experience with the long-standing and moderately well-funded Work and Technology R&D Programme shows difficulties adapting to change and in disseminating results; Fricke, 1997). Austria, Canada, Iceland, Ireland and Norway have all introduced initiatives to address some of these issues. In the group of intermediate catch-up countries, greater effort must go to ensuring that incentives are right for firms to build internal intangible assets and adopt flexible organisational structures, and that an efficient demand-driven, customer-focused business infrastructure provides appropriate information and services to firms.

- Comprehensive approaches to diffusing organisational innovation have been implemented in a few countries. Government-financed mechanisms have been developed in smaller countries, particularly in Nordic countries (notably Denmark, Finland and Norway). Individual programmes have had positive effects and have often been highly innovative and flexible (*e.g.* the BUNT programme in Norway, new approaches in Denmark and Finland). In many countries, however, there are outstanding issues which need to be addressed, including: underfunding; a relatively limited diffusion/outreach component compared with the large number of potential client firms; and insufficient co-ordination and poor articulation with education and training and labour market programmes and issues.

11.4. Raising skills to enhance adoption and impacts of high-performance workplaces

663. There is abundant evidence that past national strategies for investing in education and training have paid off in terms of faster productivity growth and higher levels of productivity at the aggregate level, and higher earnings and employability at the individual level (OECD, 1997*bb*; 1998*e*). Firm-level high-performance workplaces and work practices depend on "high-skill" strategies that make better use of and continuously renew human capital. This suggests two essential elements in national strategies to reinforce wider adoption of high-performance work practices: *(i)* provide the broad infrastructure for compulsory and basic education, improve the quality of education and encourage a larger proportion of people to obtain post-secondary degrees, including improved technical and vocational qualifications; and *(ii)* improve training and retraining of workers, and strengthen incentives for employers and employees to undertake training. These can be summed up in the concept of "lifelong learning".

664. In many countries a large share of the adult labour force has low levels of qualifications, despite evidence that improving education levels raises labour force participation, increases earnings and reduces unemployment (Table 11.4 and OECD, 1997*bb*; 1998*e*). Leaving aside the general education system, various reforms have been undertaken by individual countries to provide a stronger skill base for organisational change and the adoption of high-performance work practices.

665. Examples of initiatives designed to enhance skills and link skill development more directly with working life include initiatives in Canada to develop a culture of lifelong learning and in the United

Kingdom to put education at the top of the government agenda. In the United States, although the federal government does not have direct responsibility for education, it is taking measures to ensure that children have access to newest computer technologies. Other initiatives include: in Iceland, strengthening secondary education, particularly vocational and practical training; in Sweden, adopting a broad strategy to raise educational attainment, expand the number of places in regular, adult and higher education, with special attention to science, technology and languages, and attempting to enhance basic initial education to develop skills critical for workplace flexibility. In Ireland, the setting up of a Future Skills Identification Group with representatives of Enterprise Development and higher education agencies, and Departments of Education, Enterprise and Finance to assess existing and emerging skill needs and how to address them, has led to substantial increases in third-level places in languages and IT.

Labour market and vocational training

666. Raising the skills of the labour force will contribute to the spread of improved "high-skill" work practices and enable higher productivity growth and job creation. Training has the greatest impact on enterprise performance when undertaken in connection with changes in work organisation and job structure, when it is widely accessible, and when adequate financial incentives exist for enterprises and individuals to invest in it (OECD, 1997*bb*; 1998*e*). Skills can be raised through government-funded training, through incentives for employers and individuals, or through unaided efforts by employers and individuals. The following discussion focuses mainly on aggregate measures of inputs – training effort – not outputs (*e.g.* skills and productivity growth), it does not take into account informal and on-the-job training, and it does not assess the quality of training effort. Although not all training is directly related to the spread of high-performance work practices, upskilling across a broad front will benefit both firms, in terms of productivity payoff, and individuals, in terms of employability.

667. The recent picture of government efforts to improve skills through labour market training and support for youth training is mixed. Most money goes to labour market training and, over the period 1990-96, almost equal numbers of OECD countries increased and decreased expenditure (Table 11.5). Government efforts tend to be relatively low, considerably less than 0.5 per cent of GDP, with only Denmark, Finland and Sweden spending more. Within total labour market training, most expenditure goes to train unemployed adults and those at risk; expenditure thus tends to be cyclical and follows unemployment rates. Furthermore, training for this category may not lead to employment or satisfactory employment, so that impacts may be limited in providing a wider and deeper skill base for high-performance work practices. These strategies also have elements of overcoming well-recognised training gaps, where there is little or no training in many service occupations, in small enterprises, for the most precarious employment, and for the most disadvantaged groups in the workforce.

Table 11.5. **Public expenditure and participant inflows in labour market programmes in OECD countries**

	Labour market training				*Of which:* Training for employed adults and those at risk				*Of which:* Training for employed adults				Support of apprenticeship and related forms of general youth training			
	Public expenditure as a % of GDP		Participant inflows as a % of the labour force		Public expenditure as a % of GDP		Participant inflows as a % of the labour force		Public expenditure as a % of GDP		Participant inflows as a % of the labour force		Public expenditure as a % of GDP		Participant inflows as a % of the labour force	
	1990	1996	1990	1996	1990	1996	1990	1996	1990	1996	1990	1996	1990	1996	1990	1996
Australia (1990-91/1995-96)	0.07	0.15	1.9	4.8	0.07	0.14	1.9	4.2	. .	0.01	. .	0.6	0.04	0.03	0.7	0.9
Austria	0.10	0.13	1.3	. .	0.10	0.13	1.3	. .	. .	. .	. .	. .	. .	. .	. .	. .
Belgium (1995)	0.22	0.28	7.5	9.2	0.14	0.16	1.9	3.0	0.08	0.12	5.6	6.2	. .	0.08	. .	0.7
Canada (1990-91/1996-97)	0.27	0.26	1.9	1.9	0.23	0.25	1.2	1.9	0.04	0.01	0.7	. .	. .	0.01	. .	0.3
Czech Republic (1991)	0.01	0.01	0.1	0.2	0.01	0.01	0.1	0.2	. .	. .	. .	. .	. .	. .	. .	. .
Denmark (1995)	0.27	1.15	6.7	9.3	0.17	0.75	1.3	4.5	0.11	0.39	5.4	. .	. .	. .	. .	. .
Finland	0.25	0.57	1.4	4.7	0.25	0.56	1.4	4.7	. .	0.01	. .	. .	0.04	0.11	0.3	0.9
France (1995)	0.34	0.38	4.3	3.5	0.28	0.34	2.5	2.8	0.06	0.04	1.9	0.7	0.14	0.17	2.0	1.9
Germany	0.38	0.45	2.5	1.6	0.35	0.45	1.9	1.6	0.03	. .	0.6	. .	0.01	0.01	0.2	0.3
Greece (1995)	0.24	0.09	1.0	1.4	0.05	0.01	0.1	0.1	0.19	0.08	0.9	1.3	0.03	0.03	0.3	0.4
Hungary (1992/1995)	0.15	0.13	1.0	0.8	0.14	0.13	1.0	0.7	. .	. .	0.1	0.1	. .	. .	. .	. .
Ireland	0.49	0.23	2.5	4.1	0.33	0.14	0.7	1.6	0.16	0.08	1.8	2.5	0.18	0.13	0.7	0.6
Italy (1990/1992/1994)	0.03	0.02	. .	. .	0.03	0.02	. .	. .	. .	. .	. .	. .	0.34	0.55	3.3	2.0
Japan (1990-91/1995-96)	0.03	0.03	. .	. .	0.03	0.03	. .	. .	. .	. .	. .	. .	. .	. .	. .	. .
Luxembourg	0.02	0.01	. .	. .	0.01	0.01	. .	. .	. .	. .	. .	. .	0.06	0.07	. .	. .
Netherlands	0.21	0.12	1.6	0.4	0.20	0.12	1.6	0.4	. .	. .	. .	. .	0.05	0.03	0.8	0.5
New Zealand (1990-91/1995-96)	0.39	0.33	5.0	. .	0.39	0.33	5.0	. .	. .	. .	. .	. .	0.01	0.08	0.3	. .
Norway	0.36	0.19	2.7	2.8	0.36	0.19	2.7	2.8	. .	. .	. .	. .	. .	. .	. .	. .
Poland (1992)	0.02	0.02	0.4	0.5	0.02	0.02	0.4	0.5	. .	. .	. .	. .	0.15	0.06	2.3	1.7
Portugal (1995)	0.14	0.38	1.1	3.7	0.01	0.06	0.1	0.1	0.13	0.32	1.0	. .	0.16	0.20	0.8	. .
Spain	0.17	0.35	1.9	0.8	0.14	0.26	1.5	0.5	0.03	0.09	0.4	0.3	. .	. .	. .	. .
Sweden (1990-91/1995-96)	0.53	0.51	2.2	3.4	0.52	0.50	1.7	2.8	0.01	0.02	0.5	0.6	. .	. .	. .	. .
Switzerland (1996/1995)	0.01	0.08	0.2	1.6	0.01	0.08	0.1	1.5	. .	. .	0.1	. .	. .	. .	. .	. .
United Kingdom (1990-91/1995-96)	0.21	0.10	1.1	1.0	0.20	0.09	1.1	0.9	0.01	0.01	. .	. .	0.17	0.12	0.8	1.0
United States (1990-91/1995-96)	0.08	0.04	0.9	0.7	0.08	0.04	0.9	0.7	. .	. .	. .	. .	. .	. .	0.1	. .

Source: Adapted from OECD, *Employment Outlook*, various issues.

668. Canada, Ireland, New Zealand, the United Kingdom and the United States decreased labour market training expenditure in the 1990-96 period, paralleling improving labour market conditions and declining unemployment from 1992-93 in these countries. Australia was the exception in this group, increasing its labour market training efforts. Northern European countries mostly increased labour market training expenditure, except Luxembourg, the Netherlands, Norway and Sweden. Southern Europe was equally divided between increases and decreases. Participation is high in some countries, with over 3 per cent of the labour force in labour market training in 1996 in Australia, Belgium, Denmark, Finland, France, Ireland, Portugal and Sweden. All except Denmark had unemployment rates above the total OECD, suggesting that these programmes mostly serve to mop up the unemployed. More countries are improving "outreach" and doing more with less, with rising participation and falling expenditure, possibly through shorter participation in programmes and adoption of counselling services. However, given the level of training needed by some adults, the appropriateness of reducing costs per enrolment can be questioned.

669. Government efforts to train employed adults are of more direct relevance to the spread of high-performance workplaces and practices, as those in work are likely to be more skilled, and payoffs to employers and employees likely to be more direct. Scattered data suggest that most countries appear to be increasing their efforts to train employed adults, including in a few countries which were cutting back total labour market training expenditure. The exception is France, where training expenditure for employed adults and participation rates were both down through to the mid-1990s (although from relatively high levels). Participation in adult training is particularly high in Belgium, Denmark and Ireland.

Vocational training

670. Vocational apprenticeships and related youth training provide the base of applied skills and represent an important mechanism to initiate lifelong learning (OECD, 1997*bb*; 1998*e*). Government expenditure in this area is relatively low in all countries, and lower than general labour market training everywhere except Italy, Poland and the United Kingdom. However, more countries stepped up efforts in the 1990s, and where apprenticeship and labour market training expenditure went in opposite directions, it was mostly due to increasing apprenticeship support (Table 11.5). In most countries, participation in government-financed apprenticeships is low, below 1 per cent of the total labour force except for France, Italy, Poland and the United Kingdom (OECD, 1997*bb*, p. 10; 1998*e*).

671. Recent efforts to improve the efficiency and relevance of vocational training in around one-half of OECD countries will strengthen the base for high-skill work practices. Efforts are particularly notable in English-speaking countries, where past emphasis has been on general education. However, there have also been measures in southern Europe (Italy, Portugal, Spain) to establish or expand vocational training, as well as northern Europe (Austria, France, Finland, the Netherlands, Norway, Switzerland) and Japan to fine-tune existing arrangements and improve their interface with general education and university level studies (OECD, 1997*e*; *Employment Outlook*, various issues).

672. More specifically, the United Kingdom has developed a set of initiatives including Modern Apprenticeships and National Traineeships as well as Investors in People and the promotion of IT and management training to address weaknesses (Department of Trade and Industry, 1997); the United States is revamping and consolidating over 100 federal programmes; in Austria, initiatives include development of *Fachhochschulen*, technical college reforms and adjustment of dual system apprenticeships, while Germany is attempting to bring vocational training in line with enterprise requirements, updating existing regulations and introducing new ones for evolving occupations, and providing SMEs with low interest, long-term loans to take on apprentices; Iceland and Norway have

focused on retraining and adult education to increase business skills; Sweden is promoting adult education, industry-based training and greater interaction between regular and private education, enterprises and social partners; Hungary is developing vocational education and training; while Ireland is developing a better quality assurance system for training and human resource development to assist SMEs overcome skills barriers.

Firm-based training

673. Firm training effort is increasing as measured by training expenditure and the proportion of employees who participate, according to data for Australia, Canada, Finland, France, Germany, the United Kingdom and the United States. More qualified people are more likely to receive training, the gap between high-skilled and low-skilled participation is growing, and large firms, which often employ more qualified people, train more than small firms. However, there appears to be an overall decline in the average duration of training, with greatest declines for the lowest skilled and those with shortest tenure, in temporary employment, or in the most precarious occupations. Overall, training appears to be more widespread, but it also appears that it is being rationalised. Training duration is being reduced as the costs and benefits of different kinds of training are understood, more effective "just-in-time" training is introduced, and on the job experience is seen to provide benefits and reduce time in formal training. This has led firms, particularly large ones, to focus less on firm-wide expenditure on formal training, and more on the distribution of training, and alternatives to formal training, for achieving learning outcomes (OECD, 1998*d*).

674. Few policies or incentives encourage employer training or employees to train. Tax treatment of employer training expenditure is favourable in virtually all OECD countries insofar as it is treated as an operating cost. Expenditure is currently deductible in the same way as R&D and other intangibles, although eligibility criteria are often tight. There may also be disincentives in the way that employer training is treated in the taxation of individuals, if employees are taxed on the benefit of training received from employers (see section below). Deductible expenses usually include payments to external training and education institutions. Two countries have tax-related incentives (essentially levies) to encourage firms to spend a defined minimum on training. France has had a compulsory initiative in place since 1971, setting the minimum expenditure on vocational training at 1.1 per cent of the total wage bill (currently 1.5 per cent). Most firms, particularly large ones, spend considerably more; firms spending less pay the difference to the public treasury. Hungary has introduced a similar scheme. Despite the long-established experience with the training incentive in France and a generally rising level of expenditure on training, there has been relatively little analysis of the outcomes for employees (wages, skill levels, career paths) or employers (labour productivity, profitability, product quality).

675. A few other countries have somewhat more limited systems to collect or aggregate funds from enterprises through levies or similar collections to oblige firms to increase funding of training.[59] Countries which have levy systems on employers at national or sector level include Belgium, Denmark, Ireland, Italy, the Netherlands, Spain and Portugal. Most are based on small levies on employers' total payroll (0.5 per cent or less), which finance training at national or sector level.[60] Sweden allocated 10 per cent of pre-tax profits for the 1985 tax year to a compulsory reserve for expenditure on training and R&D. This probably added an extra 5 per cent of funding onto enterprise education and training

59. Details from *Formation professionnelle Continue* (FORCE), reporting system on access, quality and volume of continuing vocational training in Europe, 1996.

over the 1986-90 period, although much of this could have been displacement rather than additional funding (OECD, 1995*e*).

676. From 1990-94 Australia operated a Training Guarantee Scheme which obliged firms to spend a minimum 1 per cent of payroll (1.5 per cent from 1992-93) on formal employment-related training. Allowable costs included trainee wages. Employers not reaching the minimum were required to pay the difference to the tax authorities. It was seen to be effective in raising awareness particularly for medium-sized business, improving training methods, and maintaining training effort through the recession of the 1990s. However, it did not improve training in many service industries which have experienced high employment growth, nor did it increase training in very small firms which were not covered or in firms which were covered but on the low end - and training inequalities appeared to grow. Overall it was seen that such policies would be more effective if they were better targeted (*i.e.* on specific low-training sectors or problems), focused on strengthening training incentives and emphasized outputs (such as ability to organise skills to improve quality or productivity) rather than simply raising training inputs (Fraser, 1996).

677. The United Kingdom's sectoral training funds, organised on a tripartite basis and financed by a common levy were discontinued in the 1980s, to be succeeded by locally organised, private sector led Training and Enterprise Councils (TECs). The government contracts with TECs to provide support to employers, including the facilitation of enterprise-based training. Their performance depends very much on local capabilities and is related to their organisational ability to engage and work with local employers. In Canada, Sector Councils deliver adjustment programmes, administer training funds and establish industry human resource standards. Sector Councils operate in over 20 sectors, with government support and management and labour representation. The federal government transferred responsibilities for labour market training programmes to the provinces in 1996, and several provinces saw an important role for sectoral initiatives. Experience until then suggested that sectoral approaches were effective in a decentralised federal system, that the diversity of approaches was beneficial and that Councils provided innovative approaches to business-labour co-operation for human resource development (Centre for the Study of Living Standards, 1996).

678. Overall, interest in firm-based training is high, but incentives to increase training are weak, apart from tax treatment of training expenditure which can be deducted as an operating cost. Experience with compulsory levies is very scattered. They do increase training expenditure, but there has been little analysis or evidence of whether such levies improve firm productivity and performance, or whether there are shifts in the distribution of training opportunities towards particular training or skill problems.

Incentives for individuals to train

679. Incentives and enabling mechanisms are variable for human capital investment and further training for individuals. The most obvious incentive is the payoff in higher earnings and employability, where the payoffs to formal education and training are substantial. Evaluating returns to further training on the job is more difficult, in part because the outcomes are more difficult to measure and signal. Available evidence suggests that further training does generate substantial rates of return (OECD,

60. Denmark is the only country to have a substantial employee levy. The vocational education and training levy for adults (*arbejdsmarkedsbidrag*) is 8 per cent of payroll to a state labour market fund. The fund pays vocational education and training for employed and unemployed insured adults. The primary training system is the AMU-Center (Ministry of Labour) which is almost 100 per cent financed through this fund, directly or indirectly. Technical and commercial colleges (Ministry of Education) are also major training providers.

1997*bb*; 1998*e*). Potential returns to individuals are constrained by the fact that a great deal of further training is not adequately certified and often not recognised by other employers, and is therefore not transferable.

680. In the tax system there are three barriers to individual incentives to train. First, training may not generally be eligible for deduction. Some countries only allow maintenance of current qualifications, while others allow upgrading. Most countries do not allow costs leading to new qualifications. Second, threshold levels (*i.e.* the amounts that individuals can automatically deduct from taxable income as being necessarily connected with gaining that income) determine the after-tax cost of expenditure. If thresholds are high, there will be little tax incentive to train, as individuals must spend large amounts on training to take them over the threshold. Lower thresholds allow deduction of greater shares of training expenditure. Third, countries vary in actual costs which can be deducted. Taking all three factors into account, some countries have been very restrictive in providing tax incentives for individual training and professional development, allowing few activities and categories of deductible costs (Japan, the United Kingdom). France and Belgium had very high thresholds, so few individuals actually claim expenses. Other countries have been more generous, with wider eligibility of activities and cost categories, low standard allowances and generous allowances for professionals (Germany, the Netherlands and the United States).

681. Numerous countries (*e.g.* the United States and the United Kingdom) have been exploring how to strengthen incentives for, and the financial capacity of, individuals to train and pursue lifelong learning, strengthening the "high-skill" foundations of high-performance work practices. Schemes being considered include individual training/learning accounts and credits to cover the direct cost of training and of wages foregone. In a recent initiative in the United States, individuals can receive a "lifetime learning" tax credit of 20 per cent of all educational costs up to US$5 000/year (US$10 000/year after the year 2000) (Gore, 1997). There have also been initiatives to remove disincentives to training, by excluding employer training and education expenditure from employee income for tax purposes (*e.g.* in the United Kingdom, employers may deduct costs of employee training from taxable business income, and employees are not taxed on the benefit of the training they receive from their employers). Different general approaches to financing lifelong learning are evaluated in OECD (1997*cc*, Table 8.22).

682. In summary, broad directions for education and training policy reform are displayed in Table 11.4. Most countries also need to strengthen incentives for employers and employees to undertake work-related training. Few direct incentives exist for firms to undertake training apart from tax-deductibility of training costs; training levies are relatively rare. Tax incentives to individuals are even less common, with incentives weak in many countries, although some have been trying to strengthen such incentives.

Strengthening incentives to invest in intangibles, particularly technology and human resources

683. A major reason for underinvestment in intangible assets, such as technology and human resources, is their lack of visibility.[61] The importance of human resources, R&D, organisational structures, market development efforts and software exceeds the current ability to measure and manage

61. For the importance of intangible assets, see OECD (1997*dd*, Chapters 3, 14, 15, 16); Drake (1998).

them internally within firms, and to report about them externally. This deficiency is widely evident, from national statistics to business management literature, company accounts and capital markets.

684. Measures such as Tobin's Q, which show the difference between book and market values of firms, have consistently widened over a long period in most countries. High-growth "new" firms operating in technology and service sectors have large divergences between market and book value, at least in part due to inadequacies in valuing their intangible assets. At the level of the enterprise, the gap is particularly evident in financial statements and annual shareholder reports, in which information on human resources and other intangibles is absent or incomplete and difficult to interpret because of its lack of comparability with information from other enterprises.

685. Enterprises increasingly recognise that it is important to effectively manage intangibles in order to enhance adaptability and provide a sound basis for sustained corporate growth and profitability. Companies adopt innovations, ranging from attempts to improve measurement of intangible assets, to the creation of vice presidents for "knowledge management" to encourage investment in and better management of knowledge, know-how and learning. But investment in human resources and other intangibles is hindered by the inability of enterprises to report externally, in a credible and transparent way, the extent and quality of their intangible assets, and the degree to which managing them effectively can improve company performance. This lack of external visibility also weakens the incentive to improve the internal management of intangible assets.

686. This poses a problem for enterprises and society at large. It may lead to misallocation of capital towards less productive investments. Further, it will depress development of new and improved products and processes, hamper the diffusion of productivity-enhancing innovations and decrease productivity growth, upskilling and job creation. Overall, better disclosure would help strengthen incentives to invest in and manage intangibles, improving resource allocation and enhancing prospects for more favourable economy-wide employment performance.

687. One way to fill these gaps in information is for enterprises to produce, and report externally, more information on human resources and other intangibles. A number of individual companies have consistently attempted to disclose information on their intangibles with the double aim of managing them better and improving their performance and ratings in financial markets. The advantages of such spontaneous development by firms is that information is developed and reported in ways which are designed to improve management of intangibles and provide useful information to capital markets, while reflecting the firm- and sector-specific diversity of intangible assets. The overall coverage of intangibles in company reporting is probably best in Nordic countries, where Skandia is well known for its efforts. This follows on the experience with environmental "accounting", where strong social and environmental performance on the part of enterprises appears to be both appreciated by the public and rewarded in the market-place (Chapter 10). Reporting on intangibles is also developing in other countries, *e.g.* France, where social account reporting (the *bilan social*) and the training incentive have helped to focus attention on the value of and need for disclosing information on human resource aspects of intangibles.

688. However, incentive and co-ordination problems hamper firms' initiatives in reporting and disclosure. Firms fear that disclosure will reveal strategic information on investments in technology and human resources to competing firms; they have a perception that changes in reporting practices may eventually lead to changes in the way that intangibles are treated for tax purposes, reducing current tax advantages for some firms. In addition, reporting and disclosure may be formalised in a static way that will not capture further developments of firm-level intangible assets and their reporting. Furthermore,

managers who do not perform well will have an incentive not to report on the management and development of intangibles in a way which allows for easy cross-firm comparisons.

689. For such reasons, it is unlikely that relying on individual enterprises will lead to nationally and internationally comparable reporting that will strengthen intangibles management and capital market resource allocation across large numbers of firms and countries. Interest in improving comparability and strengthening the incentives for disclosure has been growing, notably in the Netherlands, the Nordic countries, the United Kingdom and the United States. Probably the best example of policy developments in this area comes from Denmark, where a set of descriptions of intangibles in company accounts has been prepared as a tool to measure, manage and report corporate intangibles on a comparable basis. This work is now entering a second phase, where the taxonomy will be used in a larger group of companies, and to test investors' assessment of the approach (Erhvervs udviklings rådet, 1997).

690. There are also initiatives to explore the feasibility of financial disclosure in accounting practice, notably through the International Accounting Standards Council (IASC), where intangible assets include scientific or technical knowledge, design and implementation of new processes or systems, intellectual property, market knowledge and computer software (International Accounting Standards Committee, 1997). However, current measurement and valuation difficulties and accounting conventions limit the extent to which indicators of investment in, and management of, human resources and other intangibles can be put into the balance sheet of a company's financial statement. Furthermore, the usual bodies competent to advise financial market regulators on the reporting of financial information may have neither the expertise nor the mandates to advise on the disclosure of non-financial information.[62] Overall, it appears that some kind of structured and systematic reporting and disclosure of non-financial information on intangibles is potentially useful to both management and capital market actors as a basis for evaluating the prospects of a company. At the same time, public policy is hampered by lack of knowledge and understanding of the importance of intangibles and human resource development in enterprise strategies and practices.

691. For the short term, it is essential to improve understanding, appreciation and reporting of intangibles by enterprises, while eliminating policy conditions which unnecessarily discriminate against investment in such assets. For the longer term, building on the experience with firm-level creativity and diversity in internal and external reporting, it appears desirable to develop a set of indicators of intangible assets along with a reporting structure which facilitates comparability and helps to guide and monitor voluntary disclosure of additional information. In this manner, policy makers should seek to underpin: *(i)* improved internal management of intangibles; and *(ii)* the development of a reliable external guide to the value of intangibles for capital markets and other resource providers. This requires a better understanding of: *(i)* the benefits for firms of improved reporting, *(ii)* the balance between benefits to firms of improved reporting and the costs and burdens on firms of such reporting; and *(iii)* how improved reporting enhances management and improves resource allocation in capital markets.

62. For more detail, see OECD and the Ernst & Young Center for Business Innovation (1997).

11.5. Encouraging greater labour-related flexibility

692. To enhance efficiency, firms adopt strategies ranging from "high-skill", "high-trust" organisation through to changing the quantities of labour used. The approach underlying the following is that: *(i)* high-performance work practices will be more productive if they involve innovative pay systems such as pay for performance, profit-sharing or bonuses; and *(ii)* flexibility is enhanced and experimentation encouraged where fewer restrictions exist on working arrangements, but where the benefits associated with standard working (particularly training and skill development) apply also to non-standard arrangements, prorated as appropriate.

Matching compensation and performance

693. Performance-related compensation is designed to strengthen employee incentives and increase the returns to trust and commitment and, to a lesser extent, to allow enterprises to link part of the wages bill to corporate performance. This type of compensation could be expected to become more widespread as enterprises seek to exploit the innovative capacities of employees and, overall, enhance the "high-trust" workplace by linking pay more directly to specific firms and establishments and employee characteristics.[63] Such compensation helps reinforce the high-trust workplace by creating self-policing incentives to improve performance. Relatively little attention has been paid to the dynamics and design of such schemes, however, despite their potential impact on productivity and performance (Nalbantian and Schotter, 1997).

694. Different kinds of compensation include: pay for individual or team performance; profit-sharing, gain-sharing and employee stock ownership plans (ESOPs); pay for qualifications/ competence or for attributes such as flexibility or commitment; and one-off payments for suggestions. These occur singly or as part of a package of compensation measures. Variable pay practices are often associated with flexible and high-performance work practices, and are increasingly linked with high-skill enterprise strategies in Canada and the United States. In Sweden, reorganised enterprises are more likely to have a larger wage spread associated with pay for performance, although differential pay practices are probably not as prevalent there as in many other countries (OECD, 1998*d*). Across Europe, a recent survey showed that pay for skills and qualifications and direct participation in organisational change are closely linked. Output bonuses were most common in Germany, profit-sharing in France and the United Kingdom, and ESOPs in the United Kingdom. Group work was often linked with bonuses, which, with pay for flexibility, were particularly effective (European Foundation for the Improvement of Living and Working Conditions, 1997).

695. Various forms of profit- and gain-sharing have legislative or institutional support. While the overall incidence of profit-sharing is low, it has increased over the previous decade (OECD, 1995*d*). It is most prevalent in Canada, France, Germany, Italy, Japan, Mexico, the Netherlands, the United Kingdom and the United States. Except for Finland, Nordic countries showed little policy interest. Legislation to encourage or expand profit-sharing has been introduced in Finland, France, Mexico, the Netherlands and the United Kingdom. Profit-sharing tends to have positive impacts on enterprise performance, particularly where employee participation is high. Firms most likely to be successful designed their employee incentive programmes to reward as large a base as possible (Bassi *et al.*, 1997). Profit-sharing and other performance-based rewards appear to be strongly associated with

63. The Commission of the European Communities (1997) identified "how to change wage systems along with the organisational structures on which they are based" as a key policy challenge.

high-performance work practices and higher-skilled workers. The positive firm-level benefits associated with various forms of reward for performance suggest that there will be economy-wide benefits from their diffusion.

696. Such practices may contribute to the growing inequalities in labour income seen in almost all OECD countries, and may undermine the abilities of "peripheral" and low-skilled workers to access, for example, training to improve their performance. Performance-related pay may be more widespread in North America, but it is increasingly being used in other countries. In almost all countries, it is reflected in a falling share of labour income to the low-income group while that going to the high-income group is rising, and income inequality has risen over time (the exceptions are France and Germany, see Chapter 1).

Working time

697. As enterprises adopt new organisational structures and work practices to achieve further flexibility they may vary the quantity of labour input by varying working time, as well as through occupational restructuring and changes in recruiting, training and compensation practices. Variations in working time have recently taken the form of greater part-time employment. In manufacturing, enterprises increasingly use staggered and reorganised hours to raise utilisation rates. Outside manufacturing, employer interest in flexible working time has been more closely linked to the nature of output, consumer preferences and containing costs.

Annualisation of working time and unusual working hours

698. Flexibility among full-time employees can be achieved through annualisation and modulation of working time. Annualisation allows employers to vary hours within a previously agreed average, typically over one year. "Modulated" arrangements are versions of annualised hours where a fixed distribution of hours conforms to high and low activity. Although these approaches are not necessarily related to the adoption of high-performance work practices, they provide flexibility by allowing employers to adapt supply more closely to demand. In the more restrictive European setting, changes in legislation have allowed use of annualised hours in Belgium, France, Spain and Switzerland. Other forms of flexible working practices such as unusual working hours may also increase. High-growth industries have tended to show high incidences of this kind of work. Demand is likely to increase with relaxation in shop opening hours in some European countries and the provision of other services outside traditional working hours. Overall, regulations restricting unusual working hours have been eased in France, Finland, Greece, Italy and Spain, and are under consideration in Austria and Germany.

Part-time and temporary working

699. A number of factors are driving increases in part-time and temporary (non-standard) employment. These include on the demand side, greater operating flexibility, possible lower costs because part-time or temporary workers may not be entitled to some benefits. Such employment may also be used to screen potential full-time employees. On the supply side, a major influence on the incidence of part-time work is women's preferences. There are also a variety of institutional arrangements that influence the incidence of part-time and temporary employment, including differences in non-wage labour costs (training or pension contributions for example) when earnings or hours fall below certain threshold levels, while for temporary employment there may be more relaxed dismissal regulations.

700. During the 1990s, the share of part-time employment grew in most OECD countries (except Denmark, Iceland, Norway, Turkey and the United States). Women made up at least two-thirds of this employment, and often more than four-fifths, in all countries. Part-time employment increased across all industries, although it has typically grown faster in services. Overall, there are signs that recent trends in part-time work are driven by firm demand as well as by supply-side developments, such as a shift in preferences towards this type of work by employees. The OECD has recommended easing constraints on part-time work in Austria, Finland, Germany, Italy and Switzerland (OECD, 1997*a*).

701. In some OECD countries, a certain number of fixed hours must be worked before employer benefit contributions are payable, giving employers incentives to create jobs just below the threshold. The overall trend is to reduce such thresholds to promote new forms of flexibility. A small number of countries set thresholds on employer social security contributions (France, Germany, Ireland and the United Kingdom). In the areas of health, pensions and unemployment benefits, there are wider cross-country differences, with Germany and Japan having the highest thresholds (OECD, 1998*f*). There is also a general disincentive for employers to train part-time employees in that training is "lumpy" (the same training effort is needed for employees working fewer hours, so the productivity payoff is spread over longer periods). On the other hand, lower levels of employer social security provision for part-time work encourage employers to hire those who are disadvantaged in the labour market, increasing employment of disadvantaged workers. Special policy measures may be warranted to ensure that part-time employees are adequately trained and that the pillars on which high-performance work practices are built – skill development, lifelong learning and trust/security – are not undermined.

702. Firm flexibility may also involve using temporary employees to a greater extent. Recourse to temporary employment may reduce employer incentives to adopt essential elements of high-skill work practices, and may undermine employee access to skill formation and benefits which will improve productivity. Temporary employment varies greatly across OECD countries. It is high and increasing in Australia and Spain, and increasing in importance in France and the Netherlands. There have been few major changes in other countries, but there are few countries where it decreased to the mid-1990s. Young people in particular have increasingly been in temporary employment and the incidence of temporary employment increased across all age groups in a range of countries (Australia, France, Germany, Ireland, Italy, the Netherlands, Spain, Sweden) (OECD, 1996*l*).

703. There is also evidence that temporary employment through agencies has increased, at least in countries that have not severely restricted it; in the United States agency employment has grown significantly. A number of countries are moving to encourage flexible employment while seeking to minimise the insecurity associated with it. In the Netherlands, private employment agencies are estimated to account for over 3 per cent of total employment, and legislation was introduced in 1997 to clarify such work and bring it within the usual status of employment contracts, with attendant benefits after half a year. This provides employers with increased labour force flexibility and employees with improved job security within flexible employment (Ministerie van Sociale Zaken en Werkgelegenheid, 1997).

Concentration of work and working hours

704. Technological and organisational change may also affect employment for various demographic groups. With increased demand for skills and flexibility, groups such as older workers may become marginalised. There is evidence of a move towards a more narrowly defined core of full-time employees and more widespread incidence of part-time and non-standard employment. Linked with firm-level reorganisation, there is also evidence that the proportions of employees working long or

short usual hours increased in at least some OECD countries. The incidence of long hours increased significantly in Australia, the United Kingdom and the United States. These developments raise concerns about whether marginalised workers have adequate access to skill formation to make them more qualified and adaptable, and increase their productivity. It also raises questions regarding whether the spread of such work patterns could unnecessarily exclude older workers and those unwilling to work long hours on a regular basis, undermining incentives for widespread lifelong learning.

Policy directions

705. Policy directions to encourage greater labour-related flexibility in ways which will enhance the spread and impacts of high-performance work practices can be summarised as follows

- Performance-related compensation appears to be increasing across OECD countries. This is often associated with high-performance workplaces, productivity gains and improved performance. There is a case for expanding information on the benefits to be drawn from such practices. Finland, France, Mexico, the Netherlands and the United Kingdom have moved in this direction over the last decade or so; other countries including Scandinavian ones should consider following suit and modifying legislation where it prevents the spread of such practices.

- Flexible working hours and greater variability in work time (such as annualisation of hours) are probably useful adjuncts to the spread of high-performance work practices as they allow enterprises to more closely align activity with demand. Recent initiatives have been taken in Finland, France, Greece, Italy and Spain (the OECD recommended easing constraints in Austria, France and Greece; OECD, 1997*a*).

- Part-time employment increased in most OECD countries in the 1990s. High-skill, high-trust strategies based on skill formation and security may be undermined to the extent that such employees do not receive benefits and training. To promote new forms of flexibility, countries are generally reducing thresholds in hours worked below which employees cannot receive benefits, although Germany and Japan maintain relatively high thresholds. To the extent that thresholds inhibit skill formation they should be reviewed and eliminated, or other targeted policy action taken to overcome them.

- Evidence for achieving organisational flexibility is apparent in the growth of "agency work" (typically a small proportion of total employment), most notably in the United States but increasing in other countries. The development of a competitive agency-work industry could help to provide flexibility to employers and more stability to temporary employees. Agency work and standard employment need to be subject to similar rules. Recent initiatives in the Netherlands are a good example, providing employers with labour force flexibility and employees with necessary security.

- Evidence on part-time and temporary work highlights "marginalisation" of younger and older workers. Apart from major issues of social cohesion, to the extent that these developments undermine more widespread adoption of productivity-enhancing work practices, they require attention, including, for example, generating greater "equality" between standard and non-standard forms of employment, and increasing coverage and portability of, *e.g.* pensions and health benefits, and improving access to training across groups of individuals.

Industrial relations and collective bargaining

706. There are new opportunities and roles for trade unions in the context of organisational change and new workplace practices, although they demand fundamental changes to the way that unions operate within firms, and strategies for reversing declining unionisation rates in almost all OECD countries. Flexible firm strategies and approaches to work organisation affect relations between employers and employees by changing the boundary of the firm, demarcations between occupations and the determinants of enterprise competitiveness. Forces towards "individualisation", ranging from increased individual responsibility in the workplace to individualised pay-setting and contracting arrangements (often involving contingent employment), may leave little room for traditional collective approaches.

707. There is a further logic in decentralising collective bargaining to enterprise or plant level. This should enable maximum flexibility for firms and employees in setting working and compensation arrangements, and allow experimentation and maximum use of both employee potential and liberalised work settings. Although recent work has shown that there is little correlation between different bargaining systems and economic performance across countries (OECD, 1997*c*), it can be argued that firm-level economic performance may be enhanced by decentralising the details of bargaining and setting work practice conditions to enterprise or plant levels, within broader sectoral or national frameworks focused on more general outcomes. The Canadian Sector Councils may be one model of such an approach.

708. Such changes put pressure on the traditional structure of industrial relations systems and the collective bargaining agenda, and on unions and representative organisations to devise and provide new services, particularly regarding human resource development. New roles for unions include providing training, enhancing workplace skills and employability, and working to develop high-skill, high-trust forms of workplace practices.

709. Two different kinds of development can be envisaged, diverging from traditional roles and strategies. In "market-driven" countries, with typically adversarial worker-management relations, a growing number of new partnerships with business have been set up to develop skills and devise strategies for workplace change. Examples include: in the United Kingdom, the UNISON union/public sector employers training partnerships, and the Trades Union Congress (TUC) Bargaining for Skills initiatives with the TECs; initiatives in the United States, such as the Consortium for Worker Education organised in partnership between trade unions, business and industry, local government and educational establishments; and in the more consensual national setting in Ireland, new forms of firm-level work and management systems are developing (Munro *et al.*, 1997; European Trade Union Confederation *et al.*, 1997). In consensual social-partnership countries there are further needs and opportunities to develop new kinds of services to members to adapt traditional union roles to new circumstances (OECD, 1996*m*).

11.6. Co-ordinating and delivering policy

710. The key ingredients in policy to improve the spread and impacts of high-performance work practices and foster investments in intangibles are: encouraging innovation and entrepreneurship; improving information flows and demonstrating the benefits of high-performance work practices; ensuring that education and training systems and incentives provide a large pool of skilled employees and that firms undertake appropriate training; and ensuring that labour market regulations do not unnecessarily hinder the adoption of flexible strategies, and that attention is paid to access to benefits such as training and employee security, and that social cohesion issues are taken into account.

711. These need to be implemented so that they enhance organisational experimentation and market-led adoption by firms and employees. The agenda cuts across departmental and ministerial responsibilities in most countries. Co-ordinated and integrated approaches are likely to be most efficient (in the allocation and use of government resources) and effective (in enhancing firm uptake of high-performance work practices). The areas of responsibility that need to be involved in co-ordination cover science, research, industry, education and labour markets. Policy must be planned coherently, involving dialogue and co-operation with other actors (industry associations, labour representatives and other institutions), delivered at the appropriate level to reach targets (*e.g.* SMEs), and monitored and evaluated to ensure that it meets criteria such as accountability, value for money and the achievement of objectives (Chapter 5). The elements essential for policy design and delivery can be found in approaches adopted by a few countries.

712. In Canada, there is clear recognition of the need to integrate industrial policies with human resource development responsibilities to develop microeconomic strategies for the "knowledge-based economy", jobs and growth. Science and innovation responsibilities reside with the industry portfolio, and labour market and some training functions with the human resource development portfolio. There is recognition that this co-ordinated strategy ranges from developing coherent approaches to measuring impacts of workplace change on enterprises and employees through to building closer contacts for devising and delivering policy. In principle, decentralisation of many responsibilities and programmes to provincial level (for example, training programmes and Sector Councils) will help marry broad strategy development with efficient delivery of programmes at the local level. However, it remains to be seen how the new division of responsibilities and operations will work in practice.

713. Denmark is giving priority to enterprise flexibility and framework conditions for organisational change. This involves close co-operation between Business and Industry, Education, Labour, and Research Ministries. This co-ordinated approach has involved dialogue on management, organisation and competences with enterprises, business and infrastructure organisations (technical service and training institutions, business schools, universities). Wide-ranging initiatives have been developed, often based on reorienting or sharpening the focus of existing programmes and institutions to: provide better information on best practices for organisational change and change management; improve skills and competences in the consultancy sector; encourage closer interaction between suppliers and users of supplementary labour force training; and increase co-operation between higher education and enterprises.

714. In Finland, the National Workplace Development Programme involves co-operation between public administration, labour market organisations and research and education institutions. The four year programme launched in 1996 builds on experience with the previous tripartite National Productivity Campaign. The management group includes the Economic Council (led by the Prime Minister), Ministry of Labour, labour market organisations, the national entrepreneurs organisation, plus the Ministry of Trade and Industry, National Board of Education, Ministry of Social Affairs and Health, Academy of Finland, Work Environment Fund, and Centre for Industrial Safety. Although it is too soon to judge outcomes in terms of identification, development and diffusion of workplace reforms, it at least involves the necessary actors and has a reasonably long time-frame for operations and substantial budgetary resources.

715. Similar broad approaches to organisational and workplace change have been adopted in a few other countries to improve efficiency in policy delivery and expedite change. In Norway, collaboration is being built through an Enterprise Development programme designed to increase knowledge of strategies, practices, working methods and infrastructure to enable Norwegian enterprises to reach

international best practice. It is being carried out with extensive tripartite co-operation with the Norwegian Federation of Trade Unions and the Confederation of Norwegian Business and Industry and funding bodies to put ideas into practice. In Iceland, since 1995 a co-ordinated policy focused on SMEs and competitiveness issues has been devised and implemented through a committee of employer and employee representatives, the Ministry of Industry and Commerce and other ministries. Finally, focusing more on skills issues, in 1996 Ireland set up a Future Skills Identification Group with representatives of enterprise development and higher education agencies, and the Departments of Education, Enterprise and Finance to assess existing and emerging skill needs and develop plans to address them.

716. Common threads run through these approaches:

- recognising the complexity of workplace change and adopting co-ordinated approaches;
- focusing on important elements in the national setting (information, demonstration, skills);
- involving business and labour organisations to ensure that initiatives are demand-led;
- working with specialised delivery agencies to ensure effective contact with target groups;
- choosing appropriate levels at which to co-ordinate policies and at which to deliver programmes.

GLOSSARY OF ABBREVIATIONS, ACRONYMS AND TERMS

ABA	Australian Broadcasting Authority
ABS	Australian Bureau of Statistics
ACE-net	Angel Capital Electronic Network
ACTS	Advanced Communications Technologies and Services
ADEPA	*Agence de la Productique* Agency for Development of Automated Production (France)
AFMA	American Film Marketing Association
AIM	Alternative Investment Market (United Kingdom)
ALMI	*ALMI Företagspartner AB* [ALMI Business Partner (Sweden)]
AMT	Advanced Manufacturing Technology
AMTAP	Advanced Manufacturing Technology Application Program (Canada)
AMTEX	American Textile Partnership
AMU	Training for the Labour Market (Denmark)
ANVAR	*Agence Nationale pour la Valorisation de la Recherche* [National Agency for the Valorisation of Research (France)]
AOL	America Online
APCE	*Agence Pour la Creation d'Entreprises* [Agency for the Creation of New Businesses (France)]
APICNET	Asia-Pacific Interactive Communication NETwork
APRODI	*Association pour la Promotion et le Développement Industriel* [Association for Promotion and Industrial Development (France)]
ARC	*Aide au Recrutement des Cadres* (France)
ARI	*Aide au Recrutement pour l'Innovation* (France)
ATOUT	*Programme d'aide à la diffusion technologique* (France)
ATP	Advanced Technology Program (United States)
ATYCA Initiative	*Iniciativa de Apoyo a la Tecnología, la Seguridad y la Calidad Industrial* [Support Initiative for Technology, Security and Industrial Quality (Spain)]
BBC	British Broadcasting Corporation
BBMKB	SME Credit Guarantee Decree (Netherlands)
BDB	Business Development Bank (Canada)

BERD Expenditure on R&D in the Business Enterprise Sector

BES Business Expansion Scheme (United Kingdom)

BIE Bureau of Industrial Economics (Australia)

BJTU *Beteiligungskapital für Junge Technologie-unternehmen* [Venture Capital for Young High Technology Firms (Germany)]

BMBF *Bundesministerium für Bildung, Wissenschaft, Forschung und Technologie* [Ministry of Education, Science, Research and Technology (Germany)]

BRI Basic Research Intensity

BTS *Bedrijfsgerichte Technologische Samenwerking* [Business-Oriented Technological Co-operation (Netherlands)]

BTU *Beteiligungskapital für Junge Technologie-unternehmen* [Venture Capital for Young High Technology Firms (Germany)]

BUNT Business Development Using New Technology (Norway)

BURGES *Bürges Förderungsbank Gesellschaft m.b.H. des Bundesministeriums für wirtschaftliche Angelegenheiten* [BURGES Small Business Guarantee Bank (Austria)]

CAD/CAM Computer-aided Design and Computer-aided Manufacturing

CARAD Civil Aircraft Research and Demonstration (United Kingdom)

CCDSP Centers for the Commercial Development of the Space Program (United States)

CD-ROM Compact Disk – Read Only Memory

CDA Communications Decency Act (United States)

CERN *Conseil Européen pour la Recherche Nucleaire* [European Organization for Nuclear Research – European Laboratory for Particle Physics]

CFC Chloro-Fluorocarbon

CIFRE *Convention Industrielle de Formation par la Recherche* (France)

CIM Computer-Integrated Manufacturing

CIS Community Innovation Survey (European Commission)

CITR Corporate Income Tax Rate

CNC *Centre National de la Cinématographie* [National Center for Cinema (France)]

CNE *Comité National d'Evaluation* (France)

CNER *Comité National d'Evaluation de la Recherche* (France)

CNR *Consiglio Nazionale delle Ricerche* [National Research Council (Italy)]

CNRS *Centre National de la Recherche Scientifique* [National Scientific Research Council (France)]

CONACYT *Consejo Nacional de Ciencia y Tecnología* [National Council for Science and Technology (Mexico)]

CORDIS Community Research and Development Information Service (European Commission)

CORTECHS *Convention de Recherche pour les Techniciens Supérieurs* (France)

CRADA Cooperative Research and Development Agreement (United States)

CRITT *Centre Régional d'Innovation et de Transfert Technologique* [Regional Centre for Innovation and Technological Transfer (France)]

CRT *Centre de Recherche Technique* [Technical Research Centre (France)]

CRTC Canadian Radio and Telecommunications Commission

CSA *Conseil Supérieur de l'Audiovisuel* [The Higher Council of Audio-visual (France)]

CSIRO Commonwealth Scientific Industrial Research Organisation (Australia)

CSSP Canadian Space Agency's Space Station Programme

DG Directorate General (European Commission internal terminology)

DOD Department of Defense (United States)

DOE Department of Energy (United States)

DOH Department of Health (United States)

EASDAQ European Association of Securities Dealers Automated Quotation

EBI Environmental Business International

EBN European Business and Innovation Centre Network

ECM Error Correction Model

EDI Electronic Data Interchange

EIF European Investment Fund

EIRMA European Industrial Research Management Association

EIS Enterprise Investment Scheme (United Kingdom)

EMS Environmental Management System

ERATO Exploratory Research for Advanced Technology (Japan)

ERISA Employment Retirement Income Security Act (United States)

ERP European Recovery Programme

ESA European Space Agency

ESOP Employee Stock Ownership Plan

ESPRIT European Strategic Programme for Research and development in Information Technologies

EU European Union

EUREKA Programme for co-operation between European firms and research institutes in the field of advanced technologies

EURO.NM *Réseau Européen des Nouveaux Marchés* [European Market for Shares of Innovative High Growth Companies]

FCPI *Fonds Commun de Placement Innovation* (France)

FDI Foreign Direct Investment

FFRDC Federally Financed R&D Centre (United States)

FGB Finnish Guarantee Board

FGG *Finanzierungsgarantie-Gesellschaft* (Austria)

FORCE *Formation professionnelle Continue* [Continuing Vocational Training (EU)]

FOTEK *Det Fødevareteknologiske Udviklings- og Forskningsprogram* [The Danish Research and Development Programme for Food Technology]

FRAC Regional Fund for Consultancy Support (France)

G7 Group of Seven leading industrialised nations: Britain, Canada, France, Germany, Italy, Japan, the United States

GBAORD Government Budget Appropriations or Outlays for R&D

GBLP Guaranteed Business Loan Program

GDP Gross Domestic Product

GERD Gross Domestic Expenditure on R&D

GIMV Investment Company for Flanders (Belgium)

GRI *Chungbu Chulyun Yunku Kigwan* [Government-supported Research Institute (Korea)]

GTS *Godkendte Teknologiske Serviceinstitutter* [Technological Service Institutes (Denmark)]

GUF General University Funds

HAN *Seondo Kisul Gaebal Saup* [Highly Advanced National project (Korea)]

HERD Expenditure on R&D in the Higher Education Sector

HERMES Harmonised Econometric Research for Modelling Economic Systems

HMO Health Maintenance Organization (United States)

HPCCP High Performance Computing and Communications Program

IAP Internet Access Provider

IAPMEI *Instituto de Apoio às Pequenas e Médias Empresas e ao Investimento* [Institute for the Support of SMEs and Investment (Portugal)]

IASC International Accounting Standards Council

ICNN Innovatie Centra Netwerk Nederland [Netherlands' Innovation Centres Network]

ICP Internet Content Provider

ICT Information and Communication Technology

IDC International Data Corporation

IIF Innovation Investment Fund (Australia)

IMF International Monetary Fund

IMT Innovation Management Techniques

INESCOP *Instituto Tecnológico del Calzado y Conexas* [Technological Footwear Institute (Spain)]

INETI *Instituto Nacional de Engenharia e Tecnologia Industrial* [National Institute for Engineering and Industrial Technology (Portugal)]

IPF *Forschungsförderungsfond für die Gewerbliche Wirtschaft (FFF)* [Industrial Research Promotion Fund (Austria)]

IPOs Initial Public Offerings

IPR Intellectual Property Rights

IRAP Industrial Research Assistance Program (Canada)

ISTAT *Istituto Nazionale di Statistica* [National Institute of Statistics (Italy)]

IT Information Technology

ITF *Innovations- und Technologiefonds* [Innovation and Technology Fund (Austria)]

JASDAQ Japanese Association of Securities Dealers Automated Quotation

KfW *Kreditanstalt für Wiederaufbau* (Germany)

KIM *Kennisdragers in het Midden- en Kleinbedrijf* [Specialists in SMEs Scheme (Netherlands)]

KIR *Kompetenzzentren – Impulsprogramme – Regierungsinitiativen* [Centres of competence/excellence – Impulse programmes – Government initiatives (Austria)]

KOSEF Korea Science and Engineering Foundation

LGS Loan Guarantee Scheme

LINK A UK Government-funded initiative, LINK promotes partnership in research between industry and the research base.

LSVCC Labour-Sponsored Venture Capital Corporation (Canada)

MBO Management Buy-out

MEP Manufacturing Extension Partnership (United States)

METIM *Mercato Telematico per le Medie Imprese* [Telematic Market for Medium-Sized Enterprises (Italy)]

MICs Management and Investment Companies

MINT Managing Integration of New Technology

MITI Ministry of International Trade and Industry (Japan)

MONITOR EU programme in the field of strategic analysis, forecasting and evaluation in matters of research and technology

MUP Research and Development Programme for Materials Technology (Denmark)

NAFIN/CNB *Nacional Financiera* [National Banking (Mexico)] *Comision Nacional Bancaria y de Valores* [National Banking and Securities Commission (Mexico)]

NAFTA North American Free Trade Agreement

NAIRU Non-Accelerating Inflation Rate of Unemployment

NASA National Aeronautics and Space Administration (United States)

NASDAQ National Association of Securities Dealers Automated Quotation (United States)

NAWRU Non-Accelerating Wage Rate of Unemployment

NBIA National Business Incubation Association (United States)

NC Network Computer

NCRA National Cooperative Research Act (United States)

NEDO New Energy and Industrial Technology Development Organization (Japan)

NFP *Nationale Forschungprogramm* [National Research Programme (Switzerland)]

NIS National Innovation System

NIST National Institute of Standards and Technology (United States)

Nordic countries Denmark, Finland, Iceland, Norway, Sweden

North America and/or North American countries Canada, Mexico, the United States

NSF National Science Foundation (United States)

NTBF New Technology-based Firm

NUTEK *Närings- och teknikutvecklingsverket* [National Board for Industrial and Technical Development (Sweden)]

OFTEL Office of Telecommunications (United Kingdom)

OTC Over-the-Counter market

P/PP Public/Private Partnership

PAC Pollution Abatement and Control

PATS Programmes in Advanced Technology (Ireland)

PBS Public Broadcasting Service (United States)

PC Personal Computer

PDFs Pooled Development Funds

PEDIP *Programa Especifico de Desenvolvimento da Industria Portuguesa* [Specific Program for the Development of Portuguese Industry]

PGS Plant Genetic Systems

PMTSs Participation Company for New Technology-Based Firms (Netherlands)

PNGV Partnership for a New Generation of Vehicles (United States)

PNP Private Non-Profit

PPM Private Participation Guarantee Order Scheme (Netherlands)

PREDIT *Programme de Recherche et de Développement pour l'Innovation et la Technologie dans les Transports Terrestres* [Research and Development Program for Innovation and Technology in Land Transport (France)]

PSTN Public Switch(ed) Telephone Network

R&D Research and Development

RDI Research Development and Innovation

RFI *Réseaux Régionaux de Financeurs de l'Innovation* (France) (Regional Networks of Innovation Funders)

ROAME-F Rationale, Objectives, Appraisal, Monitoring, Evaluation, Feedback (United Kingdom)

RTA Revealed Technological Advantage

RTD Research and Technological Development

S&T Science and Technology

SBA Small Business Administration (United States)

SBICs Small Business Investment Companies (United States)

SBIR Small Business Innovation Research (United States)

SBLA Small Business Loan Guarantee Programme (United States)

Scandinavian countries sDenmark, Iceland, Norway, Sweden

SEMATECH Semiconductor Manufacturing Technology (United States)

SEP Scottish Equity Partnership

SINPEDIP Productive investment incentive of PEDIP (*cf.* PEDIP)

SISTEC *Sistema de Informacion sobre Servicios Tecnologicos* [Information System on Technological Services (Mexico)]

SITRA National Fund for Research and Development (Finland)

SME Small and Medium-sized Enterprise

SMIPC Small and Medium Industry Promotion Corporation (Korea)

SOFARIS *Société Française pour l'Ássurance du Capital-Risque des Petites et Moyennes Entreprises* [Risk Capital Insurance for SMEs (France)]

SPEAR Support Programme for the Evaluation of Activities in the field of Research (EU)

SPRINT Strategic Programme for Innovation and Technology Transfer (EU)

SPRU Science Policy Research Unit (United Kingdom)

SURE Seemingly Unrelated Regression

TAP Technology Access Programme (Australia)

[TC]2 Textile/Clothing Technology Corporation (United States)

TCS Teaching Company Scheme (United Kingdom)

TEC Training and Enterprise Council (United Kingdom)

TEFT *Teknologiformidling fra Forskningsinstitutter til SMB* [Programme for Technology Transfer from Research Institutes to SMEs (Norway)]

TEKES *Teknologian Kehittämiskeskus* [Technology Development Centre (Finland)]

TESI *Suomen Teollisuussijoitus Oy* [Industry Investment (Finland)]

TFP Total Factor Productivity

TIC *Teknologiske Informationscentre* [Technological Information Centre (Denmark)]

TLO Technology Licensing Organisation (Japan)

TNO *Nederlandse Organisatie voor Toegepast-Natuurwetenschappelijk Onderzoek* [Netherlands Organization for Applied Scientific Research]

TOK Technical Development Credits Scheme (Netherlands)

TPC	Technology Partnerships Canada
TRIPS	Agreement on Trade-related Aspects of Intellectual Property Rights
TRP	Technology Reinvestment Project (United States)
TUC	Trades Union Congress (United Kingdom)
USPTO	United States Patent and Trademark Office
VCT	Venture Capital Trust Scheme (United Kingdom)
VEC	Venture Enterprise Center (Japan)
VTT	*Valtion Teknillinen Tutkimuskeskus* [Technical Research Centre of Finland]
WBSO	*Wet Bevordering Speur- en Ontwikkelingswerk* [Innovation Fund for Technology and Vocational Education (Netherlands)]
WIFI	*Wirtschaftsförderungs-Institut* [Institute for the Promotion of the Economy (Austria)]
WIPO	World Intellectual Property Organization
WTO	World Trade Organization
WWW	World Wide Web

BIBLIOGRAPHY

ACS, Z. (1997), "Innovation, Small Firms and Public Policy", The University of Baltimore, MD, unpublished.

ACS, Z. and D. AUDRETSCH (1993), "Innovation and Firm Size: The New Learning", *International Journal of Technology Management, Special Publication on Small Firms and Innovation.*

ADAMS, J. (1991), "Fundamental Stock of Knowledge and Productivity Growth", *Journal of Political Economy* 98(4), pp. 673-702.

ALMEIDA, P. and B. KOGUT (1997), "The Exploration of Technological Diversity and the Geographic Localization of Innovation", *Small Business Economics* 9 (1), pp. 21-31.

AMABLE, R., R. BARRE and R. BOYER (1997), *Les systèmes d'innovation a l'ère de la globalisation*, Éd. Economica, Paris.

ANDERSSON, T. and R. SVENSSON (1994), "Entry Modes for Direct Investment Determined by the Composition of Firm-specific Skills", *The Scandinavian Journal of Economics*, Vol. 96, No 4. pp. 551-560.

APCE (AGENCE POUR LA CREATION D'ENTREPRISES) (1997), <http://www.apce.com>.

ARTHUR ANDERSON ECONOMIC CONSULTING (1995), *The Economic Consequence of Independent Film Making*, report commissioned by American Film Marketing Association, Los Angeles, CA.

ARUNDEL, A., G. VAN DE PAAL and L. SOETE (1995), *Innovation Strategies of Europe's Largest Industrial Firms: Results of the PACE Survey for Information Sources, Public Research, Protection of Innovations and Government Programmes*, European Communities, Luxembourg.

ARVANITIS, S. and H. HOLLENSTEIN (1997), "Evaluating the Promotion of Advanced Manufacturing Technologies (AMT) by the Swiss Government Using Micro-level Survey Data: Some Methodological Considerations", in *Policy Evaluation in Innovation and Technology: Towards Best Practices*, OECD, Paris.

ATLAS, M. and R. FLORIDA (1997), "Why do Firms Adopt Green Design? Organisational Opportunity, Organisational Resources, Cost or Regulation", Working Paper, Carnegie Mellon University, Pittsburgh, PA.

AUSTRALIAN BUREAU OF STATISTICS (1994), "Innovation in Australian Manufacturing 1994", ABS Bulletin 8116.0.

AUSTRALIAN BUREAU OF STATISTICS (1996*a*), *Business Use of Information Technology, 1993-94*, p. 5, Australian Government Publishing Service, Belconnen, ACT.

AUSTRALIAN BUREAU OF STATISTICS (1996*b*), *Household Use of Information Technology, February 1996*, Australian Government Publishing Service, Belconnen, ACT.

AUTIO, E. and A. LUMME (1995), "Does the Innovator Role Affect the Perceived Potential for Growth? Analysis of Four Types of New, Technology-based Firms", *Frontiers of Entrepreneurship Research*, Babson College, MA.

AUTIO, E. and H. YLI-RENKO (1997), "New, Technology-based Firms in Small Open Economies – An Analysis Based on the Finnish Experience", Helsinki University of Technology, unpublished.

AYALA, F.J. (1995), "La Ciencia Espanola en la Ultimata Decada" in *Political Cientifica*, Comision Interminesterial de Ciencia e Tecnologia, Secretaria de Estado de Universidades e Investigacion, Madrid.

BALDWIN, J. (1997), "The Importance of Research and Development for Innovation in Small and Large Canadian Manufacturing Firms", Research Paper Series No. 107, Statistics Canada, Ottawa.

BALDWIN, J. and M. DAPONT (1996), "Innovation in Canadian Manufacturing Enterprises", Catalogue No. 88-513, Statistics Canada, Ottawa.

BALDWIN, J., B. DIVERTY and J. JOHNSON (1995), "Technology Use and Industrial Transformation: Empirical Perspectives", Research paper No. 75, Statistics Canada, Ottawa.

BALDWIN, J. and J. JOHNSON (1996), "Business Strategies in More- and Less-innovative Firms in Canada", *Research Policy* 25.

BASSI, L.J., B. LEV, J. LOW and G.A. SIESFELD (1997), "Accounting for and Measuring the Impact of Corporate Investments in Human Capital", December, mimeo.

BERGLUND, D. and C. COBURN (1995), *Partnerships: A Compendium of State and Federal Cooperative Technology Programs*, Battelle, Columbus, OH.

BERKHOUT, A.J., P.F. WOUTERS and H. SHAFFERS (1997), *Technologie voor de Maatschappij van Morgen*, Amsterdam.

BERNSTEIN, J. (1986), "The Effects of Direct and Indirect Tax Incentives on Canadian Industrial R&D Expenditures", *Canadian Public Policy* 12(3).

BERNSTEIN, J. and I. NADIRI (1990), "Rates of Return on Physical and R&D Capital and Structure of the Production Process: Cross Section and Time Series Evidence", in B. Raj (ed.), *Advances in Econometrics and Modelling*, Kluwer, London.

BESSANT, J. (1995), "Networking as a Mechanism for Enabling Organisational Innovations: The Case of Continuous Improvements", in *Europe's Next Step: Organisational Innovation, Competition and Employment*, United Kingdom.

BIRCH, A. (1994), *Who's Creating Jobs?*, Cognetics, Cambridge, MA.

BIRCH, A. (1997), "Evaluation of the GTS System in Denmark, 1995-97", in *Policy Evaluation in Innovation and Technology: Towards Best Practices*, OECD, Paris.

BLOOM, N., R. GRIFFITHS and J. VAN REENEN (1997), "Do R&D Tax Credits Work? Evidence from an International Panel of Countries, 1979-94", paper presented at the TSER Conference on Innovation, Competition and Employment, 21-22 August, China.

BOSTON CONSULTING GROUP (1996), informal discussions.

BOSWORTH, K., P. STONEMAN and U. SINHA (1996), "Technology Transfer, Information Flows and Collaboration: An Analysis of the CIS", *EIMS Publication* No. 36, European Commission, Luxembourg.

BRAAKSMA, R.M. (1995), *A Close Look at Technostarters*, EIM, Zoetermeer.

BRADBURY, M. and M. DAVIES (1998), "The Evaluation of Support Programmes: The Example of the United Kingdom", *STI Review*, No. 21, OECD, Paris.

BROPHY, D. (1996), "United States Venture Capital Markets: Trends and Prospects", in "Venture Capital and Innovation", OCDE/GD(96)168, OECD, Paris.

BRUEDERL, J., C. BUEHLER and R. ZIEGLER (1993), "Beschaeftigungswirkung Neugegruendeter Betriebe", *Mitteilungen aus der Arbeitsmarkt-und Berufsforschung*, No. 4, pp. 521-528.

BUNDESMINISTERIUM FÜR BILDUNG, FORSCHUNG UND TECHNOLOGIE, WISSENSCHAFT (1996), "Bundesbericht Forschung 1996", and previous issues, Bonn.

BUREAU OF INDUSTRY ECONOMICS (1993), "R&D, Innovation and Competitiveness: An Evaluation of the R&D Tax Concessions", *Research Report 50*, Australian Government Publishing Service, Canberra.

CALDERINI, M. and P. SWANN (1996), "Product Complexity and Organizational Structure in Small and Medium Enterprises: An Empirical Study", paper for the J.A. Schumpteter Society Conference.

CARACOSTAS, P. (1998), "Towards Systemic Policy at the European Level: Five Key Challenges For the Future", forthcoming in *STI Review*, No. 22, OECD, Paris.

CENTRE FOR THE STUDY OF LIVING STANDARDS (1996), *Sector Councils in Canada: Future Challenges*, Ottawa.

CHABBAL, R. (1995), "Characteristics of Innovation Policies for SMEs", in *STI Review*, No. 16, Special Issue on Innovation and Standards, OECD, Paris.

CHABBAL, R. (1997), "Un plan d'action pour les PME innovantes", European Business and Innovation Centre Network, EC-BIC Observatory, Brussels.

COCKBURN, I. and R. HENDERSON (1996), "Public-private Interaction in Pharmaceutical Research", paper presented at the Strasbourg Conference on the Economics and Econometrics of Research, ADRES, June.

COLOMBO, M. and P. GARRONE (1994), "Infra-muros R&D and Technological Agreements in Information Technology Industries: Empirical Evidence and Policy Implications", paper presented at the conference on "R&TD Co-operation", Vienna, December.

COMMISSION OF THE EUROPEAN COMMUNITIES (1997), *Partnership for a New Organisation of Work*, Green Paper, COM(97)128final, Luxembourg.

CONFERENCE BOARD (1997), *Perspectives on a Global Economy; Technology, Productivity and Growth: US and German Issues*, Winter.

COOPERS & LYBRAND (1998), "Economic Benefits of the R&D Tax Credit", Report to the R&D Credit Coalition, Washington, DC.

CORDES, J. (1989), "Tax Incentives and R&D Spending: A Review of the Evidence", *Research Policy* 18.

CRÉPON, B. and J. MAIRESSE (1994), "R-D, qualification et productivité des entreprises", in *Innovation et compétitivité*, INSEE-Economica, Paris.

DAGENAIS, M., P. MOHNEN and P. THERRIEN (forthcoming), "Do Canadian Firms Respond to Fiscal Incentives to Research and Development?", *Cahier du CIRANO*.

DAVID, P. (1991), "Computer and Dynamo: The Modern Productivity Paradox in the Not Too-Distant Mirror", *American Economic Review* 80(2).

DE LIND VAN WINJNGAARDEN, K.I. (1995), *Dutch SMEs in International Perspective: Start-ups in the Netherlands*, EIM, Zoetermeer.

DE MONGOLFIER, P. and J.P. HUSSON (1995), "The Impact of EC R&D Policy on the European Science & Technology Community – National Impact Studies", Synthesis Final Report to the European Commission, Brussels.

DeBRESSON, C., H. XIAOPING, I. DREJER and B-Å. LUNDVALL (1997), "Innovative Activity in the Learning Economy", draft report to the OECD.

DEPARTMENT OF TRADE AND INDUSTRY (1997), *Competitiveness UK: Our Partnership with Business*, London.

DICKINSON, P. and G. SCIADAS (1996), "Access to the Information Highway", Statistics Canada Services, Science and Technology Division, Analytical Paper Series No. 9, Ministry of Industry, Ottawa.

DJC RESEARCH, QUANTUM LEAP INC. and INDUSTRY CANADA INFORMATION TECHNOLOGY INDUSTRY BRANCH (1995), *IMAT: Survey of the Multimedia Industry in Canada*, DJC Research, Toronto.

DOMS, M., T. DUNNE and K.R. TROSKE (1997), "Workers, Wages and Technology", *Quarterly Journal of Economics* 112, No. 1, pp. 253-290.

DORSMAN, M. (1997), "Evaluation of Industrial R&D Support in the Netherlands: The Wage Tax and Social Insurance Allowances Act/R&D Allowance", in *Policy Evaluation in Innovation and Technology: Towards Best Practices*, OECD, Paris.

DRAKE, K. (1998), "Promoting Competitiveness in Knowledge-based Economies", *OECD Observer*, April/May, OECD, Paris.

EBN (EUROPEAN BUSINESS AND INNOVATION CENTRE NETWORK) (1996), *EC-BIC Observatory*, Brussels.

ECONOMIST (1997), "Coping with Unwelcome News", 26 April, p. 65.

EIM SMALL BUSINESS RESEARCH AND CONSULTANCY (1993, 1994, 1995, 1996), The European Observatory for SMEs, Annual Reports to Directorate-General XXIII (Enterprise Policy, Distributive Trades, Tourism and Co-operatives) of the Commission of the European Communities.

EIRMA (EUROPEAN INDUSTRIAL RESEARCH MANAGEMENT ASSOCIATION) (1997), *R&D Survey*, Paris.

ENTORF, H. and F. KRAMARZ (1995), "The Impacts of New Technologies on Wages: Lessons from Matching Panels on Employees and on their Firms", paper presented at the OECD/Department of Commerce Conference on the Effects of Technology and Innovation on Firm Performance and Employment, 1-2 May, Washington, DC.

ERGAS, H. (1987), "Does Technology Policy Matter?" in B. Guile and H. Brooks (eds.), *Technology and Global Industry*, Washington, DC.

ERHVERVS UDVIKLINGS RADET (1997), *Videnregnskaber: Rapportering og styring af videnkapital* ("Intellectual Capital Accounts, Reporting and Managing Intellectual Capital"), Copenhagen.

EUROPEAN COMMISSION (1992), *A Guideline for Survey-Techniques in Evaluation of Research*, Monitor/SPEAR Report EUR 14339 EN, Luxembourg.

EUROPEAN COMMISSION (1994), *Analysis of Experience in the Use of Verifiable Objectives*, Monitor/SPEAR Report EUR 15634 EN, Luxembourg.

EUROPEAN COMMISSION (1996*a*), *MEANS Handbook, No. 6 – Evaluating the Contribution of the Structural Funds to Employment*, Luxembourg.

EUROPEAN COMMISSION (1996*b*), *Good Practices in the Transfer of University Technology to Industry*, European Innovation Monitoring System (EIMS).

EUROPEAN COMMISSION (1996*c*), *Innovation Management Tools: A Review of Selected Methodologies*, European Innovation Monitoring System (EIMS).

EUROPEAN COMMISSION (1997*a*), *Second European Report on S&T Indicators, 1997 – Report*, EUR 17639, Luxembourg.

EUROPEAN COMMISSION (1997*b*), *Evaluating EU Expenditure Programmes: A Guide for Ex-post and Intermediate Evaluation*, Luxembourg.

EUROPEAN COMMISSION (1997*c*), "Making Markets Work: Support Service for Equity Markets for Emerging Growth Companies in Europe", report by Graham Bannock & Partners Ltd. (United Kingdom) and Essor Europe (France), EIMS Project No. 96/141.

EUROPEAN FOUNDATION FOR THE IMPROVEMENT OF LIVING AND WORKING CONDITIONS (1997), *New Forms of Work Organisation. Can Europe Realise its Potential?*, Office for Official Publications of the European Communities, Luxembourg.

EUROPEAN TRADE UNION CONFEDERATION, TRADE UNION ADVISORY COMMITTEE TO THE OECD and EUROPEAN TRADE UNION INSTITUTE (ETUI) (1997), *Jobs First: Trade Unions and Modernisation of the Labour Market*, ETUI, Brussels.

EUROSTAT (1997), "Working Papers: An Estimate of Eco-Industries in the European Union for 1994", Luxembourg.

FINANCIAL TIMES (1996*a*), "Measuring the Benefits of Research Spending is Not an Easy Task – Intangible Assets", 21 May, p. 10.

FINANCIAL TIMES (1996*b*), "IT: US Report", 2 October, Special Supplement, p. XII.

FINANCIAL TIMES (1997*a*), 13 March.

FINANCIAL TIMES (1997*b*), 30 June.

FINANCIAL TIMES (1997*c*), 16 June.

FINANCIAL TIMES (1997*d*), 5-6 June.

FINANCIAL TIMES (1997*e*), 16 July.

FINANCIAL TIMES (1997*f*), 16 January.

FÖLSTER, S. (1988), "The Incentive Subsidy for Government Support of Private R&D", *Research Policy* 17, pp. 105-112.

FÖLSTER, S. (1991), *The Art of Encouraging Innovation: A New Approach to Government Innovation Policy*, The Industrial Institute of Economic and Social Research, Stockholm.

FOUNDATION FOR RESEARCH, SCIENCE AND TECHNOLOGY (1997), *The Benefits of Meat Research in New Zealand: A Pilot R&D Outcome Review*, Wellington.

FRASER, D. (1996), *The Training Guarantee: Its Impact and Legacy 1990-94*, Department of Employment, Education, Training and Youth Affairs, Canberra.

FRICKE, W. (1997), "Evaluation of the German Work and Technology Programme from an Action Research Point of View", in T. Alasoini, M. Kyllönen and A. Kasvio (eds.), *Workplace Innovations – A Way of Promoting Competitiveness, Welfare and Employment*, National Workplace Development Programme, Yearbook 1997, Helsinki.

FRITZ, O., G. HUTSCHENREITER and D. STURN (1997), "Evaluation of RTD Programmes: Best Practice and the Austrian Experience", *Plattform Technologieevaluierung*, Newsletter 3/1997.

FUJIMOTO, T. (1998), "A Case of the Capability Evolution: Toyota and Japanese Auto Industry", *La lettre du Gerpisa*, No. 119, January.

GARDNER, J. and A. KENYON (1994), "Business Incubators in Australia – An Evaluation".

GARNSEY, E. and A. CANNON-BROOKS (1993), "The Cambridge Phenomenon Revisited: Aggregate Change among High Technology Companies since 1985", *Entrepreneurship and Regional Development* 5.

GAUDIN, T. (1997), *Introduction à l'économie cognitive*, Editions de l'aube, Paris.

GEORGHIOU, L. (1997), "Issues in the Evaluation of Innovation and Technology Policy", in *Policy Evaluation in Innovation and Technology: Towards Best Practices*, OECD, Paris.

GIBBONS, M. *et al.* (1994), *The New Production of Knowledge*, Sage, London.

GORE, A. (1997), "Remarks at Lifelong Learning Conference", 18 November, Washington, DC.

GOVERNMENT OF CANADA and OECD (1997), *Changing Workplace Strategies: Achieving Better Outcomes for Enterprises, Workers, and Society*, report on the International Conference organised by the Government of Canada and the Organisation for Economic Co-operation and Development, Ottawa, Canada, 2-3 December 1996, Ottawa and Paris.

GRÉGOIRE, P. (1995), "Au-delà du mystère ou des préjugés : jalons pour une évaluation des mesures fiscales à la R&D industrielle", Ministère de l'Industrie, du Commerce et de la Technologie, mimeo.

GUELLEC, D. and E. IOANNIDIS (forthcoming), "Determinants of Business R&D Expenditure: A Quantitative Analysis", *STI Working Paper*, OECD, Paris.

GUELLEC, D. and B. VAN POTTELSBERGHE (1998), "Government Support to Business R&D: A Quantitative Contribution", OECD, Directorate for Science, Technology and Industry, mimeo.

GULBENKIAN FOUNDATION (1995), "Report on the Restructuring of Social Sciences", report by an international expert group led by I. Wallerstein, Lisbon.

HALL, B. (1992), "R&D Tax Policy During the Eighties: Success or Failure?", NBER Working Paper No. 4240, Cambridge, MA.

HALL, B. (1996), "Fiscal Policy Towards R&D in the United States", in "Fiscal Measures to Promote R&D and Innovation", OCDE/GD(96)165, Paris.

HERVIK, A. (1997), "Evaluation of User-oriented Research in Norway: The Estimation of Long-run Economic Impacts", in *Policy Evaluation in Innovation and Technology: Towards Best Practices*, OECD, Paris.

HINES, J. (1994), "Taxes, Technology Transfer, and the R&D Activities of Multinational Firms", NBER Working Paper No. 4932, Cambridge, MA.

HORGAN, J. (1996), *The End of Science*, Broadway Books, New York.

INDUSTRY CANADA (1995), "Focusing on Results: A Guide to Performance Measurement", Discussion Paper, March.

INDUSTRY COMMISSION (1995), *Research & Development*, Canberra.

INTERNATIONAL ACCOUNTING STANDARDS COMMITTEE (1997), *Proposed International Accounting Standard. Intangible Assets*, Exposure Draft E60, London.

INTERNATIONAL FEDERATION OF THE PHOTOGRAPHIC INDUSTRY (IFPI) (1996), *IFPI World Sales 95*, London, April.

ISTITUTO NAZIONALE DI STATISTICA (ISTAT) (1995), "Anni 1990-92", *Notiziario*, serie 4.

JARMIN, R. and J. JENSEN (1997), "Evaluating Government Technology Programmes: The Case of Manufacturing Extension" in *Policy Evaluation in Innovation and Technology: Towards Best Practices*, OECD, Paris.

JOHNSON, J., J.R. BALDWIN and B. DIVERTY (1995), "The Implications of Innovation and Technological Change for Employment and Human Resource Strategy", paper presented at the OECD/Department of Commerce Conference on the Effects of Technology and Innovation on Firm Performance and Employment, 1-2 May, Washington, DC.

KIRCHHOFF, B. (1995), "Growth Contributions of Highly Innovative Small Firms", paper presented at the OECD High-level Workshop on SMEs: Employment, Innovation and Growth, 16-17 June, Washington, DC.

KLEINSCHMIDT, M. and U. PEKRUHL (1994), *Kooperative Arbeitstrukturen und Gruppenarbeit in Deutschland*, Institut Arbeit und Technik, Gelsenkirchen.

KLEPPER, S. and K. SIMONS (1996), "Technological Extinctions of Industrial Firms: An Enquiry into their Nature and Causes", paper presented at the 1996 EARIE conference, Vienna.

KRUEGER, A.B. (1993), "How Computers Have Changed the Wage Structure: Evidence from Microdata 1984-1989", *Quarterly Journal of Economics*, February, pp. 33-60.

KRUGMAN, P. (1991), "Increasing Returns and Economic Geography", *Journal of Political Economy 99*, pp. 483-500.

KUHLMANN, S. (1995), "Patterns of Science and Technology Policy Evaluation in Germany", in *Research Evaluation, Special Issue on National Systems for Evaluation of R&D in the European Union*, Vol. 5, No. 1.

KUHLMANN, S. (1997), "Evaluation as a Medium of Science and Technology Policy: Recent Developments in Germany and Beyond", in *Evaluation in Innovation and Technology Policy: Towards Best Practices*, OECD, Paris.

KUNTZE, U. and K. HORNCHILD (1995), "Evaluation of the Promotion of R&D Activities in Small and Medium-Sized Enterprises", in G. Becher and S. Kuhlmann (eds.), *Evaluation of Technology Policy Programmes in Germany*, Dordrecht.

LANJOUW, J.O. and A. MODY (1995), *Stimulating Innovation and International Diffusion of Environmentally Responsive Technology*, World Bank, Washington, DC.

LARÉDO, P. (1997), "Evaluation in France: A Decade of Experience", in *Policy Evaluation in Innovation and Technology: Towards Best Practices*, OECD, Paris.

LARÉDO, P. and M. CALLON (1990), "L'impact des programmes communautaires sur le tissu scientifique et technique français", Ministère de la Recherche et de la Technologie, Paris, January.

LATTIMORE, R. (1997), "Research and Development Fiscal Incentives in Australia: Impact and Policy Lessons", in *Policy Evaluation in Innovation and Technology: Towards Best Practices*, OECD, Paris.

LEBEAU, D. (1996), "Les mesures d'aide fiscale à la R&D et les entreprises québécoises", in M. Dagenais *et al.* (eds.), *L'efficacité des mesures d'aide fiscale à la R&D des entreprises du Canada et du Québec*, Conseil de la Science et de la Technologie, Gouvernement du Québec.

LECLERC, M. and J. GAGNÉ (1994), "International Scientific Cooperation: The Continentalisation of Science", *Scientometrics* 31.

LERNER, J. (1997), "An Empirical Exploration of a Technology Race", *The Rand Journal of Economics 28*, No. 2, pp. 228-247.

LICHT, G. and H. STAHL (1997), *Ergebnisse der Innovationserhebung 1996*, Zentrum fur Europaische Wirtschaftsforschung (ZEW), Mannheim.

LICHT, G., W. SCHNELL and H. STAHL (1997), "Results of the German Innovation Survey", ZEW Working Paper, Mannheim.

LINK, A. (1998), "Public/Private Partnerships as a Tool to Support Industrial R&D: Experiences in the United States", report prepared for the OECD Directorate for Science, Technology and Industry.

LIPSEY, R. and K. CARLAW (1998), "Technology Policies in Neo-classical and Structuralist-evolutionary Models", forthcoming in *STI Review*, No. 22, OECD, Paris.

LUMME, A. (1995), "Potential for Growth: Employment Creation Effects of the Most Promising Technology-based Entrepreneurial Companies in Finland", in R. Oakey (ed.), *New Technology-based Firms in the 1990s*, Volume II.

LUND, R. and A.N. GJERDING (1996), "The Flexible Company: Innovation, Work Organisation and Human Resource Management", mimeo; reported in more detail in A.N. Gjerding (ed.), 1997, in Danish, *Den fleksible virksomhed: Omstillingspres og fornyelse i dansk erhvervsliv*, The Danish Industry and Trade Development Council, Copenhagen.

LUNDVALL, B.Å. (1992), *National Systems of Innovation*, Frances Pinter, London.

LUUKKONEN, T. (1997), "The Increasing Professionalisation of the Evaluation of Mission-oriented Research in Finland: Implications for the Evaluation Process", in *Policy Evaluation in Innovation and Technology: Towards Best Practices*, OECD, Paris.

MADHURST, J. (1995), "New, Clean and Low Waste Products, Processing and Services and Ways to Promote the Diffusion of such Practices to Industry", Ecotec for the European Commission (DG III and DG V), Brussels.

MALERBA, F., F. LISSONI and L. CAMPANI (1995), "Italy: National Policies to Promote the Development of NTBFs", CESPRI, Bocconi University, Milan.

MANAGEMENT INFORMATION SERVICES (1993), "1992 US Environmental Spending Stimulates Economy, Creating $170 Billion Revenues and 4 Million Jobs", *MIS News Release*, Washington DC.

MANSFIELD, E. and L. SWITZER (1985), "The Effects of R&D Tax Credits and Allowances in Canada", *Research Policy* 14.

MARTIN, B. and B. SALTER (1996), *The Relationship between Publicly Funded Research and Economic Performance: A SPRU Review*, Science Policy Research Unit, Brighton.

McDONALD, R. and G. TEATHER (1997), "Science and Technology Evaluation Practices in the Government of Canada", in *Evaluation in Innovation and Technology Policy: Towards Best Practices*, OECD, Paris.

METCALFE, S. (1995), "The Economic Foundations of Technology Policy: Equilibrium and Evolutionary Perspectives", in P. Stoneman (ed.), *Handbook of the Economics of Innovation and Technical Change*, pp. 409-512, Blackwell, London.

METCALFE, S. and L. GEORGHIOU (1998), "Equilibrium and Evolutionary Foundations of Technology Policy", forthcoming in *STI Review*, No. 22, OECD, Paris.

MINISTERIE VAN SOCIALE ZAKEN EN WERKGELEGENHEID (1997), "Bill on Flexibility and Security", *Info*, April, The Hague.

MINISTRY OF LABOUR (1996), *Flexible Enterprise, Finnish Survey*, Helsinki.

MOHNEN, P. (1996), "R&D Externalities and Productivity Growth", *STI Review*, No. 18, OECD, Paris.

MOHNEN, P. (1997), "R&D Tax Incentives: Issues and Evidences", UQAM and CIRANO, mimeo.

MOTOHASHI, K. (1998), "Technology, Productivity and Employment: Insights from Firm-level Datasets in France, Japan and the United States", *STI Working Paper* 1998/2, OECD, Paris.

MOWERY, D. (1992), "The US National Innovation System: Origins and Prospects for Change", *Research Policy* 21.

MOWERY, D. (1995), "The Practice of Technology Policy", in P. Stoneman (ed.), *The Handbook of the Economics of Innovation and Technological Changes*, Oxford.

MOWERY, D. (1997), "Rapporteur's Summary of the Seoul Conference on International Technology Co-operation", DSTI/STP/TIP(97)14, Paris.

MOWERY, D. (1998), "Market Failure or Market Magic? Structural Change in the US National Innovation System", forthcoming in *STI Review*, No. 22, OECD, Paris.

MUNRO, A., H. RAINBIRD and L. HOLLY (1997), *Partners in Workplace Learning*, UNISON, London; see also unsigned article, "Training in Unison – Forging Partnerships with Employers", *Employee Development Bulletin*, Number 92, August.

MUSTAR, P. (1995), "The Creation of Enterprises by Researchers: Conditions for Growth and the Role of the Public Authorities", paper presented at the OECD High Level Workshop on "SMEs: Employment, Innovation and Growth, 16-17 June", Washington DC.

NADIRI, I. (1993), *Innovations and Technological Spillovers*, NBER Working Paper, No. 4423, Cambridge, MA.

NAKAMOTO, M. (1997), "Online Ordering: NEC to Use Net for 90 per cent of Procurement," *Financial Times*, 28 May.

NALBANTIAN, H.R. and A. SCHOTTER (1997), "Productivity Under Group Incentives: An Experimental Study", *The American Economic Review*, Vol. 87, No. 3.

NARIN, F., K.S. HAMILTON and D. OLIVASTRO (1997), "The Increasing Linkage between US Technology and Public Science", *Research Policy* 26, pp. 317-330.

NATIONAL ACADEMY OF ENGINEERING (1995), *Risk & Innovation: The Role and Importance of Small High-Tech Companies in the US Economy*, National Academy Press, Washington, DC.

NATIONAL BUREAU OF ECONOMIC RESEARCH (1995), "Trade in Ideas: Patenting and Productivity in the OECD", in J. Eaton and S. Kortum (eds.), NBER Working Paper No. 5049, Cambridge, MA.

NATIONAL INSTITUTE OF STANDARDS AND TECHNOLOGY (1996), <http://www.mep.nist.gov>.

NATIONAL RESEARCH COUNCIL OF CANADA (1990), "IRAP Evaluation Study", Final Report, December, Ottawa.

NATIONAL SCIENCE BOARD (1996), *Science & Engineering Indicators – 1996*, US Government Printing Office (NSB-21) Washington DC.

NATIONAL SCIENCE FOUNDATION (1996), *Science and Engineering Indicators*, <http://www.nsf.gov/sbe/srs/seind96/start.htm>.

NATIONAL SCIENCE FOUNDATION (1997*a*), "R&D Exceeds Expectations Again, Growing Faster than the US Economy during the Last Three Years", Data brief, NSF 97328, November.

NATIONAL SCIENCE FOUNDATION (1997*b*), *Federal Funds for Research and Development – Fiscal Years 1995, 1996, and 1997*, Vol. 45, and previous issues.

NATIONAL SCIENCE FOUNDATION (1997*c*), *Federal R&D Funding by Budget Function – Fiscal Years 1995-97*, and previous issues.

NATIONAL SCIENCE FOUNDATION (1997*d*), "National Patterns of R&D Resources: 1997" (advanced tables), <http://www.nsf.gov/sbe/srs/natpat97/start.htm>.

NATURE (1996), 11 January.

NBIA (NATIONAL BUSINESS INCUBATION ASSOCIATION) (1995), *10th Anniversary Survey of Business Incubators*, Athens, OH.

NERLINGER, E. (1995), "Die Gründungsdynamik in technologieorientierten Industrien: Ein Analyse der IAB-Beschäftigtenstatistik", Discussion Paper No. 95-17, Mannheim.

NEW YORK TIMES (1996), Section D8, 25 April.

NEW YORK TIMES (1997), "Gold Rush From Software Animates Silicon Valley," 13 January.

NEWTON, K. (1996), "The Human Factor in Firms' Performance: Management Strategies for Productivity and Competitiveness in the Knowledge-based Economy", Occasional Paper No. 14, Industry Canada, Ottawa.

NIEDERSÄCHSISCHES INSTITUT FÜR WIRTSCHAFTSFORSCHUNG (Hannover), DEUTSCHES INSTITUT FÜR WIRTSCHAFTSFORSCHUNG (Berlin), FRAUNHOFER FÜR SYSTEMTECHNIK UND INNOVATIONSFORSCHUNG (Karlsruhe), and ZENTRUM FÜR EUROPÄISCHE WIRTSCHAFTSFORSCHUNG (Mannheim) (1996), "Germany's Technological Performance", report submitted to the Federal Ministry of Education, Science Research and Technology.

OECD (1982), *The Future of University Research*, Paris.

OECD (1986*a*), *The OECD and the Environment*, Paris.

OECD (1986*b*), *Flexibility in the Labour Market: The Current Debate*, Paris.

OECD (1989), *Labour Market Flexibility: Trends in Enterprises*, Paris.

OECD (1992), *Technology and the Economy: The Key Relationships*, Paris.

OECD (1993*a*), *Science, Technology and Innovation Policies, Iceland*, Paris.

OECD (1993*b*), *Competition Policy and a Changing Broadcast Industry*, Paris.

OECD (1994), *The OECD Jobs Study*, Paris.

OECD (1995*a*), *Science, Technology and Innovation Policies, Denmark*, Paris.

OECD (1995*b*), *Impacts of National Technology Programmes*, Paris.

OECD (1995*c*), "Joint Consultation Meeting on Environmental Policy and Bioremediation/Bioprevention Technologies", COM/DSTI/ENV(95)112/REV1, Paris.

OECD (1995*d*), *Employment Outlook*, Paris.

OECD (1995*e*), *Boosting Businesses: Advisory Services*, Paris.

OECD (1996*a*), *Technology and Industrial Performance*, Paris.

OECD (1996*b*), *Technology, Productivity and Job Creation*, Paris.

OECD (1996*c*), *Science and Technology Policy Review, Korea*, Paris.

OECD (1996*d*), "Public Support to Industry. Report by the Industry Committee to the Council at Ministerial Level", OCDE/GD(96)82, Paris.

OECD (1996*e*), *Regulatory Reform and Innovation*, Paris.

OECD (1996*f*), *Venture Capital in OECD Countries, Financial Market Trends, No. 63*, Paris.

OECD (1996*g*), "Information Infrastructure Convergence and Pricing: The Internet", OCDE/GD(96)73, Paris.

OECD (1996*h*), "Competition Policy and Film Distribution", Committee on Competition Law and Policy, *Roundtable Series on Competition Policy, No. 3*, OCDE/GD(96)60, Paris.

OECD (1996*i*), "Employment in the Environmental Goods and Services Industry", OECD/DSTI/IND(96)12, Paris.

OECD (1996*j*), *The Global Environmental Goods and Services Industry*, Paris.

OECD (1996*k*), "Interim Definition and Classification of the Environment Industry. Prepared in conjunction with OECD/Eurostat Informal Working Group on the Environment Industry", OCDE/GD(96)117, Paris.

OECD (1996*l*), *Employment Outlook*, Paris.

OECD (1996*m*), "Evolving Enterprise Structure and Strategy: The Trade Union Role", Labour/Management Programme, OCDE/GD(96)116, Paris.

OECD (1997*a*), *Implementing the OECD Jobs Study: Lessons from Member Countries' Experience*, Paris.

OECD (1997*b*), *Information Technology Outlook* 1997, Paris.

OECD (1997*c*), *Employment Outlook*, Paris.

OECD (1997*d*), "An Empirical Comparison of National Innovation Systems: Various Approaches and Early Findings", DSTI/STP/TIP(97)13, Paris.

OECD (1997*e*), *Economic Outlook*, No. 62, December, Paris.

OECD (1997*f*), "Session on Globalisation – Internationalisation of Industrial R&D: Patterns and Trends", DSTI/IND/STP/SWP/NESTI(97)2, Paris.

OECD (1997*g*), "Technology and Productivity: A Three-Country Study Using Micro-level Databases", DSTI/EAS/IND/SWP(97)7, Paris.

OECD (1997*h*), "Decomposition of Industry-level Productivity Growth: A Micro-Macro Link", DSTI/EAS/IND/SWP(97)6, Paris.

OECD (1997*i*), *The OECD Report on Regulatory Reform*, Volume II, Paris.

OECD (1997*j*), *National Innovation Systems*, Paris.

OECD (1997*k*), *Policy Evaluation in Innovation and Technology: Towards Best Practices*, Paris.

OECD (1997*l*), "Evaluation of Scientific Research: Selected Experiences", OCDE/GD(97)194, Paris.

OECD (1997*m*), *Science and Technology in the Public Eye*, Paris.

OECD (1997*n*), "Advanced Technology Programmes", DSTI/STP/TIP(97)3, Paris.

OECD (1997*o*), "Foreign Access to Technology Programmes", OCDE/GD(97)209, Paris.

OECD (1997*p*), "International Technology Co-operation: Proceedings of the Seoul Conference", DSTI/STP/TIP(97)14, Paris.

OECD (1997*q*), "Diffusing Technology to Industry: Government Programmes and Policies", OCDE/GD(97)60, Paris.

OECD (1997*r*), *OECD Economic Survey – The United States*, Paris.

OECD (1997*s*), "Government Programmes for Venture Capital", DSTI/STP/TIP(96)10/REV2, Paris.

OECD (1997*t*), "Technology Incubators: Nurturing Small Firms", OCDE/GD(97)202, Paris.

OECD (1997*u*), *Communications Outlook 1997*, Paris.

OECD (1997*v*), "Measuring Electronic Commerce", OCDE/GD(97)185, Paris.

OECD (1997*w*), *Reforming Environmental Regulation in OECD Countries*, Paris.

OECD (1997*x*), *Environmental Performance Reviews*, various countries, Paris

OECD (1997*y*), "Greener Public Purchasing", Background paper for the OECD International Conference on Green Public Purchasing, Biel, Switzerland.

OECD (1997*z*), *Evaluation of Economic Instruments for Environmental Policy*, Paris.

OECD (1997*aa*), "The Role and Importance of Small and New Technology-based Firms", internal working paper, Paris.

OECD (1997*bb*), "Lifelong Learning to Maintain Employability", OCDE/GD(97)162, Paris.

OECD (1997*cc*), *Lifelong Learning for All*, Paris.

OECD (1997*dd*), *Industrial Competitiveness in the Knowledge-based Economy: The New Role of Governments*, Paris.

OECD (1998*a*, forthcoming), *International Flows of Government R&D Funds*, Paris.

OECD (1998*b*, forthcoming), *Science, Technology and Industry Outlook 1998*, Paris.

OECD (1998*c*, forthcoming), *Biotechnology for Clean Industrial Products and Processes*, Paris.

OECD (1998*d*, forthcoming), *Flexible Enterprises*, Paris.

OECD (1998*e*), *Pathways and Participation in Vocational and Technical Education and Training*, Paris.

OECD (1998*f*, forthcoming), *Employment Outlook*, Paris.

OECD and THE ERNST & YOUNG CENTER FOR BUSINESS INNOVATION (1997), *Enterprise Value in the Knowledge Economy*, Paris and Cambridge, MA.

OFFICE OF TECHNOLOGY ASSESSMENT (1995), *Innovation and Commercialisation of Emerging Technologies*, US Government Printing Office, September.

OFFICE OF TECHNOLOGY POLICY (1996), *Effective Partnering: A Report to Congress on Federal Technology Partnerships*, US Department of Commerce, Washington, DC.

OKUBO, Y. (1996), "L'internationalisation de la science", *Futuribles*, June.

ORMALA, E. (1998), "New Approaches in Technology Policy – The Finnish Example", forthcoming in *STI Review*, No. 22, OECD, Paris.

PARGER, T. (1995), "Austria: National Policies to Promote the Development of NTBFs", IfG, Vienna.

PARK, Y., Y. LIM, Z. BAE and J. LEE (1996), "Formulating and Managing the HAN Projects in Korea: Lessons and Policy Implications for Developing Countries" in *Science and Public Policy*, Vol. 23, No. 2, April.

PATEL, P. (1997), "Localised Production of Technology for Global Markets", in D. Archibugi and J. Michie (eds.), *Technology, Globalisation and Economic Performance*, Cambridge University Press, Cambridge.

PATEL, P. and K. PAVITT (1994), "The Nature and Economic Importance of National Innovation Systems", *STI Review*, No. 14, OECD, Paris

PAVITT, K. (1984), "Sectoral Patterns of Technical Change: Towards a Taxonomy and a Theory", *Research Policy* 13.

PAVITT, K. and P. PATEL (1996), "Uneven Technological Development", in X. Vence-Deza and S. Metcalfe (eds.), *Wealth from Diversity*, Kluwer Publishers, Dordrecht/Boston/London.

PIANTA, M. and G. SIRILLI (1997), "The Use of Innovation Surveys for Policy Evaluation in Italy", in *Policy Evaluation in Innovation and Technology: Towards Best Practices*, OECD, Paris.

PIRIC, A. and N. REEVE (1997), "Evaluation of Public Investment in R&D – Towards a Contingency Analysis", in *Policy Evaluation in Innovation and Technology: Towards Best Practices*, OECD, Paris.

POLT, W., E. BUCHINGER, L. JORG, A. KOPCSA, H. LEO, L. MUSTONEN, F. OLHER and S. PATSIOS (1994), "Evaluierung des ITF-Förderschwerpunktes Flex CIM", Forschungszentrum Seibersdorf, Seibersdorf, February.

PORTER, M and VAN DER LINDE (1995), "Towards a New Conception of Environment Competitiveness Relationship", *Journal of Economic Prospective.*

R&D MAGAZINE (1997), "Basic Research White Paper" <http://www.rdmag.com/BRWP/>.

REGER G. and U. SCHMOCH (eds.) (1996), *Organisation of Science and Technology at the Watershed: The Academic and Industrial Perspective*, Physica-Verlag, Heidelberg.

REPETTO, R., D. ROTHMAN, *et al.* (1996), "Has Environmental Protection Really Reduced Productivity Growth?", World Resources Institute.

RESEARCH EVALUATION (1995), *Special Issue on National Systems for Evaluation of R&D in the European Union*, Vol. 5, No. 1.

REVIEW OF BUSINESS PROGRAMS (1997), *Going for Growth: Business Programs for Investment, Innovation and Export (the "Mortimer Report")*, Canberra, June.

RIMMER, S. (1995) "Attitude and Strategy of Business Regarding Protection of the Environmental Framework", Common Environmental Framework, Eurostrategy Consultants, Brussels.

RIP, A. and B.J.R. VAN DER MEULEN (1997), "The Patchwork of the Dutch Evaluation System", in *Research Evaluation, Special Issue on National Systems for Evaluation of R&D in the European Union*, Vol. 5, No. 1.

ROMER, P. (1997), "In the Beginning was the Transistor", *Essays in Public Policy*, Hoover Digest No. 2, Hoover Institution, Stanford University Press.

ROTHWELL, R. and M. DODGSON (1993), "Technology-based SMEs: Their Role in Industrial and Economic Change", *International Journal of Technology Management, Special Publication on Small Firms and Innovation.*

SAKAKIBARA, M. (1997), "Evaluation of Government-sponsored R&D Consortia in Japan", in *Policy Evaluation in Innovation and Technology: Towards Best Practices*, OECD, Paris.

SANZ-MENÉNDEZ, L. (1995), "Research Actors and the State: Research Evaluation and Evaluation of Science and Technology Policies in Spain", in *Research Evaluation, Special Issue on National Systems for Evaluation of R&D in the European Union*, Vol. 5, No. 1.

SCHERER, F.M. (1984), *Innovation and Growth: Schumpeterian Perspectives*, MIT Press, Cambridge, MA.

SCHMOCH, U. *et al.* (1996), "Standortvoraussetzungen und technologische Trends", in Bundesamt fuer Konjunkturfragen (ed.), *Modernisierung am Technikstandort Schweiz*, VDF.

SCIENCE POLICY RESEARCH UNIT (1996), "The Relationship between Publicly Funded Research and Economic Performance", report prepared for HM Treasury, University of Sussex, Brighton.

SCOTT, J. and S. MARTIN (1998), "Financing and Leveraging Public/Private Partnerships", report prepared for the OECD Directorate for Science, Technology and Industry.

SEGERS, J.P. (1993), "Strategic Partnering Between New Technology-based Firms and Large Established Firms in the Biotechnology and Micro-electronics Industries in Belgium", *Small Business Economics* 5, pp. 271-281.

SEYVET, J. (1996), "Tax Credit for Research in France", in "Fiscal Measures to Promote R&D and Innovation", OCDE/GD(96)165, Paris.

SHAPIRA, P. (1995), "New Public Infrastructures for Small Firm Industrial Modernization in the USA", *Entrepreneurship and Regional Development*, No. 7.

SIWEK, S.E. and G. MOSTELLER (1996), *Copyright Industries in the US Economy: The 1996 Report*, Economists Inc., prepared for the International Intellectual Property Alliance, Washington, DC.

SKOIE, H. (1997), "Basic Research – A New Funding Climate?", *Science and Public Policy*, April.

SLAUGHTER, M. and P. SWAGEL (1997), "The Effect of Globalisation on Wages in the Advanced Economies", IMF Working Paper 97/43, April.

SMITH, K. (1996), "The Systems Challenge to Innovation Policy", in W. Polt and B. Weber (eds.), *Industrie und Glueck. Paradigmenwechsel in der Industrie- und Technologiepolitik*, Sonderzahl, Vienna.

SMITH, K. *et al.* (1996), *The Norwegian National Innovation System: A Pilot Study of Knowledge Creation*, STEP Report, Oslo.

SOETE, L. and A. ARUNDEL (eds.) (1993), *An Integrated Approach to European Innovation and Technology Diffusion Policy – A Maastricht Memorandum*, European Commission, Brussels-Luxembourg.

STAMPFER, M. (1997), "Science and Technology Policy Evaluation in Austria: Struggling Towards a Higher Ranking on the Policy Agenda", in *Policy Evaluation in Innovation and Technology: Towards Best Practices*, OECD, Paris.

STATISTICS CANADA (1997*a*), *Federal Scientific Activities 1997-98*, July, and previous issues.

STATISTICS CANADA (1997*b*), "Scientific and Technological Activities of Provincial Governments, 1989-90 to 1995-96", *Science and Technology Redesign Project*, March.

STATISTICS FINLAND (1997), *On the Road to the Finnish Information Society,* Statistics Finland, Helsinki.

STIGLER, G.J. and G.S. BECKER (1997), "De Gustibus Non Est Disputandum", *American Economic Review* 67, pp. 76-90.

STOREY, D. and B. TETHER (1996), "New Technology Based Firms (NTBFs) in Europe", A European Innovation Monitoring System Study, Centre for Small & Medium-sized Enterprises, University of Warwick, Coventry, United Kingdom.

SYMEONIDIS, G. (1996), "Innovation, Firm Size and Market Structure: Schumpeterian Hypotheses and Some New Themes", *OECD Economic Studies*, No. 27, OECD, Paris.

TETHER, B. and B. STOREY (forthcoming), "Smaller Firms and Europe's High Technology Sectors: A Framework for Analysis and Some Statistical Evidence", *Research Policy*.

TIDD, J., J. BESSANT and K. PAVITT (1997), *Managing Innovation: Integrating Technological, Market and Organisational Change*, John Wiley & Sons, Chichester, United Kingdom.

UNION OF INDUSTRIAL AND EMPLOYERS' CONFEDERATIONS OF EUROPE (1995), "Releasing Europe's Potential Through Targeted Regulatory Reform".

US BUREAU OF LABOR STATISTICS (1987), "The Impact of Research and Development on Productivity Growth", Bulletin 2331.

US GENERAL ACCOUNTING OFFICE (1996), *Manufacturing Extension Programs: Manufacturers' Views About Delivery and Impact of Services*, Report to the Chairwoman, Subcommittee on Technology, Committee on Science, House of Representatives, GAO/GDD/-96-75, Washington, DC.

UTTERBACK, J., M. MEYER, M. ROBERTS and G. REITBERGER (1988), "Technology and Industrial Innovation in Sweden: A Study of Technology-based Firms Formed between 1965 and 1980", *Research Policy* 17.

VENTURE ECONOMICS INVESTOR SERVICES (1997), "Historical and Current Overview of the Venture Capital Industry".

VERTOVA, A. (1997), "Technological Similarities in National Patterns of Specialisation in a Historical Perspective", paper presented at the ASEAT Conference, Manchester.

VICKERY, G. and G. WURZBURG (1998, forthcoming), "The Challenge of Measuring and Evaluating Organisational Change in Enterprises", in *Measuring Intangible Investment*, OECD, Paris.

VONORTAS, N.S. (1997), "Research Joint Ventures in the US", *Research Policy* 76, pp. 577-596.

WALL STREET JOURNAL (1996), Section A4, 25 April.

WARDA, J. (1996), "Measuring the Value of R&D Tax Provisions", in "Fiscal Measures to Promote R&D and Innovation", OCDE/GD(96)165, Paris.

WATKINS, J.D. (1997), "Science and Technology in Foreign Affairs", *Science* 277, 1 August.

WEISBROD, B.A. (1991), "The Health Care Quadrilemma: An Essay on Technological Change, Insurance, Quality of Care, and Cost Containment", *Journal of Economic Literature*, Vol. XXIX, pp. 523-552.

WESTHEAD, P. and D.J. STOREY (1994), *An Assessment of Firms Located On and Off Science Parks in the United Kingdom*, HMSO, London.

WOLFE, D.A. (1997), "The Emergence of the Region State", in T.J. Courchene (ed.), *The Nation State in a Global/Information Era: The Policy Challenge*, pp. 205-240, The Bell Canada Papers on Economic and Public Policy, Kingston, Ontario.

WORLD TRADE ORGANIZATION (1994), *The Final Act and Agreement Establishing the Word Trade Organisation (including GATT 1994)*, Uruguay Round, Marrakesh, 15 April 1994, Geneva.

YAGER, L. and R. SCHMIDT (1997), *The Advanced Technology Program: A Case Study in Federal Technology Policy*, American Enterprise Institute Studies in Policy Reform.

YOUNG, A. (forthcoming), "Government Funding of Industrial Technology", *STI Working Paper*, OECD, Paris.

OECD PUBLICATIONS, 2, rue André-Pascal, 75775 PARIS CEDEX 16
PRINTED IN FRANCE
(92 98 05 1 P) ISBN 92-64-16096-5 – No. 50165 1998

XB 2563401 1